T0182150

Computer Communications and Networks

Series editors

A. J. Sammes, Cyber Security Centre, Faculty of Technology,
De Montfort University, Leicester, UK

Jacek Rak, Department of Computer Communications, Faculty of Electronics,
Telecommunications and Informatics, Gdansk University of Technology,
Gdansk, Poland

The **Computer Communications and Networks** series is a range of textbooks, monographs and handbooks. It sets out to provide students, researchers, and non-specialists alike with a sure grounding in current knowledge, together with comprehensible access to the latest developments in computer communications and networking.

Emphasis is placed on clear and explanatory styles that support a tutorial approach, so that even the most complex of topics is presented in a lucid and intelligible manner.

More information about this series at http://www.springer.com/series/4198

Simon Parkinson · Andrew Crampton
Richard Hill
Editors

Guide to Vulnerability Analysis for Computer Networks and Systems

An Artificial Intelligence Approach

 Springer

Editors
Simon Parkinson 🅾
Department of Computer Science,
   School of Computing and Engineering
University of Huddersfield
Huddersfield, UK

Richard Hill 🅾
Department of Computer Science,
   School of Computing and Engineering
University of Huddersfield
Huddersfield, UK

Andrew Crampton 🅾
Department of Computer Science,
   School of Computing and Engineering
University of Huddersfield
Huddersfield, UK

ISSN 1617-7975   ISSN 2197-8433   (electronic)
Computer Communications and Networks
ISBN 978-3-030-06474-7   ISBN 978-3-319-92624-7   (eBook)
https://doi.org/10.1007/978-3-319-92624-7

This Springer imprint is published by the registered company Springer Nature Switzerland AG
The registered company address is: Gewerbestrasse 11, 6330 Cham, Switzerland

Preface

Performing vulnerability assessment of any computing infrastructure is an essential component towards improving a system's security. This is achieved through identifying and mitigating security weaknesses on a recurring basis. Undertaking vulnerability assessment requires in-depth knowledge of the underlying system architecture, available data sources for assessment, algorithmic techniques to assist in identifying vulnerabilities through data processing, and visualisation technologies capable of increasing human understanding and minimising cognitive load.

Artificial Intelligence has great potential to improve the Vulnerability Assessment of computing systems. This book presents key research in the discipline and aims to provide a key body of work for researchers and practitioners. This book covers various aspects of vulnerability assessment, including recent advancements in reducing the requirement on expert knowledge through novel applications of Artificial Intelligence. This book contains many case studies and can be used by security professionals and researchers as reference text, detailing how they can develop and perform Vulnerability Assessment techniques using state-of-the-art intelligent mechanisms.

Organisation

This book is organised into the following four parts:

- Part I introduces the area of Vulnerability Assessment and the use of Artificial Intelligence, as well as providing reviews into the current state of the art.
- Part II provides and discusses Vulnerability Assessment frameworks, including those for industrial control and cloud systems.
- Part III contains many applications that use Artificial Intelligence to enhance Vulnerability Assessment processes.
- Part IV presents and discussed visualisation techniques that can be used to assist the Vulnerability Assessment process.

Target Audience

This book has been created for the following audiences:

- Students and instructors will benefit from using this book as a key reference source and as a subject 'primer', describing fundamental background as well as providing educational examples of how Artificial Intelligence can be used in Vulnerability Assessment.
- Researchers will benefit from using this book as a key reference text, providing surveys of the state of the art as well as a collection of key works in the subject area.
- Security practitioners will benefit from using this book to identify the challenges of Vulnerability Assessment and using case study examples to identify how Artificial Intelligence can be used to improve the Vulnerability Assessment process.

Suggested Instructor Use

Instructors are recommended to use this book to either form an 'Artificial Intelligence for Vulnerability Assessment' module or to use aspects within the core of other Computer Security, Networking and Artificial Intelligence modules.

Each chapter contains a series end of chapter questions that can be used to form tutorial activities in taught content or as thought-provoking questions for researchers and security practitioners.

The below list provides an example of how this book's chapters can be used to create 12 teaching sessions:

- Week 1–2: Part I Introduction and State of the Art;
- Week 3–4: Part II Vulnerability Assessment Frameworks;
- Week 5–10: Part III Applications of Artificial Intelligence;
- Week 11–12: Part IV Visualisation.

Acknowledgements

The editors would like to express their sincere thanks to Saad Khan of the University of Huddersfield for assisting with editorial and administrative duties in the preparation of this book.

The authors would also like to express their thanks to the following individuals who contributed to this book's review process:

- Arosha Bandara, The Open University, UK
- Andrea Cullen, University of Bradford, UK
- Amani Ibrahim, Deakin University, Australia

- Artemios Voyiatzis, SBA Research, Austria
- David Rosado, University of Castilla–La Mancha, Spain
- Dimitrios Zissis, University of the Aegean, Greece
- Emlyn Butterfield, Leeds Beckett University, UK
- Jesus Luna Garcia, Technische Universitt Darmstadt, Germany
- John Mace, Newcastle University, UK
- Kieran Mclaughlin, the Centre for Secure Information Technologies, Belfast
- Marjan Gusev, the Ss. Cyril and Methodius University of Skopje, Macedonia
- Martin Boldt, Blekinge Institute of Technology, Sweden
- Mohamed Amine Ferrag, Guelma University, Algeria
- Sasko Ristov, University of Innsbruck, Austria
- Shujun Li, University of Surrey, UK
- Sokratis Katsikas, University of Piraeus, Greece
- Tiago Cruz, University of Coimbra, Portugal

Huddersfield, UK   Simon Parkinson
April 2018   Andrew Crampton
Richard Hill

Contents

Part I Introduction and State-of-the-art

Review into State of the Art of Vulnerability Assessment using Artificial Intelligence 3
Saad Khan and Simon Parkinson

A Survey of Machine Learning Algorithms and Their Application in Information Security 33
Mark Stamp

Part II Vulnerability Assessment Frameworks

Vulnerability Assessment of Cyber Security for SCADA Systems 59
Kyle Coffey, Leandros A. Maglaras, Richard Smith, Helge Janicke,
Mohamed Amine Ferrag, Abdelouahid Derhab, Mithun Mukherjee,
Stylianos Rallis and Awais Yousaf

A Predictive Model for Risk and Trust Assessment in Cloud Computing: Taxonomy and Analysis for Attack Pattern Detection 81
Alexandros Chrysikos and Stephen McGuire

AI- and Metrics-Based Vulnerability-Centric Cyber Security Assessment and Countermeasure Selection 101
Igor Kotenko, Elena Doynikova, Andrey Chechulin
and Andrey Fedorchenko

Artificial Intelligence Agents as Mediators of Trustless Security Systems and Distributed Computing Applications 131
Steven Walker-Roberts and Mohammad Hammoudeh

Part III   Applications of Artificial Intelligence

**Automated Planning of Administrative Tasks Using Historic Events:
A File System Case Study** 159
Saad Khan and Simon Parkinson

**Defending Against Chained Cyber-Attacks by Adversarial
Agents** 183
Vivin Paliath and Paulo Shakarian

**Vulnerability Detection and Analysis in Adversarial Deep
Learning** 211
Yi Shi, Yalin E. Sagduyu, Kemal Davaslioglu and Renato Levy

**SOCIO-LENS: Spotting Unsolicited Caller Through Network
Analysis** 235
Muhammad Ajmal Azad, Junaid Arshad and Farhan Riaz

**Function Call Graphs Versus Machine Learning for Malware
Detection** 259
Deebiga Rajeswaran, Fabio Di Troia, Thomas H. Austin and Mark Stamp

**Detecting Encrypted and Polymorphic Malware Using Hidden
Markov Models** 281
Dhiviya Dhanasekar, Fabio Di Troia, Katerina Potika and Mark Stamp

Masquerade Detection on Mobile Devices 301
Swathi Nambiar Kadala Manikoth, Fabio Di Troia and Mark Stamp

Identifying File Interaction Patterns in Ransomware Behaviour 317
Liam Grant and Simon Parkinson

Part IV   Visualisation

**A Framework for the Visualisation of Cyber Security Requirements
and Its Application in BPMN** 339
Bo Zhou, Curtis Maines, Stephen Tang and Qi Shi

Big Data and Cyber Security: A Visual Analytics Perspective 367
Suvodeep Mazumdar and Jing Wang

Index 383

Part I
Introduction and State-of-the-art

Review into State of the Art of Vulnerability Assessment using Artificial Intelligence

Saad Khan and Simon Parkinson

Abstract Vulnerability assessment is the essential and well-established process of probing security flaws, weaknesses and inadequacies in a computing infrastructure. The process helps organisations to eliminate security issues before attackers can exploit them for monetary gains or other malicious purposes. The significant advancements in desktop, Web and mobile computing technologies have widened the range of security-related complications. It has become an increasingly crucial challenge for security analysts to devise comprehensive security evaluation and mitigation tools that can protect the business-critical operations. Researchers have proposed a variety of methods for vulnerability assessment, which can be broadly categorised into manual, assistive and fully automated. Manual vulnerability assessment is performed by a human expert, based on a specific set of instructions that are aimed at finding the security vulnerability. This method requires a large amount of time, effort and resources, and it is heavily reliant on expert knowledge, something that is widely attributed to being in short supply. The assistive vulnerability assessment is conducted with the help of scanning tools or frameworks that are usually up-to-date and look for the most relevant security weakness. However, the lack of flexibility, compatibility and regular maintenance of tools, as they contain static knowledge, renders them outdated and does not provide the beneficial information (in terms of depth and scope of tests) about the state of security. Fully automated vulnerability assessment leverages artificial intelligence techniques to produce expert-like decisions without human assistance and is by far considered as the most desirable (due to time and financial reduction for the end-user) method of evaluating a systems' security. Although being highly desirable, such techniques require additional research in improving automated knowledge acquisition, representation and learning mechanisms. Further research is also needed to develop automated vulnerability mitigation techniques that are capable of actually securing the computing platform. The volume of research being

S. Khan (✉) · S. Parkinson
Department of Computer Science, University of Huddersfield, Huddersfield, UK
e-mail: saad.khan@hud.ac.uk

S. Parkinson
e-mail: simon.parkinson@hud.ac.uk

© Springer International Publishing AG, part of Springer Nature 2018
S. Parkinson et al. (eds.), *Guide to Vulnerability Analysis for Computer Networks and Systems*, Computer Communications and Networks,
https://doi.org/10.1007/978-3-319-92624-7_1

performed into the use of artificial intelligence techniques in vulnerability assessment is increasing, and there is a need to provide a survey into the state of the art.

1 Introduction

Security vulnerabilities exist in the IT infrastructures of most organisations. An infrastructure consists of software tools, network, servers, workstations, phone systems, printers and employee devices. There is a strong need to identify and eradicate security loopholes of a system to prevent financial loss, defamation and sabotage. The increasing size and importance of computing technologies in an organisation's daily business have provided attackers an incentive to develop sophisticated exploitation tools and cause increased damage [1]. While current security measures have contributed significant progress towards identification and mitigation of threats, gaps and challenges remain. The organisation itself is responsible for protecting their IT resources against potential attacks, and this will often be performed through conducting periodic security assessments. However, an organisation may not always have the necessary expertise in-house, and they will be required to pay for external consultancy. If an organisation does have in-house expertise to maintain their security, they are also required to maintain such expertise in this rapidly changing discipline. Both of these approaches incur a large financial cost. There is wide-scale motivation to decrease security management costs, as well as make an organisation more agile in that they are quicker to respond to detecting vulnerabilities as new threats develop.

1.1 Importance of Vulnerability Assessment

Performing periodic vulnerability assessment is an essential process to protect the confidentiality, availability and integrity (CIA) [2] of organisation's and user's private data. Identifying and mitigating security weaknesses on a recurring basis help to keep data secure from theft, modification and exposure, meanwhile avoiding the disruption of business operations. The research also suggests that the total amount of direct and indirect financial losses incurred after the attack [3] are usually found to be greater than the cost of consistent investment in security technologies and purchase of data protection systems. Similarly, other studies [4, 5] also demonstrate that the identification of the most crucial assets and performing continuous vulnerability assessment of them can help protect the organisation from heavy financial losses. A data breach often imposes high costs on the organisation, for example, investigating the attack, repairing and restoring the lost data, sending alerts to consumers, establishing helplines and paying legal fees and settlements [6].

In the event of cyber-attack where customer's data and private information are breached, the respective company is often faced with public criticism and defamation. For example, a 2017 ransomware attack on the UK's National Health Service [7] raised many questions on the security posture of life-critical IT systems where users are heavily reliant on them. It has also been proven that the software systems are inherently flawed due to intentional or accidental weaknesses, and a few minor vulnerabilities can be exploited to gain full access and cause large-scale damages [8]. These issues can lead towards the serious downfall of business due to customer loss [9], among other damages. According to one survey [10], there is usually an immediate loss of 11% of the number of customers when breach occurs; however, this may reduce with timely notifications to customers about what next steps they should take and provision of settlements encourages the customers.

It should also be noticed that a simple firewall or anti-virus program cannot always defend against sophisticated cyber-attacks [11], such as distributed virus/worms infection, disclosure of sensitive information, denial of service attacks and ransomware. Both internal and external system security mechanisms are being increasingly compromised by a number of methods, which can circumvent all of the existing security measures. Therefore an effective approach would be to predict, identify and eliminate the possible points of attacks before anyone exploits them. The effective management of such security loopholes through validating a strong security policy would strengthen the organisation against potential damages. For instance, routinely managing file system access control permissions according to a clearly defined policy might defend the organisation against ransomware attacks [12]. Similarly, the continuous monitoring and analysis of abnormal file system activities can also help in protecting the data against ransomware attacks [13]. Therefore, it is in the best interest of both organisations and their customers to employ such strategies that can proactively search for known vulnerabilities and frequently remove them before any attack occurs.

1.2 Motivation

The motivation behind this work is to signify the importance of security evaluations, and explores the currently used manual, assistive and automated vulnerability assessment solutions. In addition, the survey identifies the weaknesses and lacking in those solutions that can be improved to increase the quality and productivity of vulnerability management. Another reason to perform this research is to survey up-to-date literature in a centralised manner and establish a theoretical framework of ideas that can help in creating future vulnerability assessment models.

The chapter is organised as follows: the first and second sections survey existing manual and assistive vulnerability assessments techniques and determine their drawbacks and challenges. The third section presents how artificial intelligence is being applied in the vulnerability assessment using machine learning, automated planning and expert system solutions. The section further discussed identified knowledge gaps and presents future recommendations for further research.

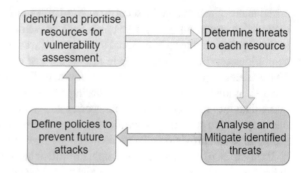

Fig. 1 Generic steps to conduct Vulnerability Assessment

2 Manual Vulnerability Assessment

A manual vulnerability assessment is a multi-step procedure. It subjectively evaluates various aspects of the resources under consideration and produces a list of security issues alongside solutions. The general principle behind vulnerability assessment process (as identified in: [14–16]) for any computing resource is shown in Fig. 1. The steps are described in the following:

1 The first step is to identify computing resources that have the potential to affect one or more mission-critical systems. The resources can also be assessed upon the users requirement. A few example resources are network, file system, operating system and (custom) applications;
2 Prioritise the resources or assets based on their importance level. This is done based on several factors, such as data sensitivity, frequency of usage, type of application and cost. The assessment process starts from the resource, which has the highest priority;
3 Determine threats to each resource and discover potential point of vulnerabilities. This step carries the most importance and is conducted by one or more security auditing experts. The quantity and quality of identified security flaws depend on the ability of experts;
4 Based on the determined threats and impact levels, the most serious potential problems are removed. Depending on the threat, it is eliminated by applying various security measures, such software patching, reconfigurations, managing access control permissions, network monitoring and encryption; and
5 Create and document a security policy or guideline in human understandable format that can aid the minimisation of consequences, if a future attack occurs.

Apart from the generic steps, vulnerability detection techniques are also designed for specific applications, for example, to remove the security lacking of OpenFlow protocol. A research study [17] performed a detailed assessment and proposed the implementation of a proxy server and transport layer security (TLS) protocol for network monitoring and encrypted communication, respectively. In another paper [18], the vulnerabilities of OpenStack's architectural components have been investigated and found various security flaws in the configuration of cloud server nodes. The paper further, along with [19], demonstrated that how existing operating systems vulnerabilities are also inherited into the cloud platform via virtual machine instances. Another paper [20] performed the security evaluation of face and iris recognition applications and successfully demonstrated that it is vulnerable to two kinds of attacks: direct and indirect. The direct attacks include spoofing attacks based on gummy fingers and high-quality printed images, whilst the indirect attacks include manipulating system database and using algorithms that can synthetically generate templates to match within database until system access is granted.

A recent paper [21] conducted the vulnerability assessment for supervisory control and data acquisition (SCADA) systems, where data integrity and availability is of the highest priority. The paper identified seven types of security flaws, such as replay attacks, write to master/remote terminal unit and response alteration, which causes loss of control, time and product features. Another paper [22] performed the categorisation of known vulnerabilities in Android operating system for smart phone devices. Some of the categories are corrupting or modifying private data, blocking and eavesdropping on services and abusing processor-intensive services and functions. A similar study [23] performed the vulnerability assessment of OAuth (protocol for authorisation) implementations in Android applications and proposed a multi-stage model for detection. The evaluation is based on 15 different OAuth service providers and 100 public applications. It is claimed that 86.2% of the application is vulnerable to user-agent hijacking, impersonation and various other network attacks.

Beside software applications, researchers have also examined the security posture of various kinds of systems. Multiple studies [24, 25] are available that determine the privacy and security risks associated with social media sites. A diverse set of security threats has been discovered regarding the anonymity of a user's identity, communication privacy, account hijacking, identity thefts and service unavailability. Similarly, in other research [26], the vulnerabilities of e-government websites are discussed using online data analysis, information security auditing and network security. Many lacking were identified regarding authentication, encryption, egress traffic monitoring and intrusion detection systems and blocking open network ports. Another study [27] performed the security assessment of autonomic networks and services and argued that there is lack of configuration management, network forensics and monitoring. A research study [28] discussed the potential wireless body area network security vulnerabilities, such as insufficient authentication, limitation of address space and routing issues while node mobility, energy management and environmental obstacles. The security reviews and knowledge gaps of Fog platform have also been assessed in several surveys, such as [29]. Fog computing has become an integral part of smart utility meters, 5G mobile networks, vehicular safety, food traceability networks and so on. For the autonomous identification of vulnerabilities in Fog network, [30] proposed a graph-based security anomaly detection (GraphBAD) approach that converts security configuration and audit log data into a graph and identifies irregular sub-graphs.

Similarly, a paper [31] analysed the control and communication components of a smart grid system and presented several attack scenarios to data integrity, service availability, power fluctuation and network communication. Another paper [32] conducted the vulnerability assessment of the aviation systems and found different false data injection and interception attacks in wireless network-based communications. One research study [33] proposes a quantitative risk and impact assessment framework to evaluate the security of general cloud computing platforms. The framework determines six security threats alongside their impact and severity. The threats include spoofing, tampering, repudiation, information disclosure, denial of service and escalation of privileges. A multi-dimensional vulnerability assessment of unmanned aerial vehicles (UAVs) has also been conducted [34]. This survey shows that UAVs are susceptible to wide range of data security issues within communication systems, sensors and autonomous control. Another interesting study identified the security loopholes of dynamic random access memory (DRAM) by launching 'Rowhammer' attack using a JavaScript code within website [35]. A Rowhammer attack modifies the content of a memory cell without having write permissions and actually accessing it. The steps include: finding and reloading two memory addresses in different rows in a high frequency, and exploiting them with bit-flipping attack.

An operating systems event logs are an important resource to discover security incidents and breaches. They have the potential to provide a timeline of what has occurred on a system. The advance persistent threats (APTs) and stealthy attacks can be identified by recognising patterns or sequences in system event log entries. The pattern recognition processes mostly rely on manual analysis and become a tedious task as event log entries are generated in hight frequency. However, some research studies suggest the use of pattern recognition algorithms from machine learning [36, 37] and rule-based engine [38, 39] can potentially increase the efficiency of process. In addition to those, many tools are available that can help in understanding as well as visualising the event log data, such as ManageEngine's EventLog Analyzer,[1] SolarWinds's Log and Event Manager,[2] LOGalyze[3] and NetVizura's EventLog Analyzer.[4]

2.1 Example

This section presents an example of manual vulnerability assessment. The example is based on finding vulnerabilities [40] in a Web application that can be exploited by an attacker to access and expose data, perform database fingerprinting, causing denial of service, bypassing authentication, executing remote commands and performing privilege escalation without authorisation. SQL injection is considered as the top threat to Web application [41], where the attacker can execute queries with a high level of permissions, either by inserting malicious SQL code or appending dynamic

---

[1]https://www.manageengine.com/products/eventlog/

[2]https://www.solarwinds.com/log-event-manager

[3]http://www.logalyze.com/

[4]https://www.netvizura.com/

```
URL: http://www.example.com/showProducts.php?catergory=SQLI
Effect: If there is no category named ''SQLI'' in application,
it might show: ''Warning: mysql_fetch_assoc(): supplied argument
is not a valid MySQL result resource in /var/www/example.com
/showProducts.php on line 34'' for MySQL. In MSSQL, the error
''Exception Details: System.Data.SqlClient.SqlException:
Invalid column name 'SQLI'.''

URL: http://www.example.com/showProducts.php?catergory=SQLI'
Effect: Putting single quote (') at the end can trigger syntax
error ''You have an error in your SQL syntax; check the manual
that corresponds to your MySQL server version for the right
syntax to use near ''SQLI''' at line 1''

URL: http://www.example.com/showProducts.php?catergory=bik'+'es
Effect: Vulnerable application will concatenate both input
strings as ''Bikes'' and show results.
```

Fig. 2 Three cases of manipulating user input parameters to confirm if SQL injection vulnerability exists in a Web application

SQL queries. There are various potential points in both databases and applications where SQL injection vulnerabilities can exist, such as incorrectly handling escape characters in user input, custom data types, insecure cookies and misconfiguration in server variables. There are different types of SQL injection [42]:

- *Error-based*—attacker generates and analyses the error to understand the design and structure of database server;
- *Union-based*—employs the *union* SQL operator to merge two or more *select* statements within single HTTP response;
- *Blind Boolean-based*—malicious user input into an application forces the database to respond differently based on if query was correct or incorrect, which can be used to deduct information;
- *Blind Time-based*—same as Blind Boolean-based vulnerability, but instead of different response, it forces the database to wait for specific time period before responding; and
- *Out-of-band*—relies on the features of database server, which are enabled and being used by the web application.

An error-based SQL injection is presented as an example as it is commonly used and considered a first step in the assessment procedure. Let us assume that there is an eCommerce Web application (http://www.example.com), which is selling certain products. The first step is to trigger a SQL error for verifying whether the application is prone to SQL injection. This can be done in numerous ways as shown in Fig. 2.

It should be noticed here that a Web server can react in different ways to database errors in response to malformed requests. It can show SQL errors on the web page return data that is entirely different from the requested one, hide all errors or display a blank page. Similarly, the application can also react in different manners when it receives database error. For example, the lack of exception handling can crash the application with an 500 'Internal Server Error' message. It can also show result of the query, even if there are unexpected parameters or redirect to some other page. All these cases point towards the possible presence of SQL injection vulnerability.

After identifying the SQL errors, the presence of SQL injection vulnerabilities are confirmed by converting the errors into valid SQL queries. The first step is to determine the data types of parameters (either numeric or string). This can be done by adding quotation marks, as the mismatch in the number of quotation marks would be displayed in the error. The numbers parameters do not use quotes, whilst strings do. The next step is to apply inline or termination technique to change the functionality of the back-end query. Consider a query "Select * from users where username='admin' and password='admin'" that is used to authenticate the administrative access. The inline technique would convert the query into "Select * form users where username='' or 1=1 or '2'='2' and password=''" and bypass the entire process. The termination technique would convert the same query into "Select * form users where username='' or 1=1; -- ' and password = ''" or "Select * form users where username='admin'; -- ' and password = ''" or "Select * form users where username='admin'/*' and password = '*/'" and also bypass the entire process. Different database servers have different ways of commenting SQL. The MSSQL and Oracle uses '--' and '/* */', whilst MySQL uses '#', '--+' and '/* */'. Using these techniques, multiple statements can also be executed simultaneously, like in this URL "http://www.example.com/welcome.aspx?user=45; select * from users having 2=2; --". If both inline and termination are failed; i.e. there are no errors shown on web page, injecting 'Time Delay' queries can be useful for the identification of successful query execution. A MySQL query would be "http://www.example.com/basket.php?id=89; Select Benchmark (150000000, Encode ('time', 'delay'));#", whereas a MSSQL query would be "http://www.example\penalty\z@.com/basket.aspx?uid=59; wait for delay '0:0:9'; --".

Another method of finding SQL injection vulnerability is the static and dynamic analysis of source code. In static analysis, code is reviewed line by line to find vulnerabilities, whilst dynamic analysis is performed at runtime. Both methods aim to find taint-style vulnerabilities, which allow data from untrusted source, such as a user. If tainted data is not properly sanitised before sending it to database server, it can create SQL injection points, also known as *sinks*. A sink can be originated via Web forms, parameters and cookies. A simple example of sink in PHP is: $data = mysql_query("select * from table where column = '$_GET["value"]'");. It is vulnerable because a user's input is passed directly to database server without validation. Similarly, if user input parameters are directly passed into a query of stored procedures, they are also vulnerable to SQL injection.

2.2   Drawbacks and Challenges of Manual Techniques

It is evident from the previous discussions in Sects. 2 and 2.1 that the manual vulnerability assessment requires acute attention to the details of an underlying product that stems from expert knowledge and experience. In addition, doing a similar assessment for other product will require the reiteration of the same process, which can be tedious task for a human being. Considering these issues, the main drawbacks and challenges of manual assessment include the lacking of expert knowledge for a given product, consistent effort needed to acquire and maintain the latest security knowledge, high time consumption and possibility of human error. The issues are briefly explained in the following:

Drawback – 1 *Manual vulnerability assessment requires the presence of experts alongside deep understanding of the given infrastructure and output results.*

Challenge – 1 *Security experts are in short supply [43], and they might not possess a sufficient amount of knowledge regarding particular computing resource.*

It is difficult for a non-expert to conduct the security evaluation and undertake mitigation activities without first spending significant time to acquire the necessary expertise. This also requires a careful selection of knowledge source. Furthermore, due to the dynamic nature of evaluation process and various types of infrastructure complications, there is an absence of a standardised or a 'one-fits-all' solution. Hence, the results of manual assessment would be based on the subjective opinion and experience of expert, which might not be correct in every case.

Drawback – 2 *The vulnerability assessment procedures require a latest knowledge and wide experience in identifying and patching the known and unknown security flaws of products.*

Challenge – 2 *It is a challenging and time-consuming responsibility to always keep updating knowledge, and even doing so, one would still not be able to determine and remove unknown (zero-day) vulnerabilities.*

The security-related concerns are rapidly growing due to constant expansion of software applications and electronic systems. It is not possible to know and understand every known vulnerability for developed systems. It can also become more strenuous with the introduction of unknown vulnerabilities that are prone to exist and can be exploited by the attacker at any time. Hence for manual assessments, the expert might or might not be able to resolve the security concerns due limitations in knowledge.

Drawback – 3 *The manual assessment is conducted by humans, which can be incomplete and erroneous due to mistakes and absent knowledge. Manual assessments also require large amount of time and effort.*

Challenge – 3 *In a large-scale infrastructure, the evaluation of each machine would be labour intensive task and require due diligence, which is hard to maintain in manual operations.*

Human error, either by malicious intention or an accident, is another important factor to consider during the manual vulnerability assessment. It might lead towards the inaccurate and incomplete results, whilst consuming large amount of time, effort and money. It is also evident from the aforementioned example in Sect. 2.1 that the manual vulnerability assessment is very time-consuming and requires in-depth expertise. As it is a manual process, there is also potential for many security flaws can be missed. Furthermore, it is difficult to design analysis tools for every given application. This creates a dilemma that can compromise the productivity of whole assessment process; however, all given issues can be resolved by the development of assistive and automated vulnerability assessment tools [44].

Based on the issues stated in Sect. 2.2, it is of vital importance to utilise assistive tools and framework that increase the quality and productivity of vulnerability assessment process, while minimising human intervention. This section reviews and analyses such assistive technologies.

2.3 Tools and Frameworks

Most organisations have complex and widespread integrated IT infrastructures that store and process a large amount of data on frequent basis. Companies also typically implement their own set of rules and regulations, and therefore are distinctive in terms of security requirements. The available set of policies and user requirements demands a subjective assessment of the given infrastructure. The manual assessment requires large amount of time, effort, and there is always a possibility of human error. Fortunately, there are many open-source and proprietary tools available that can help in improving the productivity and reliability of vulnerability assessment process. Some of the tools and frameworks are discussed below:

Metasploit

Metasploit [45] is a multi-platform penetration testing framework, which is used to simulating attacker's malicious activity. The framework includes security scanners, exploits and payloads for various operating systems and applications. Few of the many uses of this framework include launching SQL injection, network traffic eavesdropping, network stress testing, account hijacking and remote access attacks.

AirCrack

AirCrack [46] is a collection of tools that are used for evaluating the security of wireless access points and connections. These tools are primarily for Linux-based systems. All tools are customisable and operated via command line. The main features of AirCrack include wireless packet capturing, performing replay attacks, deauthentication of connected devices, fragmentation attack, creating fake access points and cracking wireless protocol encryptions.

Nmap

Nmap [47] is an open-source tool to conduct network scanning and security auditing for all major operating systems. It includes various features, such as bypassing firewalls and intrusion detection systems, port scanning, low-level packet crafting and guessing the operating system of remote machines. Nmap also contains a Nmap Scripting Engine (NSE) that allows the user to write (and effectively share) scripts for automating auditing tasks.

Burp Suite

Burp suite [48] is a commercial product aimed at automated discovery of Web application vulnerabilities, such as cross-site scripting, code injection, dropping payloads and malicious redirections. The tool can intercept bi-directional Web traffic by intelligently recognising several encoding formats. The product also contains a 'Burp Extender API' that can be used to customise and integrate it other tools.

SQLMap

Sqlmap [49] is an open-source tool that is specifically designed for exploiting database servers. It has many useful features, such as database fingerprinting, database process user privilege escalation, retrieving data from the database and remotely accessing the underlying file system. It supports all types of SQL injection techniques and is capable of probing multiple database management systems, for example MySQL, Oracle, PostgreSQL, Microsoft SQL Server and SQLite.

Wireshark

Wireshark [50] is an open-source packet capture solution. It is mainly used for analysing and troubleshooting the issues in live network traffic, when one or more parties are communicating. It is a cross-platform tool for both wired and wireless connections and also has a graphical front-end. It has many capabilities like filtering and searching in network packets, saving network and USB data streams in files, port mirroring, network taps and supports various communication protocols.

Other Tools

Many other tools are available to perform the vulnerability assessments. For example, the Open Vulnerability Assessment System (OpenVAS)[5] and Nessus,[6] which are similar to the Metasploit framework; however, they differ in terms of the range of security vulnerabilities that they can identify. Similarly, there is another collection of tools called Samurai,[7] which are used to target software applications. A tool called Nikto[8] is also widely used for determining Web application issues. It supports both HTTP and HTTPS protocols and performs the tests based on server configurations.

---

[5]http://www.openvas.org/

[6]https://www.tenable.com/products/nessus-vulnerability-scanner

[7]http://samuraism.jp/samurai/en/index.html

[8]https://cirt.net/Nikto2

2.4 Patent Literature

Many patents have been developed that propose different vulnerability assessment techniques that do not require manual input or human assistance to complete the process. For example, a network appliance is developed that can evaluate the security of multiple networks concurrently [51]. The network can be remote or on-site, and the product will perform internal and external audit. The assessment results will be communicated via encrypted channel for experts to fix them. Likewise, another invention [52] presents a method for rules-driven multi-phase network vulnerability assessment. It performs the scan for devices in a network and compares the results with a pre-defined rules set to identify vulnerabilities. A similar network security assessment tool [53] has been developed that emulates the attacks for finding vulnerabilities, and also recommends security solutions. The tool is scalable to thousands of customers at a time and minimises business disruption as it conducted remotely using an internet connection. The developed solution is highly compartmentalised containing a database, command engine, tester, report generator and other modules.

Another patented work [54] provides a local and portable scanner, which is capable of finding and repairing vulnerabilities in workstations and network servers. The scan request is launched using browser, which then contacts the server through network to download and install the scanner within browser. Another mechanism [55] actively analyses the network traffic based on a given policy and context. Upon finding a vulnerability, it allows the user to access complete information and recommends remedial procedures. There is also a patent [56] available to assess the vulnerability of a mobile device using a remote cloud-based service. The mobile device sends the scan request alongside required operative objects. The service identifies potential issues, which are then communicated back to mobile device. Such specific evaluations methods are limited in use, albeit they provide deep insight into the underlying environment.

2.5 Drawbacks and Challenges of Assistive Techniques

The discussions in Sects. 2.2 and 2.3 show that, although, assistive vulnerability assessment techniques aid the reduction of expert knowledge and increase the overall performance. However, due to having a static knowledge base, they are unable to understand the context state and configuration of underlying system, which might lead towards inaccurate and inadequate results. In addition, they are limited to the encoded knowledge and cannot detect unknown and new threats. Based on these issues, the main drawbacks and challenges of assistive assessment include: the requirement to maintain a deep understanding of tools and methodologies and lack of learning abilities to utilising new knowledge. The issues are briefly explained in the following:

Drawback – 1 *The tools and frameworks have static knowledge and therefore cannot detect unseen and zero-day vulnerabilities.*

Challenge – 1 *By integrating machine learning and artificial intelligence into vulnerability assessment process, the tools may be able to detect new and unknown issues without human intervention [57, 58].*

Many techniques use static knowledge, which is constant over and remains unchanged over a period of time. It does not increase and as such does not provide anything new. The problem with such knowledge in security assessment processes is that it will be incompatible with new or unseen environments. Hence, there is need to consolidate artificial intelligence in the evaluation process that can introduce automated knowledge acquisition and learning schemes [59] to combat the aforementioned challenge. The intelligent agents become aware of previously unseen computing environments and configurations through using cognitive abilities. Using such agents would be beneficial in detecting vulnerabilities [60], which are not hardcoded into the tool in the form of conditional statements and facts. Moreover, the agent might be able to identify zero-day vulnerabilities before a malicious attacks exploits them [61]. Apart from these, the machine learning algorithm can reduce the manual effort required for recognising and grouping vulnerabilities using classifier and clustering algorithms.

Drawback – 2 *Based on the experimental results [62], the tools have high number of false negatives and positives due to limitations in the implementation and lack of support for commonly used technologies.*

Challenge – 2 *The modern software applications, whether for a desktop, Web or mobile, are constantly increasing in complexity and the analysis tools require intelligence to discern or probe their structure, input and design features.*

Due to the large number of programming languages, development frameworks and computing infrastructures, it is challenging to create and embed universal evaluation processes in a tool that will be compatible with all software applications. For this reason, the tools do not have capabilities to identify all existing vulnerabilities. Furthermore, there are many versions and implementations of the same application for different operating systems and hardware. These issues motivate the need for an intelligent, autonomous tool which can comprehend an applications design and environment to provide useful and reliable vulnerability assessment results.

Drawback – 3 *Assistive vulnerability assessment requires a thorough understanding of tools, detailing how they can be utilised and how the results based on the given infrastructure can be interpreted. The tools also lack in capabilities to perform basic remedial actions against identified threats.*

Challenge – 3 *Learning to use the tools and frameworks for resolving identified security issues has a large dependency on human expertise and will be time-consuming. Another challenge is to understand the feasibility and compatibility of tools with respect to the underlying system and user requirements.*

The process of security vulnerability assessment requires careful thought and planning due to both lack of expertise and the abundance of tools. Choosing a right tool for a given problem involves a wealth of experience, requiring thorough comprehension of underlying infrastructure and business operations. After selecting a suitable tool, the next step is to appropriately configure, utilise and decode the output in accordance with the underlying system and user requirements. This motivates the need to develop autonomous tools, which can independently perform corrective actions against identified issues. This is necessary as the mere identification of vulnerabilities does not actually reduce the threats and improve the security. The advantages of a vulnerability assessment rely on the willingness of an administrator or security practitioner to resolve identified issues. Building an autonomous tool would be a challenging task, which would include automated knowledge learning to determine and resolve threats, planning a mitigation strategy in terms of the given system and a mapping mechanism to convert remedial actions, and then conversion into corresponding operating system and software commands.

3 Research in Artificial Intelligence for Vulnerability Assessment

Artificial intelligence is becoming increasingly utilised in many domains (e.g. manufacturing, transport, healthcare) to reduce the reliance on expert knowledge. This is certainly the case with cyber security where it is becoming increasingly used. It is evident from Sects. 2 and 2.2 that the manual and assistive assessment methodologies require improvements in several areas, mainly in automated knowledge learning, representation and utilisation for increased productivity, performance and quality of vulnerability assessment process. This section provides a survey of artificial intelligent techniques that are currently being integrated into vulnerability assessment, along with knowledge gaps and future recommendations.

3.1 Literature Review

This section reviews existing literature and taxonomies solutions into corresponding sub-categories of artificial intelligence. The categories include machine learning, autonomous learning and planning, and expert systems. The articles are manually gathered from renowned research outlets, such as ACM, IEEE, Springer, Elsevier using the Google Scholar search engine. The keywords used to search for articles are, for example, "use of machine learning in vulnerability assessment", "vulnerability assessment expert systems", "vulnerability assessment using automated planning techniques" and so on.

3.1.1 Machine Learning Techniques

Machine learning is used to build predictive models for vulnerabilities classification, clustering and ranking. Some commonly used algorithms that have good characteristics on a wide range of problems are: support vector machines (SVM), Naive Bayes and random forests. For determining the performance, various evaluation metrics are used, such as precision and recall and the f-score [63]. It is often the case that security threats facing a computing system are defined by one or more set of vulnerabilities. One study claims that by finding and analysing the causal connections among these issues, a risk analysis model can be developed that will proactively determine and prioritise security loopholes [64]. The risk analysis model employed a Bayesian network and ant colony optimisation techniques to represent risk factors and defined vulnerability propagation paths based on knowledge observed from case studies and domain experts. Another research has proposed a similar mechanism, but a key differences is that it uses fuzzy decision theory [65]. Besides observation and expert approval, this paper has taken advantage of events and their cause–consequence relations to add value in the quality of assessment process. Another paper [66] proposed an approach to determine abnormal behaviours, incorrect configurations and critical security flaws in the vulnerability assessment data of network of 44 devices. The approach is based on unsupervised learning and uses pattern recognition and clustering (K-means) algorithms. The technique is claimed to have extracted useful information from data that was previously unknown.

Bayesian networks are also being used to assist system administrators in calculating the chances of compromise on different layers of network. According to the paper [67], a Bayesian attack graph (BAG) has been developed by modelling the atomic network attacks and their causal relationships. The BAG includes the attributes for each attack alongside the likelihood of happening and respective security measures. The BAG can be utilised in unknown environment, whereas the quantification of threats might also help in building efficient security management and threat mitigation plans. Another paper [68] presents a hybrid technique to identify gaps within security controls deployed in a system. It consists of decision-making trial and evaluation laboratory to define relationships security controls, analytic network process to establish probability ratings and fuzzy linguistic quantifiers-guided maximum entropy order-weighted averaging to determine accumulative impact values, which are further assessed by experts. The results presented in the paper have shown successful evaluation as well as determining the prominent controls for better security.

As the machine learning techniques require training data, a paper [69] proposed a method to utilise publicly available databases of past vulnerabilities in training classification algorithm. This method is claimed to serve various purposes, such as determining the taxonomy of newly identify vulnerability and predicting how a vulnerability can be exploited. The support vector machine classifier was used to train 10,020 positive and 3,745 negative examples. Another paper [70] presents a technique to discover unknown and variants of known mobile device vulnerabilities, mainly in the domain of wireless and communication networks. The technique uses a combination of four machine learning algorithms: random forest, Bayesian networks, k-nearest neighbours and radial basis function and have achieved significant accuracy in identifying potential malware and back doors. The features used to train the algorithms are related to phone call, text messaging and Web services. A dynamic vulnerability assessment method [71] has been developed that can identify transient instability vulnerabilities in a self-healing smart grid structure and also recommend (sometimes perform) corrective actions. The method uses support vector machine algorithms and performs pattern recognition to discover instabilities with high performance and accuracy.

Machine learning techniques are also used to identify the security vulnerabilities of Web application, such as SQL injection, denial of service. In one paper [72], researchers generated SQL injection datasets from known attack patterns using a custom application and trained a support vector machine classifier to build a predictive model. The resultant model was able to identify SQL injection vulnerabilities with high precision and accuracy. Likewise, another paper developed an architecture, called Bait and Decoy Web servers [73]. This architecture uses random tree machine learning algorithm to learn the patterns of legitimate Web traffic and applied it to recognise distributed denial of service attack. They claimed to build a lightweight, scalable server that can be integrated with intrusion detection systems to determine security flaws in unforeseen traffic. Similarly, to identify vulnerabilities in the source code of PHP-based Web application, a hybrid approach is presented that uses a combination of static and dynamic code analysis to determine SQL injection, cross-site scripting, remote code execution and file inclusion vulnerabilities. The logistic regression and random forest algorithms were trained for supervised, whilst co-trained random forest algorithm was used for semi-supervised learning to produce vulnerability predictors with reasonable accuracy.

In one patented work [74], the authors proposed an intelligent technique that can specifically identify the unauthorised access vulnerabilities in a system using rule-based machine learning. Different commands are executed to collected data regarding workstations or network components, which then lead to decisions being made by retrieving rules stored in a database. Another patented technique [75] presents a system that analyses the mobile applications in three steps (surface, runtime and static analysis) to identify malicious behaviour. The system uses both source code and data, acquired during mobile application execution as input and subsequently uses clustering algorithms like hierarchical clustering and k-means to determine the anomalous behaviour. The tool is executed in sandbox environment and allows one or more users at a time.

It should be noticed here that some research studies such as by Sommer and Paxson [76] and Huang et al. [77] suggest that machine learning is not ready for practical use. They claim that despite of having extensive academic research done in applying machine learning techniques in security-related areas, the real-world applications are 'surprisingly' limited. They raised concerns are lack in outlier detection, semantic gaps, contrasting feature spaces, assumptions in training data, high cost of errors due to large amount of false positives and diversity of security issues. One such example is an open-source tool, called Vdiscover [78], which takes lightweight static and dynamic features to determine vulnerabilities using convolutional neural networks and logistic regression model. The tool also allows the training of a new vulnerability prediction model. They have successfully evaluated the tool on 1039 Debian programs with reasonable accuracy and performance.

3.1.2 Automated Planning

As discussed in Sect. 2.3, many tools and frameworks are available to perform expert-like security assessment through simulated attacks on different systems. The challenge with such frameworks is that expert knowledge, and large amounts of effort are required to manually choose and execute the attacks. Although some security weaknesses such as unpatched software and insecure ports can be identified by vulnerability scanning tools, their results might not always be comprehensive [79]. On the other hand, a study suggests that if the attack plans are generated by the aid of computer, there is potential to discover more plans than human experts due to intelligent algorithms and fast processing power [80]. The paper also demonstrates that autonomous plan generation can help non-experts to avoid the complexity of learning new knowledge, whilst save time, effort and resources.

Automated planning (AP) is the process of selecting and organising purposeful actions in achieving expected outcomes [81]. The Planning Domain Definition Language (PDDL) and its extensions are commonly used for encoding domain knowledge [82]. Given the knowledge is encoded into PDDL domain action model and a problem file, various classical and forward heuristic planners are available, such as FF-Metric [83], which use problem-solving techniques to generate attack plans. They can generate plans to improve quality and reduce any time-based constraints [84].

Existing literature shows that there have been successful exploration of the use of AP in different cyber security domains. The main area of focus is in generating attack plans that can assess the security of underlying system [85]. According to National Institute of Standards and Technology (NIST), attack graphs are used to model a multiple set of security vulnerabilities that can be used for launching an attack [86]. The vulnerabilities are essentially states that are represented in the form of conditions. The transitions among the states, linking initial and goal states, enumerate attack sequences. In other words, the real-time steps of an attacker are modelled and represented in the form of attack graphs [87]. One initial piece of work involved the use of classical planning to generate hypothetical attack scenarios to exploit the system [88]. The study simulates realistic adversary courses of action and mainly focuses on malicious insider's threat. The domain model includes 25 different objects (basic elements of computing), 124 predicates (information about system components and their input parameters) and 56 actions (adversary objectives), whereas each problem contains between 200 to 300 facts.

In another work [89], courses of actions are generated by taking system configurations an input. The output actions are adversarial in nature, and their aim is to compromise the system in the most efficient way, albeit by a trusted security professional (widely termed white-hat hacking). Another paper [90] uses planning to assess network security. First, a transformation algorithm is used to convert attack models into PDDL representation. Attack information containing requirements and exploits is encoded into a domain file, while information about system such as networks, machines, operating systems, ports and running services is stored in problem files. The object types are the system properties such as privileges and operating systems, while predicates essentially depict the relationship among objects. This paper analyses the whole network, has up-to 1800 actions and hosts 700 exploits. However, the main drawback here is that it uses classical planning, which is why the system cannot handle incomplete knowledge. The research has continued the development of AP for penetration testing [91] discussing the need to overcome scalability limitations.

Partially observable Markov decision processes (POMDP) can also be used to overcome limitations on incomplete knowledge by generating attack plans even if the planner is given incomplete knowledge and uncertainties [92]. POMDPs are capable of prioritising actions based on expected reward that is composed of asset value, time and risk of detection to find the optimal terminal state. Further research [93] investigates how to produce better attack plans for a particular machine within short period of time. Their solution applies intelligent vulnerability scanning actions through using POMDPs to find feasible attacks for each separate machine and inquires targeted network structure approximations on-demand. Despite all the advantages of POMDPs, they are complicated and require large computational resources. It is also difficult to design the 'initial belief' for every real-world problem. As a solution, a paper [94] presents a middle ground between classical planning and POMDPs called Markov decision processes (MDPs). The actions work same as before, but they do not perform scanning. Every outcome of action (effect) is assigned a probability regardless of host configuration predicates. The probability value depends on the level of attacker's uncertainty in launching that particular action. As PDDL is not equipped to tackle these uncertainties, the paper also suggests a PDDL-like language that can allow probability values inside actions.

It should be noticed that there is a fundamental difference between penetration testing (intended to exploit a series of vulnerabilities for adversarial gain) and vulnerability assessment (aim is to search and prioritise vulnerabilities that exist and mitigate them) [95]. Regardless of their differences in term of motivations and objectives, the generation of attack plans using AP assists in evaluating the security of the underlying system. The vulnerability assessment usually comes before penetration testing because it is the first step towards maturing the security state of entire system and focuses on breadth over depth of analysis. Some recent studies have also pursued the use of hypothesis development, rather than attack graph planning, for identifying potential malware infections within a network [96, 97]. Their aim is to generate plausible hypotheses that can elaborate the given set of observations from analysing the network traffic. The malware life cycles are encoded into domain model with the help of an expert. The actions explain whether the sequence of observations is malicious or benign with a certain probability.

A commercial tool is also available, called Core Impact, that uses AP to generate possible attack plans and performs real-time penetration testing [98]. It is capable of extending attack graphs models with new exploits, and handling probabilistic and numerical effects for choosing a correct sequence of actions. The system also constructs AND-OR trees to determine candidate attacks paths towards a particular asset. The tool is efficient in terms of execution time and in the generated network traffic. Its computational complexity is $O(n \log n)$, where n is the total number of actions in domain file. Similar work has been done by [91], where contingent (or conditional) plan trees are constructed for simulated penetration testing.

The process of generating domain models requires additional expertise in modelling complex domain actions. Writing domain models manually can be labour intensive and prone to errors. This has resulted in a pursuit of autonomously processing available data sources to learn domain knowledge. The domain models can be acquired from various knowledge sources such as plan traces and human experts [99]. This autonomous knowledge acquisition process is efficient and has facilitated the exploitation of AP in new areas. However, there are significant challenges, such as gathering correct and complete knowledge, adapting the incremental growth of knowledge and encoding the knowledge into efficient and error-free action schemas.

3.1.3 Expert Systems

The expert systems are also being utilised to identify the vulnerabilities. An expert system is a software application that mimics the decision-making abilities of human beings. The decisions are generated by the inference or reasoning engine through using knowledge base [100]. The inference engine can use one of two techniques, forward or backward chaining [101]. Forward-chaining engines deduce conclusions from the given facts while backward chaining draws facts from the given conclusions. The forward-chaining engines are faster as they have data-driven approach and use bottom-up reasoning, whilst backward-chaining engines show all wide range of possible conclusions (sets of known alternative goals) as they involve goal-driven search [102]. The knowledge base (KB) represents the vulnerability assessment process in various formats, such conditional statement (if-then), fuzzy logic decision rules and ontology [103].

A research study developed a Predictive, Probabilistic Cyber Security Modelling Language (P^{2}CySeMoL) that can determine the overall cyber security of enterprise architectures using reasoning and path planning [104]. The P^{2}CySeMoL generates the qualitative relationships of assets, attacks and defences and determines possible vulnerabilities using decision-making abilities. The inputs include the attributes of various components, such as operating system and firewall. The value of attributes is used to make a decision with a likelihood of whether an attack will be successful or a countermeasure will be functional. It should be noticed that the P^{2}CySeMoL is successor and improved version of CySeMoL [105]. Various other vulnerability description languages are also available, such as Open Vulnerability and Assessment Language (OVAL) [106] and National Vulnerability Database (NVD) [107], which are understandable by machines, and hence aids in automating the evaluation process. OVAL along with its interpreter is used to represent the system configurations, determine vulnerabilities, find the configurations gaps and lack of patch states and reporting the results [108]. NVD includes security checklists, software flaws, impact metric and misconfiguration details and is used for security assessment automation and complaints. The knowledge is represented in Extensible Markup Language (XML) in both OVAL and NVD. A tool, called Enterprise Vulnerability Modelling and Assessment Tool (EVMAT) [109] uses a combination of OVAL, NVD and various metric formulas to determine the vulnerability level of an enterprise and provides a risk management solution.

There are many tools that use an reasoning engine to automatically finds security loopholes; however, most of them are dependent on input from network vulnerability scanners. A tool, called multi-host, multi-stage, vulnerability analysis (MulVAL), is developed that determines the security issues of a network of Linux machines [110]. The knowledge base is modelled in Datalog language that contains security issue specifications, configurations, logical rules, permissions etc. The tool was tested on a large scale, where it detected policy violations caused by software vulnerabilities. Another researched developed an assessment framework for the cloud platforms, called 'Vulcan' [14]. They argued that when multiple services are combined using Service-oriented Architecture (SoA) environments, the overall security state is not determine and many loopholes are left behind. The Vulcan framework can determine vulnerabilities of software application and cloud by utilising reasoning logic from ontology knowledge base. Similar to MulVAL and Vulcan, there are some other tools as well, such as Topological Analysis of Network Attack Vulnerability (TVA) [111] and Network Security Planning Architecture (NETSPA) [112]. For both tools, the core idea is to build and utilise a dependency graph that can depict a possible set of attacks. The graph consists of multiple cause and effect conditions that provide complete information about a certain attack.

Fuzzy logic techniques have also been utilised for improving the vulnerability assessment process. The fuzzy rules [113] are not crisp conditional statements; they range between true and false. The fuzzy logic determines the extend to which fuzzy facts match the rules using a membership functions. Fuzzy logic is considered appropriate for the vulnerability assessment [114] because the level of uncertainty of results is quite high, modelling of rules is vague, quantitative values are not present and assets have different impact values based on importance. A patented work used goal-oriented fuzzy logic decision rules to determine the vulnerability level of a network [115]. The rules were developed using the expertise from security engineers. The tool models the given network into system object model database and then assigns each object to respective vulnerability analysis program, which takes the decision based on fuzzy rules. Another paper uses fuzzy cognitive maps (FCMs) to provide a lightweight-risk assessment method, which can be used to subjectively evaluate any particular system [116]. The system first defines causal dependencies and assign weights to the assets, use FCM-based reasoning based on various security standards and guidelines to calculate risks alongside financial loss. Another paper [117] presents the fuzzy logic-based system (FLS) to determine code injection vulnerabilities in Web applications along with code-level metrics to establish vulnerability impact levels. The proposed system analyses the source code based on expert knowledge extracted from online vulnerability databases and also suggests fixing measures.

There are various tools available that uses ontologies for vulnerability assessment. Security ontologies are also considered as a viable solution as the information security-based semantic technologies [118] can precisely define the entities and relationships with each other as there are always contradictory opinions among security experts and conflicts in data collected from online resources. In an ontology, each security threat and countermeasure can be modelled along with cost, effort and loss metrics [119]. A paper further claims that the ontologies can represent both external threats and internal vulnerabilities simultaneously using concepts, taxonomies, relations, characteristics, axioms and restraints [120]. One such system is called VuWiki that uses ontology to classify and annotate of vulnerability assessment processes [121]. This ontology was developed using 55 vulnerability assessment studies and aims at providing a central, structured and unified platform for assessment details based on a specific criteria. This tool also allows the collaborative work feature to add updated knowledge on regular bases. There is another tool called ontology for vulnerability management (OVM) [122], that developed created the ontology using common attack patterns and applies high-level reasoning and decision-making for vulnerability analysis and management.

3.2   Knowledge Gaps and Recommendations

In the light of Sect. 3.1, it is evident that many artificial intelligence techniques have been developed and integrated into the vulnerability assessment. This has resulted in the increase of quality, quantity and performance of security threat identification and mitigation. Another important aspect to consider is that these techniques are designed to provide assistance and reduce the effort of the human non-experts, instead of fully replacing them. There are, however, many knowledge gaps, and improving them will further increase the application, usability and effectiveness of automated vulnerability assessment. The main gaps are in the domain of automated knowledge acquisition and learning, limitations in computing power and memory, extracting human understandable results and autonomous resolution of identified issues. Following is the detailed explanation:

Knowledge Gap – 1 *Despite the advancements in machine learning techniques, the possibility of overfitting or underfitting still exists while training a model [123]. These issues stem from bias (erroneous data) and variance (random noise) in training data.*

Recommendation – 1 *Acquire balanced data that has complete set of observations with similar amount of positives and negatives. Reduce the dimensions of data alongside eliminating wrong observations. Moreover, use k-fold cross-validation technique [124] to estimate the performance of model before utilising it.*

It is clear from the literature that the vulnerability assessment comprises of vague, subjective and incomplete procedure. Moreover, expert observations can be indecisive and contain conflicting knowledge. This creates a dilemma for assessment processes as they can cause overfitting or underfitting issues, which are already part of various machine learning algorithms [125]. Both of these errors can be described in terms of bias and variance. Bias is the algorithm's tendency to train on incorrect data, whereas variance is the tendency to learn random and irrelevant instead of correct observations [126]. Having bias and variance in training data causes the model's predictions to deviate from the correct value. The overfitting issue (low bias, but high variance) arises when algorithm starts to memorise the training data, instead of learning a general trend or relationship among concepts. It also occurs when the data have more number of parameters than observations. This is why an overfitted model has high accuracy on training data, but performs poor on previously unseen data. On the other hand, the underfitting problem (high bias, but low variance) occurs when the algorithm misses important relationships and results in rather a simplistic model due to having incomplete training data. The underfitted model has low accuracy on training data as well as real-time data.

Both overfitting and underfitting issues can be solved by having a balanced trade-off between bias and variance [127]. A simple model that consists of clear decision boundaries would provide better results and performance. The data should have similar amount of positives and negatives and cover all possible scenarios, without having large number of data points [128]. Another good practice is to perform data normalisation or preprocessing before training using dimension (parameters) reduction and feature rescaling, subtraction and standardisation techniques [129].

Knowledge Gap – 2 *The existing autonomous knowledge acquisition solutions have various lacking, such as needing human assistance in collecting and representing domain knowledge and conflicts and ambiguity in the knowledge of human experts, crowd-sourcing, observations and experiments.*

Recommendation – 2 *There is a need for systematic autonomous learning and representation approaches that utilise data mining, machine learning, pattern recognition, classifier or other similar algorithms to extract knowledge from online data streams. This will consistently provide updated and applicable knowledge in a dynamic, adaptable and flexible manner [130].*

The accuracy and completeness of automated vulnerability assessment depend on the quality of knowledge acquisition and representation. Having a flawed knowledge will result in incorrect security evaluations. Based on the literature, there are many different sources available, for example crowd-sourcing models [131] and involving human experts [132] to collect vulnerability assessment knowledge. The creation of such knowledge sources requires a large amount of manual effort and time, reduction of human error, conflict resolution and elimination of ambiguities. These issues motivate the need of developing autonomous approaches, which can learn and utilise domain knowledge directly from data streams, without prior knowledge and human aid. One such solution [133] is developed to autonomously acquire and represent knowledge from security event logs using unsupervised learning techniques (association rule mining and novel technique to produce causal connections). Assuming the event logs were generated by expert evaluation and configuration activities, the knowledge acquired would be capable of suggesting vulnerability assessment procedures. The development of more similar solutions by identifying other knowledge sources will reduce the human effort, meanwhile expanding the amount and correctness of security evaluation schemes.

Another important aspect to consider is the representation of knowledge as it can increase or decrease the productivity of entire process based on difficulty levels. According to the literature review, there are various formats available, for example propositional rules [134], chains of reasoning [135] and variants of PDDL. There is a need for automated encoding of knowledge as it too requires the manual effort and expertise in domain modelling. In addition to that, similar to assistive vulnerability assessment lacking described in Sect. 2.5, the automated assessment also requires the development and integration of tools, which can take corrective, remedial actions in mitigating the identified security threats.

4 Conclusion

This purpose of this chapter is to highlight the importance of vulnerability assessment in rapidly growing IT infrastructures and review the existing tools and methodologies that can be used in order to improve the quality and productivity of security evaluation. According to the literature, it is concluded that the vulnerability assessment is conducted in three major method: manual, assistive and automated, and each method has advantages and disadvantages. The manual vulnerability assessment is performed by a human expert who can subjectively comprehend the underlying system and user requirements to provide better results. However, this method is cost intensive and requires a large amount of time and effort alongside expertise and experience. The assistive vulnerability assessment is conducted with the help of tools and framework that are both commercially and freely available, but they are based on static knowledge, and each evaluation method is hard-coded inside them. Due to this reason, the assistive tools are unable to understand the system's environment and configurations and possibly produce irrelevant and inaccurate results. Both manual and assistive methodologies require human interference and might not suitable for effectiveness, efficiency and coverage of vulnerability assessment.

It is evident from the literature that adding artificial intelligence into the vulnerability assessment is feasible and provisions expert assessment knowledge without any human expert present. This poses significant number of advantages as the quality 'manual-like' vulnerability assessment is performed in an automated manner, without exerting much time, effort and money. Moreover, it eliminates the need for understanding the given system, performs in-depth analysis and enables any non-expert to identify the vulnerabilities. However, many knowledge gaps are present in integrating artificial intelligence techniques (machine learning, expert system and automated planning) with the assessment procedures that should be improved in order to increase the usability of automated vulnerability assessment in practical environments. This chapter also suggests some future recommendations to alleviate the issues regarding, training data for machine learning and automated knowledge acquisition, representation and learning. Another important concern raised and discussed in this chapter is need for automated mitigation tool for identified vulnerabilities that can further aid the reduction of human effort.

5   Questions

1. Explain the five steps of manual Vulnerability Assessment process.
2. Why do Vulnerability Assessment processes vary between different organisations? Provide three reasons.
3. Explain two drawbacks of manual Vulnerability Assessment processes?
4. Provide a list and brief description of three tools that can assist in the Vulnerability Assessment of a large-scale infrastructure.
5. Is there any difference between Assistive and Artificial Intelligence based Vulnerability Assessment techniques? Elaborate your answer.
6. What is the significant benefit of Artificial Intelligence in Vulnerability Assessment? Explain with an example.
7. What machine learning techniques are available to improve the Vulnerability Assessment process? Discuss their advantages and disadvantages.
8. How can Automated Planning help in penetration testing?
9. Are there any Artificial Intelligence based systems available that can enable a non-expert to conduct Vulnerability Assessment?
10. Explain a knowledge gap in Artificial Intelligence based Vulnerability Assessment? Also discuss the possible ways to fill that gap.

References

1. Sadeghi A, Bagheri H, Garcia J Malek S (2017) A taxonomy and qualitative comparison of program analysis techniques for security assessment of android software. IEEE Trans Softw Eng 43(6):492–530
2. Cherdantseva Y, Hilton J (2013) A reference model of information assurance and security. In: 2013 eighth international conference on availability, reliability and security (ARES), IEEE, pp 546–555
3. Smith GS (2004) Recognizing and preparing loss estimates from cyber-attacks. Inf Syst Sec 12(6):46–57
4. Jerman-Blažič B et al (2008) An economic modelling approach to information security risk management. Int J Inf Manag 28(5):413–422
5. Butler, S.A (2002) Security attribute evaluation method: a cost-benefit approach. In: Proceedings of the 24th international conference on software engineering, ACM, pp 232–240

6. Romanosky S, Telang R, Acquisti A (2011) Do data breach disclosure laws reduce identity theft? J Policy Anal Manag 30(2):256–286
7. O'dowd A (2017) Major global cyber-attack hits NHS and delays treatment. BMJ: British Med J (Online) 357
8. Shahzad M, Shafiq MZ, Liu AX (2012) A large scale exploratory analysis of software vulnerability life cycles. In: Proceedings of the 34th international conference on software engineering, IEEE Press, pp 771–781
9. Lystrup O (2017) Customer loss after a breach is real, but dont lose focus. https://continuum.cisco.com/2017/02/06/customer-loss-after-a-breach-is-real-but-dont-lose-focus/. Accessed 04 Dec 2017
10. Ablon L, Heaton P, Lavery DC, Romanosky S (2016) Consumer attitudes toward data breach notifications and loss of personal information. Rand Corporation, California
11. Keller S, Powell A, Horstmann B, Predmore C, Crawford M (2005) Information security threats and practices in small businesses. Inf Syst Manag 22(2):7
12. Parkinson S (2017) Use of access control to minimise ransomware impact. Netw Sec 7:5–8
13. Kharraz A, Robertson W, Balzarotti D, Bilge L, Kirda E (2015) Cutting the gordian knot: a look under the hood of ransomware attacks. In: International conference on detection of intrusions and malware, and vulnerability assessment, Springer, pp 3–24
14. Kamongi P, Kotikela S, Kavi K, Gomathisankaran M, Singhal A (2013) Vulcan: Vulnerability assessment framework for cloud computing. In: 2013 IEEE 7th international conference on software security and reliability (SERE), IEEE, pp 218–226
15. Jøsang A, AlFayyadh B, Grandison T, AlZomai M, McNamara J (2007) Security usability principles for vulnerability analysis and risk assessment. In: Twenty-third annual computer security applications conference, 2007. ACSAC 2007, IEEE, pp 269–278
16. Baker GH (2005) A vulnerability assessment methodology for critical infrastructure sites. In: DHS symposium: R and D partnerships in homeland security
17. Benton K, Camp LJ, Small C (2013) Openflow vulnerability assessment. In: Proceedings of the second ACM SIGCOMM workshop on hot topics in software defined networking, ACM, pp 151–152
18. Ristov S, Gusev M, Donevski A (2014) Security vulnerability assessment of openstack cloud. In: 2014 sixth international conference on computational intelligence, communication systems and networks (CICSyN), IEEE, pp 95–100
19. Khan S, Parkinson S, Crampton A (2017) A multi-layered cloud protection framework. In: Companion proceedings of The 10th international conference on utility and cloud computing, ACM, pp 233–238
20. Gomez-Barrero M, Galbally J, Fierrez J (2014) Efficient software attack to multimodal biometric systems and its application to face and iris fusion. Pattern Recognit Lett 36:243–253
21. Cherdantseva Y, Burnap P, Blyth A, Eden P, Jones K, Soulsby H, Stoddart K (2016) A review of cyber security risk assessment methods for scada systems. Comput Sec 56:1–27
22. Shabtai A, Fledel Y, Kanonov U, Elovici Y, Dolev S, Glezer C (2010) Google android: a comprehensive security assessment. IEEE Sec Privacy 8(2):35–44
23. Wang H, Zhang Y, Li J, Liu H, Yang W, Li B, Gu D (2015) Vulnerability assessment of oauth implementations in android applications. In: Proceedings of the 31st annual computer security applications conference, ACM, pp 61–70
24. Zhang C, Sun J, Zhu X, Fang Y (2010) Privacy and security for online social networks: challenges and opportunities. IEEE Netw 24(4)
25. Zhao J, Zhao SY (2015) Security and vulnerability assessment of social media sites: an exploratory study. J Educ Busin 90(8):458–466
26. Zhao JJ (2010) Zhao SY (2010) Opportunities and threats: a security assessment of state e-government websites. Gov Inf Q 27(1):49–56
27. Barrere M, Badonnel R, Festor O (2014) Vulnerability assessment in autonomic networks and services: a survey. IEEE Commun Surv Tutor 16(2):988–1004
28. Movassaghi S, Abolhasan M, Lipman J, Smith D, Jamalipour A (2014) Wireless body area networks: a survey. IEEE Commun Surv Tutor 16(3):1658–1686

29. Khan S, Parkinson S, Qin Y (2017) Fog computing security: a review of current applications and security solutions. J Cloud Comput 6(1):19
30. Parkinson S, Qin Y, Khan S, Vallati M (2017) Security auditing in the fog. In: Proceedings of the second international conference on internet of things and cloud computing, ACM, p 191
31. Hahn A, Ashok A, Sridhar S, Govindarasu M (2013) Cyber-physical security testbeds: architecture, application, and evaluation for smart grid. IEEE Trans Smart Grid 4(2):847–855
32. Kumar SA, Xu B (2017) Vulnerability assessment for security in aviation cyber-physical systems. In: 2017 IEEE 4th international conference on cyber security and cloud computing (CSCloud), IEEE, pp 145–150
33. Saripalli P, Walters B (2010) Quirc: A quantitative impact and risk assessment framework for cloud security. In: 2010 IEEE 3rd international conference on cloud computing (CLOUD), IEEE, pp 280–288
34. Hartmann, K, Steup, C (2013) The vulnerability of UAVS to cyber attacks-an approach to the risk assessment. In: 2013 5th international conference on cyber conflict (CyCon), IEEE, pp 1–23
35. Gruss D, Maurice C, Mangard S (2016) Rowhammer. js: a remote software-induced fault attack in javascript. Detection of intrusions and malware, and vulnerability assessment. Springer, Berlin, pp 300–321
36. Ma S, Hellerstein JL (2001) Mining partially periodic event patterns with unknown periods. In: 17th international conference on data engineering, 2001. Proceedings, IEEE, pp 205–214
37. Li W (2013) Automatic log analysis using machine learning: awesome automatic log analysis version 2.0. Uppsala universitet
38. Anthony R (2013) Detecting security incidents using windows workstation event logs. SANS Institute, InfoSec Reading Room Paper
39. Mehdiyev N, Krumeich J, Enke D, Werth D, Loos P (2015) Determination of rule patterns in complex event processing using machine learning techniques. Proc Comput Sci 61:395–401
40. Clarke-Salt J (2009) SQL injection attacks and defense. Elsevier, Amsterdam
41. OWASP T (2013) Top 10-2013. The ten most critical web application security risks
42. Kindy DA, Pathan A-SK (2011) A survey on SQL injection: Vulnerabilities, attacks, and prevention techniques. In: 2011 IEEE 15th international symposium on consumer electronics (ISCE), IEEE, pp 468–471
43. Gavas E, Memon N, Britton D (2012) Winning cybersecurity one challenge at a time. IEEE Sec Privacy 10(4):75–79
44. Halfond WG, Orso A (2005) Amnesia: analysis and monitoring for neutralizing SQL-injection attacks. In: Proceedings of the 20th IEEE/ACM international conference on automated software engineering, ACM, pp 174–183
45. Holik F, Horalek J, Marik O, Neradova S, Zitta S (2014) Effective penetration testing with metasploit framework and methodologies. In: 2014 IEEE 15th international symposium on computational intelligence and informatics (CINTI), IEEE, pp 237–242
46. dOtreppe, T (2013) Aircrack-ng
47. Lyon GF (2009) Nmap network scanning: the official nmap project guide to network discovery and security scanning. Insecure, USA
48. Garn B, Kapsalis I, Simos DE, Winkler S (2014) On the applicability of combinatorial testing to web application security testing: a case study. In: Proceedings of the 2014 workshop on joining academia and industry contributions to test automation and model-based testing, ACM, pp 16–21
49. Damele B, Stampar M (2012) Sqlmap. http://sqlmap.org
50. Chappell L, Combs G (2010) Wireshark network analysis: the official wireshark certified network analyst study guide. Chappell University, USA, Protocol Analysis Institute
51. Webb EM, Boscolo CD, Gilde RG (2016) Network appliance for vulnerability assessment auditing over multiple networks. Google patents. US Patent App. 15/079,224
52. Gleichauf R, Shanklin S, Waddell S, Ziese K (2001) System and method for rules-driven multi-phase network vulnerability assessment. Google patents. US Patent 6,324,656

53. Bunker N, Laizerovich D, Bunker E, Van Schuyver J (2001) Network vulnerability assessment system and method. Google patents. US Patent App. 09/861,001
54. Taylor P, Mewett S, Brass PC, Doty TR (2007) Vulnerability assessment and authentication of a computer by a local scanner. Google patents. US Patent 7,178,166
55. Cooper G, Valente LFP, Pearcy DP, Richardson HA (2008) Policy-based vulnerability assessment. Google patents. US Patent 7,451,488
56. Oberheide J, Song D, Goodman A (2016) System and method for assessing vulnerability of a mobile device. Google patents. US Patent 9,467,463
57. Tyugu E (2011) Artificial intelligence in cyber defense. In: 3rd international conference on cyber conflict (ICCC), IEEE, pp 1–11
58. Harel Y, Gal IB, Elovici Y (2017) Cyber security and the role of intelligent systems in addressing its challenges. ACM Trans Intell Syst Technol (TIST) 8(4):49
59. Bareiss R (2014) Exemplar-based knowledge acquisition: a unified approach to concept representation, classification, and learning, vol 2. Academic Press, Cambridge
60. Saad K, Simon P (2016) Towards a multi-tiered knowledge-based system for autonomous cloud security auditing. AAAI
61. Li T, Hankin C (2016) Effective defence against zero-day exploits using Bayesian networks. In: International conference on critical information infrastructures security, Springer
62. Doupé A, Cova M, Vigna G (2010) Why johnny cant pentest: an analysis of black-box web vulnerability scanners. In: International conference on detection of intrusions and malware, and vulnerability assessment, Springer, pp 111–131
63. Edkrantz M, Said A (2015) Predicting exploit likelihood for cyber vulnerabilities with machine learning. Unpublished Masters Thesis, Chalmers University of Technology Department of Computer Science and Engineering, Gothenburg, Sweden
64. Feng N, Wang HJ , Li M (2014) A security risk analysis model for information systems: causal relationships of risk factors and vulnerability propagation analysis. Inf Sci 256:57–73
65. de Gusmão APH , e Silva LC, Silva MM, Poleto T, Costa APCS (2016) Information security risk analysis model using fuzzy decision theory. Int J Inf Manag 36(1):25–34
66. Corral G, Armengol E, Fornells A, Golobardes E (2007) Data security analysis using unsupervised learning and explanations. Innovations in hybrid intelligent systems. Springer, Berlin, pp 112–119
67. Poolsappasit N, Dewri R, Ray I (2012) Dynamic security risk management using bayesian attack graphs. IEEE Trans Depend Sec Comput 9(1):61–74
68. Lo C-C, Chen W-J (2012) A hybrid information security risk assessment procedure considering interdependences between controls. Expert Syst Appl 39(1):247–257
69. Bozorgi M, Saul LK, Savage S, Voelker GM (2010) Beyond heuristics: learning to classify vulnerabilities and predict exploits. In: Proceedings of the 16th ACM SIGKDD international conference on knowledge discovery and data mining, ACM, pp 105–114
70. Damopoulos D, Menesidou SA, Kambourakis G, Papadaki M, Clarke N (2012) Gritzalis S (2012) Evaluation of anomaly-based ids for mobile devices using machine learning classifiers. Secur Commun Netw 5(1):3–14
71. Cepeda, J, Colomé, D, Castrillón N (2011) Dynamic vulnerability assessment due to transient instability based on data mining analysis for smart grid applications. In: IEEE PES conference on innovative smart grid technologies (ISGT latin America), IEEE, pp 1–7
72. Uwagbole SO, Buchanan WJ, Fan L (2017) Applied machine learning predictive analytics to SQL injection attack detection and prevention, pp 1–4
73. Ndibwile JD, Govardhan A, Okada K, Kadobayashi Y (2015) Web server protection against application layer ddos attacks using machine learning and traffic authentication. In: Computer software and applications conference (COMPSAC), 2015 IEEE 39th annual, vol 3, IEEE, pp 261–267
74. Benjamin P (2010) System for intrusion detection and vulnerability assessment in a computer network using simulation and machine learning. Google patents. US Patent 7,784,099
75. Titonis TH, Manohar-Alers NR, Wysopal CJ (2017) Automated behavioral and static analysis using an instrumented sandbox and machine learning classification for mobile security. Google patents. US Patent 9,672,355

76. Sommer R, Paxson V (2010) Outside the closed world: on using machine learning for network intrusion detection. In: 2010 IEEE symposium on security and privacy (SP), IEEE, pp 305–316
77. Huang L, Joseph AD, Nelson B, Rubinstein BI, Tygar J (2011) Adversarial machine learning. In: Proceedings of the 4th ACM workshop on security and artificial intelligence, ACM, pp 43–58
78. Grieco G, Grinblat GL, Uzal L, Rawat S, Feist J, Mounier L (2016) Toward large-scale vulnerability discovery using machine learning. In: Proceedings of the sixth ACM conference on data and application security and privacy, ACM, pp 85–96
79. Holm H, Sommestad T, Almroth J, Persson M (2011) A quantitative evaluation of vulnerability scanning. Inf Manag Comput Secur 19(4):231–247
80. Khan S, Parkinson S (2017) Towards automated vulnerability assessment
81. Ghallab M, Nau D, Traverso P (2004) Automated planning: theory and practice. Elsevier, Amsterdam
82. McDermott D, Ghallab M, Howe A, Knoblock C, Ram A, Veloso M, Weld D, Wilkins D (1998) Pddl-the planning domain definition language
83. Hoffmann J (2003) The metric-ff planning system: translating "ignoring delete lists" to numeric state variables. J Artif Intell Res 20:291–341
84. Valenzano R.A, Sturtevant N, Schaeffer J, Buro K, Kishimoto A (2010) Simultaneously searching with multiple settings: an alternative to parameter tuning for suboptimal single-agent search algorithms. In: Third annual symposium on combinatorial search
85. Amos-Binks A, Clark J, Weston K, Winters M, Harfoush K (2017) Efficient attack plan recognition using automated planning. In: 2017 IEEE symposium on computers and communications (ISCC), pp 1001–1006
86. Singhal A, Ou X (2017) Security risk analysis of enterprise networks using probabilistic attack graphs. Network security metrics. Springer, Berlin, pp 53–73
87. Kotenko I, Doynikova E (2014) Security assessment of computer networks based on attack graphs and security events. In: Information and Communication Technology-EurAsia Conference, Springer, pp 462–471
88. Boddy MS, Gohde J, Haigh T, Harp SA (2005) Course of action generation for cyber security using classical planning. In: ICAPS, pp 12–21
89. Riabov A, Sohrabi S, Udrea O, Hassanzadeh O (2016) Efficient high quality plan exploration for network security. In: International scheduling and planning applications workshop (SPARK)
90. Obes JL, Sarraute C, Richarte G (2013) Attack planning in the real world. arXiv preprint arXiv:1306.4044
91. Shmaryahu D (2016) Constructing plan trees for simulated penetration testing. In: The 26th international conference on automated planning and scheduling, p 121
92. Sarraute C, Buffet O, Hoffmann J (2013) Penetration testing== pomdp solving? arXiv preprint arXiv:1306.4714
93. Sarraute C, Buffet O, Hoffmann J (2013) Pomdps make better hackers: accounting for uncertainty in penetration testing. arXiv preprint arXiv:1307.8182
94. Hoffmann J (2015) Simulated penetration testing: from "dijkstra" to "turing test++". In: ICAPS, pp 364–372
95. Shah S, Mehtre BM (2015) An overview of vulnerability assessment and penetration testing techniques. J Comput Virol Hacking Tech 11(1):27–49
96. Sohrabi S, Udrea O, Riabov AV (2013) Hypothesis exploration for malware detection using planning. Edited By: Nicola Policella and Nilufer Onder, 29
97. Sohrabi S, Riabov A, Udrea O, Hassanzadeh O (2016) Finding diverse high-quality plans for hypothesis generation. In: Proceedings of the 22nd European conference on artificial intelligence (ECAI)
98. Sarraute C, Richarte G, Lucángeli Obes J (2011) An algorithm to find optimal attack paths in nondeterministic scenarios. In: Proceedings of the 4th ACM workshop on security and artificial intelligence, ACM, pp 71–80

99. Shah M, Chrpa L, Jimoh F, Kitchin D, McCluskey T, Parkinson S, Vallati M (2013) Knowledge engineering tools in planning: state-of-the-art and future challenges. Knowl Eng Plan Sched 53
100. Liao S-H (2005) Expert system methodologies and applicationsa decade review from 1995 to 2004. Expert Syst Appl 28(1):93–103
101. Sharma T, Tiwari N, Kelkar D (2012) Study of difference between forward and backward reasoning. Int J Emerg Technol Adv Eng 2(10):271–273
102. Al-Ajlan A (2015) The comparison between forward and backward chaining. Int J Mach Learn Comput 5(2):106
103. Uren V, Cimiano P, Iria J, Handschuh S, Vargas-Vera M, Motta E, Ciravegna F (2006) Semantic annotation for knowledge management: requirements and a survey of the state of the art. Web Semant Sci Serv agents World Wide Web 4(1):14–28
104. Holm H, Shahzad K, Buschle M, Ekstedt M (2015) P2cysemol: Predictive, probabilistic cyber security modeling language. IEEE Trans Depend Sec Comput 12(6):626–639
105. Holm H, Sommestad T, Ekstedt M, Nordstro ML (2013) Cysemol: a tool for cyber security analysis of enterprises. In: 22nd international conference and exhibition on electricity distribution (CIRED 2013), IET, pp 1–4
106. X-z Chen, J-h Li (2007) A novel vulnerability assessment system based on oval. Minimicro Syst-Shenyang- 28(9):1554
107. O'Reilly PD (2009) National vulnerability database (NVD)
108. Chen X, Zheng Q, Guan X (2008) An oval-based active vulnerability assessment system for enterprise computer networks. Inf Syst Front 10(5):573–588
109. Wu B, Wang AJA (2011) Evmat: an oval and nvd based enterprise vulnerability modeling and assessment tool. In: Proceedings of the 49th annual southeast regional conference, ACM, pp 115–120
110. Ou X, Govindavajhala S, Appel AW (2005) Mulval: a logic-based network security analyzer. In: USENIX security symposium, pp 8–8, Baltimore
111. Jajodia S, Noel S, OBerry B (2005) Topological analysis of network attack vulnerability. Managing cyber threats. Springer, Berlin, pp 247–266
112. Lippmann R, Scott C, Kratkiewicz K, Artz M, Ingols KW (2007) Network security planning architecture. Google patents. US Patent 7,194,769
113. Klir G, Yuan B (1998) Fuzzy sets and fuzzy logic, vol 4. Prentice Hall, New Jersey
114. Aleksić A, Stefanović M, Tadić D, Arsovski S (2014) A fuzzy model for assessment of organization vulnerability. Measurement 51:214–223
115. Fox K, Henning R, Farrell J, Miller C (2007) System and method for assessing the security posture of a network and having a graphical user interface. Google patents. CA Patent 2,396,988. https://www.google.ch/patents/CA2396988C?cl=en
116. Szwed P, Skrzyński P (2014) A new lightweight method for security risk assessment based on fuzzy cognitive maps. Int J Appl Math Comput Sci 24(1):213–225
117. Shahriar H, Haddad H (2014) Risk assessment of code injection vulnerabilities using fuzzy logic-based system. In: Proceedings of the 29th annual ACM symposium on applied computing, ACM, pp 1164–1170
118. Yao Y, Ma X, Liu H, Yi J, Zhao X, Liu L (2014) A semantic knowledge base construction method for information security. In: 2014 IEEE 13th international conference on trust, security and privacy in computing and communications (TrustCom), IEEE, pp 803–808
119. Singhal A, Wijesekera D (2010) Ontologies for modeling enterprise level security metrics. In: Proceedings of the sixth annual workshop on cyber security and information intelligence research, ACM, p 58
120. Wang JA, Guo M (2009) Security data mining in an ontology for vulnerability management. In: International joint conference on bioinformatics, systems biology and intelligent computing, 2009. IJCBS'09. IEEE, New York, pp 597–603
121. Khazai B, Kunz-Plapp T, Büscher C, Wegner A (2014) Vuwiki: an ontology-based semantic wiki for vulnerability assessments. Int J Disaster Risk Sci 5(1):55–73

122. Wang JA, Guo M (2009) OVM: an ontology for vulnerability management. In: Proceedings of the 5th annual workshop on cyber security and information intelligence research: cyber security and information intelligence challenges and strategies, ACM, p 34
123. Dietterich T (1995) Overfitting and undercomputing in machine learning. ACM Comput Surv (CSUR) 27(3):326–327
124. Bengio Y, Grandvalet Y (2004) No unbiased estimator of the variance of k-fold cross-validation. J Mach Learn Res 5:1089–1105
125. Domingos P (2012) A few useful things to know about machine learning. Commun ACM 55(10):78–87
126. Bishop CM (2006) Pattern recognition and machine learning. Springer, Berlin
127. Li A, Shan S, Gao W (2012) Coupled bias-variance tradeoff for cross-pose face recognition. IEEE Trans Image Process 21(1):305–315
128. Srivastava N, Hinton GE, Krizhevsky A, Sutskever I, Salakhutdinov R (2014) Dropout: a simple way to prevent neural networks from overfitting. J Mach Learn Res 15(1):1929–1958
129. Le QV (2013) Building high-level features using large scale unsupervised learning. In: 2013 IEEE international conference on acoustics, speech and signal processing (ICASSP), IEEE, pp 8595–8598
130. Angelov P (2012) Autonomous learning systems: from data streams to knowledge in real-time. Wiley, New Jersey
131. Zhuo HH (2015) Crowdsourced action-model acquisition for planning. In: AAAI, pp 3439–3446
132. Long K, Radhakrishnan J, Shah R, Ram A (2009) Learning from human demonstrations for real-time case-based planning
133. Khan S, Parkinson S (2017) Causal connections mining within security event logs. In: The 9th international conference on knowledge capture, ACM
134. Zhu Y, Fathi A, Fei-Fei L (2014) Reasoning about object affordances in a knowledge base representation. In: European conference on computer vision, pp 408–424, Springer
135. Neelakantan A, Roth B, McCallum A (2015) Compositional vector space models for knowledge base inference. In: 2015 AAAI spring symposium series

A Survey of Machine Learning Algorithms and Their Application in Information Security

Mark Stamp

Abstract In this survey, we touch on the breadth of applications of machine learning to problems in information security. A wide variety of machine learning techniques are introduced, and a sample of the applications of each to security-related problems is briefly discussed.

1 Introduction

Machine learning plays a major role in computer science research, and such research has already had an impact on real-world applications. Within the field of information security, it is difficult to overstate the potential applications for machine learning.

In this survey, we introduce a wide variety of machine learning techniques that are outside of the neural network paradigm. For each technique discussed, we provide an overview, followed by a representative sample of security-related applications where the technique has proved useful. The information presented here is intended to provide a gentle introduction to the field, and to give the reader a sense of the wide variety of applications where machine learning can play a useful role.

The remainder of this chapter is organized as follows. In Sect. 2, we discuss hidden Markov models (HMM) and some of the many applications of this powerful machine learning technique. Then, in Sect. 3, we cover profile hidden Markov models (PHMM), which can be viewed as highly specialized versions of HMMs. Section 4 covers principal component analysis (PCA), which is a popular technique focused on dimensionality reduction. The ever-popular and powerful method of support vector machines (SVM) is the focus of Sect. 5. The basics of clustering are covered in Sect. 6. Vector quantization (VQ) is the topic of discussion in Sect. 7. VQ can be viewed as generalization of the well-known k-means clustering algorithm.

Linear discriminant analysis (LDA) is the topic of Sect. 8. While LDA is certainly useful in its own right, it is also interesting due to its close connections to both SVM

M. Stamp (✉)
San Jose State University, San Jose, California, USA
e-mail: mark.stamp@sjsu.edu

© Springer International Publishing AG, part of Springer Nature 2018   33
S. Parkinson et al. (eds.), *Guide to Vulnerability Analysis for Computer Networks and Systems*, Computer Communications and Networks,
https://doi.org/10.1007/978-3-319-92624-7_2

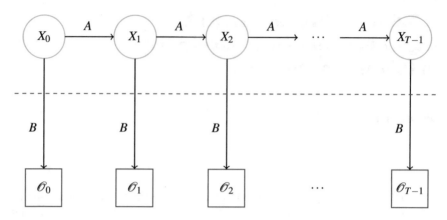

Fig. 1 Hidden Markov model

and PCA. Arguably, the simplest machine learning technique is k-nearest neighbours (k-NN), which we consider in Sect. 9. In spite of—or perhaps because of—its simplicity, k-NN is often among the most effective machine learning strategies. Section 10 covers random forests™ (RF™), which are a generalization of simple decision trees. As with k-NN, RFs often perform surprisingly well when compared to other machine learning approaches. Finally, in Sect. 11, we discuss boosting, whereby a collection of weak classifiers can be used to construct a strong classifier.

2 Hidden Markov Models

2.1 Overview of Hidden Markov Models

This brief overview of hidden Markov models (HMM) follows the author's tutorial [1]. The classic introduction by Rabiner [2] is also recommended, as is the seminal work by Cave and Neuwirth [3].

As the name suggests, a hidden Markov model includes a Markov chain (typically, of order one) that is not directly observable. An HMM also includes a set of observations that are probabilistically related to this Markov process. Thus, from the observations, we can gain useful (probabilistic) information about the underlying Markov process.

A generic view of an HMM is given in Fig. 1. In this figure, the dashed line can be thought of as a "curtain" that blocks our view of the underlying (hidden) Markov process.

Each of the following three problems can be solved efficiently within the framework of an HMM.

1. Given an HMM and a sequence of observations, we can *score* the sequence against the model.
2. We can *uncover* the "best" hidden state sequence. For HMMs, "best" is defined as the state sequence that maximizes the expected number of correct states. In contrast, a dynamic program determines the highest scoring overall path.
3. We can *train* a model to match a given observation sequence. The HMM training method can be viewed as a discrete hill climb on the (high-dimensional) parameter space.

2.2 Security Applications of HMMs

Hidden Markov models have found wide application in a vast number of fields. In the realm of information security, HMMs have proven useful for malware detection and analysis [4–7], among many other applications.

Today, the most widely used method of malware detection is based on pattern matching with predetermined signatures. Some advanced forms of malware can evade signature-based scanning, and HMMs have been applied with success in many cases where signature scanning fails. For example, in [7], it is shown that HMMs can easily detect various classes of metamorphic malware—an advanced form of malware that changes its internal structure with each infection as a means of evading signature detection.

The paper [8] provides an outline for a metamorphic malware generator that is provably immune to signature detection. In [9], it is shown that HMMs can effectively distinguish malware that is based on the technique in [8]. This work nicely illustrates the potential benefit of machine learning—as compared to standard signature detection—in the field of malware detection.

HMMs are also a staple item in intrusion detection system (IDS) research; see, for example [10, 11]. In the IDS subfield of masquerade detection, the goal is to detect an intruder, even when the intruder attempts to mimic the behaviour of a legitimate user. A large number of research papers focus on masquerade detection based on UNIX commands; see the excellent survey by Bertacchini and Fierens [12]. In most of the more than 40 research papers (as of 2009) discussed by Bertacchini and Fierens, HMM-based results serve as a—if not *the*—benchmark to which new research results are compared. Examples of masquerade detection research papers that apply HMMs include [13, 14].

Other security-related research where HMMs have played a significant role includes such diverse topics as detection of pirated software [15, 16], "stealthy" ciphertext [17] (i.e. ciphertext that is made to look like plaintext so as to evade some types of automated scanning), credit card fraud [18], and network-based attack detection [19–22].

A relatively simple example involving English text analysis illustrates many of the strengths of HMMs—and machine learning, in general. This English text example was apparently first given by Cave and Neuwirth [3]. For this example, suppose

Table 1 Sample converged B^T for English text ("⌣" is word space)

	State 1	State 2		State 1	State 2		State 1	State 2
a	0.13845	0.00075	j	0.00000	0.00365	s	0.00000	0.11042
b	0.00000	0.02311	k	0.00182	0.00703	t	0.01102	0.14392
c	0.00062	0.05614	l	0.00049	0.07231	u	0.04508	0.00000
d	0.00000	0.06937	m	0.00000	0.03889	v	0.00000	0.01621
e	0.21404	0.00000	n	0.00000	0.11461	w	0.00000	0.02303
f	0.00000	0.03559	o	0.13156	0.00000	x	0.00000	0.00447
g	0.00081	0.02724	p	0.00040	0.03674	y	0.00019	0.02587
h	0.00066	0.07278	q	0.00000	0.00153	z	0.00000	0.00110
i	0.12275	0.00000	r	0.00000	0.10225	⌣	0.33211	0.01298

that we train an HMM with two hidden states on a sequence of letters extracted from English text. All punctuation, numbers, and special characters are removed, and all upper-case letters are converted to lower-case, leaving 27 distinct observation symbols. If we train an HMM on such an observation sequence of sufficient length, we obtain a model for English text. An example of the resulting observation probability matrix—the B matrix in the notation of Fig. 1—for such a model appears in Table 1. In this case, it is clear that the two hidden states correspond to consonants and vowels. When training an HMM, the hidden states are not specified, and yet the HMM was able to extract important (and intuitive) statistical information from the data. This provides an easily duplicated and easily appreciated example of "learning" within the context of machine learning.

3 Profile Hidden Markov Models

3.1 Overview of Profile Hidden Markov Models

From the discussion of HMMs in Sect. 2.1, it is clear that a hidden Markov model gives us an overall view of an observation sequence, without explicitly accounting for positional information within a sequence. However, in some applications, the position of an element within a sequence provides crucial information. For such applications, a profile hidden Markov model (PHMM) may give better results, since a PHMM accounts for positional information.

PHMMs were originally developed for bioinformatics application, but have been applied more widely—although not as widely as many other machine learning techniques. For an introduction to PHMMs in bioinformatics, the book [23] is the obvious choice. On the other hand, for an introduction to PHMMs with information security as the backdrop, the author is partial to the presentation in [24].

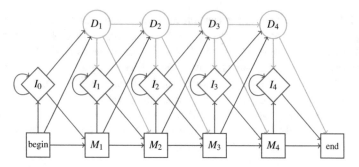

Fig. 2 Profile hidden Markov model

Since an HMM is statistical in nature, an occasional missing or extraneous observation is of little concern. In contrast, any missing or extraneous element in a PHMM will result in a misalignment. Hence, we must explicitly account for insertions and deletions within a PHMM. Consequently, the state transitions of a PHMM are far more complex than those of an HMM.

A generic view of the state transitions in a PHMM is given in Fig. 2. Note that this figure only deals with the state transitions and does not include the observations.[1] That is, Fig. 2 is the PHMM equivalent of the part above the dashed (i.e. the state transitions) in Fig. 1.

Training a PHMM consists of two steps: first, we generate a multiple sequence alignment (MSA) by aligning a collection of training sequences. Then, based on this MSA, we, in effect, define a particularly simple HMM at each position within the MSA. The resulting PHMM can be used for scoring in an analogous manner as an HMM.

3.2 Security Applications of PHMMs

Although much less widely used (in general) than HMMs, PHMMs have nevertheless been applied with success to selected research problems in information security. For example, in [25], PHMMs perform well at detecting several challenging classes of malware, when trained on API call sequences. In contrast, the work in [26] shows that for certain features (specifically, extracted mnemonic opcode sequences), PHMMs often perform poorly, as compared to HMMs. These papers indicate that sequential information is inherently much stronger in (dynamic) API calls than in (static) opcode sequences. This is intuitive, since it is relatively easy to shuffle the order of static opcodes, while the order of API calls is critical to the proper functioning of the code. Another perspective on malware-related research involving PHMMs can be found in [27].

---

[1] Observations are invariably known as "emissions" in a PHMM.

PHMMs have also been applied with success to the masquerade detection problem. In [28], it is shown that for masquerade detection based on UNIX commands, a PHMM significantly outperforms an HMM in cases where limited training data is available. Consequently, an effective strategy for this particular problem is the following: train a PHMM when a (small) threshold on the size of the training data has been reached, and use this model until a much larger collection of training data has been accumulated. Once sufficient data is available, train an HMM on this larger set and from that point on, and use the resulting HMM for detection. This enables us to have an effective masquerade detection system in place much sooner than if we had to wait until we have collected sufficient training data for the HMM. A similar topic is discussed in the book [29].

PHMMs are applied to the problem of protocol identification in [30, 31], which has relevance in information security in the context of firewalls and network-based intrusion detection. In [32], PHMMs are applied to encrypted VoIP traffic and in [33], PHMMs are used to analyse applications based on network traces. Although this latter paper is not presented from a security perspective, such a technique would clearly be relevant in the field of anomaly-based intrusion detection.

Again, outside of bioinformatics, PHMMs have not been applied as extensively as the other machine learning techniques discussed here. But even the small sample of applications discussed in this section shows that there is great potential for PHMMs to make a significant contribution to information security.

4 Principal Component Analysis

4.1 Overview of Principal Component Analysis

Principal component analysis (PCA) is a linear algebraic technique that provides a powerful tool for dimensionality reduction. Here, we provide a very brief introduction to the topic; for more details, Shlens' tutorial is highly recommended [34], while a good sources for the maths behind PCA is [35]. The discussion at [36] provides a brief, intuitive, and fun introduction to the subject.

Geometrically, PCA aligns a basis with the (orthogonal) directions having the largest variances within the dataset. These directions are defined to be the principal components. A simple illustration of such a change of basis appears in Fig. 3.

Intuitively, larger variances correspond to more informative data—if the variance is small, the training data is clumped tightly around the mean and we have limited ability to distinguish between samples. In contrast, if the variance is large, there is a much better chance of separating the samples based on the characteristic (or characteristics) under consideration. Consequently, once we have aligned the basis with the variances, we can ignore those directions that correspond to small variances without losing significant information. In fact, small variances often contribute only noise,

Fig. 3 A better basis

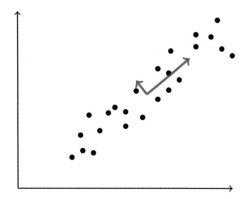

in which cases we can actually improve our results by neglecting those directions that correspond to small variances.

The linear algebra behind PCA training (i.e. deriving a new-and-improved basis) is fairly deep, involving eigenvalue analysis. Yet, the scoring phase is simplicity itself, requiring little more than the computation of a few dot products, which makes scoring extremely efficient and practical.

Note that we treat singular value decomposition (SVD) as a special case of PCA, in the sense that SVD provides a method for determining the principal components. It is possible to take the opposite perspective, where PCA is viewed as a special case of the general change of basis technique provided by SVD. In any case, for our purposes, PCA and SVD can be considered as essentially synonymous.

4.2 Security Applications of PCA

PCA has proven useful in a variety of security applications including malware analysis [37, 38] and image spam detection [39]. This latter application is not surprising, since PCA is a well-known (and powerful) technique for image classification [40]. Executable files can also be treated as images, which provides a natural setting for applying image processing techniques—such as PCA—to the malware detection problem [41, 42].

Other security-related applications of PCA include network-based intrusion detection [43], and problems related to anomaly-detection [44], as well as biometric applications [45, 46]. Not surprisingly, PCA is a classic technique for facial recognition [47].

Fig. 4 Maximizing the
margin

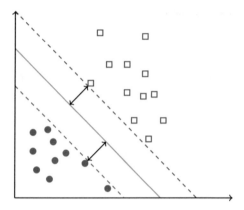

5   Support Vector Machines

5.1   *Overview of Support Vector Machines*

As with many machine learning techniques, an SVM is conceptually simple, yet
gaining a deep understanding can be surprisingly difficult. From a high-level perspective, an SVM simply separates labelled training samples using a hyperplane (if
possible), while maximizing the "margin", i.e. the distance from the hyperplane to
the classes. Such a hyperplane is illustrated in Fig. 4.

In an SVM, the data is typically mapped to a higher-dimensional space, which
makes separation using a hyperplane easier. The so-called kernel trick enables us to
work in a higher-dimensional space without paying a significant performance penalty.
In this sense, SVMs provide an interesting contrast to PCA, where dimensionality
reduction is the overriding concern.

Verifying the details of the kernel trick can be accomplished using Lagrange
multipliers. Although not simple, this is well worth the effort, as the kernel trick is
the key to understanding SVMs. For more detail on SVMs, see [48–50] or Berwick's
delightfully titled notes [51].

5.2   *Security Applications of SVMs*

SVMs have proven to be strong performers in the field of malware detection [52, 53].
In [54], for example, it is shown that an SVM-based score is particularly robust in the
face of common malware obfuscation techniques. In a somewhat similar vein, the
paper [55] shows that SVMs perform well in the challenging task of detecting new
and novel forms of malware. In [56], linear SVMs are used due to their analysability.

That is, in addition to generating a useful scoring technique, a linear SVM often enables us to learn something about the malware in the training set.

Other security applications where SVMs have been used with success include image spam detection and analysis [39, 57, 58], intrusion detection [59–61], and (text-based) spam analysis [62]. Analysis of network-based attacks [63], steganographic analysis [64], and biometric identification [65] is additional examples of the numerous security-related applications of SVMs.

On the other hand, a targeted attack based on contaminating SVM training data is considered in [66]. Due to the geometric nature of the SVM training process, such attacks are relatively straightforward, which might be considered a weakness in comparison to other machine learning techniques, particularly in security applications.

6 Clustering

6.1 Overview of Clustering

In clustering, our goal is to split a dataset into subsets (typically, disjoint) where all data in a subset share similar characteristics. Clustering is usually applied in a "data exploration" mode; that is, we use clustering to try to derive some insight into mysterious data. There are many good sources of information on clustering, including [67–70]. Clustering animations can be particularly enlightening; see [71] and [72] for k-means and EM clustering animations, respectively.

The most popular method of clustering is k-means, which is based on an extremely simple iterative process where we alternate between computing cluster centroids (i.e. centre of mass of each cluster) and assigning data points to clusters. Expectation maximization (EM) clustering follows a similar procedure, but uses probability distributions for its "distance" measure. An example of EM clustering (based on Gaussian distributions) appears in Fig. 5. Note that Gaussian distributions allow for elliptical clusters, while other distributions can yield clusters with more exotic shapes.

6.2 Security Applications of Clustering

Clustering has been used in a large number of research studies focused on malware detection, malware analysis, and malware classification. For example, malware clustering results form the basis for the research in each of the papers [4, 73–76].

Various forms of clustering have been applied to a wide variety of other information security problems, including spam analysis [77] and network-based attacks [78]. In addition, cluster analysis has proven useful in intrusion detection [79], botnet traffic detection [80], and in dealing with various privacy issues [81], among many other applications.

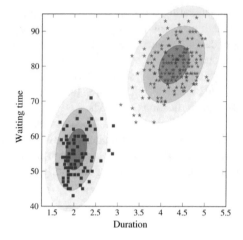

Fig. 5 EM clustering of old faithful eruption data

Fig. 6 Rounding as VQ

7 Vector Quantization

Vector quantization (VQ is a form of clustering where we have a so-called codebook
of vectors,[2] each of which is viewed as a prototype for a collection of other vectors.
A codebook vector can be viewed as an approximation of all of its associated vectors.

Rounding to the nearest integer is a particularly simple, one-dimensional example
of VQ, where the integers serve as the codebook, with non-integers approximated by
the nearest (in the rounding sense) integer. Rounding as VQ is illustrated in Fig. 6,
where, for example, the integer 1 is an element of the codebook, and its associated
"vectors" consist of all numbers in the interval from 0.5 to 1.5 (including 0.5, but
not 1.5, since we are assuming that we round up, as usual).

From a clustering perspective, the prototype vectors in VQ can be viewed as
centroids, with the set of vectors associated with a particular codebook prototype
representing a cluster. While there are many approaches to VQ clustering, the most
popular technique is the Linde–Buzo–Gray (LBG) algorithm [83].

---

[2]These VQ codebook vectors are not to be confused with a codebook cipher [82].

7.1 Security Applications of VQ

Vector quantization (VQ) is a very general technique with wide application. Examples of security-related applications of VQ include image encryption [84], digital watermarking [85] and steganography [86], intrusion detection [87], and malware detection [88].

8 Linear Discriminant Analysis

Based on the typical derivations of PCA (using eigenvector analysis) and SVM (using Lagrange multipliers), it would appear that PCA and SVM have little—if anything—in common. However, LDA provides the "missing link" between PCA and SVM and is well worth studying for this reason alone. Of course, LDA is also interesting and useful in its own right. For more information on LDA, Farag and Elhabian's fine tutorial [89] is recommended, and [90–92] are also insightful.

To illustrate the LDA projection process, consider the examples that appear in Fig. 7a and b. In Fig. 7a, we have projected the two classes (circles and squares) onto a hyperplane where the classes are not well-separated. In contrast, the projected data in Fig. 7b is better separated. In LDA, we want to project the training data onto the hyperplane that "best" separates the training sets, as determined by a measure that incorporates both between-class separation (which, ideally, should be large) and the within-class spread (which, ideally, should be small).

At first blush, it might seem better to determine the LDA projection based solely on maximizing the separation between the projected means. While such an approach would be simple to implement, the examples in Fig. 8 show that this can yield poor results. The projection onto the x-axis in Fig. 8a better separates the means, yet the projection in Fig. 8b yields better separation between the classes. This example shows that it is not sufficient to maximize the separation between the means—we will also need to account for the (projected) within-class scatter.

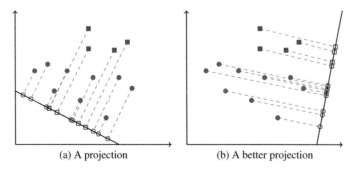

(a) A projection   (b) A better projection

Fig. 7 Projecting onto hyperplanes

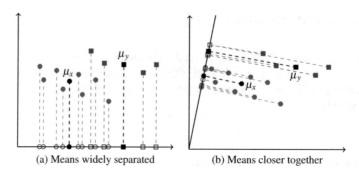

(a) Means widely separated   (b) Means closer together

Fig. 8 Projecting the means

The Fisher discriminant is a relatively simple function that combines both the projected between-class means and projected within-class scatter. Training in LDA consists of maximizing the Fisher discriminant [93].

8.1 Security Applications of LDA

LDA has been successfully applied to biometric problems, including facial recognition [94–96] and gait recognition [97].

9 *k* Nearest Neighbour

It is difficult to imagine a simpler technique than k-NN, where data is classified simply based on its nearest neighbour (or neighbours) in a given training set. For k-NN, there is no explicit training phase, as once the training set is specified, there is nothing more to do to train the model. Further information on k-NN can be found in [98], which includes illustrative examples of decision boundaries.

9.1 Security Applications of k-NN

The k-NN technique has been used in such diverse security applications as intrusion detection [99], biometric authentication based on keystroke dynamics [100], and securing queries in the cloud [101].

Fig. 9 Decision tree
example

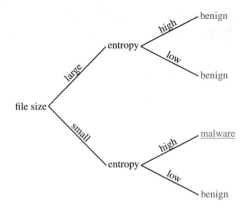

10 Random Forests

Random forests™ (RF™) are surely among the most popular of machine learning
techniques. Since RFs™ are based on decision trees, the basic concepts are easy to
understand, yet the details are somewhat involved.

Decision trees are extremely simple and require little data to construct. In addition,
decision trees are intuitive and easy to combine with other techniques. The primary
drawback to a decision tree is that it will tend to overfit the training data, which is
usually undesirable in a learning algorithms.

To illustrate a decision tree, suppose that we have a labelled training set consisting
of malware and benign samples. From this training set, we observe that malware
samples tend to be smaller in size and have higher entropy, as compared to benign
samples. We could use this information to construct the decision tree in Fig. 9, where
the thresholds for "large" versus "small" (size) and "high" versus "low" (entropy)
would be based on the training data. This decision tree could then be used to classify
any sample as either malware or benign, based on its size and entropy.

We might want to consider features in a different order. For example, file size and
entropy, as illustrated in Fig. 9, could instead be considered in the opposite order as
illustrated in Fig. 10.

Observe that in Fig. 9, a "large" sample will always be classified as benign regardless of its entropy, whereas for the feature ordering in Fig. 10, a "low" entropy sample
will always be classified as benign. In general, splits made closer to the root will tend
to have more influence on the final classification. Therefore, we want to make decisions that are based on more distinguishing information closer to the root of the
tree. In this way, the decisions for which the training data is less informative are
made later in the process, where such decisions will have less influence on the final
classification.

The information gain provided by a feature can be defined as the expected reduction in entropy when we branch on that particular feature. In the context of a decision
tree, information gain can be computed as the entropy of the parent node minus the

Fig. 10 Features in different order

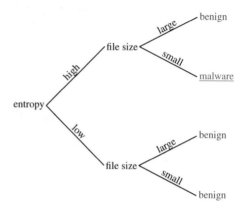

average weighted entropy of its child nodes. When constructing a decision tree, we can measure the information gain for each feature and select features in a greedy manner based on this measure. In this way, features with the highest gain will be closest to the root. This is desirable, since we will reduce the entropy as rapidly as possible. An additional benefit of such an approach is that it enables us to simplify the tree by trimming features that provide little or no information gain.

To reduce the tendency of decision trees to overfit the training data, "bagging" can be used. Bagging consists of selecting (overlapping) subsets of the training data, and constructing a decision tree for each subset. Then, to obtain an overall classification, we can, for example, use a simple majority vote of the bagged decision trees.

In a random forest, the concept of bagging is generalized further—we perform bagging on both the data and the features. For more information on RF™, see [102–104] or go to the original source [105].

10.1 Security Applications of RFs

Random forests™ have been applied extensively to problems in information security. The security applications of RFs™ include intrusion detection [106, 107], malware detection [108–110], and malicious PDFs [111], phishing detection [112], facial recognition [113], and detecting vulnerable software [114], among many others.

11 Boosting

Boosting is a general technique whereby we combine multiple (weak) classifiers into one (much stronger) classifier [115]. Many machine learning techniques can be applied in a manner that is similar to boosting. For example, we might combine

Table 2 Test data for Fig. 11 ($n = 100$)

L	Hits	
	51	52
1000	482	518
500	246	254
250	124	126

an HMM score, a PCA score, and an LDA score by using an SVM to construct a classifier [24]. But the real beauty of boosting is that the individual classifiers can be extremely weak—anything better than a coin flip can be used. And, provided that we have a sufficient number of usable classifiers, boosting enables us to construct an arbitrarily strong classifier.

AdaBoost (shorthand for "adaptive boosting") is the best-known and most widely used boosting algorithm. At each iteration of AdaBoost, a greedy strategy is used, in the sense that we select the individual classifier (and compute its associated weight) that improves our overall classifier the most. It is an adaptive approach, since we build each intermediate classifier based on the classifier that was determined at the previous step of the algorithm.

It is interesting to note that AdaBoost is not a hill climb—we select the best available classifier at each step, but there is no guarantee that this selection will improve our overall classifier. We will see that it can be advantageous to continue, even when the overall classifier gets worse at a given iteration.

To illustrate the concepts behind boosting, we outline an example of AdaBoost where all of the available classifiers are extremely weak. For a particular dataset, we have 100 labelled samples; that is, we have (X_i, z_i), for $i = 1, 2, \ldots, 100$, where each X_i is a data point, and each $z_i \in \{-1, +1\}$ is the correct classification of X_i. Furthermore, we have available $L = 1000$ classifiers c_ℓ. Of these 1000 classifiers, there are 482 for which $c_\ell(X_i) = z_i$ for exactly 51 of the 100 data points X_i, while each of the remaining 518 classifiers satisfies $c_\ell(X_i) = z_i$ for exactly 52 of the 100 data points X_i. In other words, each of the classifiers c_ℓ has an accuracy of 51% or 52%, with approximately the same number of classifiers having 51% accuracy as those having 52% accuracy.

We experimented using all 1000 of these classifiers c_ℓ, and we also considered the case where we only use the first 500 classifiers, and the case where we use the first 250 of the c_ℓ. Details on these classifier subsets are provided in Table 2, where "hits" is the number of correct classifications.

The results of our AdaBoost experiments on this data are summarized in Fig. 11. The darker (blue) line is the case where all 1000 classifiers are available, the medium (red) line represents the case where 500 of the classifiers are used, and the lighter (green) line is for the case where only 250 of the classifiers are used. In each case, we have graphed the classification accuracy of the intermediate classifiers C_m,

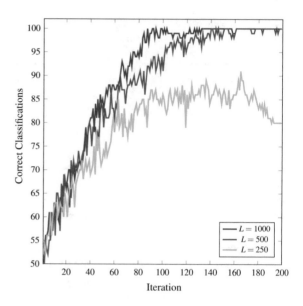

Fig. 11 Correct classifications versus iteration ($n = 100$)

for $m = 1, 2, \ldots, 200$, which were constructed using the AdaBoost algorithm, as given in [116].

From Fig. 11, we see that with $L = 1000$ classifiers—each of which is just marginally better than flipping a coin—we can obtain ideal accuracy using about 100 classifiers. On the other hand, with $L = 500$ classifiers available, we need about 140 iterations before we achieve ideal classification, and with "only" $L = 250$ weak classifiers, we never reach more than about 90% accuracy.

Why do we obtain better results in Fig. 11 when more classifiers are available? With more classifiers to choose from, the improvement provided by each iteration of the adaptive algorithm used in AdaBoost will tend to be larger.

Given the weakness of the individual classifiers, each of the cases in Fig. 11 is impressive. But, these results do indicate that AdaBoost is likely to require a large number of weak classifiers.

It is worth noting that in practice, boosting may not achieve quite such impressive results. Unfortunately, boosting algorithms in general tend to be extremely sensitive to noise. Also, since an exponential weighting function is used in AdaBoost, outliers can cause difficulties.

11.1 Security Applications of Boosting

AdaBoost has proven useful, for example, in intrusion detection [117], phishing detection [118], and malware analysis [119, 120]. Boosting also figures prominently in the facial recognition literature [121].

12 Conclusion

In this chapter, we have brief discussed a veritable alphabet soup of machine learning techniques, including HMM, PHMM, PCA (and SVD), SVM, VQ, LDA, k-NN, and RF, not to mention clustering and boosting. In each case, we also provided examples of the variety of security-related applications where the technique has proven useful. A large number of pointers to the relevant literature have been given, including references to tutorials and other introductory articles on each of the various techniques. For deeper study of the topics covered here, your humble author is partial to [24], which includes illustrative applications that are covered in depth.

13 Questions

1. Describe the following terms and their difference: 'Hidden Markov Models' and 'Profile hidden Markov Model'?
2. How Profile Hidden Markov model is used to detect malware?
3. What is principal component analysis? What are its security applications?
4. Elaborate support vector machines and k Nearest Neighbour.
5. List common algorithms that can be used for clustering in terms of security application.
6. Explain the following applications of Random Forest: malicious PDF detection and phishing.
7. Provide an example of decision tree in terms of security.
8. What is Fisher's discriminant?
9. Why 'Boosting' is a better approach in machine learning techniques?
10. What is the relationship between correct classification and iterations?

References

1. Stamp M (2004) A revealing introduction to hidden Markov models. https://www.cs.sjsu.edu/~stamp/RUA/HMM.pdf
2. Rabiner LR (1989) A tutorial on hidden Markov models and selected applications in speech recognition. Proc IEEE 77(2):257–286
3. Cave RL, Neuwirth LP (1980) Hidden Markov models for English. In: Ferguson JD (ed) Hidden Markov models for speech, IDA-CRD, Princeton, pp 16–56
4. Annachhatre C, Austin TH, Stamp M (2015) Hidden Markov models for malware classification. J Comput Virol Hacking Tech 11(2): 59–73. https://doi.org/10.1007/s11416-014-0215-x
5. Austin TH, Filiol E, Josse S, Stamp M (2013) Exploring hidden Markov models for virus analysis: a semantic approach. In: 46th Hawaii international conference on system sciences, HICSS 2013, Wailea, USA, 7–10 Jan 2013, pp 5039–5048. IEEE Computer Society?. https://doi.org/10.1109/HICSS.2013.217

6. Kalbhor A, Austin TH, Filiol E, Josse S, Stamp M (2015) Dueling hidden Markov models for virus analysis. J Comput Virol Hacking Tech 11(2): 103–118. https://doi.org/10.1007/s11416-014-0232-9

7. Wong W, Stamp M (2006) Hunting for metamorphic engines. J Comput Virol 2(3): 211–229. https://doi.org/10.1007/s11416-006-0028-7

8. Borello J-M, Mé L (2008) Code obfuscation techniques for metamorphic viruses. J Comput Virol 4(3):211–220

9. Venkatachalam S, Stamp M (2011) Detecting undetectable metamorphic viruses. In: Proceedings of 2011 international conference on security & management. SAM'11, pp 340–345

10. Cho S-B, Park H-J (2003) Efficient anomaly detection by modeling privilege flows using hidden Markov model. Comput Secur 22(1): 45–55. https://doi.org/10.1016/S0167-4048(03)00112-3

11. Hu J, Yu X, Qiu D, Chen H-H (2009) A simple and efficient hidden Markov model scheme for host-based anomaly intrusion detection. IEEE Netw Mag Glob Internet Working 23(1): 42–47. https://doi.org/10.1109/MNET.2009.4804323

12. Bertacchini M, Fierens P (2009) A survey on masquerader detection approaches. In: Proceedings of V Congreso Iberoamericano de Seguridad Informática, Universidad de la República de Uruguay, pp 46–60

13. Okamoto T, Ishida Y (2007) Framework of an immunity-based anomaly detection system for user behavior. In: International conference on knowledge-based and intelligent information and engineering systems. Springer, Berlin, pp 821–829

14. Posadas R, Mex-Perera C, Monroy R, Nolazco-Flores J (2006) Hybrid method for detecting masqueraders using session folding and hidden Markov models. In: Proceedings of the 5th Mexican international conference on artificial intelligence. MICAI'06. Springer, Berlin, pp 622–631

15. Kazi S, Stamp M (2013) Hidden Markov models for software piracy detection. Inf Secur J Glob Perspect. 22(3):140–149. https://doi.org/10.1080/19393555.2013.787474

16. Rana H, Stamp M (2014) Hunting for pirated software using metamorphic analysis. Inf Secur J Glob Perspect 23(3): 68–85. https://doi.org/10.1080/19393555.2014.975557

17. Simova M, Stamp M, Pollett C (2005) Stealthy ciphertext. In: Arabnia HR, Joshua R (eds) Proceedings of the 2005 international conference on internet computing. ICOMP 2005. CSREA Press, pp 380–388

18. Srivastava A, Kundu A, Sural S, Majumdar A (2008) Credit card fraud detection using hidden Markov model. IEEE Trans Dependable Secur Comput 5(1): 37–48. https://doi.org/10.1109/TDSC.2007.70228

19. Ariu D, Tronci R, Giacinto G (2011) HMMPayl: an intrusion detection system based on hidden Markov models. Comput Secur30(4): 221–241 (2011). https://doi.org/10.1016/j.cose.2010.12.004

20. Okamoto T, Ishida Y (2011) Towards an immunity-based anomaly detection system for network traffic. Int J Knowl Based Intell Eng Syst 15(4): 215–225. https://doi.org/10.3233/KES-2011-0223

21. Oza A, Ross K, Low RM, Stamp M (2014) HTTP attack detection using n-gram analysis. Comput. Secur 45: 242–254. https://doi.org/10.1016/j.cose.2014.06.002

22. Sperotto A, Sadre R, de Boer P-T, Pras A (2007) Hidden Markov model modeling of SSH brute-force attacks. In: Bartolini C, Gaspary LP (eds) Proceedings of 20th IFIP/IEEE international workshop on distributed systems: operations and management (DSOM 2009). Lecture notes in computer science, vol 5841. Springer, Berlin, pp 164–176

23. Durbin R, Eddy S, Krogh A, Mitchison G (1998) Biological sequence analysis: probabilistic models of proteins and nucleic acids. Cambridge University Press, Cambridge

24. Stamp M (2017) Introduction to machine learning with applications in information security. Chapman and hall/CRC, Boca Raton

25. Vemparala S, Troia FD, Visaggio CA, Austin TH, Stamp M (2016) Malware detection using dynamic birthmarks. In: Verma RM, Rusinowitch M (eds) Proceedings of the 2016 ACM on international workshop on security and privacy analytics, IWSPA 2016. ACM, USA, pp 41–46. https://doi.org/10.1145/2875475.2875476

26. Attaluri S, McGhee S, Stamp M (2009) Profile hidden Markov models and metamorphic virus detection. J Comput Virol 5(2):151–169. https://doi.org/10.1007/s11416-008-0105-1
27. Ravi S, Balakrishnan N, Venkatesh B (2013) Behavior-based malware analysis using profile hidden Markov models. In: Proceedings of 2013 international conference on security and cryptography, SECRYPT
28. Huang L, Stamp M (2011) Masquerade detection using profile hidden Markov models. Comput Secur 30(8): 732–747. https://doi.org/10.1016/j.cose.2011.08.003
29. Pathan A-SK (2014) The state of the art in intrusion prevention and detection. Auerbach publications, Boston, USA
30. Wright C, Monrose F, Masson GM (2004) HMM profiles for network traffic classification. In: Proceedings of the 2004 ACM workshop on visualization and data mining for computer security, VizSEC/DMSEC '04. ACM, USA, pp. 9–15. https://doi.org/10.1145/1029208.1029211
31. Wright CV, Monrose F, Masson GM (2005) Towards better protocol identification using profile HMMs, Information security institute, Johns Hopkins university, JHU Technical Report JHU-SPAR051201. https://www.cs.jhu.edu/~cwright/hmm-techreport.pdf
32. Wright CV, Ballard L, Coull SE, Monrose F, Masson GM (2010) Uncovering spoken phrases in encrypted voice over ip conversations. ACM Trans Inf Syst Secur 13(4): 35–13530. https://doi.org/10.1145/1880022.1880029
33. Yadwadkar NJ, Bhattacharyya C, Gopinath K, Niranjan T, Susarla S (2010) Discovery of application workloads from network file traces. In: Proceedings of the 8th USENIX conference on file and storage technologies, FAST'10. USENIX Association, Berkeley, USA, pp 183–196. http://dl.acm.org/citation.cfm?id=1855511.1855525
34. Shlens J (2005) A tutorial on principal component analysis. http://www.cs.cmu.edu/~elaw/papers/pca.pdf
35. Shalizi C Principal component analysis. https://www.stat.cmu.edu/~cshalizi/uADA/12/lectures/ch18.pdf
36. Stack exchange: making sense of principal component analysis (2015). https://stats.stackexchange.com/questions/2691/making-sense-of-principal-component-analysis-eigenvectors-eigenvalues
37. Deshpande S, Park YH, Stamp M (2014) Eigenvalue analysis for metamorphic detection. J Comput Virol Hacking Tech 10(1): 53–65. https://doi.org/10.1007/s11416-013-0193-4
38. Jidigam RK, Austin TH, Stamp M (2015) Singular value decomposition and metamorphic detection. J Comput Virol Hacking Tech 11(4): 203–216. https://doi.org/10.1007/s11416-014-0220-0
39. Annadatha A, Stamp M (2017) Image spam analysis and detection. J Comput Virol Hacking Tech [online first] 1–14. https://doi.org/10.1007/s11416-016-0287-x
40. Norko A (2015) Simple image classification using principal component analysis (PCA). https://ece.gmu.edu/~hayes/courses/MachineLearning/Projects/Presentations/Norko.pdf
41. Nataraj L, Karthikeyan S, Jacob G, Manjunath BS (2011) Malware images: visualization and automatic classification. In: Proceedings of the 8th international symposium on visualization for cyber security, VizSec '11. ACM, USA, pp. 4–147. https://doi.org/10.1145/2016904.2016908
42. Selvin VRS (2017) Malware scores based on image processing. Master's project, Department of computer science, San Jose state university. http://scholarworks.sjsu.edu/etd_projects/546
43. Wang W, Battiti R (2006) Identifying intrusions in computer networks with principal component analysis. In: The first international conference on availability, reliability and security, ARES 2006. IEEE, USA. https://doi.org/10.1109/ARES.2006.73
44. Chandola V, Banerjee A, Kumar V (2009) Anomaly detection: a survey. ACM computing surveys (CSUR) 41(3):15
45. Chen T, Hsu YJ, Liu X, Zhang W (2002) Principle component analysis and its variants for biometrics. In: 2002 international conference on image processing, proceedings. IEEE, USA. https://doi.org/10.1109/ICIP.2002.1037959
46. Sprager S, Zazula D (2009) A cumulant-based method for gait identification using accelerometer data with principal component analysis and support vector machine. WSEAS Trans Signal Process 5(11):369–378

47. Turk M, Pentland A (1991) Eigenfaces for recognition. J Cogn Neurosci 3(1): 71–86. https://doi.org/10.1162/jocn.1991.3.1.71
48. Cristianini N, Shawe-Taylor J (2000) An introduction to support vector machines and other Kernel-based learning methods. Cambridge University Press, Cambridge
49. Law M (2011) A simple introduction to support vector machines. http://www.cise.ufl.edu/class/cis4930sp11dtm/notes/intro_svm_new.pdf
50. OpenCV: introduction to support vector machines. http://docs.opencv.org/doc/tutorials/ml/introduction_to_svm/introduction_to_svm.html
51. Berwick R (2003) An idiots guide to support vector machines (SVMs). http://www.svms.org/tutorials/Berwick2003.pdf
52. Firdausi I, lim C, Erwin A, Nugroho AS (2010) Analysis of machine learning techniques used in behavior-based malware detection. In: Proceedings of the 2010 second international conference on advances in computing, control, and telecommunication technologies. ACT '10. IEEE Computer Society, Washington, USA, pp. 201–203. https://doi.org/10.1109/ACT.2010.33
53. Ye Y, Li T, Adjeroh D, Iyengar SS (2017) A survey on malware detection using data mining techniques. ACM Comput Surv 50(3):41–14140. https://doi.org/10.1145/3073559
54. Singh T, Troia FD, Visaggio CA, Austin TH, Stamp M (2016) Support vector machines and malware detection. J Comput Virol Hacking Tech 12(4):203–212. https://doi.org/10.1007/s11416-015-0252-0
55. Rieck K, Trinius P, Willems C, Holz T (2011) Automatic analysis of malware behavior using machine learning. J Comput Secur 19(4):639–668
56. Arp D, Spreitzenbarth M, Gascon H, Rieck K (2014) DREBIN: effective and explainable detection of android malware in your pocket
57. Chavda A (2017) Image spam detection. Master's project, Department of computer science, San Jose State University. http://scholarworks.sjsu.edu/etd_projects/543/
58. Krasser S, Tang Y, Gould J, Alperovitch D, Judge P (2007) Identifying image spam based on header and file properties using c4.5 decision trees and support vector machine learning. In: Proceedings of information assurance and security workshop, IAW '07. IEEE, USA. http://ieeexplore.ieee.org/xpl/mostRecentIssue.jsp?punumber=4267526
59. Hu W (2003) Robust support vector machines for anomaly detection. In: Proceedings of 2003 international conference on machine learning and applications, ICMLA03, pp. 23–24
60. Khan L, Awad M, Thuraisingham B (2007) A new intrusion detection system using support vector machines and hierarchical clustering. VLDB J 16(4):507–521. https://doi.org/10.1007/s00778-006-0002-5
61. Mukkamala S, Janoski G, Sung A (2002) Intrusion detection using neural networks and support vector machines. In: Proceedings of the 2002 international joint conference on neural networks, IJCNN'02, vol. 2. IEEE, USA, pp 1702–1707
62. Drucker H, Wu D, Vapnik V (1999) Support vector machines for spam categorization. IEEE Trans Neural Netw 10(5)
63. Sohn T, Seo J, Moon J (2003) A study on the covert channel detection of tcp/ip header using support vector machine. In: Qing S, Gollmann D, Zhou J (eds) Information and communications security (ICICS 2003), vol 2836. Lecture notes in computer science. Springer, Berlin, pp 313–324
64. Lyu S, Farid H (2004) Steganalysis using color wavelet statistics and one-class support vector machines. Proc SPIE 5306:35–45
65. Heisele B, Serre T, Prentice S, Poggio TA (2003) Hierarchical classification and feature reduction for fast face detection with support vector machines. Pattern Recognit 36(9):2007–2017. https://doi.org/10.1016/S0031-3203(03)00062-1
66. Biggio B, Nelson B, Laskov P (2012) Poisoning attacks against support vector machines. In: Proceedings of the 29th international conference on machine learning, ICML'12. Omnipress, USA, pp 1467–1474. http://dl.acm.org/citation.cfm?id=3042573.3042761
67. Jain AK, Dubes RC (1988) Algorithms for Clustering Data. Prentice-Hall, USA

68. Mirkin B (2011) Choosing the number of clusters. http://www.hse.ru/data/2011/06/23/1215441450/noc.pdf
69. Mooi E, Sarstedt M (2011) Cluster analysis. In: A concise guide to market research. Springer, Berlin, pp 237–284. Chap 9
70. Tan P-N, Steinbach M, Kumar V (2005) 8. Cluster analysis: basic concepts and algorithms, pp. 487–568. Addison-Wesley, Boston (2005)
71. Shabalin AA K-means clustering. http://shabal.in/visuals/kmeans/1.html
72. Lad A. EM algorithm for estimating a Gaussian mixture model. http://www.cs.cmu.edu/~alad/em/
73. Kinable J, Kostakis O (2011) Malware classification based on call graph clustering. J Comput Virol 7(4):233–245. https://doi.org/10.1007/s11416-011-0151-y
74. Narra U, Troia FD, Visaggio CA, Austin TH, Stamp M (2016) Clustering versus SVM for malware detection. J Comput Virol Hacking Tech 12(4): 213–224. https://doi.org/10.1007/s11416-015-0253-z
75. Pai S, Troia FD, Visaggio CA, Austin TH, Stamp M (2017) Clustering for malware classification. J Comput Virol Hacking Tech 13(2):95–107. https://doi.org/10.1007/s11416-016-0265-3
76. Perdisci R (2012) Vamo: towards a fully automated malware clustering validity analysis. In: Proceedings of the 28th annual computer security applications conference, ACSAC '12. ACM, New York, USA, pp 329–338. https://doi.org/10.1145/2420950.2420999
77. Wei C, Sprague A, Warner G (2009) Clustering malware-generated spam emails with a novel fuzzy string matching algorithm. In: Proceedings of the 2009 ACM symposium on applied computing, SAC '09. ACM, New York, USA, pp 889–890. https://doi.org/10.1145/1529282.1529473
78. Perdisci R, Lee W, Feamster N (2010) Behavioral clustering of http-based malware and signature generation using malicious network traces. In: Proceedings of the 7th USENIX conference on networked systems design and implementation, NSDI'10. USENIX Association, Berkeley, USA, pp. 26–26. http://dl.acm.org/citation.cfm?id=1855711.1855737
79. Portnoy L, Eskin E, Stolfo S (2001) Intrusion detection with unlabeled data using clustering. In: Proceedings of ACM CSS workshop on data mining applied to security (DMSA-2001), pp 5–8
80. Gu G, Perdisci R, Zhang J, Lee W (2008) Botminer: clustering analysis of network traffic for protocol- and structure-independent botnet detection. In: Proceedings of the 17th conference on security symposium, SS'08. USENIX Association, Berkeley, USA, pp 139–154. http://dl.acm.org/citation.cfm?id=1496711.1496721
81. Vaidya J, Clifton C (2003) Privacy-preserving k-means clustering over vertically partitioned data. In: Proceedings of the Ninth ACM SIGKDD international conference on knowledge discovery and data mining, KDD '03. ACM, New York, USA, pp. 206–215. https://doi.org/10.1145/956750.956776
82. Stamp M (2011) Information security: principles and practice, 2nd edn. Wiley, USA (2011)
83. Linde Y, Buzo A, Gray RM (1980) An algorithm for vector quantizer design. IEEE Trans Commun 28:84–95
84. Chen T-S, Chang C-C, Hwang M-S (1998) A virtual image cryptosystem based upon vector quantization. IEEE Trans Image Process 7(10):1485–1488
85. Cox IJ, Kilian J, Leighton FT, Shamoon T (1997) Secure spread spectrum watermarking for multimedia. IEEE Trans Image Proces 6(12):1673–1687
86. Chang C-C, Tai W-L, Lin M-H (2005) A reversible data hiding scheme with modified side match vector quantization. In: 19th international conference on advanced information networking and applications, AINA 2005, vol. 1. IEEE, USA, pp. 947–952
87. Zheng J, Hu M (2006) An anomaly intrusion detection system based on vector quantization. IEICE Trans Inf Syst 89(1):201–210
88. Ichino M, Kawamoto K, Iwano T, Hatada M, Yoshiura H (2015) Evaluating header information features for malware infection detection. J Inf Process 23(5):603–612

89. Farag AA, Elhabian SY (2009) A tutorial on data reduction: linear discriminant analysis (LDA). http://www.di.univr.it/documenti/OccorrenzaIns/matdid/matdid437773.pdf
90. Balakrishnama S, Ganapathiraju A (2007) Linear discriminant analysis — a brief tutorial. http://www.music.mcgill.ca/~ich/classes/mumt611_07/classifiers/lda_theory.pdf
91. Raschka S (2014) Linear discriminant analysis — Bit by bit. http://sebastianraschka.com/Articles/2014_python_lda.html
92. Welling M. Fisher linear discriminant analysis. http://www.ics.uci.edu/~welling/classnotes/papers_class/Fisher-LDA.pdf
93. Farag AA, Elhabian SY (2008) A tutorial on data reduction: linear discriminant analysis (LDA). http://www.di.univr.it/documenti/OccorrenzaIns/matdid/matdid437773.pdf
94. Kan M, Shan S, Xu D, Chen X (2011) Side-information based linear discriminant analysis for face recognition. BMVC 11:1–12
95. Liu C, Wechsler H (2002) Gabor feature based classification using the enhanced fisher linear discriminant model for face recognition. IEEE Trans Image Process 11(4):467–476. https://doi.org/10.1109/TIP.2002.999679
96. Lu J, Plataniotis KN, Venetsanopoulos AN (2005) Regularization studies of linear discriminant analysis in small sample size scenarios with application to face recognition. Pattern Recog Lett 26(2):181–191
97. Boulgouris NV, Chi ZX (2007) Gait recognition using radon transform and linear discriminant analysis. IEEE Trans Image Process 16(3):731–740
98. Zakka K (2016) A complete guide to k-nearest-neighbors with applications in python and R. https://kevinzakka.github.io/2016/07/13/k-nearest-neighbor/
99. Liao Y, Vemuri VR (2002) Use of k-nearest neighbor classifier for intrusion detection. Comput Secur 21(5):439–448
100. Hu J, Gingrich D, Sentosa A (2008) A k-nearest neighbor approach for user authentication through biometric keystroke dynamics. In: IEEE international conference on communications, ICC'08. IEEE, USA, pp 1556–1560
101. Elmehdwi Y, Samanthula BK, Jiang W (2014) Secure k-nearest neighbor query over encrypted data in outsourced environments. In: 30th international conference on data engineering, ICDE 2014. IEEE, USA, pp 664–675
102. Chen E (2011) How does randomization in a random forest work? https://www.quora.com/How-does-randomization-in-a-random-forest-work
103. Liaw A, Wiener M (2011) Classification and regression by randomforest. R News 2(3):18–22
104. Lin Y, Jeon Y (2002) Random forests and adaptive nearest neighbors, Technical Report 1055, Department of statistics, University of Wisconsin. https://www.stat.wisc.edu/sites/default/files/tr1055.pdf
105. Breiman L, Cutler A (2001) Random forests™. https://www.stat.berkeley.edu/~breiman/RandomForests/cc_home.htm
106. Thaseen S, Kumar CA (2013) An analysis of supervised tree based classifiers for intrusion detection system. In: 2013 International conference on pattern recognition, informatics and mobile engineering, PRIME 2013. IEEE, USA, pp 294–299
107. Zhang J, Zulkernine M (2006) A hybrid network intrusion detection technique using random forests. In: Proceedings of the first international conference on availability, reliability and security, ARES '06. IEEE, USA, pp 262–269. https://doi.org/10.1109/ARES.2006.7
108. Santos I, Brezo F, Ugarte-Pedrero X, Bringas PG (2013) Opcode sequences as representation of executables for data-mining-based unknown malware detection. Inf Sci 231:64–82
109. Sanz B, Santos I, Laorden C, Ugarte-Pedrero X, Bringas PG, Álvarez G (2013) Puma: permission usage to detect malware in Android. In: International joint conference CISIS12-ICEUTE′ 12-SOCO′, vol. 189. Springer, Berlin, pp 289–298
110. Shabtai A, Fledel Y, Elovici Y (2010) Automated static code analysis for classifying Android applications using machine learning. In: International conference on computational intelligence and security, CIS 2010. IEEE, USA, pp 329–333
111. Smutz C, Stavrou A (2012) Malicious pdf detection using metadata and structural features. In: Proceedings of the 28th annual computer security applications conference. ACM, USA, pp 239–248

112. Ma L, Ofoghi B, Watters P, Brown S (2009) Detecting phishing emails using hybrid features. In: Symposia and workshops on ubiquitous, autonomic and trusted computing, UIC-ATC'09. IEEE, USA, pp 493–497
113. Ghosal V, Tikmani P, Gupta P (2009) Face classification using Gabor wavelets and random forest. In: Canadian conference on computer and robot vision, CRV'09. IEEE, USA, pp 68–73
114. Nguyen VH, Tran LMS (2010) Predicting vulnerable software components with dependency graphs. In: Proceedings of the 6th international workshop on security measurements and metrics. ACM, USA, p 3
115. Rojas R (2009) AdaBoost and the super bowl of classifiers: a tutorial introduction to adaptive boosting. http://www.inf.fu-berlin.de/inst/ag-ki/adaboost4.pdf
116. Stamp M (2017) Boost your knowledge of adaboost. https://www.cs.sjsu.edu/~stamp/ML/files/ada.pdf
117. Hu W, Maybank S (2008) Adaboost-based algorithm for network intrusion detection. IEEE Trans Syst Man Cyber Part B (Cybernetics) 38(2): 577–583
118. Miyamoto D, Hazeyama H, Kadobayashi Y (2007) A proposal of the adaboost-based detection of phishing sites. In: Proceedings of the joint workshop on information security
119. Aswini A, Vinod P (2014) Droid permission miner: Mining prominent permissions for android malware analysis. In: 2014 fifth international conference on the applications of digital information and web technologies (ICADIWT). IEEE, USA, pp. 81–86
120. Khan MS, Siddiqui S, McLeod RD, Ferens K, Kinsner W (2016) Fractal based adaptive boosting algorithm for cognitive detection of computer malware. In: 5th international conference on cognitive informatics & cognitive computing, ICCI*CC. IEEE, USA, pp 50–59
121. Yang P, Shan S, Gao W, Li SZ, Zhang D (2004) Face recognition using ada-boosted Gabor features. In: Proceedings of sixth IEEE international conference on automatic face and gesture recognition. IEEE, pp 356–361

Part II
Vulnerability Assessment Frameworks

Vulnerability Assessment of Cyber Security for SCADA Systems

Kyle Coffey, Leandros A. Maglaras, Richard Smith, Helge Janicke,
Mohamed Amine Ferrag, Abdelouahid Derhab, Mithun Mukherjee,
Stylianos Rallis and Awais Yousaf

Abstract Supervisory control and data acquisition (SCADA) systems use programmable logic controllers (PLC) or other intelligent electronic devices (IED),
remote terminal units (RTU) and input/output (I/O) devices to manage electrome-
chanical equipment in either local or distributed environments. SCADA systems
cover a range of industrial sectors and critical infrastructures such as water treatment
and supply, electricity generation and distribution, oil refining, food production and
logistics. Several factors have contributed to the escalation of risks specific to control

K. Coffey · L. A. Maglaras (✉) · R. Smith · H. Janicke
De Montfort University, Leiceter, U.K.
e-mail: leandros.maglaras@dmu.ac.uk

K. Coffey
e-mail: P13211535@my365.dmu.ac.uk

R. Smith
e-mail: rgs@dmu.ac.uk

H. Janicke
e-mail: heljanic@dmu.ac.uk

M. A. Ferrag
Department of Computer Science, Guelma University, Guelma, Algeria
e-mail: mohamed.amine.ferrag@gmail.com

A. Derhab
Center of Excellence in Information Assurance, King Saud University, Riyadh,
Saudi Arabia
e-mail: abderhab@ksu.edu.sa

M. Mukherjee
Guangdong Provincial Key Lab of Petrochemical Equipment Fault Diagnosis,
Guangdong University of Petrochemical Technology, Maoming, China
e-mail: m.mukherjee@ieee.org

S. Rallis
General Secretary of Digital Policy, Athens, Greece
e-mail: Strallis@gmail.com

A. Yousaf
University of Engineering and Technology, Lahore, Pakistan
e-mail: mr.awais.yousaf@ieee.org

© Springer International Publishing AG, part of Springer Nature 2018
S. Parkinson et al. (eds.), *Guide to Vulnerability Analysis for Computer Networks
and Systems*, Computer Communications and Networks,
https://doi.org/10.1007/978-3-319-92624-7_3

systems, including the adoption of standardized technologies with known vulnerabilities, interconnectivity with other networks, use of insecure remote connections and widespread availability of technical information about control systems. This chapter discusses vulnerability assessment of SCADA systems, focusing on several aspects such as asset discovery, identification of vulnerabilities and threats, mitigation of attacks and presentation of major privacy issues.

1 Introduction

In the winter of 2014, the lights went out for over 70 million Americans across the North East, fear spread as a lack of power combined with sub-zero temperatures. Banks lost operations, hospitals were blacked out, air traffic was shut down, Internet and communications were lost [1]. What was the cause of this national meltdown? A group of hacktivists decided to spread panic by attacking critical infrastructure. The attack revealed how dependent we have become on a single point of failure, energy. Energy generation and distribution are getting smarter, no more stand-alone units for the massive network of devices; this is the digital age. Energy is transformed into data, new threats, emerging risks, countless cyber attacks. Our comfort and lifestyles are at risk, financial institutions, communications, hospitals are vulnerable. Critical infrastructure is interdependent; a failure in one and may lead to an uncontrollable chain reaction. The security and economic robustness of any country must be protected; therefore, energy cyber security has become a strategic concern. New energy cyber security solutions, along with energy device performance databases, are needed to continually mitigate and counter vulnerabilities. If we are connected to the grid, everyone is connected to us; therefore, we must know exactly how vulnerable energy assets are. Also in December 2016, a power blackout in Ukraine's capital Kiev was caused by a cyber attack and preliminary findings indicated that workstations and SCADA systems, linked to the 330 kw substation north, were influenced by external sources outside normal parameters [2].

Leveraging off "traditional" threats and possible attacks associated with information and communication technologies (ICT) such as denial of service, spoofing, message tampering, new and more sophisticated threats and methods of attacks via vulnerable points of access such as smart meters, and more generally, sensor weaknesses are continually being discovered. Load altering attacks (LAA) [3] attempt to alter a group of unsecured controllable loads in order to damage the grid through circuit overflow or other such mechanisms. Attacks can be either static (leading "simply" to offsets in node/network load volume), or dynamic, (when they evolve over time according to an attack scheme, leading to the progressive degradation of a network's state. During an LAA attack, the same smart meter is exploited to give the attacker critical network sensing information needed to develop and reinforce the attack over time.

Other areas of cyber security research have demonstrated the feasibility of the so-called unidentifiable false data injection attacks [4], which are attacks that cannot be detected by the network state estimator. Increased connectivity of billions of energy devices, smart meters, photovoltaic modules, home automation systems will see an equally exponential rise in vulnerable access points via the modern energy grid that will forever change the ways in which we must think about the many complex multidimensional levels of protection needed to defend against all external threats.

2 SCADA Systems

Industrial control systems (ICS) and SCADA systems are an integral aspect of the modern industrial environment and the critical national infrastructure (CNI). For many years, SCADA and ICS networks were a completely independent sector of any business or agency, where the field devices and industrial mechanisms which interacted with physical assets were separate from the corporate networks or Intranet. However, as Internet technologies became ever more integrated into modern society, and as corporations began to grow exponentially around the globe, the demand for remote auditing and control of industrial systems increased. This resulted in the merging of Internet Protocol (IP) and SCADA/ICS technologies, which in turn exposed the older field devices to a new set of attack vectors, leading to unprecedented vulnerabilities when integrated with IP [5]. In an age where threats from the cyber domain are ever evolving, the tools used to perform security audits and penetration tests against IP systems are subsequently being used on the older SCADA/ICS networks. These tools, without the correct configuration, could not be effective or even cause substantial damage to the SCADA devices connected to a business's infrastructure, rather than helping to protect and audit them [6].

SCADA and ICS technologies are prevalent not only within manufacturing industries, but also within the organizations responsible for the safety and well-being of citizens around the globe [7]. Water treatment facilities, electrical grids and nuclear power stations all rely on a combination of SCADA and IP networks in order to control the distribution and regulation of the services they provide [8]. As these industries have become greater in both scale and complexity, the automation and upkeep of all the technology within these environments must be handled by machines and computers. Having the ability to remotely monitor and control large industrial sights allows companies and industries to expand their capabilities in order to provide more services to the general public, whilst at the same time making the data accessible to the staff responsible for operating and engineering the technologies in question. All the examples stated above contain resources which are not only essential to the operation of modern-day life, but could potentially have devastating consequences if any of these systems were to malfunction. Not only do these systems threaten the lives of the people who use this technology, but also the environments and the civilizations which surround these facilities.

Cyber attacks against SCADA systems are considered extremely dangerous for CNIs operativeness and must be addressed in a specific way. As an example, one of the most adopted attacks to a SCADA system is based on fake commands sent from the SCADA to the RTUs. Among others, STUXNET worm infection perfectly represents the frailty of the regulatory systems devoted to control CNIs [9]. First isolated in mid-June 2010, STUXNET is a computer virus specifically designed for attacking Windows-based industrial computers and taking control of PLCs, influencing the behaviour of remote actuators and leading to instability phenomena or even worse. The paradox is that CNIs massively rely on newest interconnected (and vulnerable) ICT technologies, while the control equipment is typically old, legacy software/hardware. Such a combination of factors may lead to very dangerous situations, exposing the systems to a wide variety of attacks.

Similar to when a cyber attack is launched against a company's database or Web server, the exploitation or misuse of the devices found on a SCADA network can have negative effects on both the clientele and the corporation [10]. However, unlike the IP networks in abundance today, SCADA systems are not only threatened by hackers wishing to exploit vulnerabilities in software or firmware, but also by the tools commonly associated with monitoring, auditing and securing networks. Cyber attacks or misuse of security tools could cause the devices to become unresponsive [11] or alter the data being received by the device or being stored on the device [10]. In such an event, field devices including water pumps, electricity generators or pneumatic instruments could either stop functioning or begin to behave erratically, causing damage to either the devices themselves, the products they interact with, or the customers who use their facilities. Whereas IP networks can cause significant damage to intellectual property and personal privacy, there is evidence that malfunctioning SCADA systems have caused physical damage [12].

3 Detecting Assets

Reconnaissance, whether passive or active, lawful or malicious, remains one of the most important parts of any strategic cyber security operation [13]. Network scans help visualize the configuration of a communications infrastructure and help identify possible methods of entry or exploitation. Reconnaissance can be achieved through service detection and operating system fingerprinting, two key features of many network scanning tools [14]. Conducting reconnaissance within the cyber domain has become even more vital as the CNIs of various countries are now governed and controlled using computer networks. These systems are responsible for the auditing and control of national grids, power stations, water treatment plants and industrial production lines.

Passive Scanning: Passive scanning methods use the monitoring of network traffic to identify services, hosts and clients. An observation point is setup on the network, requiring assistance from the network administrators or network engineers to configure these systems for optimum results. As referenced in [15], passive scanners can be run continuously for large periods of time without disrupting regular network traffic or interacting with the devices themselves, as the input data for passive scanning tools is a direct feed of the network's traffic. This means that algorithms can be created in order to dissect each protocol. This has the potential to extract important information and identifiers from each packet. An independent passive scanner designed by [16] demonstrates how a simple algorithm can be created to extract Modbus traffic from a network, gain information about master and slave devices as well as monitoring the status of Modbus transactions. Although the algorithms used in this project demonstrate the versatility of passive scanners, the tools are still only limited to analysing a single SCADA protocol. The validity of the algorithms could also be challenged as this system was designed and implemented in 2007. There is a significant chance that changes may have been made to this particular protocol which makes the extraction and parsing system redundant [13].

Active Probing: The process of active probing has one significant difference to passive sniffing: live interaction with the devices. Bartlett, Heidemann and Papadopoulos [17] define active probing as "*attempting to contact each service at each host. Sending packets to each host and monitoring the response*". Another definition is given by Deraison and Gula [18], which says "*any use of a network scanner to find hosts, services and vulnerabilities is an active assessment.*".

In evaluating the information given in the previous sources, the process of passively scanning a network seems to be far more applicable to gaining information about devices on an ICS or SCADA network. As referenced in both Bartlett, Heidemann and Papadopoulos [17] and Deraison and Gula [18] active methods require some form of interaction with the devices on the network, which could be one of the potential ramifications of using active tools against SCADA devices. As opposed to the passive methodologies discussed in Xu et al. [15] which run for a longer period at an "*observation point*" on the network, removing the need to send or receive data from any devices that are connected. Active reconnaissance is also a type of computer attack in which an intruder engages with the targeted system to gather information about vulnerabilities [19]

3.1 Existing Tools

From discussing the key advantages and disadvantages of each scanning methodology, attention can then be brought to the current technologies and tools available in the public domain.

Nmap: Bartlett, Heidemann and Papadopoulos [17] discuss the use of Nmap as an example of active network probing. The conditions on which Nmap is used are confined to a very limited set of network technologies. The main focus seems to be standard corporate networks with services such as HTTP, SSL, MySQL, SMTP. The application of Nmap against these services demonstrates how active probing works in a TCP/IP environment; however, it fails to address how Nmap is used on more bespoke networks such as SCADA and ICS. Bodenheim [20] gives a more relevant example of Nmap being used on the networks of interest. This paper provides explanations behind specific Nmap commands and how it achieves the desired output. Jaromin, [21] supports the information presented in Bartlett, Heidemann and Papadopoulos [17], enforcing the fact that Nmap is an active probing mechanism.

Nessus: This tool developed by Tenable Network Security. Peterson [22] discusses how Nessus can be used to scan for vulnerabilities within a control system environment. Peterson goes on to explain how Nessus works and how it can be tailored to facilitate SCADA networks. Nessus could have on an ICS/SCADA system by stating that due to the number of plugins associated with the tool, some of the extended functionality may cause control systems to crash. **Passive Vulnerability Scanner (PVS)**: Maintained by the same organization responsible for Nessus, PVS is a passive accompaniment to the suite of network scanning tools provided by Tenable Network Security. Deraison and Gula [18] define a passive tool to be a mechanism which "*sniffs network traffic to deduce a list of active systems*". What is interesting within this paper is that PVS and passive scanning as a whole are associated with the "*sniffing of a network, as opposed to scanning*". Xu et al. [15] and Gonzalez and Papa [16] clearly identify how passive technology works and give examples of live experiments. From the information provided within these sources, it seems that the use of passive network sniffers over a longer period of time is the most beneficial and non-intrusive way of performing reconnaissance on SCADA systems.

Zmap: With similar functionality to Nmap, Zmap is an open-source active network prober designed to perform Internet-scale scans. The probing of large area networks (LANs) is achieved using TCP SYN and ICMP echo scans. This is addressed in Durumeric, Wustrow and Halderman [23]. Not only is the active technology behind Zmap discussed in detail, each element of the Zmap functionality is dissected and explained at a substantial technical level, including its modular framework for dissecting different protocols. Amongst this information, reference is made to limitations of certain networks which may result in the tool not working correctly, particularly when the scan rate of the probing packets being sent is too high for the target infrastructure. An experiment was conducted to investigate whether there is a correlation between "*scan rate*" and "*hit rate*" when probing a network, analysing the efficiency and success of the tool itself. Li et al. [24] also make reference to Zmap and its ability to probe a multitude of different protocols through the use of plug-in modules. There is evidence to suggest that Zmap can be used to probe protocols such as DNP3, Modbus and Siemens S7.

Shodan: Shodan is a service which acts as a search engine to identify and index Internet-facing devices. Shodan has become of significant interest as many ICS and SCADA systems are identifiable via this tool. Bodenheim [20] directly explores how the technology behind Shodan impacts the devices connected to ICS.

Table 1 provides a summary of these tools. This table gives a concise breakdown of the key information about each of the tools referenced within this section.

Moreover, network scanners interact with SCADA devices and may cause significant disruption to the way these devices operate. Based on this idea, authors in [25] explore, test and critically analyse the use of network scanning tools against bespoke SCADA equipment in order to identify the issues with conducting asset discovery or service detection on SCADA systems with the same tools used on conventional IP networks. The observations and results of the experiments conducted evaluated the

Table 1 A summary of existing active and passive network scanning tools

Tool	Summary
NMap + ZMap	• Open source, active
	• Uses a combination of ping sweeping, SYN scanning and TCP connecting to determine which hosts reside on a network and which services they are operating
	• Version detection or full TCP connection could cause legacy systems to misbehave
	• NMap Scripting Engine has allowed for bespoke modules to be created for SCADA protocols such as Modbus
	• ZMap has an almost identical capability but can scan large area networks
Nessus	• Commercial, active
	• Working on a "policy" framework, Nessus allows users to conduct host discovery and vulnerability analysis in a similar way to NMap, again using ICMP, TCP and ARP scanning
	• Unlike NMap, Nessus has the capability actively probe each service to report on potential vulnerabilities
Passive vulnerability scanner	• Commercial, passive
	• Uses interface packet sniffing to dissect and analyse the data being sent over the network in order to gain information about the assets and services being deployed
	• Although it does not require any form of direct probing with nodes, PVS must be continuously ran in order to gain a better understanding of the network it is monitoring
	• The time it takes to analyse traffic is significantly higher than the active alternatives
Shodan	• Open source/membership based, active
	• Uses similar techniques to NMap, ZMap and Nessus to find the services that are running on Internet-facing devices
	• All results are then stored in a database for users of the Shodan search engine to query against
	• Shodan has the potential to bring unwanted malicious attention to ICS/SCADA networks through the storing and reporting of information about ICS infrastructures

feasibility of running network scanners against these bespoke devices and whether they have a negative impact on how they operate.

In order to protect SCADA systems, a lot of methods and mechanisms were recently proposed, most of which include a passive or active scanner as an internal part. Some of these systems are intrusion detection systems (IDS) for embedded platforms or distributed IDS for SCADA [26], device-level anomaly detection [27] and classification, IDS solutions combining network traces and physical process control data [28], detection based on traffic and protocol models or approaches based on semantic analysis [29], just to mention a few. A thorough analysis that presents which IT security methods could be applied to SCADA systems is presented in [30].

4 Vulnerabilities and Threats

Due to advanced functionalities and several heterogeneous third-party components, a single misconfiguration leads to vulnerability issue, resulting in catastrophic damage and equipment failure [31–33]. It is important to note that apart from vulnerability from outside attackers such as hackers and industrial competitors, inside attacks may come from ex-employees, vendor personnel, site engineers, etc. To mitigate cyber threats coming from the Internet due to the increased connectivity among internal and external networks, firewall and other similar control technologies can be used at the network perimeter. A misconfiguration in any of the equipment affects the network security, since it may not suppress the security threat due to lack of knowledge of the network architecture [31]. Also, if the backbone network is controlled by another third party, then the network components are shared with external vendors, resulting in other security threats for SCADA systems. [31] In the following subsections, we discuss several vulnerability issues and risks that SCADA systems face nowadays.

4.1 Vulnerabilities of SCADA Systems

- **Unidentified Interfaces**: Several components are equipped with specific functions and services in order to help suppliers and management personnel to configure network or software. These interfaces allow personalized configuration and functionality [34]. However, weak authentication and possible insecure interface from field devices result in a threat to the SCADA systems.
- **Firewall Management**: A network firewall controls the data flow between control servers and corporate systems in the SCADA. The misconfiguration of the firewall [31] due to lack of information about the network or lack of specific knowledge, results to poor control on the data that flows inside a SCADA system.
- **Unknown Services Provided by Third-Party Software**: Third-party software is developed for promoting interoperability and for supporting a wide-range services. However, all of the services may not be required, therefore, could be turned off.

The system suppliers are unaware of the services that might be needed to support the full functionality of the system. Moreover, these unknown services provided by the third-party software may arise vulnerability issues for SCADA systems [35].

- **Logical and Physical Configuration Mismatch**: Network segregation is an important security measure for SCADA systems. Although in general, the logical dimensions reveal a clear separation of the network, different physical components might be implemented in a single physical entry, for instance configuring a switch (or router) to separate some of the network parts as a separate logical network, although the physical devices are connected to the same switch (or router). Moreover, in cases when malicious packages alter the configuration of a single device, all connected components might be compromised.

- **Extended Access to SCADA systems**: In an ideal scenario, logical access to a SCADA system must reside within the physical security coverage. The physical security coverage refers to the protection of the physical location by fencing, guarding and other similar precautions. However, due to increased use of portability and wireless connectivity, the logical access is extended beyond secure physical location. Therefore, the uncontrolled and inadequate security of the logically extended access arise new vulnerability issues [31].

4.2 Threats of SCADA Systems

The above vulnerabilities arise new threats that have a negative impact on the performance of SCADA systems [36]. Some of the threats are presented here:

- **DoS/DDoS Attack**: Denial-of-service (DoS)/distributed DoS (DDoS) attacks [37] overload the resources such a way that the intended tasks cannot be performed.

- **Replay Attack**: In a replay attack [38], a valid message with valid data is repeated for the unlimited times, resulting in a serious threat to the SCADA systems.

- **Man-in-the-Middle (MITM) Attack**: By spoofing attack, an outsider gains illegitimate access to the system, whereas the intruder can monitor the message circulating over the SCADA network in sniffing attack [39].

- **Malicious Software**: Malicious software (such as worms, Trojan horses and backdoors) affect the integrity and confidentiality of the SCADA systems [40].

- **Password Pilfering**: In password pilfering, an intruder can get the access control. Thus, the confidentiality and the level of authority are compromised [40].

- **Advanced Persistent Threats**: During an APT threat [41], unauthorized person aims to steal data from SCADA systems in a hidden manner.

Traditional SCADA systems lack in proper vulnerability measurements. Several attacks can damage expensive equipment and jeopardize human health and safety in SCADA systems. Therefore, adequate threat mitigation and privacy measurements become the essential part of SCADA systems.

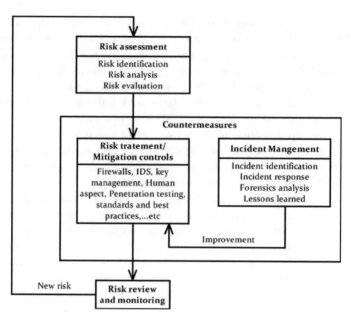

Fig. 1 Mitigation process for SCADA system

5 Mitigation

To defend against cyber attacks, a mitigation process is required to reduce the organization's cyber risk to an acceptable level. The mitigation process, as shown in Fig. 1, is built in the following three phases:

- *Prior implementation of mitigation controls*: In this phase, a cyber risk assessment methodology [42] is conducted to identify, analyse and evaluate the risks, rank them and allocate the budget from the highest risk to the lower ones until an acceptable level of SCADA security is reached or the budget is consumed.
- *Implementation of mitigation controls*: In this phase, the security controls, which mitigate the risks of the previous phase to an acceptable level, are implemented such as intrusion detection systems, key management, security standards and best practices.
- *Post implementation of mitigation controls*: In this phase, the risks are continuously reviewed and monitored to identify any new risks and feed them to the risk assessment component. In addition, the lessons learned from the security incidents that occur in the system will help improving the mitigation controls.

5.1 Cyber Security Risk Assessment Methods for SCADA Systems

In the literature, many cyber security risk assessment methodologies of SCADA system have been proposed [42]. They are either designed for generic SCADA [43], or they are developed for the following domains such as: rail road sector [44], energy sector [45], nuclear plant [46], electric power sector [47], chemical plants [48], hydro-power plant [49] and power grids [50] .

5.2 Countermeasures

Many different tools or methodologies have been proposed in the literature that can defend a SCADA systems.

SCADA security standards and best practices—The following major security standards [7, 51] have been proposed for SCADA security.

- *ISO/IEC 27002*: It has been developed by the International Organization for Standardisation (ISO). It represents a generic standard for implementation of information security management in organizations, and it covers many components such as human resources security, physical security, access control and incident management.
- *NIST System Protection Profile*: In 2004, the National Institute of Standards and Technology (NIST) released a document titled System Protection Profile Industrial Control Systems, which covers the security and objectives of SCADA systems.
- *API-1164 Security Standard*: American Petroleum Institute produced Standard 1164, Pipeline SCADA Security to provide security guidelines to pipeline operators.
- *NISCC Firewall Deployment Guide*: In 2005, the National Infrastructure Security Coordination Center (NISCC) published a good practice guide for firewall deployment in SCADA networks.
- *NIST SP 800-82*: In 2008, NIST released this security guideline to Industrial Control Systems, and it was updated in 2011.
- European Union Agency for Network and Information Security (ENISA) released in 2013 recommendations for Europe on SCADA patching.

Penetration testing—Security tools such as Metasploit, Nessus and Core IMPACT can be used to perform penetration testing and make sure that the SCADA system is free from known exploits and vulnerabilities [7]. Sploitware [52] is a tool that was developed specifically for penetration testing of SCADA systems.

Honeynets—SCADA Honeynets, such as the SCADA Honeynet Project [53], are used to deter adversaries from attacking the real system. They can be used to collect information about the attack without exposing an actual system to exploitation risk and hence improve the SCADA security.

Firewall and network segmentation—Network segmentation classifies IT assets into specific groups and then restricts access to these groups using firewalls. By placing resources into different segments of a network, a compromise of one segment cannot lead to the compromise of the entire system, which is recommended in the case of industrial control systems .

Intrusion detection systems – In the literature, various intrusion detection systems (IDS) have been proposed for SCADA systems. Almalawi et al. [54] proposed an unsupervised anomaly-based IDS for the detection of integrity attacks. Using the data-driven clustering technique, an IDS that can identify normal and critical states of SCADA network is proposed [55]. Lin et al. [29] designed an IDS to detect the control commands related to attacks in SCADA. A multilayer cyber security framework for protecting SCADA against intrusions is proposed in [56]. The traffic behaviour and frequent patterns of the network are used to detect SCADA attacks [57]. A one-class SVM to detect intrusions in SCADA is proposed in [58]. Shitharth et al. [59] proposed an intrusion weighted particle-based cuckoo search optimization (IWP-CSO) and hierarchical neuron architecture-based neural network (HNA-NN) techniques to detect intrusions in SCADA

The false data injection is designed to impact the state estimation of the SCADA system. This attack is based on the assumption that an attacker has compromised one or several meters and hence falsified data that are injected into the SCADA centre. False data injection attacks against the state estimation of power system can lead to dangerous situations like blackout or causing the control centre to make wrong decisions. To detect this attack, different solutions [60–63] have been proposed.

Key management—SCADA communicates with different devices such as: remote terminal units (RTUs) and intelligent electronic devices (IEDs). To ensure confidentiality of the transmitted data, a key management scheme is required. Several key management schemes for SCADA networks have been proposed. The key distribution architecture of the scheme can be either centralized [64, 65] or decentralized [66, 67].

Incident management—The incident management process start by the identification phase, which checks if the event is a security incident. Then, it is followed by the response phase, which aims to limit the damage of the incident, isolate the affected systems and return back to the normal state. After that, a forensic analysis is conducted to discover the cause of the incident so the system can be hardened to prevent future incidents. In the last phase, lessons are learned from the incident to improve the mitigation controls.

Human aspect—Humans are always considered as the weakest link of the security of a cyber physical system [7, 68]. It has been observed that social engineering has largely been used to compromise SCADA systems by exploiting user's little knowledge on security [69]. In order to deal with this issue, an organization must develop, among other security measures, a training programme that enhances the security awareness of its employees.

Table 2 Summary of privacy-preserving schemes for SCADA system in smart grid architecture

Scheme	Communication and system model	Privacy model	Countermeasures	Performances (+) and limitations (−)
Wen et al. (2013) [70]	Residential area composed of a control centre, two cloud servers, a requester and some residential users	- Query privacy	- Hidden vector encryption	+ Efficient compared to the scheme [71] in terms of communication overhead, computation complexity and response time; - No threat model presented.
Wen et al. (2014) [72]	Smart grid marketing architecture with main three parts, including energy sellers, energy buyers, and auction managers (with two servers: a registration server (RS) and an auction server)	- Privacy of the energy buyers	- Public key encryption with keyword search;	+ Efficient compared to the scheme [73] in terms of the computation and communication overhead in the one keyword search process;
			- Secure cryptographic hash function;	- No threat model presented;
				- Ranked search and personalized search are not considered.
Fahad and Mahmood (2014) [74]	SCADA data publishing	- Data privacy	- Clustering concept	+ Deal with multivariate data;
				+ Improve the data utility;
				+ Enhancing the privacy level;
				- Computational time is high.

(continued)

Table 2 (continued)

Scheme	Communication and system model	Privacy model	Countermeasures	Performances (+) and limitations (-)
Li et al. (2014) [75]	Smart grid marketing architecture with main four parts, including electricity generators, retailers, data centre, and filtering centre	- Query privacy	- Paillier encryption;	+ Can achieve ranked search and personalized search simultaneously compared to [72];
			- Secure cryptographic hash function;	+ Efficient in terms of computation and communication overhead;
				- No threat model presented;
				- Energy costs are not considered.
Jiang et al. (2015) [76]	SCADA in smart grid with three main components, namely, human-machine interface, master terminal unit, and remote terminal unit	- Availability under privacy of users;	- Dual directional hash chains	+ Minimize the computation, memory, communication, and energy costs;
		- Forward secrecy;		- Many assumptions about the privacy needed to understand implementation.
		- Backward secrecy;		
Ferrag (2017) [77]	Three types of network architecture (i.e., NAN, BAN, and HAN), including a control centre (CC) and some cloud servers	- Data privacy	- Identity-based encryption;	+ Resilience against data replay attack, availability attack, modification attack, man-in-the-middle attack, and Sybil attack;
		- Gateway privacy	- Secure cryptographic hash function;	- Query privacy is not considered.

(continued)

Table 2 (continued)

Scheme	Communication and system model	Privacy model	Countermeasures	Performances (+) and limitations (-)
Rahman et al. (2017) [78]	Three entities in the system: (a) energy supplier as registration manager, (b) automation server as bidding manager, and (c) virtual end nodes as bidders	- Anonymity;	- ElGamal public key encryption;	+ No impersonation;
		- Untraceability;	- Schnorr signature scheme;	+ Non-repudiation;
		- Non-linkability;		+Verifiability;
				- Query privacy is not considered.

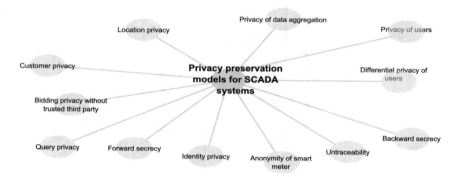

Fig. 2 Classification of privacy preservation models for SCADA system

6 Privacy Issues in SCADA Systems

In this section, we review several privacy-preserving schemes for SCADA systems in smart grid architecture. Based on the classification of privacy-preserving schemes for smart grid in [79], privacy-preserving schemes for SCADA system in smart grid architecture can be classified according to privacy models. The summary of privacy-preserving schemes for SCADA system in smart grid architecture is presented in Table 2. In addition, Fig. 2 shows the classification of privacy preservation models for SCADA system in smart grid architecture.

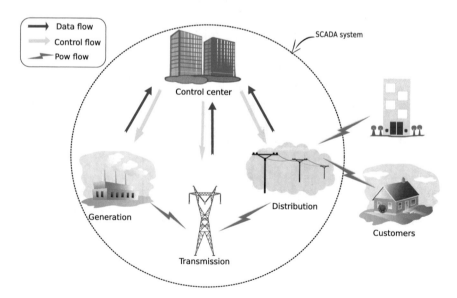

Fig. 3 SCADA system in smart grid architecture

Wen et al. in [70] proposed a scheme, called PaRQ, for a typical residential area composed of a control centre, two cloud servers, a requester and some residential users. Based on three main phases, namely construction of the range query predicate, encrypted data deposit, range query, PaRQ can provide data confidentiality and privacy by introducing an HVE technique. In addition, PaRQ is efficient compared to the scheme [71] in terms of communication overhead, computation complexity and response time, but no threat model is presented. Wen et al. [72] proposed a scheme called SESA which considers the privacy of the energy buyers in smart grid marketing architecture with main three parts, including energy sellers, energy buyers and auction managers (with two servers: a registration server (RS) and an auction server). Based on three main phases, namely bidding, pre-filtering and decision-of-winner, the SESA scheme is efficient compared to the scheme in [73] in terms of computation and communication overhead in the one keyword search process. Ranked search and personalized search are not considered in the SESA scheme.

To preserve the SCADA data publishing, Fahad and Mahmood [74] introduced a privacy-preserving framework, named PPFSCADA. To deal with multivariate network attributes, the PPFSCADA framework uses three similarity measurements. As an advantage, PPFSCADA can deal with multivariate data, improve the data utility, and enhance the privacy level, but the computational time is high. Similarly to PaRQ scheme [70] in the context of query privacy, Li et al. in [75] proposed a scheme called EMRQ in smart grid marketing architecture with main four parts, including electricity generators, retailers, data centre, and filtering centre. The EMRQ scheme can provide not only secure transactions between sellers and buyers, but can also achieve confidentiality of keywords, authentication, data integrity and query privacy.

Based on the conceptual model of National Institute for Standards and Technology (NIST), Fig. 3 shows an example of a system model used in smart grid architecture based on SCADA system, which is based on four main components, namely generation, transmission, distribution, and customer, feature two-way power and information flows in smart grid. Jiang et al. in [76] considered the availability under the privacy of users in smart grid with three main components, namely human–machine interface, master terminal unit and remote terminal unit. Based on the dual directional hash chains, Jiang et al. proposed a scheme called LiSH+ that is capable of solving the availability problem in resource-constrained SCADA system. Specifically, LiSH+ uses four main phases, namely (1) rekeying; (2) self-healing mechanism, (3) adding new member nodes and (4) re-initialization mechanism. Rahman et al. [78] proposed a secure and private bidding protocol for incentive-based demand response system. Without relying on any trusted third party, the protocol [77] can preserve the anonymity, untraceability and non-linkability. In 2017, Ferrag [77] proposed an efficient privacy-preserving energy consumption scheme with updating certificates, called EPEC. Using the identity-based encryption and secure cryptographic hash function, the EPEC scheme can achieve privacy of data and gateway and can resist to data replay attack, availability attack, modification attack, man-in-the-middle attack and Sybil attack.

According to the study published in 2017 in [80], the process of proposing a new privacy-preserving scheme for SCADA system should pass on the following eight phases:

1. Definition of the network model;
2. Definition of the attack models (e.g. identity-based attacks, location-based attacks, eavesdropping-based attacks, manipulation-based attacks and service-based attacks);
3. Definition of the privacy model (e.g. location privacy, identity privacy, anonymity, traceability, interest privacy, backward privacy and content-oriented privacy);
4. Identification of areas of vulnerability and possible interdependencies of the system;
5. Selection of the countermeasures (e.g. cryptographic methods);
6. Proposition of the main phases of scheme (e.g. system initialization, nodes registration);
7. Prove the robustness of the scheme using various security analysis techniques (e.g. game theoretic approaches, GNY logic, AVISPA tool, ProVerif and BAN logic); and
8. Evaluate the scheme's performance in terms of storage cost, computation complexity, communication overhead and delay overhead.

7 Conclusions

Whereas IP networks can cause significant damage to intellectual property and personal privacy, malfunctioning SCADA systems can lead to physical damage. Reconnaissance, whether passive or active, lawful or malicious, remains one of the most important parts of any strategic cyber security operation. Conducting reconnaissance within the cyber domain has become even more vital as the CNIs of various countries are now governed and controlled using computer networks. This chapter discussed vulnerability assessment of SCADA systems, focusing on several aspects such as asset discovery, identification of vulnerabilities and threats, mitigation of attacks and presentation of major privacy issues. The chapter presents a recently proposed process, which consists of eight phases, that should be followed when proposing a new privacy-preserving scheme for SCADA system.

8 Questions

1. What are the main differences between an IP and a SCADA system?
2. What is active and what is passive reconnaissance? Can it be used for attack purposes?
3. Explain an efficient privacy-preserving process for SCADA systems.

4. Can you describe an example mitigation process for SCADA systems?
5. What are the main components used to mitigate cyber risks in SCADA systems?
6. Briefly describe the eight phases of a privacy-preserving scheme for SCADA systems.
7. Discuss the main cause of vulnerabilities in the SCADA systems.
8. How can third-party vendors and extended physical access to the SCADA create vulnerabilities in the SCADA systems?
9. Describe how unidentified interfaces can compromise the security in the SCADA systems.
10. What are the major threats in the classical SCADA systems?

References

1. Walters R (2014) Cyber attacks on US companies in 2014. Herit Found 4289:1–5
2. Polityuk P, Vukmanovic O, Jewkes S (2017) Ukraines power outage was a cyber attack: Ukrenergo
3. Skorobogatov SP (2005) Semi-invasive attacks: a new approach to hardware security analysis. Ph D thesis, University of Cambridge Ph D dissertation
4. Skorobogatov SP, Anderson RJ et al (2002) Optical fault induction attacks. In: CHES, vol. 2523. Springer, Berlin, , pp 2–12
5. Radvanovsky R, Brodsky J (2016) Handbook of SCADA/control systems security, 2nd edn. CRC press LLC, Boca Raton
6. Stouffer K, Falco J, Scarfone K (2011) Guide to industrial control systems (ics) security. NIST Spec Publ 800(82):16–16
7. Nicholson A, Webber S, Dyer S, Patel T, Janicke H (2012) Scada security in the light of cyber-warfare. Comput Secur 31(4):418–436
8. Franz M (2003) Vulnerability testing of industrial network devices. In: Cisco critical infrastructure assurance group (Ciag), ISA industrial network security conference (2003)
9. Langner R (2011) Stuxnet: dissecting a cyberwarfare weapon. IEEE Secur Priv 9(3):49–51
10. Duggan D, Berg M, Dillinger J, Stamp J (2005) Penetration testing of industrial control systems. Sandia national laboratories
11. Byres E, Lowe J (2004) The myths and facts behind cyber security risks for industrial control systems. Proc VDE Kongr 116:213–218
12. Kerr PK, RollinsJ, Theohary CA (2010) The Stuxnet computer worm: harbinger of an emerging warfare capability
13. Rodofile NR, Radke K, Foo E (2016) DNP3 network scanning and reconnaissance for critical infrastructure. In: Proceedings of the Australasian computer science week multi conference. ACM, p 39
14. Knapp ED, Langill JT (2011) Industrial network security: securing critical infrastructure networks for smart grid, SCADA , and other industrial control systems syngress ???
15. Xu Y, Bailey M, Vander Weele E, Jahanian F (2010) Canvus: context-aware network vulnerability scanning. In: International workshop on recent advances in intrusion detection. Springer, Berlin , pp 138–157
16. Gonzalez J, Papa M (2007) Passive scanning in modbus networks. Crit Infrastruct Prot 175–187
17. Bartlett G, Heidemann J, Papadopoulos C (2007) Understanding passive and active service discovery. In: Proceedings of the 7th ACM SIGCOMM conference on internet measurement. ACM, pp 57–70
18. Deraison R, Gula R (2004) Blended security assessments, combining active, passive and host assessment techniques. Tenable network security

19. Chen C-Y, Ghassami A, Mohan S, Kiyavash N, Bobba RB, Pellizzoni R, Yoon M-K (2017) A reconnaissance attack mechanism for fixed-priority real-time systems. arXiv:1705.02561
20. Bodenheim RC (2014) Impact of the shodan computer search engine on internet-facing industrial control system devices. Technical report, Air force institute of technology wright-patterson AFB OH graduate school of engineering and management
21. Jaromin RM (2013) Emulation of industrial control field device protocols. Technical report, air force inst of tech wright-patterson AFB OH graduate school of engineering and management
22. Peterson D (2006) Using the nessus vulnerability scanner on control systems. Digital bond white paper
23. Durumeric Z, Wustrow E, Halderman JA (2013) Zmap: fast internet-wide scanning and its security applications. USENIX Secur Symp 8:47–53
24. Li F, Durumeric Z, Czyz J, Karami M, Bailey M, McCoy D, Savage S, Paxson V (2016) You've got vulnerability: exploring effective vulnerability notifications. In: USENIX security symposium, pp 1033–1050
25. Coffey K, Smith R, Maglaras L, Janicke H (2018) Vulnerability analysis of network scanning on SCADA systems. Secur Commun Netw
26. Cruz T, Rosa L, Proença J, Maglaras L, Aubigny M, Lev L, Jiang J, Simões P (2016) A cybersecurity detection framework for supervisory control and data acquisition systems. IEEE Trans Ind Inf 12(6):2236–2246
27. Zaddach J, Bruno L, Francillon A, Balzarotti D (2014) Avatar: A framework to support dynamic security analysis of embedded systems' firmwares. In: NDSS
28. Gao W, Morris T, Reaves B, Richey D (2010) On scada control system command and response injection and intrusion detection. In: eCrime researchers summit (eCrime). IEEE, pp 1–9
29. Lin H, Slagell A, Kalbarczyk Z, Sauer P, Iyer R (2016) Runtime semantic security analysis to detect and mitigate control-related attacks in power grids. IEEE Trans Smart Grid
30. Cook A, Janicke H, Maglaras L, Smith R (2017) An assessment of the application of it security mechanisms to industrial control systems. Int J Internet Technol Secur Trans 7(2):144–174
31. Johansson E, Sommestad T, Ekstedt M (2009) Issues of cyber security in SCADA-systems - on the importance of awareness. In: Proceedings of the IEEE 20th international conference and exhibition on electricity distribution–part 1, pp 1–4
32. Singh A, Prasad A, Talwar Y (2016) SCADA security issues and FPGA implementation of AES: a review. In: Proceedings of the IEEE 2nd international conference on next generation computing technologies (NGCT), pp 899–904
33. Babu B, Ijyas T, Muneer P, Varghese J (2017) Security issues in SCADA based industrial control systems. In: Proceedings of the IEEE 2nd international conference on anti-cyber crimes (ICACC), pp 47–51
34. Expo I, Fink RK, Spencer DF, Wells RA (2006) Lessons learned from cyber security assessments of SCADA and energy management systems
35. Mahboob A, Zubairi JA (2013) Securing SCADA systems with open source software. In: Proceedings of the IEEE high capacity optical networks and emerging/enabling technologies, pp 193–198
36. Sajid A, Abbas H, Saleem K (2016) Cloud-assisted IoT-based SCADA systems security: a review of the state of the art and future challenges. IEEE Access 4:1375–1384
37. Davis CM, Tate JE, Okhravi H, Grier C, Overbye TJ, Nicol D (2006) SCADA cyber security testbed development. In: Proceedings of the IEEE 38th North American power symposium, pp 483–488
38. Wang Y (2011) sSCADA: securing SCADA infrastructure communications. Int J Commun Netw Distrib Syst 6(1):59–78
39. Cagalaban G, Kim T, Kim S (2010) Improving SCADA control systems security with software vulnerability analysis. In: WSEAS international conference on automatic control, modelling & simulation, pp 409–414
40. Yang Y, McLaughlin K, Littler T, Sezer S, Im EG, Yao ZQ, Pranggono B, Wang HF (2012) Man-in-the-middle attack test-bed investigating cyber-security vulnerabilities in smart grid SCADA systems. In: International conference on sustainable power generation and supply (SUPERGEN 2012), pp 1–8

41. Bere M, Muyingi H (2015) Initial investigation of industrial control system (ICS) security using artificial immune system (AIS). In: Proceedings of the international conference emerging trends networks and computer communication (ETNCC), pp 79–84

42. Cherdantseva Y, Burnap P, Blyth A, Eden P, Jones K, Soulsby H, Stoddart K (2016) A review of cyber security risk assessment methods for scada systems. Comput Secur 56:1–27

43. Francia III GA, Thornton D, Dawson J (2012) Security best practices and risk assessment of SCADA and industrial control systems. In: Proceedings of the international conference on security and management (SAM), p 1 (2012). The steering committee of the world congress in computer science, computer engineering and applied computing (WorldComp)

44. Chittester CG, Haimes YY (2004) Risks of terrorism to information technology and to critical interdependent infrastructures. J Homel Secur Emerg Manag 1(4)

45. Ten C-W, Manimaran G, Liu C-C (2010) Cybersecurity for critical infrastructures: attack and defense modeling. IEEE Trans Syst Man Cybern Part A Syst Hum 40(4):853–865

46. Song J-G, Lee J-W, Lee C-K, Kwon K-C, Lee D-Y (2012) A cyber security risk assessment for the design of i&c systems in nuclear power plants. Nucl Eng Tech 44(8):919–928

47. LeMay E, Ford MD, Keefe K, Sanders WH, Muehrcke C (2011) Model-based security metrics using adversary view security evaluation (advise). In: 2011 Eighth international conference on quantitative evaluation of systems (QEST). IEEE, pp 191–200

48. Cárdenas AA, Amin S, Lin Z-S, Huang Y-L, Huang C-Y, Sastry S (2011) Attacks against process control systems: risk assessment, detection, and response. In: Proceedings of the 6th ACM Symposium on Information, Computer and Communications Security. ACM, pp 355–366

49. Markovic-Petrovic J, Stojanovic M (2014) An improved risk assessment method for scada information security. Elektron ir Elektrotech 20(7):69–72

50. Yan J, Govindarasu M, Liu C-C, Vaidya U (2013) A PMU-based risk assessment framework for power control systems. In: 2013 IEEE power and energy society general meeting (PES). IEEE, pp 1–5

51. Leszczyna R (2018) Cybersecurity and privacy in standards for smart grids-a comprehensive survey. Comput Stand Interfaces 56:62–73

52. Nazir S, Patel S, Patel D (2017) Assessing and augmenting scada cyber security: a survey of techniques. Comput Secur 70:436–454

53. Pothamsetty V, Franz M (2005) Scada honeynet project: Building honeypots for industrial networks. Cisco Systems, Inc.,[Online]. Available http://scadahoneynet.sourceforge.net/. Accessed 18 Jan 2018

54. Almalawi A, Yu X, Tari Z, Fahad A, Khalil I (2014) An unsupervised anomaly-based detection approach for integrity attacks on scada systems. Comput Secur 46:94–110

55. Almalawi A, Fahad A, Tari Z, Alamri A, AlGhamdi R, Zomaya AY (2016) An efficient data-driven clustering technique to detect attacks in SCADA systems. IEEE Trans Inf Forensics Secur 11(5):893–906

56. Yang Y, McLaughlin K, Sezer S, Littler T, Im EG, Pranggono B, Wang H (2014) Multiattribute scada-specific intrusion detection system for power networks. IEEE Trans Power Deliv 29(3):1092–1102

57. Sayegh N, Elhajj IH, Kayssi A, Chehab A (2014) SCADA intrusion detection system based on temporal behavior of frequent patterns. In: 2014 17th IEEE Mediterranean electro technical conference (MELECON). IEEE, pp 432–438

58. Maglaras LA, Jiang J, Cruz T (2014) Integrated ocsvm mechanism for intrusion detection in scada systems. Electron Lett 50(25):1935–1936

59. Shitharth S et al (2017) An enhanced optimization based algorithm for intrusion detection in scada network. Comput Secur 70:16–26

60. Esmalifalak M, Liu L, Nguyen N, Zheng R, Han Z (2014) Detecting stealthy false data injection using machine learning in smart grid. IEEE Syst J

61. Yu W, Griffith D, Ge L, Bhattarai S, Golmie N (2015) An integrated detection system against false data injection attacks in the smart grid. Secur Commun Netw 8(2):91–109

62. Deng R, Xiao G, Lu R, Liang H, Vasilakos AV (2017) False data injection on state estimation in power systemsattacks, impacts, and defense: a survey. IEEE Trans Ind Inform 13(2):411–423

63. Guo Z, Shi D, Johansson KH, Shi L (2017) Optimal linear cyber-attack on remote state estimation. IEEE Trans Control Netw Syst 4(1):4–13

64. Rezai A, Keshavarzi P, Moravej Z (2016) Advance hybrid key management architecture for scada network security. Secur Commun Netw 9(17):4358–4368

65. Jiang R, Lu R, Luo J, Lai C, Shen XS (2015) Efficient self-healing group key management with dynamic revocation and collusion resistance for scada in smart grid. Secur Commun Netw 8(6):1026–1039

66. Rezai A, Keshavarzi P, Moravej Z (2013) Secure scada communication by using a modified key management scheme. ISA Trans 52(4):517–524

67. Ebrahimi A, Koropi F, Naji H (2014) Increasing the security of SCADA systems using key management and hyper elliptic curve cryptography. In: Proceedings of the 9th symposium advanced science and technology, Mashhad, pp 17–24

68. Evans M, Maglaras LA, He Y, Janicke H (2016) Human behaviour as an aspect of cybersecurity assurance. Secur Commun Netw 9(17):4667–4679

69. Greene T (2008) Experts hack power grid in no time. Network world (2008)

70. Wen M, Lu R, Zhang K, Lei J, Liang X, Shen X (2013) PaRQ: a privacy-preserving range query scheme over encrypted metering data for smart grid. IEEE Trans Emerg Top Comput 1(1): 178–191. https://doi.org/10.1109/TETC.2013.2273889

71. Shi E, Bethencourt J, Chan T-HH, Song D, Perrig A (2007) Multi-dimensional range query over encrypted data. In: 2007 IEEE symposium on security and private (SP '07). IEEE, pp 350–364. https://doi.org/10.1109/SP.2007.29

72. Wen M, Lu R, Lei J, Li H, Liang X, Shen XS (2014) SESA: an efficient searchable encryption scheme for auction in emerging smart grid marketing. Secur Commun Netw 7(1): 234–244. https://doi.org/10.1002/sec.699

73. Liu Q, Wang G, Wu J (2009) An efficient privacy preserving keyword search scheme in cloud computing. In: 2009 International conference on computational science and engineerings. IEEE, pp 715–720. https://doi.org/10.1109/CSE.2009.66

74. Fahad A, Tari Z, Almalawi A, Goscinski A, Khalil I, Mahmood A (2014) PPFSCADA: privacy preserving framework for SCADA data publishing. Future Gener Comput Syst 37:496–511. https://doi.org/10.1016/j.future.2014.03.002

75. Li H, Yang Y, Wen M, Luo H, Lu R (2014) EMRQ: An efficient multi-keyword range query scheme in smart grid auction market. KSII Trans Internet Inf Syst 8(11): 3937–3954 (2014). https://doi.org/10.3837/tiis.2014.11.015

76. Jiang R, Lu R, Luo J, Lai C, Shen XS (2015) Efficient self-healing group key management with dynamic revocation and collusion resistance for SCADA in smart grid. Secur Commun Netw 8(6), 1026–1039 (2015). https://doi.org/10.1002/sec.1057

77. Ferrag MA (2017) EPEC: an efficient privacy-preserving energy consumption scheme for smart grid communications. Telecommun Syst 66(4): 671–688 (2017). https://doi.org/10.1007/s11235-017-0315-2

78. Rahman MS, Basu A, Kiyomoto S, Bhuiyan MZA (2017) Privacy-friendly secure bidding for smart grid demand-response. Inf Sci (Ny) 379:229–240 (2017). https://doi.org/10.1016/j.ins.2016.10.034

79. Ferrag MA, Maglaras LA, Janicke H, Jiang J, Shu L (2018) A systematic review of data protection and privacy preservation schemes for smart grid communications. Sustain Cities Soc. https://doi.org/10.1016/j.scs.2017.12.041

80. Ferrag MA, Maglaras L, Ahmim A (2017) Privacy-preserving schemes for Ad Hoc social networks: A Survey. IEEE Commun Surv Tutor 19(4): 3015–3045. https://doi.org/10.1109/COMST.2017.2718178

A Predictive Model for Risk and Trust Assessment in Cloud Computing: Taxonomy and Analysis for Attack Pattern Detection

Alexandros Chrysikos and Stephen McGuire

Abstract Cloud computing environments consist of many entities that have different roles, such as provider and customer, and multiple interactions amongst them. Trust is an essential element to develop confidence-based relationships amongst the various components in such a diverse environment. The current chapter presents the taxonomy of trust models and classification of information sources for trust assessment. Furthermore, it presents the taxonomy of risk factors in cloud computing environment. It analyses further the existing approaches and portrays the potential of enhancing trust development by merging trust assessment and risk assessment methodologies. The aim of the proposed solution is to combine information sources collected from various trust and risk assessment systems deployed in cloud services, with data related to attack patterns. Specifically, the approach suggests a new qualitative solution that could analyse each symptom, indicator, and vulnerability in order to detect the impact and likelihood of attacks directed at cloud computing environments. Therefore, possible implementation of the proposed framework might help to minimise false positive alarms, as well as to improve performance and security, in the cloud computing environment.

1 Introduction

Cloud computing environment combines known technologies, such as virtualisation, big data, data warehousing, and data mining. The advantages that it provides are increased performance, ease of deployment, elasticity of a service, and anytime-anywhere access. A cloud computing environment with the aforementioned benefits,

A. Chrysikos (✉)
Cyber Security Research Group, School of Computing and Digital Media,
London Metropolitan University, London, UK
e-mail: A.Chrysikos@londonmet.ac.uk

S. McGuire
Department of Computer Science, University of Huddersfield,
Huddersfield, UK
e-mail: S.Mcquire@hud.ac.uk

© Springer International Publishing AG, part of Springer Nature 2018
S. Parkinson et al. (eds.), *Guide to Vulnerability Analysis for Computer Networks and Systems*, Computer Communications and Networks,
https://doi.org/10.1007/978-3-319-92624-7_4

81

as well as its dynamic resource sharing and its cost-effectiveness, draws the attention of many enterprises and individual users [1]. Especially, for technological developments such as mobile applications and Internet of Things (IoT), a cloud computing environment becomes the preferred way of deployment.

Cloud services are provided dynamically to its users in a non-transparent manner. Due to its complex infrastructure, it exhibits heterogeneous capabilities of services and resources [2, 3]. Therefore, users might not be confident in terms of controlling the data stored in the cloud. In addition, safeguarding users' privacy and providing secure cloud-based transactions are challenging. Establishing consistent operational practices and performance as well as reliable cloud services has also a level of difficulty. Therefore, from a cloud user point of view, the reliability of a cloud service is an important issue [4].

Every day a new announcement is released regarding cloud computing threats and security risks. Furthermore, security is highlighted as the most critical obstacle in adapting cloud computing for a service [5]. As a result, cloud computing security issues lead to difficulties in terms of developing a well-defined assessment structure regarding the actual impact on security. This is justified by two key reasons. Firstly, basic vocabulary terms, such as vulnerability, risk, and threat, are usually adopted interchangeably. Secondly, not all issues identified are specifically related to cloud computing [6, 7]. In order to establish a clear understanding about cloud-specific security issues, an analysis of how cloud computing influences security issues is required. A key factor is security vulnerabilities [8, 9]. This is important because security vulnerabilities could function as indicators that could in turn help detect cloud computing-based attack patterns and vulnerabilities. Before expanding on that, though, it is important to first establish what is 'vulnerability'?

2 Vulnerability: An Overview

Vulnerability is characterised as a prominent risk factor [10]. Specifically, the ISO 27000 defines risk as "the potential that a given threat will exploit vulnerabilities of an asset or group of assets and thereby cause harm to the organisation" [11]. The Open Group has developed an overview of the factors contributing to risk [12]. Specifically, as presented in Fig. 1 it uses the same two top-level risk factors as ISO 27000, the likelihood of a harmful event (in diagram: loss event frequency) and its consequence (in diagram, probable loss magnitude). The probable loss magnitude's sub-factors influence a harmful event's ultimate cost (see Fig. 1 on the right). On other hand, the loss event's frequency sub-factors occur when a threat agent, for instance a hacker, successfully exploits a vulnerability (see Fig. 1 on the left). The frequency with which that develops is based on two factors:

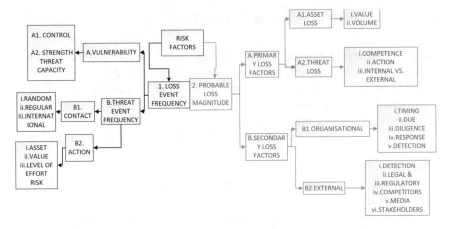

Fig. 1 Taxonomy of risk factors (Open Group) based on [11]

- The frequency is determined by both the agent's motivation and how much access the agents have to the attack targets. What is the level of effort? What is the risk level for the attackers? What can they gain from the attack?
- The difference between the threat agents' attack capabilities and the system's strength to resist the attack [11, 12].

2.1 Definition of Vulnerability

According to the aforementioned Open Group's risk taxonomy factors, a useful definition of vulnerability is developed. Vulnerability is defined as the probability that an asset will be unable to resist the actions of a threat agent. It exists when there is a difference between the force being applied by the threat agent and an object's ability to resist that force [13].

Thus, vulnerability should always be expressed in terms of resistance to a certain attack type. For instance, in a real-world example, a car not able to protect its driver against injury when hit frontally by a truck travelling at 60 mph is vulnerability. The resistance of the car's crumple zone is simply too weak compared to the truck's force. On the other hand, against the "attack" of a biker, or even a small car driving at a more moderate speed, the car's resistance strength is perfectly adequate [12].

Computer vulnerability can also be described as a removal or weakening of a certain resistance strength. For example, buffer overflow vulnerability weakens a system's resistance to arbitrary code execution. Whether attackers can exploit this vulnerability, or not, depends on how capable they are [5].

2.2   Vulnerabilities in Cloud Computing

Having defined and explained the term "vulnerability", this section examines how cloud computing can influence the risk factors presented in Fig. 1. From a cloud customer perspective, the right-hand side is related to the probable magnitude of future loss. Similarly to conventional IT infrastructure, in cloud computing the consequences and ultimate cost of, for instance, data confidentiality breach are the same [14]. From a cloud service perspective, it looks a bit different. Cloud computing systems were previously separated on the same infrastructure; therefore, a loss event could be more affective. However, this fact can be easily included into a risk assessment, as no conceptual work is required to adapt impact analysis to cloud computing [8].

The left-hand side, in Fig. 1, deals with the loss event frequency. Cloud computing could potentially alter the probability of a harmful event's occurrence. Specifically, cloud computing could cause significant changes in the vulnerability factors, because moving to a cloud infrastructure might alter the attackers' access level and motivation, as well as effort and risk [15]. To support a cloud-specific risk assessment, it is important to start investigating the exact nature of cloud-specific vulnerabilities. However, is there such thing as "cloud-specific" vulnerability? If so, certain factors in a cloud computing environment should make vulnerability cloud-specific.

A cloud computing environment consists of many components with different roles that need to interact with each other. Depending on the context, the nature of interaction may differ. Trust is an essential aspect to achieve confidence-based interactions amongst various entities in a cloud computing environment. Therefore, the taxonomy of trust models and classification of information sources for cloud-specific risk assessment is needed for an effective trust assessment in a cloud computing environment. This in return might help identify factors that make vulnerability cloud-specific.

Trust assessment in a cloud computing environment requires facilitation of a wide range of aspects involving services; such as software, platform, and infrastructure as a service, and deployment models; such as private, public, community, and hybrid [16]. For that reason, the evolving dynamic of trust relationships amongst those entities makes trust assessment a vital area that needs addressing. In the following sections, the taxonomy of trust assessment models, trust assessment information sources, and trust dimensions in cloud computing are presented.

3   Trust Assessment Models in Cloud Computing

A trust model is defined as a collection of rules, elements, and process to develop trust amongst the different entities in any computing paradigm. Specifically, cloud computing environment components such as databases, virtual machines, cloud service providers, cloud service customers, and cloud services are examples of different entities. Trust models are classified in two categories, decision models and evaluation

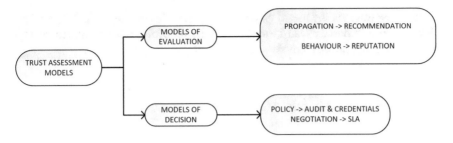

Fig. 2 Taxonomy of trust model based on [17]

models [17]. These models are applied to the cloud computing paradigm and are further developed through their connection with trust assessment techniques. This leads to the development of taxonomy of trust models and trust assessment techniques. Figure 2 presents taxonomy of trust models; in the following sections, a detailed description is provided.

3.1 Decision Models

The aim of a decision model is to provide an access control decision as a unique trust decision instead of following a relatively complex mechanism that includes authentication and authorisation [5]. Decision models are categorised into two types, as policy models and negotiation models. The policy model employs credentials and policies in order to control access to different resources. Specifically, credentials and policies signify the essential permissions required to access various resources. The other type is the negotiation model that applies negotiation strategies in order to establish trust between two different entities [17].

Cloud service providers may apply different audits and compliance standards to provide assurance to their users about the offered software, platforms, and services [18]. To increase the level of security, third-party assessment is provided by auditors. This involves issuing the audit certificates based on the audit compliance. However, cloud service providers are not required to disclose the audit reports to the users [19]. A trust assessment technique, though, can employ credentials and policies of cloud service providers to customers in order to make a trust decision. Such credentials and policies may be set by applying standards such as X.509, digital certificates, or public key infrastructure (PKI). In the cloud computing environment context, a service level agreement (SLA) can be applied as a policy-based method that may provide trust assessment [6]. An SLA describes the functional- and quality-related facets of the offered cloud service [20]. The details of those aspects are specified during the negotiation process between cloud providers and cloud customers. Nevertheless, authenticating claims made by a cloud service provider as part of the SLA documentation necessitates an experienced and trusted third party [19]. In general, establishing trust via the use of credentials and policies can be difficult to achieve. Hence, it is considered as hard trust [20]. In the following section, the second type of trust models, evaluation models, is examined.

3.2 Evaluation Models

Evaluation models are defined as computational trust models; this is because trust assessment is dependent on evaluation of different parameters. Specifically, these parameters categorise the evaluation models in behaviour models and propagation models [6]. In behaviour models, the aim is to compute the trust of the previously mentioned entities by measuring relevant factors such as reliability and performance. In propagation models, a new trust relationship is developed through the data distribution of pre-existing trust values in communication paths to other entities [21].

In the behaviour model, a reputation technique may be applied as trust assessor of a cloud service. In particular, trust is measured via the combination of ratings submitted by a number of cloud users for a cloud service [19]. The measurement of trust may employ various methods like addition or averaging and fuzzy logic. The resulting value of trust signifies the degree of cloud users' trust to a specific cloud service [20].

On the other hand, the propagation models are using a recommendation-based technique. Essentially, in this technique a cloud user develops a trust for a cloud service based on recommendations by trusted third-party cloud users [20].

Overall, both reputation and recommendation techniques employ factors such as feedback regarding trust assessment and ratings. Therefore, establishing trust through those elements is classed as soft trust [6].

4 Trust Assessment Information Sources in Cloud Computing

The cloud users' service-related needs are constantly changing in the diverse environment of cloud computing. Consequently, the role of various factors, such as feedback, ratings, and Quality of Service (QoS), in trust assessment is very important. In the following paragraphs, four trust assessment information sources are examined, specifically, direct and indirect interaction, cloud service provider declarations, and third-party assessment [6]. These information sources are, then, correlated with various factors of the cloud computing environment. The outcome was a taxonomy of information sources for trust assessment that is presented in Fig. 3 and then explained in the following sections.

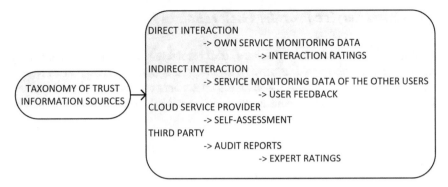

```
DIRECT INTERACTION
              -> OWN SERVICE MONITORING DATA
                        -> INTERACTION RATINGS
INDIRECT INTERACTION
                  -> SERVICE MONITORING DATA OF THE OTHER USERS
                            -> USER FEEDBACK
CLOUD SERVICE PROVIDER
                -> SELF-ASSESSMENT
THIRD PARTY
              -> AUDIT REPORTS
                      -> EXPERT RATINGS
```

TAXONOMY OF TRUST INFORMATION SOURCES

Fig. 3 Taxonomy of trust information sources based on [6]

4.1 Direct Interaction

When a cloud user has past experiences with cloud services, then the source of information is the direct interaction between those two sides. Specifically, this type of information can be expressed as ratings provided by the cloud user after interacting with a cloud service. The factors for trust assessment can be in the form of QoS parameters and can be documented through monitoring during the process of interaction between a cloud service and a cloud user. The advantage of storing and reviewing a cloud user's previous experiences is that the most relevant information can be used for trust assessment. However, such reviews will also include information that is insufficient, and as a result, not suitable for the purpose of trust assessment [19].

4.2 Indirect Interaction

When a cloud user has insufficient, or no past experience with cloud services, then the source of information is the indirect interaction between a cloud user and a cloud service. Specifically, assessment factors are calculated based on third-party users' experiences and can be in the form of feedback and/or ratings that are provided by third-party cloud users regarding their cloud service experiences. In addition, this type of information could be acquired through the processing of data recorded by the cloud service provider. Consequently, the assessment conducted by employing this type of information could be considered of better validity. On the other hand, the information retrieved by third-party users may be biased in terms of feedback quality that is a potential concern. Therefore, the feedback collected as part of indirect interaction could be employed as initial assessment until direct interaction is made available [21].

4.3   Cloud Service Provider Declarations

A cloud service provider incorporates a set of parameters of cloud services that may include information related to privacy, security, integrity, and compliance. Nevertheless, all this information is based on the assessment conducted and published by the cloud service providers themselves. Therefore, the data authenticity needs to be confirmed [20].

4.4   Third-Party Assessment

Third-party auditor (TPA) in cloud computing is a mechanism that inspects cloud services by reflecting on parameters such as privacy, performance, and security. The reports generated by TPA form an objective and a formal source of information that may be used for trust assessment [22].

5   Trust Dimensions in Cloud Computing

A trust model measures the security strength and computes a trust value. A trust value comprises of various parameters that are necessary dimensions to measure cloud services security. In the consequent sections, the dimensions regarding effective trust assessment are identified.

5.1   Multi-criteria

Trust assessment evaluation needs to entail various parameters like availability and reliability, in order to describe relevant qualities of the cloud provider and/or the cloud service [20]. Specifically, those parameters are categorised in objective and subjective parameters. The objective parameters incorporate real-time measurement or ratings provided by users. The subjective parameters incorporate factors such as feedback provided by third-party cloud service customers [19]. The combination of the aforementioned parameters is a challenging task. If it is successful, though, it could lead to quality trust assessment.

5.2   Context

Each type of cloud service requires different performance specification based on the various applying scenarios. Therefore, a trust model should consider the different types of cloud services applied. The types that form distinct contexts for trust assessment are Platform as a Service (PaaS) and Software as a Service (SaaS) [23].

5.3   Personalisation

In the cloud computing environment, there is a wide variety of user requirements about the trust assessment of the previously mentioned cloud services. A personalised service allows users to determine suitable requirements regarding trust evaluation from their perspective [6]. This enables users' flexibility to specify their own unique preferences, needs, and information sources about trust assessment.

5.4   (De)Centralised Trust Assessment

In the centralised trust assessment approach, the architecture consists of a centralised repository that stores the trust assessment-related data. The mechanism can be simple to implement, and the trust assessment data such as ratings and processing are conducted in a centralised entity/site. The main disadvantage is the possibility of failure of that centralised entity [21]. In the decentralised trust assessment method, the trust-related data are distributed amongst various entities/sites. Furthermore, the decentralised architecture allows computation of trust data and storage in multiple sites of the distributed cloud computing environment. Therefore, it enables the scalability and redundancy characteristic to all its users.

5.5   Adaptability

In the various applications of a cloud computing environment, there is a number of actors, such as cloud customer, cloud provider, cloud broker, cloud carrier, and cloud auditor, who could be situated around the globe. In addition, new cloud providers may be added or current users may be withdrawn from the cloud computing environment. In such a diverse environment with the potential for rapid change, alterations in the cloud infrastructure may occur constantly. Therefore, it is important for a trust model to adapt to any change seamlessly [6]. The term adaptability signifies the degree of which a trust evaluation model adapts to the aforementioned changes.

5.6   Credibility

In the trust evaluation context of a cloud computing environment, credibility refers to the degree of service parameters or the data quality given as input for the trust assessment process [21]. Therefore, encouraging the credibility of cloud services or the credibility of feedback provided by the cloud users is an essential task.

5.7 Trust Dynamics

In the dynamic cloud computing environment, associations between two or more different entities are not fixed but evolve with experience. Therefore, trust amongst entities needs to be assessed and revised regularly [21].

Having completed the presentation of the dimensions to be supported by trust management systems, an analysis of trust assessment frameworks is provided.

6 Analysis of Trust Assessment Frameworks in Cloud Computing

In the last ten years, researchers have been investigating the various aspects of trust assessment in the cloud computing environment. A series of important trust assessment frameworks are presented in the subsequent paragraphs. Specifically, the selection of the frameworks addressed is based on those involving a holistic approach focused on cloud services. In addition, the frameworks are presented in chronological order that can be seen in Table 1.

To begin with, Noor et al. proposed the design and implementation of CloudArmor [24], a reputation-based trust management framework that provides a set of functionalities to deliver Trust as a Service (TaaS). Specifically, it is an adaptive and robust model for measuring the credibility of user feedback to protect cloud services from malicious users. Furthermore, it offers comparison of the trustworthiness of cloud services. Ghosh et al. suggested a framework that evaluates the associated risk in interacting with the cloud provider [25]. This framework performs the trust assessment of cloud provider in the context of SaaS, PaaS, and IaaS. The next framework is proposed by Qu and Buyya. It is a trust evaluation framework regarding selection of cloud infrastructure services [26]. Specifically, it evaluates the trust of cloud services based on the subjective QoS requirements and preferences of the cloud user. Noor et al. recommended a generic analytical framework for trust management [2]. In the framework, interactions in cloud applications occur at three layers. For each layer, a set of dimensions is identified and used as a benchmark to evaluate and analyse existing trust management research prototypes.

The next trust assessment framework is proposed by Pawar et al. to measure the trustworthiness of an infrastructure provider [27]. It evaluates trust by employing factors such as SLA, satisfaction ratings, and providers' behaviour values. Furthermore, it takes into account the uncertainty of information during trust evaluation. Habib et al. proposed an architecture that employs a centralised method to collect trust-related

Table 1 Comparative analysis of trust assessment frameworks

Existing work	Trust assessment models	Trust assessment information sources	Trust dimensions
Noor et al. 2016 [24]	• Reputation • Credibility • Credentials • Trust assessment of cloud service using fuzzy logic	• User feedback (direct/indirect interactions, collusion attacks) • Direct interaction (Dynamic QoS parameters, such as performance, availability) • Cloud Service Provider satisfaction ratings and behaviour values	• Decentralised architecture • A technique to identify credible feedback • Availability and security of trust management system
Ghosh et al. 2015 [25]	• SLA • Reputation	• Cloud customer ratings • User feedback (direct/indirect interactions)	• Context of interaction for trust assessment • SLA-based competence assessment • Mathematical modelling of trust, reputation, competence, and risk
Qu et al. 2014 [26]	• QoS parameters • Trust assessment of cloud service using fuzzy logic	• Expert ratings (static parameters, such as security) • Direct interaction (dynamic QoS parameters, such as performance, availability)	• Dynamic trust • Personalised trust evaluation
Noor et al. 2013 [2]	• Reputation • Policy • Credentials	• User feedback (direct/indirect interactions, collusion attacks) • Direct interaction (Dynamic QoS parameters, such as performance, availability)	• Decentralised architecture • A technique to identify credible feedback • Availability and security of trust management system
Pawar et al. 2012 [27]	• Reputation • Recommendation	• cloud service provider satisfaction ratings and behaviour values • SLA indicators	• Context includes IaaS and multi-cloud environment
Habib et al. 2011 [21]	• Reputation • Recommendation	• User feedback • Expert ratings • Declarations of cloud service provider	• Personalised trust evaluation • Integration: Combining feedback and other trust-related factors from multiple sources
Alhamad et al. 2010 [28]	• SLA • Negotiation	• Cloud service provider and users experience • SLA agent reports	• Decentralised architecture

data from various sources [21]. The framework is using a number of QoS parameters determined by the users, to measure trust assessment of cloud providers. The final framework discussed here is suggested by Alhamad et al. that uses SLA and applies a business process monitoring [28]. Specifically, it takes advantage of the SLA cloud customer categorisation in various classes to enable domain-specific trust values.

Table 1 shows a comparative analysis of the aforementioned trust assessment frameworks. The table is structured by using the titles and information from the previously presented trust assessment-related sections. The first column of the table includes the existing work. This outlines the previously explained trust assessment frameworks in chronological order. The second column, trust assessment models, describes the basic trust assessment techniques used in each framework. In the third column, which is titled as trust assessment information sources, the information sources and parameters are indicated. Finally, the fourth column is the trust dimensions that presents the features of the several dimensions of trust assessment supported by the frameworks.

In the previous sections, a classification of information related to vulnerabilities (risk factors), trust assessment models, trust assessment information sources, and trust dimensions of the cloud computing environment is presented. This analysis and taxonomy of information are considered crucial to better comprehend the novel approach recommended in the current research. Before doing that, though, a description of similar approaches is presented.

7   Related Detection Approaches

When it comes to detection approaches, security researchers require a mechanism that can integrate and analyse a wide variety of data sources. Particularly, they need a mechanism that can process information that is generated by heterogeneous sources implemented in any cloud computing environment. These mechanisms should aim to detect attack patterns and reduce false positive alarms.

Hansman et al. employed five classifiers to describe different types of attack [29], specifically, classification by attack vendor, classification by attack target, classification by operational impact, classification by informational impact, and classification by defence. All this information can provide the network administrator with data on how to mitigate or deter an attack. Amer and Hamilton developed an ontology-based attack model to assess the security of an information system from an attacker's point of view [30]. The aim of the assessment process is to evaluate the effects of an attack. The process consists of four stages. The first stage consists of identifying the systems' vulnerabilities using automated vulnerability tools. These tools evaluate vulnerabilities of computer systems, applications, or networks and generate sets of scan results. The second stage involves determining the attacks that might occur due to the previously identified vulnerabilities. In the third stage, the possible effects of those vulnerabilities are analysed. In the fourth and final stage, the attack effects are calculated.

Patel et al. proposed a taxonomy with four dimensions that provides classification covering network and computer attacks [31]. Specifically, it provides assistance in improving network and computer security, as well as language consistency through attack description. The first dimension focuses on classifying the attack. The second classifies the target of the attack. The third provides vulnerability classification or uses criteria from Howard and Longstaff's taxonomy [32]. The fourth dimension addresses the effects of the attack.

Ficco et al. recommended a hybrid and event correlation approach for detecting attack patterns. The process involves detecting symptoms by collecting diverse information at several cloud levels in order to perform a complex event analysis presented in an ontology [33].

All of the previously mentioned methodologies demonstrate beneficial ontology and taxonomy that may offer informative guidelines regarding cyber intrusions and attack analysis. However, there is lack of detail required to analyse all symptoms and attacks that could in return minimise the number of false positive alarms. For instance, the same attack in two different cloud services may have a different degree of impact, but in most existing systems it would be classed as a malicious attack by both services.

The proposed framework addresses this issue, of a system generating multiple false positive alarms, through the implication of risk and trust assessment analysis in the detection process. In this approach, all actors, such as cloud providers and cloud customers, participate in the data analysis to achieve a high level of information and data processing. Before describing the proposed framework, though, the underpinning systems are presented.

7.1 Intrusion Detection System

An intrusion detection system (IDS) is very important in terms of preventing an attack against an information technology (IT) organisation. An IDS conducts a security system diagnosis to discover all suspicious activities based on detection algorithms. Specifically, those systems can help to deter and prevent actions related to security breaches, system flaws, as well as potential threats that may lead to system violations [34].

On the other hand, an IDS system may detect many false actions, but it may also lead to a number of false positive alarms and authorised users identified as intruders. In a cloud computing environment where all resources are shared amongst cloud customers, this point becomes even more critical. In order to minimise the number of false positive alarms and improve the efficiency of attack detection in all cloud computing environments, the proposed framework includes both cloud service providers and cloud customers as part of the correlation process in all cloud layers (SaaS, PaaS, IaaS).

7.2   Risk Assessment System

Risk assessment can be identified as the potential that a given attack will exploit vulnerabilities of an asset or a group of assets to cause loss or damage to the assets. According to the ISO 27005 Risk Management, risk is measured by evaluating the probability of successful attacks and the subsequent impact of those attacks, should they occur [5]. For example, as calculated in the following equation [35]:

$$Risk = Impact \times Likelihood \qquad (1)$$

Specifically, the term Impact refers to the degree of which a risk event might affect an enterprise, expressed in terms of: confidentiality, integrity, and authentication. The term Likelihood refers to the possibility that a given event may occur [5]. The implementation of the aforementioned equation in the proposed framework aims to stimulate cloud customers to evaluate security risks and simplify the analysis of all identified events.

8   Proposed Framework for Attack Pattern Detection Through Trust and Risk Assessment

The proposed framework is a predictive model that detects attack patterns based on trust assessment and risk assessment analysis. Figure 4 presents a correlation process that consists of a sequence of activities that are designed to analyse all network traffic through cloud layers [36]. The proposed framework applies a correlation process that intends to unify different steps of correlation by adding risk and trust assessment analysis in the diagnosis step, before the taxonomy step takes place.

An attack pattern is an abstraction mechanism that describes how an observed attack type is executed. Following the life cycle of cyber-attack, when an attack occurs it uses several paths, from reconnaissance to exploitation, and aims to gain unauthorised access to data [37]. Through studying the impact effects of an attack and

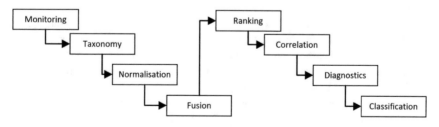

Fig. 4 Taxonomy of trust assessment information sources based on [36]

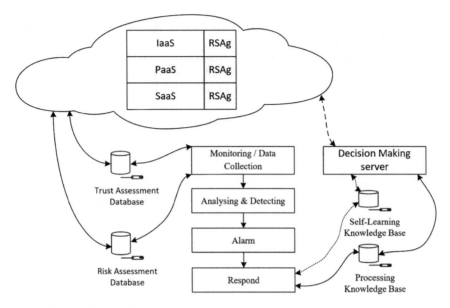

Fig. 5 Proposed framework for attack pattern detection

simplifying the analysis of monitored events, then it could be possible to minimise false positive alarms.

Figure 5 shows the proposed framework's four essential security functions: monitoring/data collection, analysing and detecting, alarm, and respond. The attack patterns are detected by collecting and analysing data from all cloud layers. The data storage is structured in two separate knowledge databases that do not communicate. These are the trust assessment database and the risk assessment database. The reason for recommending two isolated databases is to reassure cloud providers for data pseudonymisation. The cloud providers processing of personal data are conducted in a way that the data can no longer be attributed to a specific data subject without the use of additional information [38]. The pseudonymised information from those two databases is then combined in the processing knowledge base. There, the risk of the attack is calculated and a response is sent whether it represents a suspicious threat or a false positive alarm. The calculation is conducted in the Decision-Making server that determines the impact of each attack pattern and the risk of the attack. The respond function is connected to a self-learning knowledge base that classifies information about all attacks. It serves as an Advice as a Service for the Decision-Making server.

A Risk Software Agent (RSA), a goal-oriented computer program that reacts to its environment and operates without continuous direct supervision to perform its function, is related to each function defining the impact and likelihood of each detected symptom. The Decision-Making server determines the impact of each attack pattern and the risk of the attack. Employing the aforementioned framework could help minimise the rate of false positive alarms and increase the effectiveness of attack pattern detection systems.

The analysis of attack patterns is conducted by calculating the score of all indicators. Specifically, the proposed solution includes a definition for risk (Ri) as a product of the probability (Po) of a security compromise and its potential impact (Im). More specifically:

$$Ri = Po \times Im \qquad (2)$$

The recommended correlation is used to aggregate the attack scenarios, and symptoms generated by all parts in the cloud computing environment. The impact (Im) is a value consisting of the following indicators: trust assessment indicator (TaI), vulnerability (Vu) and symptoms (Sy). Each of these indicators has a different impact. The probability (Po) value is increased in relation to each indicator of an attack pattern. More specifically:

$$Im = TaI + Vu + Sy \qquad (3)$$

The impact (Im) and probability (Po) of each indicator are defined by the cloud customer and cloud provider using data collected from all cloud layers. The aim is to use attackers' behaviour to determine the impact (Im) and expose a potential attacker before an attack can take place. The value of risk (Ri) related to each attack determines whether the attack is successful or false positive alarm depending on the sensitivity of the targeted data as defined by the owner (cloud provider and cloud customer). More specifically:

$$Ri = Po \times (TaI + Vu + Sy) \qquad (4)$$

9 Recommendations for Further Research and Conclusion

In the current study, a taxonomy and analysis of risk and trust assessment techniques in the cloud computing paradigm are presented. Risk factors for a cloud-specific risk assessment are classified. Furthermore, information sources and factors for trust assessment are categorised. The analysis of the techniques studied shows that most of the approaches should involve both cloud providers and cloud customers in the process of attack pattern detection. This could be achieved by sharing common processes of data collection and analysis.

Therefore, a new framework for attack pattern detection in the cloud computing paradigm is proposed. A framework to recognise and analyse malicious actions based on risk and trust assessment factors and information sources is related to attack patterns. Specifically, the recommended framework classifies attacks by evaluating the probability of a security breach and its potential impact indicators, such as trust assessment indicator, vulnerability, and symptoms. The outcome of this evaluation gives the likelihood of an attack pattern risk. Both cloud providers and cloud customers are involved in the data collection and correlation process. This classification might aid to protect data in the cloud and provide a method that could efficiently analyse suspicious attack actions and reduce false positive alarms

In the cloud computing environment, risk and trust assessment need to be assessed continuously using multiple factors. These factors keep changing in the dynamic and constantly evolving cloud computing paradigm. In addition, multi-cloud environments demand a more risk- and trust assessment-oriented analysis. Therefore, risk and trust assessment needs of cloud providers and cloud customers have to be addressed in more detail. Finally, future work should test the implementation of the suggested framework in an actual cloud computing environment.

10 Questions

1. List and explain existing technologies that are used by Cloud computing.
2. Illustrate the taxonomy of risk factors produced by the Open Group.
3. Provide three possible vulnerabilities that might exist in Cloud computing infrastructure, and also explain their impact.
4. Which trust models are available for Cloud computing?
5. What is service level agreement?
6. Which cloud parameters are used by Third Party Auditor?
7. What is Trust-as-a-Service?
8. Explain three trust dimensions in cloud computing.
9. Explain why intrusion detection system is important in cloud. What are its benefits?
10. Why reputation is important in cloud trust model?

References

1. Dillon T, Wu C, Chang E (2010) Cloud computing: issues and challenges. In: 2010 24th IEEE international conference on advanced information networking and applications (AINA). Ieee, pp C27–33
2. Noor, T.H., Sheng, Q.Z., Zeadally, S., Yu, J.: Trust management of services in cloud environments: obstacles and solutions. ACM Comput Surv (CSUR) 46(1), 12 (2013)
3. Abbadi IM, Martin A (2011) Trust in the cloud. information security technical report 16(3–4):108–114
4. Habib SM, Ries S, Muhlhauser M (2010) Cloud computing landscape and research challenges regarding trust and reputation. In: 2010 7th international conference on ubiquitous intelligence & computing and 7th international conference on autonomic & trusted computing (UIC/ATC). IEEE, pp 410–415
5. Grobauer, B., Walloschek, T., Stocker, E.: Understanding cloud computing vulnerabilities. IEEE Secur Priv 9(2), 50–57 (2011)
6. Mouratidis, H., Islam, S., Kalloniatis, C., Gritzalis, S.: A framework to support selection of cloud providers based on security and privacy requirements. J Syst Softw 86(9), 2276–2293 (2013)
7. Heydari, A., Tavakoli, M.A., Riazi, M.: An overview of public cloud security issues. Int J Manag Excell 3(2), 440–445 (2014)

8. Catteddu D (2010) Cloud computing: benefits, risks and recommendations for information security. In: Web application security. Springer, pp 17–17
9. Islam, S., Fenz, S., Weippl, E., Kalloniatis, C.: Migration goals and risk management in cloud computing: a review of state of the art and survey results on practitioners. Int J Secur Softw Eng (IJSSE) **7**(3), 44–73 (2016)
10. Trappey, A.J., Trappey, C.V., Govindarajan, U.H., Sun, J.J., Chuang, A.C.: A review of technology standards and patent portfolios for enabling cyber-physical systems in advanced manufacturing. IEEE Access **4**, 7356–7382 (2016)
11. ISO: ISO/IEC 27000:2016 the overview of information security management systems. https://www.iso.org/standard/66435.html. Accessed 01 Feb 2016
12. Kreger H, Estefan J (2009) Navigating the soa open standards landscape around architecture. Joint Paper, The Open Group, OASIS, and OMG
13. Lemoudden M, Bouazza N, El Ouahidi B, Bourget D (2013) A survey of cloud computing security overview of attack vectors and defense mechanisms. J Theor Appl Inf Technol 54(2)
14. Fernandes, D.A., Soares, L.F., Gomes, J.V., Freire, M.M., Inácio, P.R.: Security issues in cloud environments: a survey. Int J Inf Secur **13**(2), 113–170 (2014)
15. Takabi, H., Joshi, J.B., Ahn, G.-J.: Security and privacy challenges in cloud computing environments. IEEE Secur Priv **8**(6), 24–31 (2010)
16. Subashini, S., Kavitha, V.: A survey on security issues in service delivery models of cloud computing. J Netw Comput Appl. **34**(1), 1–11 (2011)
17. Moyano F, Fernandez-Gago C, Lopez J (2012) A conceptual framework for trust models. In: International conference on trust, privacy and security in digital business. Springer, pp 93–104
18. Rimal BP, Choi E, Lumb I (2009) A taxonomy and survey of cloud computing systems. In: 2009. NCM'09. fifth international joint conference on INC, IMS and IDC. Ieee, pp 44–51
19. Huang, J., Nicol, D.M.: Trust mechanisms for cloud computing. J Cloud Comput Adv Syst Appl **2**(1), 9 (2013)
20. Pearson S (2013) Privacy, security and trust in cloud computing. In: Privacy and security for cloud computing. Springer, pp 3–42
21. Habib SM, Ries S, Muhlhauser M (2011) Towards a trust management system for cloud computing. In: 2011 ieee 10th international conference on trust, security and privacy in computing and communications (TrustCom). IEEE, pp 933–939
22. Wang C, Wang Q, Ren K, Lou W (2010) Privacy-preserving public auditing for data storage security in cloud computing. In: 2010 Proceedings Ieee Infocom. Ieee, pp 1–9
23. Mell P, Grance T et al (2011) The nist definition of cloud computing
24. Noor, T.H., Sheng, Q.Z., Yao, L., Dustdar, S., Ngu, A.H.: Cloudarmor: supporting reputation-based trust management for cloud services. IEEE Trans Parallel Distrib Syst **27**(2), 367–380 (2016)
25. Ghosh, N., Ghosh, S.K., Das, S.K.: Selcsp: a framework to facilitate selection of cloud service providers. IEEE Trans Cloud Comput **3**(1), 66–79 (2015)
26. Qu C, Buyya R (2014) A cloud trust evaluation system using hierarchical fuzzy inference system for service selection. In: 2014 Ieee 28th international conference on advanced information networking and applications (aina). IEEE, pp 850–857
27. Pawar PS, Rajarajan M, Nair SK, Zisman A (2012) Trust model for optimized cloud services. In: IFIP international conference on trust management. Springer, pp 97–112
28. Alhamad M, Dillon T, Chang E (2010) Sla-based trust model for cloud computing. In: 2010 13th international conference on network-based information systems (NBiS). Ieee, pp 321–324
29. Hansman, S., Hunt, R.: A taxonomy of network and computer attacks. Comput Secur **24**(1), 31–43 (2005)
30. Hafez Amer S, Hamilton Jr, JA (2010) Intrusion detection systems (ids) taxonomy-a short review. This is a paid advertisement. STN 13-2 June 2010: Defensive Cyber Security: Policies and Procedures 2, 23
31. Patel, A., Taghavi, M., Bakhtiyari, K., JúNior, J.C.: An intrusion detection and prevention system in cloud computing: a systematic review. J Netw Comput Appl **36**(1), 25–41 (2013)

32. Howard JD, Longstaff TA (1998) A common language for computer security incidents. Technical report, Sandia National Labs., Albuquerque, NM (US); Sandia National Labs., Livermore, CA (US)
33. Ficco M, Tasquier L, Aversa R (2013) Intrusion detection in cloud computing. In: 2013 eighth international conference on P2P, parallel, grid, cloud and internet computing (3PGCIC). IEEE, pp 276–283
34. Bace R, Mell P (2001) Nist special publication on intrusion detection systems. Technical report, BOOZ-ALLEN AND HAMILTON INC MCLEAN VA
35. Humphreys, E.: Information security management standards: compliance, governance and risk management. Inf Secur Tech Rep **13**(4), 247–255 (2008)
36. Valeur, F., Vigna, G., Kruegel, C., Kemmerer, R.A.: Comprehensive approach to intrusion detection alert correlation. IEEE Trans Dependable Secure Comput **1**(3), 146–169 (2004)
37. Shin J, Son H, Heo G (2013) Cyber security risk analysis model composed with activity-quality and architecture model. In: International conference on computer, networks and communication engineering, pp 609–612
38. Bolognini, L., Bistolfi, C.: Pseudonymization and impacts of big (personal/anonymous) data processing in the transition from the directive 95/46/ec to the new eu general data protection regulation. Comput Law Secur Rev **33**(2), 171–181 (2017)

AI- and Metrics-Based Vulnerability-Centric Cyber Security Assessment and Countermeasure Selection

Igor Kotenko, Elena Doynikova, Andrey Chechulin
and Andrey Fedorchenko

Abstract This chapter considers methods and techniques for analytical processing of cyber security events and information. The approach suggested in the chapter is based on calculating a set of cyber security metrics suited for automatic- and human-based perception and analysis of cyber situation and suits for automated countermeasure response in a near real-time mode. To fulfil security assessments and make countermeasure decisions, artificial intelligence (AI)-based methods and techniques, including Bayesian, ontological and any-time mechanisms, are implemented. Different kinds of data are used: data from SIEM systems, data accumulated during security monitoring, and data generated by the word community in external databases of attacks, vulnerabilities and incidents for typical and special-purpose computer systems. To calculate integral metrics, the analytical models of evaluation objects are applied. To specify security objects and interrelationships among them, an ontological repository is realised. It joins data from various security databases and specifies techniques of logical inference to get answers on security-related requests. The suggested approach is demonstrated using several case studies.

I. Kotenko (✉) · E. Doynikova · A. Chechulin · A. Fedorchenko
St. Petersburg Institute for Informatics and Automation of the Russian Academy
of Sciences, 39, 14 Liniya, St. Petersburg, Russia
e-mail: ivkote@comsec.spb.ru

E. Doynikova
e-mail: doynikova@comsec.spb.ru

A. Chechulin
e-mail: chechulin@comsec.spb.ru

A. Fedorchenko
e-mail: fedorchenko@comsec.spb.ru

I. Kotenko · E. Doynikova · A. Chechulin · A. Fedorchenko
St. Petersburg National Research University of Information Technologies,
Mechanics and Optics, 49, Kronverkskiy prospekt, Saint-Petersburg, Russia

© Springer International Publishing AG, part of Springer Nature 2018
S. Parkinson et al. (eds.), *Guide to Vulnerability Analysis for Computer Networks and Systems*, Computer Communications and Networks,
https://doi.org/10.1007/978-3-319-92624-7_5

1   Introduction

Modern security information and event management (SIEM) systems provide a huge amount of cyber security data about events and other security information. Unfortunately, currently applied mechanisms for security assessment and countermeasure selection do not use them efficiently. There is a need to create comprehensive artificial intelligence (AI)-based methods and techniques for analytical processing of cyber security events and information.

The approach suggested in the chapter is based on AI-based methods and generation of a set of cyber security metrics suited for automatic- and human-based perception and analysis of cyber situation. The approach is intended for the automated countermeasure response in a near real-time mode. In addition to data from the SIEM system, we use data collected during security monitoring processes, and data accumulated by the word community in the external databases of attacks, vulnerabilities and incidents for typical and special-purpose computer systems.

To specify and calculate primary cyber security metrics that characterise the analysed system, a comprehensive analysis and classification of the available source data (to convert them to the unified form) is performed. For this goal, we use a set of common security data enumeration standards (such as SCAP [1], CVSS [2], CVE [3], CAPEC [4], CWE [5], etc.) and scores from the SIEM system, open databases and experts. To calculate integral metrics, the analytical models of evaluation objects (attacks, attackers, incidents, countermeasures), that incorporate key attributes of these objects and their interaction, are applied.

To specify attack sequences, the graph models based on vulnerability exploitations are proposed to use. To specify interrelationships among objects, it is suggested to realise an ontological approach. We provide a common ontology that specifies relations between all objects of security assessment and countermeasure selection and constructs an ontological repository that jointly uses data from various security databases (such as NVD [6], CVE [3], ExploitsDB [7], CAPEC [4], CWE [5], etc.). We specify the techniques of logical inference on the basis of the ontological repository to get answers on security-related questions, including:

- What are the weak places of the analysed system?
- Is the system secured?
- What is an attacker goal?
- What are attacker future steps?
- Should we apply countermeasures?
- What countermeasures should we apply?

Besides, integrated metrics, methods and techniques applicable for the SIEM systems are proposed. They are adaptive, use entire set of available data and operate in a near real time.

To realise the adequate attack assessment and response, the profiles of attacks, attackers and incidents are generated. These profiles are based on particularities of the analysed system and possible nature and types of security incidents. Due to the dynamic character of the security situation and the necessity to consider continuously coming new data to generate assessments and security decisions, the any-time approach is implemented.

The suggested metrics, methods and techniques are demonstrated using different case studies. In these case studies, various attacks against the analysed system are specified. We show the processes of analytical modelling of objects of security assessment, including data gathering from various databases, data processing, data analysis, ontology construction and logical inference. We also demonstrate the process of dynamical reconstruction of the used models depending on the security situation and considering the current security events. Moreover, different phases of the security assessment, including metrics calculation and visual representation, as well as the dynamical recalculation of security metrics, are shown.

The main difference of the offered approach from the already suggested ones is the integration of different AI-based and vulnerability-centric functionalities in one component to achieve better results for analytical processing of cyber security events and information. The approach novelty consists also in the way of using security metrics and analytical models for comprehensive evaluation of security properties. The rest of the paper is organised as follows. In Sect. 2, the main input data for security assessment and countermeasure selection is reviewed. Section 3 discusses the solutions to correlate security events and to build the ontology of security data. Section 4 considers the analytical attack modelling approach suggested. Section 5 outlines the security metrics chosen and the security assessment and countermeasure selection techniques proposed. Section 6 presents case studies and examples of experiments. In conclusion, the main results and future research direction are considered.

2   Input Data for Security Assessment and Countermeasure Selection

Currently, there are many different security data sources. Each security data source has its own representation format and accumulates information of the specific type. Security analysis systems gather, analyse and join these data for security assessment and countermeasure selection.

The challenges in using such data are related to the following aspects [8]: (1) each data type can be provided by several sources; (2) maintenance of the same type repositories is not coordinated; (3) continuous growth of stored data volumes complicates analysis and matching of security data; (4) differences between the security data representation formats in the data stores greatly complicate their automated application.

All security information can be divided on two classes [9]: conditionally static content and dynamic content (Fig. 1). The main difference of information in these classes consists in the nature of its changing. Data with conditionally static content usually does not change after adding to a storage (excluding rare cases of information

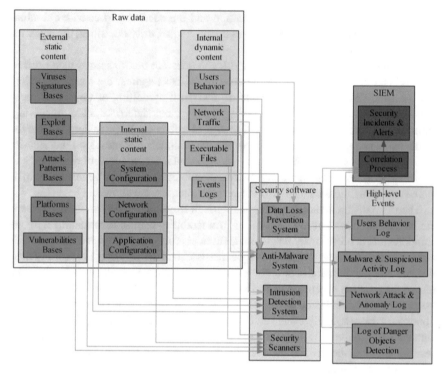

Fig. 1 Common scheme of using the input data in SIEM systems

updating or extension). Data with dynamic content represents characteristics of the described security aspects in real time. However, the usefulness of such information in any case decreases over time.

To avoid the misunderstanding, let us provide an event definition. The event is understood as result of the action (completed, denied, failed) or attempt to commit the action generated by either a source of action, or by its processing system having a predefined description format, understandable by processing system, and also having specific properties that describe the action itself. Also, the notions of the security information type and source should be clarified. The type is a separate class of objects that characterises the specific security aspect (vulnerability, weakness etc.). The source is a specific file or database that provides data on the particular information type.

Vulnerability representations are the most extensive security information type by the total volume and the number of sources. Currently, the most common vulnerability database is Common Vulnerabilities and Exposures (CVE) [3]. Key fields of the vulnerability representation in the CVE format are as follows [6]: (1) an unique source identifier; (2) textual description of the vulnerability; (3) references to the other sources of vulnerability description; (4) publishing date and (5) vulnerability status (candidate or approved vulnerability). An extended version of CVE is

National Vulnerability Database (NVD). This source contains additional fields: (1) the list and (2) vulnerable configuration of the software and hardware (in the CPE format [10]); (3) vulnerability score according to the Common Vulnerability Scoring System (CVSS) [2]; (4) vulnerability exploitation result and (5) identifier of weakness (CWE) [5] used for the vulnerability exploitation. The last field is not mandatory and usually contains the upper-level (general) weakness class. Other sources of vulnerability representation, such as OSVDB [11], X-Force [12] and BugTrack [13], contain similar fields.

Main disadvantages of these databases are non-unified representation of the vulnerable products and absence of detailed specification of their configurations. An advantage for application of different vulnerability representation sources together consists in stronger connection of information and extension of usable knowledge on security events and information.

Databases (dictionaries) of hardware and software are used to determine the current configurations of the system. On their base the vulnerabilities can be analysed. The aforementioned database of hardware and software CPE (Common Platform Enumeration) dictionary of version 2.2 [10] has the following entry fields: (1) type; (2) producer name; (3) product name; (4) version; (5) modification; (6) edition; (7) language. Version 2.3 is extended with the next fields: (1) architecture; (2) hardware platform; (3) software platform. This extension should specify different software and hardware in the dictionary more accurately. But the problems with unambiguous product identification are not rare because of the features of the entry format in the dictionary. More advanced kind of dictionary of software and hardware is a CVRF format (Common Vulnerability Reporting Framework) [14]. It represents various kinds of product hierarchically and has additional fields: build number; specification and others. But currently, there is no product dictionary in this format.

Information on exploits includes the description and practical implementation (source code, special file, etc.) of the specific vulnerability. It usually includes the following fields: (1) a unique source identifier; (2) vulnerable hardware and software; (3) exploitation details.

Configurations databases contain information on the correct and secure setting of the specific software. At present, only one open database in a formalised form with this information exists Common Configuration Enumeration (CCE) [15]. The format of this database contains the next fields: (1) a unique identifier; (2) textual description of the customisable platform component; (3) unformatted platform name; (4) configuration setting; (5) technical details of the configuration setting mechanism that indicates location of the optional fields (path in the file system, parameter name in the configuration file, registry branch, etc.); (6) references to the sources of recommendations on the current configuration setting (usually, on the platform developer Web site).

Attack patterns are the key security information type for detection and prevention of the attack actions against distributed and networked objects of the protected infrastructure. The main source of this information is CAPEC database [4]. Its representation format includes the following fields: (1) a unique source identifier; (2) identifiers of the vulnerability examples; (3) identifiers of the weaknesses used in attack;

(4) textual description of the attack; (5) references to the additional description of particular attack stages and details (used vulnerabilities, exploits, hardware and software, etc.).

Information on weaknesses related to the security is provided currently as a classification that contains in the hierarchical form the following fields: (1) categories; (2) classes; (3) base weaknesses and (4) alternatives. Each element has a unique identifier of the common source Common Weaknesses Enumeration (CWE) [5].

Stores for collection of security events include logs of operation systems, applications, services and other possible sources and sensors. Event representation formats in different logs are significantly differing from each other. Meanwhile, almost all event representation standards have the common fields (properties): (1) date and time of event occurrence; (2) global event type (information, attention, warning, error, audit success, audit failure); (3) own type that indicates a specific action described in the event; (4) event source (sensor, application, etc.) and some others. In opposite to the information with conditionally static content, the absent values of some fields in the entries can be partially restored. For example, an own event type can implicitly belong to the specific event category not provided in the entry. The similar situation exists for the categories of events properties. The task of security events storing, processing and further application is implemented in the correlation process. This process is described in the next section.

3   Correlation of Events and the Ontology of Security Data

The process of security information correlation was originally created for intrusion detection systems (IDSs). The general aim of such processes was to identify relations between network events, their aggregation and analysis to detect attacks (including distributed and multi-stage attacks) [16]. The methods of information correlation in SIEM systems were adapted from the IDS.

In general consideration, the correlation process (in a broad sense) can be divided into the following stages [16]: (1) normalisation; (2) aggregation; (3) filtering; (4) anonymisation; (5) prioritisation; (6) correlation (in the narrow sense). The presence and additional decomposition of these stages in a specific solution depends on its implementation [17].

At the moment, there are many methods, approaches and techniques for event and security information correlation. Each of them has its own advantages and disadvantages. Usually, general correlation process in existing solutions combines several methods. All methods can be conditionally divided into signature based and heuristic (behaviour analysis). These methods can apply various approaches based on similarity analysis, statistical analysis, data mining, etc.

For security evaluation and decision making regarding the countermeasures selection, the most important is the correlation of the data with the conditionally static content. One of the promising approaches for this task solution is the application of an ontological model operating by a set of types of security information. Based on

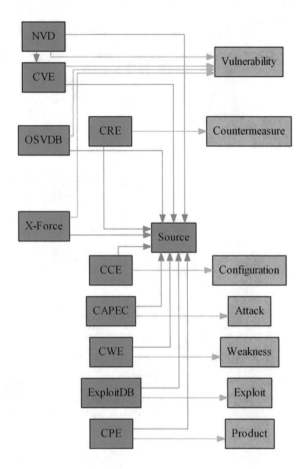

Fig. 2 Fragment of the entity hierarchy of the ontological model

this model through logical inference, it is possible to extract and use new knowledge from the data repository by integrating different sources of information and binding the semantic of various types of data.

The classes of such ontological model are determined taking into account the following types of information objects: vulnerabilities, products, weaknesses, exploits, attack patterns, configurations and countermeasures. The structure of the relationships between these objects is formed based on the analysis of the open security databases (e.g. CPE [10], CVE [3], CWE [5], CAPEC [4], etc.).

Figure 2 shows a fragment of the inheritance hierarchy of the ontological model used for the security information repository. All classes are divided into: (1) types of security information (all except the Source and Reference classes); (2) sources of security information (Source); (3) references to third-party sources with specific security data (Reference) (not shown in the figure) [18].

Direct integration (binding) of information in the security information repository is performed by defining object properties for the presented classes of the model.

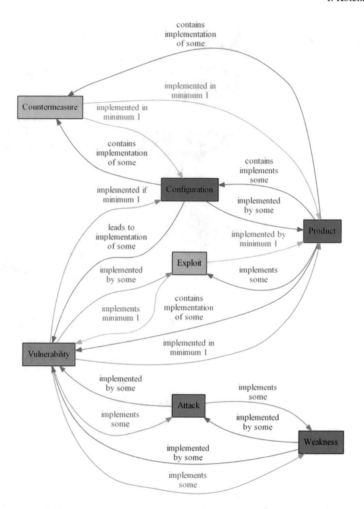

Fig. 3 Relationships and their types for main concepts of the ontological data model

The example of object properties that connect different types of security information with the indication of cardinality is presented in Fig. 3. This figure contains object domains and object properties. Flexible structure of the model allows you to add new data sources and types of security information without changing existing requirements [19].

Some of the entities that represent individual features are implemented by the isolated properties of the data. Example of this kind of property (the structure of the CVSSv2 metrics hierarchy for vulnerability description) is shown in Fig. 4 (right). In this case, an important feature of OWL2 is the ability to set a value range for a data property based on a user-defined type. For instance, the range of possible values for the "AccessComplexity" metric is given by the expression: "High", "Low",

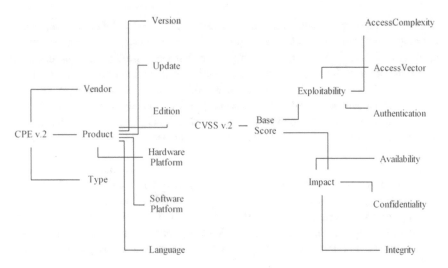

Fig. 4 Examples of data properties of the hybrid repository ontological model

"Medium". The left half of Fig. 4 shows an example of hierarchy for the product concept.

Examples of the proposed hybrid repository implementation and usage are presented in Sect. 6.

4 Analytical Attack Modelling

This section considers the suggested analytical attack modelling approach, the formal framework for analytical attack modelling, and the generalized architecture of the security analysis system based on this approach. The proposed solution for analytical processing of cyber security events and information is developed using the suggested security repository, the techniques for generation of attack trees and service dependencies, taking into account known and new attacks based on zero-day vulnerabilities, stochastic analytical modelling, and interactive decision support to develop preferred security solutions.

4.1 Common Approach

The common approach to analytical attack modelling, we have chosen, is based on the following main procedures: (1) generating the common attack graph based on current and possible vulnerabilities; (2) determining the current malefactors' actions based on current logs and alerts; (3) generating (adjusting) the attack (sub)graphs for possible sequences of malefactors' actions by modelling of malefactors' behaviour; (4) modelling possible attacks and responses (countermeasures); (5) calculating the security metrics (see Sect. 5), attack and response impacts providing comprehensive risk analysis procedures; (6) providing necessary information to the components of event and information collection, event-driven processing, decision support, reaction and countermeasures as well as the repository and visualization modules [20].

According to the main functional requirements of analytical attack modelling, we differentiate between two main modes or stages: (1) design time (or configuration) stage; (2) exploitation stage.

On the first mode (stage), we fulfil preliminary security evaluation of the network analysed (or the system under protection): determining vulnerabilities; defining possible routes (graphs) of attacks and attack goals, building and saving the common attack graph; searching probable bottlenecks ("weak places") in network topology; calculating various security metrics (see Sect. 5); defining attack and countermeasures impacts; producing common guidelines on increase of security level and solutions on security.

On the second mode (stage), we recalculate the results prepared on the first stage according to the current situation in the network analysed (or the system under protection) by processing incoming events and alerts: producing adjusted attack subtrees based on changes in the network; recalculating different security metrics; getting data about intruder's previous steps; predicting the intruder's next steps taking into account current situation; helping in correlation of events and alerts; recalculating attack and countermeasures impacts; adjusting guidelines on increase of security level and solutions on security measures/policies/tools.

According to the analysis of state of the art in attack modelling, the main functional requirements and the suggested formal framework for analytical attack modelling, we select the following key elements of the proposed architectural solutions: using the security repository (including system configuration, malefactor models, vulnerabilities, attacks, scores, countermeasures) (see Sect. 3); effective attack tree generation techniques based on Topological Vulnerability Analysis (TVA) approach which enumerates potential sequences of exploits of known vulnerabilities to build attack graphs; taking into account known and on zero-day vulnerabilities; combined use of attack graphs; security metric calculation (see Sect. 5), including attack impact, response efficiency, response collateral damages, attack potentiality, attacker skill level; interactive decision support to select the solutions on security measures/tools by defining their preferences regarding different types of requirements (risks, costs, benefits) and setting trade-off between high-level security objectives [21].

The integration of these functionalities presents the main difference between the offered approach and those already suggested for attack modelling. The novelty consists also in the way of modelling attacks (we intend to use a multi-level model of attack scenarios based on known and zero-day vulnerabilities) and applying constructed attack graphs (for different locations of malefactors) to determine a family of security metrics and evaluate security properties.

4.2 Service Dependencies

To improve the efficiency of analysing the attack sequences and the attack/response impact propagation, we investigated two possible options. In the first case, aim is to prevent exploitation of the gained privileges by the malefactor. In this case, the knowledge about service dependencies is not needed, and attack graphs' analysis can be used without any additions. In the second case, we need information regarding the attack/countermeasure impact analysis and we use the service dependencies' graphs. To form the services dependencies' graph, we need to define all services in the network and their dependencies. To do this, we extended the network model which is used for attack graphs' generation.

Instance "Service" has the following properties: (1) each dependent service has property "Request" (access from the parent service defines privileges/user credentials of this service); (2) each parent service has the property "Trust" (defines trust relationship which should be satisfied by the dependent service) and "Privileges sharing" (defines privileges shared with dependent services if dependency is satisfied).

During the attack graph generation step, we also need to perform some additional analysis. On the basis of input data (containing the network data in predefined format, the database filled by vulnerability list, the host where the malefactor is located, etc.), the attack graph generator forms the attack graph (tree).

For each attack, the output consists of some privileges obtained or revoked on a target host. As the NVD is used to generate the attack graph, for each particular attack we get an impact vector which represents the post attack effects.

For every atomic attack (each step in the attack graph), we create an additional service dependency graph. As input, it uses privileges/user credentials on some service(s) after the attack (impact vector of the vulnerability), a vulnerability list and a service structure. The privileges/user credentials are delegated by the service. If the trust relationship is satisfied by the delegated privileges, the new privileges are shared between services. As a result, we get malefactor's gain and return it as a precondition for the next attack step.

4.3 Source Data

We divide all data into two categories: input data and output data. Main input data can be two types: (1) data obtained from external sources, and (2) data obtained by analysing the network (system) and generated by users. For more detailed information, see Sect. 2. The input data, required to construct and analyse the attack graph, is separated by the data source.

The first type of input data is the data from external sources (it can be loaded from the Internet): vulnerabilities; weaknesses in code/design/architecture; attacks patterns (CAPEC), etc.

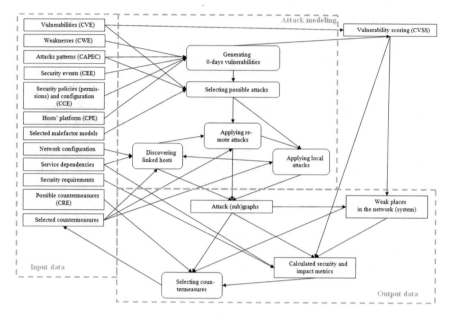

Fig. 5 Main data flows of attack modelling and security evaluation

The second type of input data is the data from internal sources (from the network generated by scanning tools and from users): network events and alerts; malefactor's model; network configuration; hosts' platform (hardware and software packages); service dependencies; countermeasures; security requirements; security policies and configuration.

The output data, obtained as the result of the attack modelling and analysis, is as follows: attack graphs; security and impact metrics; selected countermeasures; weakness places (here, the weak places are those elements of the tested network, breaking of which leads to the greatest damage). For more detailed description of security metrics and countermeasure selection process, see Sect. 5.

The data flows are presented in Fig. 5.

4.4 Attack Graph Generation

The algorithm of generating the common attack graph is based on implementation of the following sequence of actions: (1) determination of the preparatory actions which allow malefactor to move from one host to another; (2) determination of the reconnaissance actions for detection of "live" hosts; (3) determination of the reconnaissance scenarios for detected hosts; (4) determination of the attack actions based on vulnerabilities and auxiliary actions.

As the result, all attack actions are divided into the following classes: (1) reconnaissance actions; (2) preparatory actions within the limits of malefactor's privileges (these actions are used for creation of conditions needed for implementation other attack actions; (3) actions for gaining the privileges of local user and of administrator; and (4) confidentiality, integrity and availability violation.

There are three necessary conditions for adding a potential attack in the attack graph: (1) the protected system has vulnerabilities; (2) an attacker needs knowledge and resources to perform attacking activities; (3) an attack accomplishment facilitates the achievement of the malefactor goal. The first condition is determined completely by properties of the protected system. The second one is defined by both the system and malefactor model properties. The third one is determined by malefactor goals.

Respectively, at a stage of preparation and construction of attack trees a three-dimensional matrix is formed for each host according to the following information:

1. class of attacks (data gathering, preparation activities, increasing of privileges, attack goal realization);
2. needed access type (remote source without access rights, remote user of the system, local user of the system, administrator);
3. restriction for malefactors (by malefactor knowledge, zero-day vulnerabilities, etc.).

As a result, for each host a set of cortges (attack action class, access type, malefactor knowledge level) is formed, for each cortge in its turn a list of particular attacks and vulnerabilities needed for these attacks implementation is generated. The total list of vulnerabilities is formed on the base of the host software and hardware description and public vulnerability databases. Additional data sources for the detected vulnerabilities are the reports of security scanners such as Nessus, MaxPatrol, etc.

When constructing an attack graph, besides, particular vulnerabilities attack patterns described in CAPEC format are used. We use these patterns not only as input information, but also for producing new ones as the result of the security analysis. They can describe the most often used sequences of vulnerability exploitations and other actions of the attacker. The patterns also contain attack descriptions that do not use vulnerabilities, for example at the initial stage of attack the malefactor could gather information on available hosts. To specify in this case the attacker actions, the CAPEC-292 (Host Discovery) entry is used. It describes a group of various ways of scanning hosts and ports. This group contains, for example, such entries as CAPEC-285 (ICMP Echo Request Ping), CAPEC-296 (ICMP Information Request), CAPEC-299 (TCP SYN Ping), etc.

The next stage is a search of vulnerable software. The following patterns are used to describe malefactor actions: CAPEC-310 (Scanning for Vulnerable Software), CAPEC-311 (Fingerprinting Remote Operating Systems), CAPEC-300 (Port Scanning), etc. The third stage of attack graph generation both particular vulnerabilities from the CVE [3] dictionary and patterns like CAPEC-233 (Privilege Escalation) is used.

After forming matrices of potential attacks, for each host a possible malefactor type and the initial location are chosen for the analysed network.

The examples of the malefactor type are as follows:

- External hacker, a user having significant knowledge in information security field, but lacking any direct possibility to connect to the internal network. Possible intrusion points are servers which can be accessed via the Internet (Web servers, mail servers, etc.);
- Internal user, a user having basic knowledge in information security field, with local user or administrator rights.

Worm/virus/botnet, a program that can use a set of vulnerabilities specified in advance. It is supposed that in this case, a part of internal network can be already infected.

The full malefactor model includes following parameters: type (internal, external, complex); initial privileges for each host of the network (none, remote user, local user, administrator); possible access points in the network; knowledge level (defines possible attack actions).

Further for each chosen malefactor model, a list of possible goals is generated. For example, for the internal user it could be a revenge (causing maximum damage for the company). The goal of the external hacker could be the access to confidential information located on a server inside the network. For a worm at the first stage, a goal can be its distribution, while at the second one it could be carrying out DDoS attacks.

Therefore, the malefactor is presented by a pair "malefactor model, goal", which determines constraints on the usage of attack actions and possible initial intrusion point into the network. The key elements of the suggested approach are as follows: (1) for all malefactor models, the attack graph is formed in the same time on the basis of information gathered; (2) for each malefactor model, the security metrics are evaluated; (3) for each malefactor with security level higher that permitted, the list of possible countermeasures is formed.

Due to the fact that the results of attack modelling subsystem operation cannot be often computed in real-time, their usage in real-time processes is limited. However, the generated attack graphs keep their actuality for a certain period of time (until significant changes in the security policy or physical network topology occur).

Thanks to this in the frame of general system of event analysis, it is suggested to use the attack graphs constructed in advance. These attack graphs can be used when solving two main tasks: (1) predicting subsequent malefactor actions and (2) analysis and detection of their past actions which led the system into its current state.

However, in some cases the attack modelling system needs to update attack graphs. For example, this necessity occurs when host characteristics (software and hardware, criticality, etc.), network topology and a list of possible malefactors are changed, as in these cases key objects are changed (malefactor models, matrices of host properties, etc.).

However in this case attack, graphs are updated partly as the changes are calculated only for particular elements of matrices. Due to this fact, the computational complexity of the update decreases significantly.

After attack graphs' generation, they are used for security evaluation and countermeasure selection (see Sect. 5). Examples of attack modelling are presented in Sect. 6.

5   Security Assessment and Countermeasure Selection

Security assessment is one of the key processes of security management. The main goal of security assessment consists in providing valuable and sufficient information to decision makers for countermeasure selection. This information may be represented as a set of security metrics.

5.1   Security Metrics

Security metrics are quantitative or qualitative measures of specific attributes obtained using an analytical model developed for specific information needs [22]. Security metrics should be repeatable, inexpensive in computing, and numerical. Also they should have the units of measurement and correspond to a context [23].

Note that a lot of security metrics and their classifications using various attributes were suggested by the research and commercial organizations. There are classifications by objects of assessment (technical metrics, organizational metrics and management metrics), by business functions (incidents management, vulnerability managements, etc.), by computation method (primary and integral metrics), by value type and others.

From our point of view, the classification of security metrics by several attributes is the most illustrative, namely: by the objects of security assessment (configuration characteristics of the analysed system, attacks, attackers, security incidents and countermeasures) when completeness of the set of metrics depends on the coverage of characteristics of all assessment objects; by computation method (primary and integral metrics); by computation mode (static metrics and metrics that change with time, or dynamic); and, finally, by consideration of zero days (metrics that are calculated considering only known vulnerabilities and metrics that are calculated considering zero-day vulnerabilities). Examples of security metrics of different classes are provided in Table 1.

Table 1 does not comprise all the indexes we use for the security assessment and countermeasure selection. And it certainly does not contain all known security metrics. It is provided as the illustrative example of the classification we suggest. More detailed information on the various security metrics can be found, for example, in [24–27].

Here are some clarifications on the data provided in Table 1. Classification by the computation method defines if the metric is calculated directly or on the basis of other metrics. Thus, the software/hardware vulnerability is calculated directly on

Table 1 Examples of security metrics

Class: Topological metrics			
An object of assessment: Network configuration			
Security metrics	Computation method	Computation mode	0-day
Software/hardware vulnerability	Primary	Static/Dynamic	Basic
Host vulnerability	Integral	Static/Dynamic	Basic
Host criticality	Integral	Static/Dynamic	Basic
Host vulnerability to 0-day attacks	Integral	Static/Dynamic	0-day
Security level	Integral	Static/Dynamic	Basic/0-day
Attack surface	Integral	Static/Dynamic	Basic
Class: Attack metrics			
An object of assessment: Attacks			
Attack potentiality	Integral	Static/Dynamic	Basic/0-day
Attack impact	Integral	Static/Dynamic	Basic
Monetary attack impact	Integral	Static/Dynamic	Basic
Attack response costs	Primary	Static	Basic
Class: Incident metrics			
An object of assessment: Security incidents			
Incident criticality	Primary	Static	Basic
Monetary impact from incident	Primary	Static	Basic
Number of the compromised hosts	Primary	Static/Dynamic	Basic
Annual incident probability	Integral	Static/Dynamic	Basic/0-day
Class: Decision support			
An object of assessment: Countermeasures			
Countermeasure efficiency	Primary	Static/Dynamic	Basic
Collateral damage potential	Primary	Static/Dynamic	Basic
Countermeasure selection index	Integral	Static/Dynamic	Basic
Countermeasure cost	Primary	Static	Basic

the basis of number of vulnerabilities in the software/hardware instance, while host vulnerability is calculated on the basis of software/hardware vulnerability metric. Computation mode depends on the stage of system exploitation. Static metrics are calculated on the design stage, while dynamic metrics are calculated on the system exploitation stage on the basis of the security events processing and show security situation in time. Monitoring of the security situation is especially important to calculate the attack probabilities and preventive attack response. Zero-day category allows considering unknown vulnerabilities and attacks if needed.

"Good" metrics, i.e. metrics that satisfy the requirements above, are the result of correct specification of the following elements: input data, computation methods and criteria for interpreting the results. Determination of these aspects in scope of our security assessment technique is provided below.

Input data is the key element of the security assessment and countermeasure selection. Input data gathering is rather challenging task. To resolve this challenge and to automate the security assessment process, we use open security data sources and security data specifications described in Sect. 2.

In our technique, an important role is given to the interconnections among security data sources, data, analytical models and security metrics. These interconnections determine the logic of security assessment and countermeasure selection processes. For this goal, an ontological model and inference on its base are used. An ontological approach allows us to systematise available security data and to get new knowledge on their base. The developed ontology is described in details in Sect. 3, while the analytical models and their interconnections used for calculations are provided in Sect. 4. The technique for security assessment and countermeasure selection that uses all aforementioned elements and specifies the computation methods for security metrics is described in details below.

5.2 Security Assessment

The main metric of the system security level is a risk level. According to the standard definition, the risk is a combination of attack impact and attack probability [28].

The difficulty consists in calculation of the attack probability, especially considering the aforementioned challenge of security data gathering. The statistics of security incidents can be absent for the analysed network. Therefore, we suggest using Bayesian approach [29, 30]. It allows us to consider the influence of security events on the system security state, to forecast attack development and to outline previous attack steps. The central model for calculations is the Bayesian attack graph. It is generated on the basis of the attack graph described in Sect. 4 by the assignment of local, conditional and unconditional probabilities to its nodes. Thus, the attack graph is a graph $G = (S, L, \tau)$, where S contains the nodes of the graph (i.e. the set of attack actions), $L S \times S$ the set of links between actions, τ the relation between attack actions. For each graph node S, the local probability of compromise p, the discrete local conditional probability distribution Pc, and unconditional probability Pr are set.

As the chapter title implies, our approach is vulnerability-centric. This is explained by the fact that each attack action corresponds to the vulnerability exploitation. To set initial local probabilities for the attack actions (attack graph nodes), we use CVSS scores [2] for the vulnerabilities. Afterwards, we redefine the probabilities using Bayes' theorem after the events processing. This allows monitoring security in the system exploitation mode that corresponds to the dynamic computation mode in security metrics' classification.

The technique consists of the following procedures [31]:

1. Calculate the risk level for the attack graph nodes on the base of the classic equation [28]:
   $Risk = Attack Impact \times Attack Potentiality,$
   where $Attack Impact$ is an attack impact (combination of the attack damage and asset criticality); and $Attack Potentiality$ is the attack probability.
2. Determine the risk level for an attack as combination of the minimum probability for the attack nodes on the attack graph and maximum impact.
3. Define the risk level for a host as the maximum risk for attacks that go through this host.
4. Set the risk level for the network as the maximum risk for the hosts.
5. If event comes process the event and return to procedure 1 (but use another equations to calculate security metrics).

In the scope of the technique, the algorithms for calculation $Attack Potentiality$ and $Attack Impact$ are developed. Algorithm of calculation of AttackPotentiality includes three steps:

1. calculation of the local probabilities of compromise for the graph nodes;
2. calculation of the discrete conditional probability distributions; and
3. calculation of the unconditional probabilities.

We define local probabilities of compromise for the graph nodes on the base of the CVSS index Exploitability as in [29]:

$$Exploitability = 20 \times Access Vector \times Access Complexity \times Authentication$$

where $Access Vector$ determines access to the vulnerability, $Access Complexity$ sets complexity of the vulnerability exploitation, and Authentication defines if exploitation of the vulnerability requires additional authentication.

The attack graph is constructed so that transition from one state to another is possible only if there is access to the appropriate graph node. So, the equation for the $Exploitability$ can be redefined to calculate a local probability for node S_i that corresponds to the attack action and normalized to get probability value from 0 to 1:

$$\begin{cases} p(a_i) = 2 \times Access Vector \times Access Complexity \times Authentication & S_i \in S_r \\ p(a_i) = 2 \times Access Complexity \times Authentication & S_i \notin S_r \end{cases},$$

where S_r—root nodes of the graph.

Probability that node is not compromised is defined as $1-p(a_i)$.

Discrete conditional probability distributions $Pc(S_i|Pa(S_i))$ for the graph nodes (i.e. probabilities of compromise of S_i considering different combinations of states of its parents $Pa(S_i)$) are defined on the base of the reverse depth-first traversal for the graph. Two types of relations are determined for the attack graph nodes: "AND" (to compromise child node, it is necessary to compromise all parent nodes); "OR" (to compromise child node, it is necessary to compromise at least one parent node). The attack graph is constructed so that nodes of the attack path are connected with "AND" relation. "OR" relation forms different paths. We use equations that were suggested in [30] to calculate discrete conditional probability distributions in case of "AND" relations:

$$Pc(S_i|Pa(S_i)) = \begin{cases} 0, & \exists S_i \in Pa(S_i)|S_i = 0 \\ p(S_i), & \text{otherwise} \end{cases};$$

In case of "OR" relations:

$$Pc(S_i|Pa(S_i)) = \begin{cases} 0, & \forall S_i \in Pa(S_i)|S_i = 0 \\ p(S_i), & \text{otherwise} \end{cases}.$$

Unconditional probabilities for the graph nodes are defined on the base of local probabilities and discrete conditional probability distributions by equation:

$$Pr(S_1, ..., S_n) = \prod_{i=1}^{n} Pc(S_i | Pa[S_i]).$$

Attack impact metric (*AttackImpact*) for the attack graph node is determined on the base of criticality of an asset R_k ($k \in [1, l]$, l —number of all software assets of an organization) and damage level of the attack action a_i in case of successful exploitation of a vulnerability v_i ($i \in [1, m]$, m—number of all asset vulnerabilities) by their multiplication.

Asset criticality metric is calculated for the asset confidentiality $cCrit_k$, integrity $iCrit_k$ and availability $aCrit_k$ considering their value for the organization goals.

Damage from an attack action is defined on the base of the CVSS indexes as vector $[\, ConfImpact_{k,i}(c) \ IntegImpact_{k,i}(i) \ AvailImpact_{k,i}(a) \,]$, where $ConfImpact_{k,i}(c)$—damage level for the confidentiality of R_k in case of successful implementation of a_i that exploits vulnerability v_i, $IntegImpact_{k,i}(i)$—damage level for the integrity of R_k, $AvailImpact_{k,i}(a)$—damage level for the availability of R_k. $ConfImpact_{k,i}(c)$, $IntegImpact_{k,i}(i)$ and $AvailImpact_{k,i}(a)$ can take values {0.0; 0.275; 0.660} according to the CVSS indexes *confidentiality impact*, *integrity impact* and *availability impact*.

AttackImpact is defined as a sum:

$$AttackImpact = cCrit_k \times ConfImpact_{k,i}(c) + iCrit_k \times IntegImpact_{k,i}(i) +$$

$$+ aCrit_k \times AvailImpact_{k,i}(a).$$

If event *ev* comes, the probability that node *S* of an attack graph is compromised (*AttackPotentiality*) is calculated as follows:

$$p(S|ev) = \frac{p(ev|S) \times p(ev)}{p(S)} = \frac{p(ev|S) \times (p(ev|S) \times p(S) + p(ev|\neg S) \times p(\neg S))}{p(S)},$$

where $p(S)$—probability of the node compromise before security event; $p(ev|S)$—*information reliability* index for an event *ev* that determines probability that event *ev* is true; $p(ev|\neg S)$—probability that *ev* is false (false positive).

Probabilities for the child nodes of attacks that go through the compromised node are redefined taking into account the new probability of the compromise for the node for which the security event happened.

Returning to the key elements of the "good" metrics, we should specify the *criterion of interpretation* for the risk level values. Risk level value changes from 0 to 100 as minimum impact level and minimum probability level is 0, and maximum probability level is 1 and maximum impact level is 100. Risk from 0 to 0.1 is considered as low (risk can be ignored), risk from 0.1 to 1—medium (countermeasures should be implemented), risk from 1 to 10—high (countermeasures have to be implemented as soon as possible), risk from 10 to 100—critical (countermeasures have to be implemented now).

5.3 Countermeasure Selection

We determine two modes of the countermeasure selection technique: static and dynamic. The static mode can be applied on the design, deployment and exploitation stages of the system operation. The dynamic mode can be applied only on the exploitation stage of the system operation. In the static mode, security measures that increase the common system security level are selected. In the dynamic mode, measures that prevent the detected attacks are selected. For example, in the static mode the measure "Identification and authentication" can be selected and implemented using a software token. In the dynamic mode (when information on the security incidents come), this software token can be used to activate the multi-factor authentication. The main idea of the developed technique consists in selecting effective countermeasures on any stage of the system operation.

In the static mode of the technique, we propose to cover with countermeasures all objects (network objects and attack graph objects) with unacceptable risk level (i.e. objects which compromise leads to the high monetary losses). The technique starts from the launching of countermeasure selection process. This means that the security assessment is completed and the risk levels are calculated. The technique includes the following main stages:

1. Determination of the assessment level by using data in the repository. We outline three static data layers: topological, attacks and attacker. These layers are connected hierarchically from the lowermost topological layer to the attacks layer and to the highest attacker layer. Each data layer gives a higher level of security assessment accuracy (allows us to calculate the risk more accurately considering more security data).
2. Data acquisition considering the assessment level. On this stage, we get from the repository information for the countermeasure selection, including available analytical models and security metrics.
3. Countermeasure selection considering the assessment level. The result of this stage is the countermeasure list.

Figure 6 shows the flow chart of the dynamic mode. The technique includes the following main stages:

1. Waiting for the events. Each new event here signals the modification of security risks. This modification can be both the result of the security incidents and the result of the network configuration modifications. If an event comes, go to the next stage.

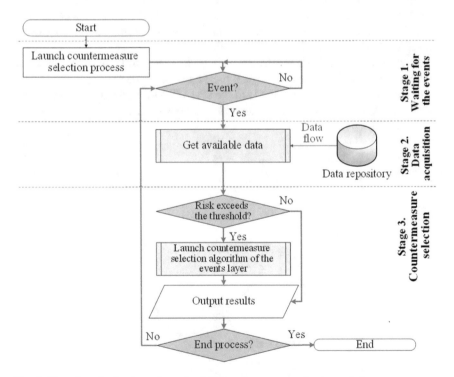

Fig. 6 Flow chart for the dynamic mode of the countermeasure selection technique

2. Data acquisition. These data incorporate information on the security incidents and the recalculated security risks.
3. Countermeasure selection. If new risk levels exceed the predefined threshold, then launch the countermeasure selection algorithm. Go to the stage (1).

6 Case Studies

6.1 Test Case

For experimental evaluation of the developed prototype, the model of a small local network was created (Fig. 7).

There are three zones in tested network. The hosts, situated in these zones, are as follows: (1) External: Malefactor; (2) DMZ: User1_Win98; User2_WinXP; User3_Linux; (3) Internal: User4_Linux; User5_Windows7. The Router and Firewall are separating these zones: Router is between External and DMZ zones and Firewall is between DMZ and Internal zones.

Let us outline the following network elements which are necessary for attack modelling: Network hardware (firewall, router, etc.); Computers with installed software (Web server, Application servers, Database servers, Users' computers); Links between the network elements (wired, wireless).

We separate malefactors for this case study according to their logical location. Separation of malefactors by the logical location depends on the topology (Fig. 8): In the internal network Malefactor 1; In the DMZ (De Militarized Zone) network - Malefactor 2; Outside of the controlled network (access via Internet) Malefactor 3.

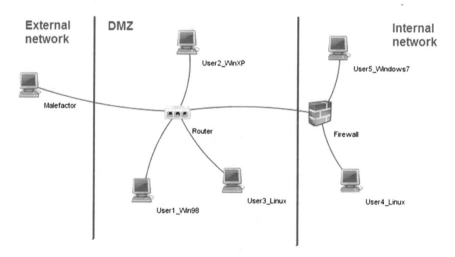

Fig. 7 Tested network view

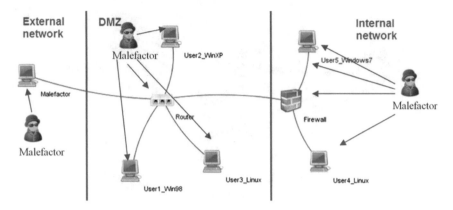

Fig. 8 Network elements and locations of malefactors

Thus, we differentiate three types of malefactors: (1) located in the internal network; (2) located in the DMZ; (3) located outside of the controlled network.

After entering the network configuration, the next step is to generate possible attack actions that depend on malefactors' knowledge and skills, installed software and network topology. Figure 9 shows the attacker knowledge about the tested network after performing all possible attacks. This figure also shows that the attacker has got the information about the topology within the DMZ network (the object Router connects all hosts inside the DMZ), but the attacker was not able to penetrate the internal network protected by Firewall.

Figure 9 illustrates different attacks traces that attacker can perform in the tested network. The attacker, carrying out attack actions, is located in the centre of the spherical representation. The icons and notations used in the attack graph are depicted in Table 2.

Figure 10 shows an example of the report about detected vulnerabilities and possible attack traces. The report also outlines the values of some security metrics and the common assessment of the security level (Orange).

When constructing the attack tree, particular attack patterns described in the CAPEC format [4] are used. The patterns contain attack descriptions that do not use vulnerabilities, for instance at the initial stage of an attack the malefactor could gather information on available hosts.

To specify in this case the attacker actions, the CAPEC-292 (Host Discovery) entry is used. It describes a group of various ways of scanning hosts and ports. This group contains, for example, such entries as CAPEC-285 (ICMP Echo Request Ping), CAPEC-296 (ICMP Information Request), CAPEC-299 (TCP SYN Ping).

The second stage is a search of vulnerable software. The examples of patterns used to describe malefactor actions are as follows: CAPEC-310 (Scanning for Vulnerable Software), CAPEC-311 (Fingerprinting Remote Operating Systems), CAPEC-300 (Port Scanning), etc.

On the third stage of the attack graph generation, both particular vulnerabilities from the CVE dictionary and patterns like CAPEC-233 (Privilege Escalation)

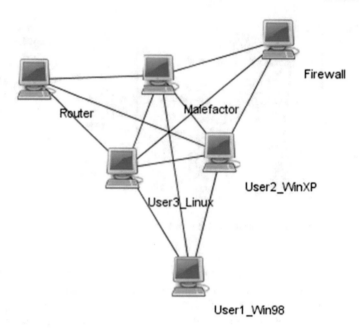

Fig. 9 Attacker's knowledge view

Table 2 Notation used in the attack graph

Notation	Description
	Malefactor initial position (name of the platform used by the malefactor as an initial location is displayed near the icon)
	Attack action (the symbol A is displayed near the icon), e.g. PING or an attack pattern (the symbol S is placed near the icon)
	Attack action which uses some vulnerability (the symbol V is placed near the icon)

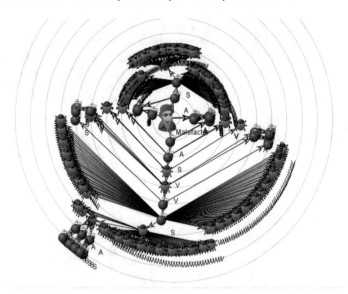

Fig. 10 Attacker tree view

are used. For instance, for the router, the attacker can use the vulnerability CVE-2016-5365 which represents stack-based buffer overflow in Huawei Honor WS851 routers with software 1.1.21.1 and earlier allows remote attackers to execute arbitrary commands with root privileges via unspecified vectors. This vulnerability enables the attacker to get full knowledge about DMZ network structure and perform some attacks directly from router. For the Windows operation system, the attacker can use vulnerability CVE-2010-2550 in the SMB Server in Microsoft Windows XP SP2 and SP3 and Windows 7. This server does not properly validate fields in an SMB request, which allows remote attackers to execute arbitrary code via a crafted SMB packet.

6.2 Metrics Calculation on the Basis of Attack Graph

Below, a simple example is presented. It shows how the attack graph is used to calculate the attack probabilities. Figure 11 illustrates a fragment of Bayesian attack graph with local, conditional and unconditional probabilities of attacks success and appropriate vulnerabilities. Calculations are as follows.

Calculation of the local probabilities: for the node A (CVE-2006-0038) CVSS *AccessComplexity* "Medium" that is equal to 0.61, *Authentication* "None" that is equal to 0.704. As soon as node A is not root, the local probability is calculated as follows $p(A) = 2 \times AccessComplexity \times Authentication = 2 \times 0.61 \times 0.704 = 0.85888$; for the node C (CVE-2001-1572) *AccessVector*

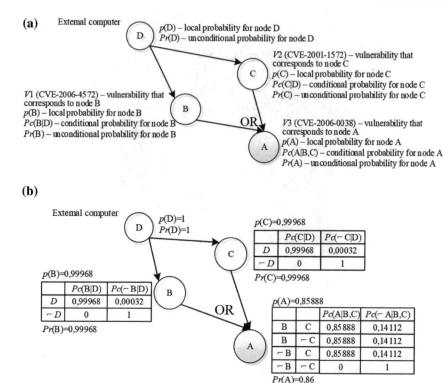

Fig. 11 A fragment of Bayesian attack graph

"Network" (numerical value 1), *AccessComplexity* "Low" (numerical value 0.71), *Authentication* "None" (numerical value 0.704). As soon as node C is root (it is available from the attacker computer), the local probability is calculated as $p(C) = 2 \times AccessVector \times AccessComplexity \times Authentication = 2 \times 1 \times 0.71 \times 0.704 = 0.99968$; for the node B (CVE-2006-4572) *AccessVector* "Network" (numerical value 1), *AccessComplexity* "Low" (numerical value 0.71), *Authentication* "None" (numerical value 0.704). As soon as node B is root, the local probability is calculated as follows $p(B) = 2 \times AccessVector \times AccessComplexity \times Authentication = 21 \times 0.71 \times 0.704 = 0.99968$. For the node D, the local probability can be set depending on the attacker profile. Set it equal to 1.

Calculation of the conditional probabilities using reverse traversal of the graph in depth: for the node A, conditional probability depends on the nodes B and C. As soon as dependence is of type "OR" $Pc(A|B,C) = p(A) = 0.85888$ for all cases except the situation when B and C are not compromised.

Table of discrete local distribution for node A is provided in Fig. 11a; for nodes B and C, the conditional probabilities depend on the node D, $Pc(B|D) = p(B) = 0.99968$ and $Pc(C|D) = p(C) = 0.99968$ if node D is not compromised. Tables of discrete local distributions for nodes B and C are provided in Fig. 11b.

Calculation of the unconditional probabilities using traversal of the graph in width:

for node D $Pr(D) = 1$;

for node C

$$Pr(C = True|D) = \sum_{D=\{True,False\}} Pc(C = True|D) \times Pr(D) = 0,99968 \times 1 + 0 \times 0;$$

for node B

$$Pr(B = True|D) = \sum_{D=\{True,False\}} Pc(B = True|D) \times Pr(D) = 0,99968 \times 1 + 0 \times 0;$$

for node A

$$Pr(A = True|B, C) = \sum_{B,C=\{True,False\}} Pc(A = True|B, C) \times Pr(B) \times Pr(C) = 0,85888$$

$$\times 0,99968 \times 0,99968 + 0,85888 \times 0,99968 \times 0,00032 + 0,85888 \times 0,99968 \times 0,00032$$

$$\approx 0,86.$$

```
PREFIX rdf: <http://www.w3.org/1999/02/22-rdf-syntax-ns#>
PREFIX owl: <http://www.w3.org/2002/07/owl#>
PREFIX rdfs: <http://www.w3.org/2000/01/rdf-schema#>
PREFIX xsd: <http://www.w3.org/2001/XMLSchema#>

PREFIX hssi: <http://comsec.spb.ru/HSSI/ontology#>

SELECT (MAX(?baseScore) AS ?maxBaseScore)
WHERE {
?vulnerability rdf:type hssi:NVD.
?vulnerability hssi:implementedIn ?product.
?vulnerability hssi:BaseScore ?baseScore.
?product hssi:type ?type.
?product hssi:vendor ?vendor.
?product hssi:product ?productName.
values(?type ?vendor ?productName)
{
("o"^^xsd:string "microsoft"^^xsd:string "windows_2003_server"^^xsd:string)
}
}
```

Fig. 12 Example of the query to the ontological database

6.3 Security Assessment and Ontological Inference

As it was said in the previous section, the ontology allows us to extend the knowledge on the security situation via queries to the ontological database.

In Fig. 12, a simple query is provided that allows calculating of software/hardware vulnerability metric for the Windows Server. More complicated queries allow us to compute other metrics used for security assessment and countermeasure selection.

7 Conclusion

The issues of analytical processing of cyber security events and information are considered by many researchers and commercial organizations. Different proposed approaches have their own advantages and disadvantages. In this chapter, we briefly described the methods, techniques and models that we suggested to use for security data gathering, processing and analysis in scope of the modern SIEM systems.

As a base, we used the methods of analytical modelling, ontologies, Bayesian inference, any-time algorithms and others. The paper described the suggested classification of security-related data, the data sources, the tools and standards we used for unified representation and automated processing of cyber security events and information.

The developed security data ontology was provided. Further, we outlined the way we generate the analytical models of security related objects, including attack graphs, service dependencies, malefactors and system configuration.

The techniques of security assessment and countermeasure selection that use these models were specified. These techniques allow us to monitor security situation and select countermeasures in case of attacks. An advantage of the described models and techniques consists in the automated joint application of heterogeneous data from various sources to get new knowledge on the security situation sufficient for decision making in any time. From our point of view, it is rather efficient for security assessment and countermeasure selection.

Finally, we provided illustrative examples for some of the proposed techniques and models. We aimed to describe the security assessments and countermeasure selection processes in the detailed and understandable way and hope that our results will be useful for the scientific and practical goals. The future research will be devoted to development of user behaviour analytics and big data mechanisms for analytical processing of cyber security events and information, detailed elaboration of all specified components and detailed experimental investigation.

8 Questions

1. Name and elaborate data sources, which are available to acquire input data for Security Information and Event Management (SIEM)?
2. Explain how SIEM is important in cyber security?
3. What are the common security data enumeration standards?
4. What are the challenges involved in using SIEM data?
5. Provide a common scheme of using the external static and internal dynamic input data in SIEM systems.
6. What is Common Vulnerability Reporting Framework?
7. What techniques are available to correlate events. What are their benefits and challenges? Explain your answers with examples.
8. Explain the steps involved in analytical attack modelling and Bayesian attack graph.
9. What are security metrics? Explain in detail.

Acknowledgements This research is being supported by the grants of the RFBR (18-07-01488), partial support of budgetary subject 16-116033110102-5, Grant 074-U01, and the Council for Grants of the President of Russia (project MK-314.2017.9, scholarship SP-751.2018.5).

References

1. Waltermire D, Quinn S, Scarfone K, Halbardier A (2011) The technical specification for the security content automation protocol (SCAP): vol. 27 Scap version 1.2. (2011)
2. First: common vulnerability scoring system SIG. https://www.first.org/cvss (2018). Accessed 27 Feb 2018
3. Mitre: common vulnerabilities and exposures. https://cve.mitre.org/data/downloads/index.html (2018). Accessed 27 Feb 2018
4. Mitre: common attack pattern enumeration and classification (2018). https://capec.mitre.org/. Accessed 27 Feb 2018
5. CWE: common weakness enumeration (2018). https://cwe.mitre.org/. Accessed 27 Feb 2018
6. NIST: national vulnerability database (2018). https://nvd.nist.gov/. Accessed 27 Feb 2018
7. Exploit-DB: offensive security's exploit database archive (2018). https://www.exploit-db.com/. Accessed 27 Feb 2018
8. Fedorchenko A, Kotenko I, Chechulin A (2015) Design of integrated vulnerabilities database for computer networks security analysis. In: 2015 23rd Euromicro international conference on parallel, distributed and network-based processing (PDP). IEEE, New York (2015), pp 559–566
9. Fedorchenko A, Kotenko IV, Chechulin A (2015) Integrated repository of security information for network security evaluation. JoWUA 6(2):41–57
10. NIST: official common platform enumeration (CPE) dictionary (2018). https://nvd.nist.gov/cpe.cfm. Accessed 27 Feb 2018
11. Choattrition J (2018) OSVDB: everything is vulnerable. https://blog.osvdb.org/. Accessed 27 Feb 2018
12. IBM: Introducing IBM X-force malware analysis on cloud (2018). https://www.ibm.com/security/xforce. Accessed 27 Feb 2018
13. SecurityFocus: vulnerabilities (2018). http://www.securityfocus.com/. Accessed 27 Feb 2018
14. ICASI: the common vulnerability reporting framework (CVRF) (2018). http://www.icasi.org/cvrf/. Accessed 27 Feb 2018

15. NIST: common configuration enumeration (CCE) details (2018). https://nvd.nist.gov/cce/index.cfm. Accessed 27 Feb 2018
16. Kruegel C, Valeur F, Vigna G (2004) Intrusion detection and correlation: challenges and solutions. Springer, USA
17. Fedorchenko A, Kotenko I, El Baz D (2017) Correlation of security events based on the analysis of structures of event types. 2017 9th IEEE international conference on intelligent data acquisition and advanced computing systems: technology and applications (IDAACS), vol 1. IEEE, New York, pp 270–276
18. Kotenko I, Chechulin A, Doynikova E, Fedorchenko A (2017) Ontological hybrid storage for security data. International symposium on intelligent and distributed computing. Springer, Berlin, pp 159–171
19. Fedorchenko A, Kotenko I, Doynikova E, Chechulin A (2017) The ontological approach application for construction of the hybrid security repository. In: 2017 XX IEEE international conference on soft computing and measurements (SCM). IEEE, New York (2017), pp 525–528
20. Kotenko IV (2014) Chechulin AA (2014) Fast network attack modelling and security evaluation based on attack graphs. J Cyber Secur Mobil 3(1):27–46
21. Doynikova EV, Chechulin AA, Kotenko IV (2017) Analytical attack modelling and security assessment based on the common vulnerability scoring system. In: Proceedings of the 20th conference of open innovations association FRUCT, vol 20
22. ISO: ISO/IEC 27004:2016: Information technology - security techniques - information security management - monitoring, measurement, analysis and evaluation (2018). https://www.iso.org/obp/ui/#iso:std:iso-iec:27004:ed-2:v1:en:en. Accessed 27 Feb 2018
23. Singhal A, Ou X (2011) Security risk analysis of enterprise networks using probabilistic attack graphs, Nist inter-agency report
24. Kotenko IV, Doynikova EV (2016) Dynamical calculation of security metrics for countermeasure selection in computer networks. In: Proceedings of the 24th Euromicro international conference on parallel. IEEE Computer Society, Los Alamitos, California, pp 558–565
25. Piliero S (2009) Security Metrics. Establishing unambiguous and logically defensible security metrics (2009). https://www.certconf.org/presentations/2009/files/WK-1.pdf. Accessed 27 Feb 2018
26. Kotenko I, Stepashkin M (2006) Attack graph based evaluation of network security. IFIP international conference on communications and multimedia security. Springer, Berlin, pp 216–227
27. Cheng Y, Deng J, Li J, Deloach S, Singhal A, Ou X (2018) Metrics of security
28. ISO: ISO/IEC 27005:2011: information technology - security techniques - information security management - monitoring, measurement, analysis and evaluation (2018). Accessed 27 Feb 2018
29. Poolsappasit N, Dewri R, Ray I (2012) Dynamic security risk management using bayesian attack graphs. IEEE Trans Depend Sec Comput 9(1):61–74
30. Frigault M, Wang L, Singhal A, Jajodia S (2008) Measuring network security using dynamic Bayesian network. In: Proceedings of the 4th ACM workshop on quality of protection, ACM, pp 23–30
31. Doynikova E, Kotenko I (2017) CVSS-based probabilistic risk assessment for cyber situational awareness and countermeasure selection. 2017 25th Euromicro International conference on parallel, distributed and network-based processing (PDP). IEEE, New York, pp 346–353

Artificial Intelligence Agents as Mediators of Trustless Security Systems and Distributed Computing Applications

Steven Walker-Roberts and Mohammad Hammoudeh

Abstract This chapter considers the emergence of a new cybersecurity paradigm—a system in which no trust exists. The brief history to this new paradigm is examined, the challenges and opportunities of such a paradigm and how to design a system implementing zero trust starting with static vulnerability analysis. The role of artificial intelligence as a selfless mediating agent is examined to resolve some issues in implementing a trustless security system, in addition to the challenges this presents.

1 A Brief History of Zero Trust

The first major development of computer security in mainstream computing was in the late 1980s, around the time of the Morris worm proliferating in 1988. At that time, firewalls were already being developed, but the sudden shock of Morris worm, effectively a Denial of Service (DoS) attack, sent the Internet into proverbial meltdown. Though the Morris worm was perhaps the first major outbreak of malicious computer code, it soon became impossible to have an internet-facing computer system without it being subject to attack. Thus, the firewall was after that widely adopted [1].

It did not take long for the world to realise the biggest limitation of a firewall, described so perfectly by [2] as an "all eggs in one basket" approach. In that paper, it was suggested that if a firewall is overcome then the largest security asset is lost. From the title of the article ("Firewall v2.0"), it becomes crystallized that as early as 1997, just a few short years after the wider adoption of firewalls in day-to-day computing, that they were rapidly becoming insufficient as the number of users on

S. Walker-Roberts (✉)
School of Computing, Manchester Metropolitan University, John Dalton Building,
Chester Street, Manchester, UK
e-mail: steven@walkerroberts.co.uk

M. Hammoudeh
Manchester Metropolitan University, John Dalton Building, Chester Street, Manchester, UK
e-mail: m.hammoudeh@mmu.ac.uk

© Springer International Publishing AG, part of Springer Nature 2018
S. Parkinson et al. (eds.), *Guide to Vulnerability Analysis for Computer Networks and Systems*, Computer Communications and Networks,
https://doi.org/10.1007/978-3-319-92624-7_6

the internet grew and the massive advancement of technology continued into the millennium.

There have been many suggestions aiming to resolve that critical issue in the literature leading up to the time of writing, but as [3] points out, they effectively work like an onion. That is, layers upon layers of security zones are designed around each other in paper after paper. Reference [4] echoes that problem, referring to the age-old computer security mantra that a good computer security configuration equates to a good M&M, hard and crunchy on the outside whilst soft on the inside. There are surprisingly few studies of the efficacy of firewalls and other intrusion detection and prevention technologies (IDPS) as a general technological capability.

Those quantitative studies that do exist, such as [5], look at improving security systems through mathematical optimisation. However, as is clear from [5], security systems are a constructionist creation that require an event to happen in order for the system to later safeguard against it, either by a process of statistical induction or constructive extension. When the attack is internal, not only is the firewall almost certainly bypassed but the security breach has to happen for a dynamic security system such as an IDPS to intervene and evaluate the breach or for an administrator to (hopefully) be notified of the early signs a novel security breach in event logs. It appears, on the basis of the near-absence of any experimental research involving perimeter security systems, that the very nature of its existence as a technology renders it a single point of failure. It is not intended for twenty-first century cybersecurity as a single means of securing a computer system nor with an IDPS as a class combination because these are both prone to the weaknesses of statistical induction and the fundamental inability to foresee 100% of zero-day threats in the future.

In light of that flaw, there is a considerable body of research investigating the "insider threat". Many studies, such as [6] use simulation to model such threats. In that particular study, a typical attack was constructed and game-theoretic equilibrium values were used to establish the relative beliefs of the system administrator and the attacker. That, it argues, provides a platform for focussing attention to security events and knowing where weaknesses lie. However, it fails to provide an overall suggestion on how to overcome the firewall "eggs in one basket" hurdle. Similarly, [7] uses Bayesian inference to build on repeated evaluation of evidence of an attack (malicious packets in their case). The problem is that whilst the research appears rigorous, it still requires malicious activity which precedes the eventual prediction of malicious insider activity. Thus, whilst it would be useful for a DDoS-type security event, it offers nothing in the way of preventing data exfiltration and sabotage, nor other modes of attack such as side-channel infiltration or pre-texting.

Some other studies take the form of case-studies, e.g. [8]. In that case study, the researchers evaluated 200 real cybersecurity breaches using technical summaries and classified them using the CAPEC industrial standard for identifying the attack steps taken to achieve intrusion. That study aimed at identifying how future technologies would need to target vulnerabilities, but did not itself propose any such technology to overcome those challenges. This is further evidenced in a later survey by that research group at the University of Oxford in [9].

What is apparent from the literature is that there are no firm proposals and no detailed research studies which have provided an academically rigorous overall answer to the malicious insider issue. A new problem which has emerged is that not only are infrastructures coping with increasingly complex and often internal attacks, there has been an increasing trend of Bring Your Own Device (BYOD). That effectively means that confidential computer systems are being accessed from devices which do not belong to, or communicate over, a network infrastructure with security preparations that are within the control of the data controller. Reference [10] studies this particular problem. That research group looked at organisational practices and feedback to develop a framework using qualitative surveys. Whilst the research surely assists with developing security processes and policies, it does not offer a suggestion as to a new technology. Reference [11] proposed a dynamic access control system on the profile of an individual or a group rather than its situation within a computer network, but the research paper did not include any simulation to evidence that approach. The literature appears otherwise lacking in significant further studies.

The term zero-trust was coined by J. Kindervaag in [4] in an initial proposal by Forrester Research, a market research company. Reference [4] argues that "zero trust" is a model and that there are three key principles which should be adhered to, then any network can be secured in modern computing across boundaries. These principles are (i) ensure all resources are accessed securely regardless of location; (ii) adopt a least privilege strategy which is strictly enforced; (iii) inspect and log all traffic. These are, it appears, extremely generalised propositions. Besides being long-standing principles which are well established in academia and in practice, much of those concepts are already current general knowledge and so regrettably add little to the discourse in cybersecurity.

The "zero-trust model" (where not already extant) was born from privately commissioned commercial research by Forrester Research. That novel model has never been formalised, and its underlying private commercial research basis is not academically rigorous. This is because "zero trust" is a security paradigm and cannot be properly described as a model. Reference [12] was Forrester's first public appraisal of their version of the model to the United States National Institute of Standards and Technology (NIST) in response to its call for evidence in the inquiry of reference RFI#130208119-3119-01 [13]. In that submission to the US Government, [12] suggests having a central router ("segmentation gateway"), implementing VLANs, having "multiple parallelised switching cores" and central management from a console is what is required to achieve a zero-trust architecture. It also proposes a new type of network known as a "Data Acquisition Network" which is essentially the same as `syslog` which has existed since the 1980s (around the time firewalls were implemented). The briefing paper entirely lacks critical analysis and discussion. That submission to NIST adds very little indeed to the state of the art of itself because it is critically flawed, even as a pamphlet, though it does invite debate on ideas which go right to the foundations of cybersecurity academia and industry—it asks whether we could have a usable computer system in which nothing is trusted. Following the OPM breach in 2015, a US sub-congressional committee investigated the efficacy of cybersecurity and made key recommendations [13] of which that question formed a pivotal part.

The most progress which seems to have been made in creating a secure unprivileged or "zero-trust" network is Google's BeyondCorp which was first technically documented in a public paper by [14]. In that technical paper, a system is overviewed by which an inventory is used in combination with identity to decide appropriate access, even over an insecure network. The proposal seems to rely on an inventory external to the system itself and secure communication as the key determinants in implementing the model. This is clearly superior to the proposals in [4, 12] which are not concretely founded on evidence.

An additional technology which emerged in 2014 was Ethereum, which is a decentralised block-chain technology in which currency is exchanged for cryptographic mining or real cash [15]. It is possible to build massively decentralised applications with this technology which are heavily cryptographic and which integrate currency into the use of the application. There are however multiple problems with this technology. Firstly, Ethereum is centred around the use of its currency "ether" which means that a significant amount of cash flow might be needed to use and integrate with the primary Ethereum network to develop "smart contracts". Secondly, Ethereum is designed to be decentralised and democratic in style, and so this is very difficult to adjust to business requirements. Finally, Ethereum only deals with trustless security in the context of networking and fails to deal with other aspects of the application of trustless methods such as the other planes of computing.

It becomes clear that the biggest challenge in the post-millennial computing era is confined no longer to making devices faster or improving power efficiency. Arguably one of the greatest challenges for computing has been keeping devices secure. With cybersecurity incidents rapidly increasing year on year almost explosively [16], it is now strikingly obvious that computer scientists and engineers need to change the way that they approach the problem of computer security. Firewalls and security zones do not mitigate sophisticated or insider attacks to computer systems, even when combined with IDPS [8].

Even the least informed know of massive cyberattacks such as Stuxnet [17], the NHS cyberattacks (used to distribute ransomware), the CIA and NSA leaks, the US OPM breach and increasingly massive commercial data breaches. Cybersecurity threats have moved beyond the virtual to the physical. It has become such a concern to the USA that President Barack Obama made an Executive Order Dated 12 February 2013, requiring the US NIST to develop new cybersecurity measures to tackle cybercrime, cyberterrorism and nation state threats. The UK has branched off a part of GCHQ, the National Cybersecurity Centre, to deal with increasingly prevalent threats. This, in combination with the Joint Committee on National Security Strategy ("JCNSS") inquiry into cybersecurity, is one of a number of steps taken by the UK to investigate ways of remaking cybersecurity in a what is a changed era when compared to the time that seminal computer security technologies such as firewalls were first proposed in the 1980s. The perimeter security model has meant that security breaches are becoming all too common, increasingly internal in origin and increasingly detrimental. Adding to the discourse is the fact that cybersecurity is now a theatre of war for nation states, terrorists and otherwise cyber criminals [17].

Within that sphere of emergence, computer networks have become increasingly connected, particularly as a result of the Internet of Things ("IoT"), which has inherently increased the complexity of keeping resources secure. As a result of that complexity, security threats have dramatically increased in number with complexity allowing for theoretically limitless attack surfaces. Computer security has consequently become "the" scientific problem posed by post-millennial computing and optimisation. Very few computer users are in a position to implement complex threat mitigation in a rapidly developing computer industry and legacy technology can stall efforts to improve this situation, thus leaving resources exposed to risk.

It is apparent that as a generality, the literature is incredibly lacking in consensus as to the best way to address externalisation of computing resources and increasingly frequent internal attacks. What is clear is that the perimeter security model and perimeter security installations are not sustainable in distributed computing networks that have no fixed trust boundary.

The literature leans towards several emerging security technology trends. The first is a move towards user-centric security which is seen in the externalisation literature and Google's BeyondCorp technical specification. The second is a move towards security of state rather than security of zone; this is seen in the progression from the onion/M&M picture of firewall zoning to the contemporary perspective of security around the user and their permissible resources. Third, the default security position is that no entity comprising a computer system should be trusted. Trust has become transient. Finally, there is a new computer security paradigm of "zero trust": trustless and unprivileged networks.

In the present day, cybersecurity has reached the frontier of human nature. The world is now asking whether it is possible to have a computer system in the present ubiquitous technology climate which does not trust any entity. It is right to consider whether this would create a dangerous computer system on the order of "SkyNet" in popular fiction or whether the boundaries of cybersecurity are simply shifting, in the same way that networking boundaries have shifted as a result of ubiquitous computing in the IoT sphere.

2   The Challenge of Achieving No Trust

When considering whether a trustless security system is feasible, one may ask a number of questions. How can one have a trustless security system which fits in a society based upon trust? How can a trustless system remain usable if the user is not trusted to use its intended functions? How can information be protected and comply with legislation if it is not controlled by a data controller? There are many other interesting challenges presented by the idea of having a trustless security system.

Given that society is a system based upon trust and reputation owing to experiential human nature, it is very difficult to imagine from a lay perspective the creation of a relevant and usable trustless security system. Generically, software development now controls as a discipline a huge portion of infrastructure creation via Infrastructure-as-Code. Software development is designed to meet user and business requirements and so is by nature focussed on making the user experience first class and any other considerations such as cybersecurity often a second-class citizen. Thus, in a trustless context, the design question begins with 'How do I make a minimum viable product with the least amount of trust?'. Consider for example a database connected to a front-end Web application. Should there be an intermediate proxy? Should data be encrypted at source? What does a user need to be able to do? How can the user be further separated from other resources? Does the system need to collect all of the user data proposed? Can resources be further segmented?

These are important considerations which would be difficult to imbue even in an experienced software developer tasked with making a simple web application. The resources available to the software developer will undoubtedly be a major factor in the evaluation of the complexity of any underlying security mechanisms. Zero trust is about security by design and so one practical challenge will be making it easy for developers to do security well in any event during the software development stage, but moreover to implement zero-trust security at the coding stage.

Another caveat for a trustless security system is how feasible it would be to manage state if it is to be assumed that nothing about the underlying application can be trusted. In contemporary environments, often distributed computing applications are made up of many stateless microservices knitted together with a front-end presentation layer and a permanent data store at the backend for holding state. If none of those microservices are trusted, the state would have to be immutable and unreadable to those microservices or highly ephemeral. In that situation, how can such microservices operate at all? The answer is that data supplied to a microservice would have to be user-derivative based upon minimal disclosure and when data is permanently stored it would need to remain in the control of the data originator and thus would likely need to be cryptographically isolated to the user based upon information they have that no other person could have.

An additional challenge for trustless security systems is that trust exists beyond software abstractions. Trust exists in the fabric of computer architecture and will therefore inevitably become an electronic design problem in the future. Given the intricacy of electronic design, this will be a difficult area in which to find specialist engineers. However, it may be a valuable starting point for developing trustless security for practical everyday use.

Unfortunately in reality, the designers of computer systems are only able to envisage a limited number of events and channels for misuse. It is often the case that the abuse of a computer system is internal in origin and as a result of neglect by the user [18]. Any trustless security system design would have to take account of the need for system administrators and software developers to address these problems entirely at the design and development stage in a relatively straightforward fashion. Often, computer systems are designed and developed first, with some later integration with an off-the-shelf security suite—this is a practice that would almost certainly need to be changed within a trustless context.

3 Legal Changes Paving Way for Trustless Security

There are a number of principles recognised by the Information Commissioner's Office as being the most pertinent to information security [19]. These are briefly (i) that data must be processed fairly and lawfully; (ii) the data must be processed for specified purposes; (iii) the processing must be adequate; (iv) data recorded about a subject must be accurate; (v) data can only be retained for a specified period of time; (vi) subjects have a number of substantive rights in relation to data held about them; (vii) data must be stored securely; (viii) there are restrictions on how data can be processed internationally. These are listed in Part 1 of Schedule 1 of the Data Protection Act 1998 and are interpreted in accordance with Schedule 2 of the Data Protection Act 1998 as referred to in s.4 Data Protection Act 1998.

According to Part II of Schedule 1 of the Data Protection Act 1998, data is processed fairly and lawfully if the information is not obtained illicitly or by means of deceit, and the data subject consents to such data being recorded or has consented to third- party processing (Sch. 2(1) Data Protection Act 1998). It is important that this is often instituted during the formation of an agreement, for example a loan agreement which requires that information be shared with credit reference agencies whom may then share that credit file with other lenders. In general, it is expected that the data subject will have been fully informed as to the purpose for which data protected under the Act about them is sought.

The processing also has to be necessary in the performance of a contract or "taking steps at the request of the data subject with a view to entering into a contract" (Sch. 2(2) Data Protection Act 1998). Data can also be lawfully collected if it is necessary to do so in order to comply with a legal obligation or in the vital interests of the data subject. There are other fair processing justifications at Sch. 2(5) such as the administration of justice and the exercise of the functions of the House of Commons.

If data is sensitive personal data, defined at s.(2) of the Data Protection Act 1998 as any information about race, political opinion, religious beliefs, etc., then the processing of sensitive personal data must be "necessary". There is a detailed list of fair processing justifications which make such processing necessary at Schedule 3 Data Protection Act 1998.

The purposes must be "specified" either in a position statement from the data controller which is provided to the data subject at the point at which they agree to provide information, or a notice must be served on the Information Commissioner particularising the same purposes (Sch. 1(5) Data Protection Act 1998). A position statement may be a policy, a contract, or official correspondence of an organisation in its capacity as a data controller directed to the Information Commissioner. Data processing is determined to be "adequate", if when any data is collected from a data subject, such data is collected minimally [20], but this is the general practice norm.

Whilst accuracy may seem like an obvious proposition, there are pitfalls. In general, accuracy must represent the position a data controller would take if they had conducted reasonable enquiries as to the accuracy of personal data. Thus, Sch.1 II(7) Data Protection Act 1998 indicates that provided the data controller took reasonable steps to verify the accuracy of any data connected with a specific purpose, it does not err. There is an additional protection for a data controller if a mistake is legitimately made—a data controller may record the fact of a dispute about the accuracy of personal data at the point within the data that there is a dispute.

Data subjects have a number of substantive rights, which if breached, lead to a breach of the sixth principle (Sch. 1(II)(8) Data Protection Act 1998). The most frequent rights exercised are the rights of subject access at ss.7-8 Data Protection Act 1998. These rights provide that a data subject may receive all records about him on a proper request under that section, and payment of any relevant fee, to which the data controller must reply within 45 days.

The data subject also has the right to object to data being processed for the purposes of direct marketing, processing likely to cause damage or distress, or processing which is subject to automated decision making that may significantly affect the data subject (e.g. reliability as an employee) (Sch 1(II)(8) Data Protection Act 1998).

The Information Commissioner's Office has prepared detailed guidance in relation to the General Data Protection Regulation (EU Regulation 2016/679) (GDPR) which replaces the Data Protection Directive 95/46/EC. The new regulation, set to come into force on May 25, 2018, relates to data controllers and data processors [21]. There are two notable new rights under the GDPR for data subjects. These are under Articles 17 and 20, respectively.

Article 17 provides a new formal right of erasure or "right to be forgotten". This essentially means that a data subject can make a request to a data controller to have information about them destroyed. This right stems from *Google Spain SL, Google Inc. v Agencia Espanola De Proteccion de Datos* (C131-12). In that case, a man was identified as having his property subject to a forced sale in a prominent newspaper in 1998. In 2010, the information was still available on Google and the male asked for it to be removed from Google. Google refused. The matter went before a number of national courts before finally being referred to the European Court of Justice (ECJ). The ECJ decided that he had a fundamental right to be forgotten because the information was no longer relevant. The judgement of the ECJ has been the subject of furious debates. This right has now been formally adopted within the GDPR—this provides data subjects with substantial control over information about them held by any data controller.

Article 20 confers a new right to data portability. For example, if a data subject wants to move to services provided by a different data controller, then they are entitled by Article 20 to obtain data in a format which allows for it to be easily transferred to a competitor. This is likely to affect online services such as Facebook and Google whom store large amounts of data and have a significant level of competition—this has wide implications for data management in the cloud.

There are significant new obligations. In principle, these are that data controllers must ensure data is kept secure by design (Article 25), controllers outside of the EU must appoint representatives in the EU and will be subject to EU law (Article 27); data controllers are required to keep records of any processing activity (Article 30), must guarantee the security of processing (Article 32) and must carry out a data protection impact assessment. A data protection officer must now be appointed in any organisation undertaking significant processing activities. The requirement to register with a data protection authority has been repealed.

In the event of a data breach, the data controller is now required to notify a supervisory authority (Article 33). Previously, the position was quite unsatisfactory in that data controllers, if they had suffered a data protection breach, were not required by law to report it. Thus, organisations failing to meet data protection standards could do so with impunity regardless of the risk to data subjects. That position has now changed, and it will likely be a criminal offence as a result of Article 84.

The data controller must also communicate the fact of the breach to the data subjects concerned (Article 34). The present position is that a data controller has to voluntarily notify data subjects of the loss or breach of their data. The GDPR will ensure that data subjects are notified so that they can seek the appropriate remedy. Failure to notify is highly likely to be a criminal offence in many jurisdictions as a result of Article 84. The penalties have now increased and are as high as 4% of the annual worldwide turnover of the organisation (Article 83(5)).

Presently, it is a criminal offence pursuant to s.55(1) of the Data Protection Act 1998 to disclose or receive information without the consent of a data controller. This offence encompasses many situations where a rogue employee or a malicious third-party misuses information. The recipient of the data can also be incorporated into the offence and prosecuted as a principle offender. There are specified circumstances where an offence would not be committed, primarily if the data is disclosed or received in order to prevent or detect crime (s.55(2)(a)(i) Data Protection Act 1998). There are other defences in s.55(2) of the Data Protection Act 1998 that protect a potential offender, such as reasonable belief that the person was entitled to make the disclosure or receive the information, as the case may be. If an offence is committed, then the Information Commissioner may serve a fixed penalty on the offender under s.55A Data Protection Act 1998.

An example case in which a fine was imposed was the recent case of the data breach at the Crown Prosecution Service in 2015 [22], in which sensitive personal data (the video interviews of victims of sexual offences) were stolen by burglars from a flat in Manchester. The Information Commissioner had found, after his investigation, that the Crown Prosecution Service had instructed a contractor (Swan Films) to make redactions to vulnerable witness interviews in preparation for Crown Court trials. Due to an issue with due diligence, the Crown Prosecution Service had allowed the contractor to store highly confidential information and had not vetted the premises in order to learn that the data would not be held securely. The data were stored on various unencrypted DVDs and hard discs which were stolen by burglars. They were later recovered but not before the Crown Prosecution Service was liable to be fined by £200, 000.

The tort of misuse of private information was devised in case law in the judgement of *Campbell v Mirror Group Newspapers Ltd* [2004] UKHL 22. Naomi Campbell sued The Mirror newspaper for photographing her outside of a drug rehabilitation clinic and claiming that she was, as a result of being placed outside there by the photographs, a drug addict. She sued claiming that Article 8 (the right to a private and family life) in Schedule 1 of the Human Rights Act 1998 was engaged and breached. She argued that the Court was required to act compatibly with the European Convention on Human Rights pursuant to s.6 Human Rights Act 1998. She won a trial at first instance, but MGN appealed to the Court of Appeal. There, it was decided that MGN were not liable. Naomi Campbell appealed to the House of Lords which decided that Naomi Campbell had a reasonable expectation of privacy, and that the balance between Naomi Campbell's Article 8 rights and MGN's Article 11 right (to freedom of expression) fell in Naomi Campbell's favour.

This case not only defines the tort, but creates in effect a two stage test. In this case, the Lords were express that "confidence" and "privacy" are interchangeable terms. The test is (i) whether the Claimant had a reasonable expectation of privacy; (ii) if so, whether that reasonable expectation outweighs the Article 11 rights of the Defendant. This precedent, however, does not give an automatic right to compensation, merely an equitable remedy such as an injunction.

Ordinarily, there is no right to claim damages as a result of a data protection breach either. That was, until, the case of *Vidal-Hall v Google Inc*[2014] EWHC 13 (QB). In those proceedings, the Claimant brought proceedings because Google had expressed a public position statement which said that it would not store cookies for the DoubleClick ad service for users of the Safari web browser without their express consent. In reality, Google had collected such data in large quantities from users without their express consent.

The Claimants claimed damages under s.13 Data Protection Act 1998. The question of law in *Vidal-Hall* was whether a Claimant could claim damages for distress under s.13 of the Data Protection Act 1998. The Court of Appeal decided that it could claim those damages. Thus, any Claimant can rely on this case as authority that they too have suffered quantifiable damage resulting from distress were it but for the breach of Defendant's duties under the Data Protection Act 1998.

An on-going class action against *WM Morrisons*, brought by approximately 6000 employees whose payroll data were stolen, is presently before the High Court. The Court has been asked whether a Claimant can claim damages as a result of a loss that did not cause any damage that the Claimant can actually prove. It is likely that the Court will decide that WM Morrisons is liable.

Even if it decides in the favour of WM Morrisons presently, when the GDPR takes effect in May 2018, Article 82 will apply to domestic civil litigation. Article 82 requires states to provide for adequate compensation and redress for any breach of the GDPR provisions. As a result, in the future it is likely an organisation can be sued and be required to pay damages even if the Claimant cannot prove they suffered a loss of any kind.

The current state of the law is that an organisation which fails to comply with the Data Protection Act 1998 is not only liable to pay compensation under s.13 of the Data Protection Act 1998 for distress, they can also be sued for the tort of misuse of private information which can result in a substantial amount of damages being awarded. In the future, businesses can be fined up to 4% of annual turnover. Any organisation or person which breaches s.55 Data Protection Act 1998 can be prosecuted or issued with a monetary fixed penalty of up to £250, 000 by the Information Commissioner pursuant to s.55 Data Protection Act 1998. The new requirements under the GDPR are onerous and so will become easier to fall foul of. In an increasingly volatile threat climate, it has become more important than ever to do cybersecurity safely so that one does not fall foul of the rules.

It is impossible to comply with the Data Protection Act 1998 or the GDPR in public cloud computing because data has to be in the hands of a third party at some point in a transitional format which is not fully compliant; thus, in order to be able to leverage public cloud services and other public infrastructures in which there is likely to exist a transitional state, new technologies need to be created which are able to mitigate a malicious cloud provider.

Presently, if services are used in the public cloud, a malicious cloud provider would mean that data at rest, in transit and during processing, is vulnerable to exploitation. All it would take is for a public cloud provider to be compromised, such as in the case of the NSA's PRISM [23] in which it was exfiltrating data on a mass scale to the ignorance of public cloud services providers. This is a significant problem and challenges the foundations of computer security.

In the future, business operations which use weak security systems will quickly become unsustainable financially because of the onerous provisions governing the relationship between data subjects and data controllers. This has substantial implications for how cybersecurity systems will be modelled in the future.

4   A Comparison of Trustful Security Technologies

Existing security technologies are generally sub-divided into rule-based technologies, dynamic technologies and a specialist sub-class of dynamic IDPS technologies: artificially intelligent security agents. These are all trustful in that they evaluate the state of trust in user agents to make decisions about access control; this is in absolute contrast to trustless security systems which start with the proposition that the access attempt is unauthorised and malicious.

Anomaly detection features as the dominant form of IDPS implementation today. A large number of high-impact research studies [24–37]) are related entirely to anomaly detection. This is likely to be because no mainstream technologies have been developed to supersede IDPS security systems.

Eleven studies confirmed that they used synthetic data to simulate IDPS detection in response to given datasets. This presents a shortfall in two ways: (i) synthetic data cannot represent unusual or novel scenarios which the designer cannot envisage; (ii) it does not represent statistically the nature and distribution of malicious activity that is likely to occur in real security incidents. Consequently, it is not surprising that TPR ("trust-positive rate") and FPR ("false-positive rate") values are markedly lower than the theoretical ideals of 1.0 and 0.0, respectively.

In the literature experimental studies, many fail to leverage real-world data and these generally have lower FPR and TPR values than studies using synthetically generated data. This tends to suggest that synthetic data could be more optimistic than real-world data. It is plausible to suggest that a shortcoming in the state of the art is that synthetic and non-synthetic outcomes are rarely compared together which can generate misleading results about the underlying viability of the IDPS class of technologies today.

IDPS systems can be divided into approximately four techniques of anomaly detection: (i) event-based statistical detection; (ii) behavioural anomaly detection; (iii) raw data anomaly detection; (iv) meta-data anomaly detection.

The majority of the detection systems used in practice across the industry today are event-based using primarily system logs. Studies related to the effectiveness of the same include [26–30, 38]; these show a generally poor TPR and FPR for this sub-class of IDPS.

Together, these IDPS sub-classes examine traffic and system actions in real time to determine whether an anomalous action has taken place. Each approach uses different methods to attain the same goal; for example, [28] describes a machine-based IDPS which makes a binary decision as to good and bad using finite-state machines. Conversely, [27, 29] use real-time log analysis of system events to determine if a malicious action has taken place. All of these methods are dependent on the amount of malicious activity taking place, the degree of abnormality in that activity and the sensitivity of the algorithm being used; this is an agreed position within each of those approaches.

All of these methods are constructionist in that they require an event to occur and re-occur in a fashion which does not desensitise the IDPS in order for detection to work. Thus, in the context of internal threats, particularly of a zero-day nature, it is possible to envisage why anomaly detection in its present form within the literature is not designed to cope with situations where one computer security breach could be malignant.

Behavioural anomaly detection works by intercepting a malicious user before they do any act of significant harm. It anticipates the danger presented by a developing behavioural profile. Reference [25] explores this in detail. In that study, only 4 of 173 participants were behaving legitimately in one experiment. The mitigation for the internal threat proposed in those circumstances was to revoke access once a certain level of malicious intent was demonstrated through interaction with honey traps.

Reference [39] provides a similar alternative in which a user has a pre-determined level of trust which reduces when they breach behavioural obligations and increases when they meet obligations. When trust level drops below a certain level, access is revoked. In comparison to a conventional IDPS, this requires malicious activity to be repeated consistently over a period of time because it is, by definition, a time-series measurement taken longitudinally, whereas a conventional IDPS sub-class can react immediately provided detection is apparent. It is therefore possible to conclude that, behavioural anomaly detection, as it is presented in these studies, is not capable of mitigating novel threats because even one breach which presents as a single incident of malicious activity (e.g. a USB file download) could be enough to cause a catastrophic security breach.

Raw data IDPS sub-classes often examine raw packets sent over a computer network which are associated with a particular user or session and thus form an important part of many network intrusion detection systems ("NIDS"). In [36], a combination of behavioural analysis and examination of the raw data in packets was used to statistically determine if the number of packets emanating from a user is normal.

Conversely in [37], raw data is examined for unusual patterns of broadcast in the same manner as a traditional IDPS class. The approach in that study is unique in that whilst the IDPS is conventional, a compromised virtual machine in which malicious activity occurs is compared to a non-compromised machine which mirrors the resource under attack. Thus, it is possible to detect and mitigate an attack in real time which is novel.

An increasing number of IDPS implementations are based upon meta-data anomaly detection and use resultant data to examine malicious inside activity—this is often achieved through deep packet inspection in real-time and so is resource expensive to perform. Reference [33] investigates application-level meta-data by analysing biometric data in alternate to the potentially more computationally expensive deep packet inspection of a conventional IDPS. Reference [27] present a novel way of identifying malicious database transactions based upon the content of the transaction at execution time. Another database-related study was [24] in which a novel way of detecting malicious activity was by examining the resultant data that a malicious user would be left with if their request for data by one means or another was allowed.

These IDPS sub-classes produce massively deviated TPR and FPR values, and so it is difficult to predict or measure with any precision how effective a given implementation of an IDPS will perform in the real world resulting from the caveat that the effectiveness of an IDPS is much dependant on the use case [40]. The uniqueness of each use case precludes any common mechanism in security, which is an additional barrier to effective implementation and measurement of IDPS systems.

There is no reliable evidence to substantiate whether one IDPS sub-class is preferred over another sub-class. However, there is a substantial body of evidence within the literature to conclude that no IDPS sub-class can have an absolute success rate (i.e. a TPR of 1.0 and an FPR of 0.0) and thus will be prone to failure so long as zero-day vulnerabilities exist, as a result of a statistical truth rather than a logical truth. This can be referred to as the "1% rule"—the idea that statistically no IDPS is capable of absolute success.

Given that IDPS systems are prone to failure, computing in general moves towards decentralised and highly secured application structures. Very few of these have been created in practice owing to the theoretical difficulties resting at the foundations of cybersecurity.

5 Designing a Trustless Security System

This section proposes a novel method of implementing trustless security in a distributed application context. Trustless in this context refers to an underlying assumption that each aspect of the computer system is compromised, and therefore, common linkages on the logical and physical levels are inherently weak.

These linkages exist across discrete functional planes of logical and physical hardware which in order to function must be intrinsically connected by some logical connection. It is proposed that those functional planes, whilst intrinsically connected, can serialise and broadcast information between each plane in a finite determinative order in such a way that no other plane or logical entity shares state or control of system events happening elsewhere within that or another functional plane, at a defined point in time and at a defined locus within the computer system. In this way across logical links and planes, the data exchange is ephemeral and serialised data is immutable and unreadable. This is referred to further as the theory of cardinal privilege. The point of exchange at a given linkage is the cardinal vector, V and the collection of resources joined by the vector are cardinal sets, S. Multiple sets form the network of logic that is the underlying "system".

Given that serialisation is often a binary process, the resulting logical relationship at a linkage is absolute and therefore exists as a boolean truth. On a given functional plane therefore, for a given finite state, the state of interconnection of logical components is absolute at a given point in time. Thus, the system can remain turing-complete whilst being separable at each juncture either on a timed basis or algebraically.

5.1   Cardinal Vectors

The ability to form cardinal vectors and the overall availability of computer resources to be allocated a state forms a global universe set, U. It is proposed that for a given logical network to exist, it must have a number of logical connections between computing resources within U. The number of connections is said to be the cardinality of the logical network overall, C. A logical resource with no cardinal vector (which would be both ephemeral and immutable) is said to have a cardinality of zero and is therefore a zero set, θ.

An ideal system should have cardinality of 1, that is to say that concerns should be separated in accordance with the separation of concerns principle [41, 42] such that the theoretical optimum is achieved: a logical network forms with the least necessary connections in order to work, in an ideal situation this would be a single connection. If a system requires a state to be serialised across multiple logical connections, then this should be carried out in a series of stages to minimise the cardinality involved in the transaction toward the ideal. Cardinality can be reduced by making data ephemeral, immutable and unreadable to all else except the present data plane. This is very similar to Saltzer's principle of least common mechanism in [43] but builds upon this much further because the goal is maximum logical isolation rather than a state of least privilege. Least privilege in isolation offers merely a single state of privilege, whereas cardinal privilege is a maintained state within a system of infinite logical continuance.

Fig. 1 Population hierarchy
of cardinal vectors

5.2 Hierarchy of Trust and Ratio of Contact

There are a number of logical planes within the cardinal privilege theory. The following planes are initially proposed in Fig. 1.

The hardware plane is the security layer concerning physical components and the security of their interaction between each other and the other functional planes across cardinal vectors at a specified point in time. The serialisation plane is the security layer concerned with the serialization of data during conversion and transport to hardware. The communication plane is the security layer concerned with all external logical network interactions. The user data plane is the security layer concerned with creating user state. The user plane is the security layer concerning the interaction of users (machine and human) with a system. The size of each layer in the pyramid represents the relative logical contact ratio at that functional plane. The pyramid is ordered according to the journey of state from the point of origin to the point of committal to hardware.

Each plane represents a mathematical set of like-for-like computing resources resting at that layer which are capable of transferring state between each other. For example, a computer network would be a group of network interfaces which can be grouped together into a set.

In an ideal theoretical system, state should begin a logical journey after creation in which it exists and remains derivative of the user agent responsible for creation of that state. In such a way, the state is ephemeral, immutable and only accessible to that user agent. In its journey to the communication plane, logical networks in communication should not be able to discover each respective network nor interpret the contents of a transaction between such networks. During serialization, the source and destination should not be revealed and the state should remain ephemeral, immutable and inaccessible to all except the immediate logical accessors. Finally, the hardware should be logically isolated maximally and positioned so that discovery and side-channel exploitation cannot take place.

The very foundation of privilege is assumed to be that every resource is malicious and is controlled covertly by a third party.

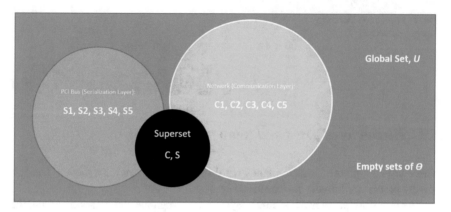

Fig. 2 Universe of cardinal vectors

5.3 Planar Privilege Modes

The logical network of sets can be represented mathematically in the following way, in the case of the above: $N = C_1, C_2, C_3, C_4, C_5$ where N represents a network, and C_n represents a network interface connecting other computing resources to the set N. The state of the network at a defined point is the privilege mode of that functional plane.

The following example represents the superset, L in Fig. 2: $L = C, S$, where C is an NIC and S is the serialization bus to it (a PCI bus with a microprocessor to serialise and deserialise data). S_n represents other buses capable of interaction with each other on the electronic level. A diagram of these two planes working together as part of the universe, U, can be seen in the figure above. The universe U represents the entire distributed computer system. Any empty space is a zero set; i.e. $\theta = $. This represents resources which have not yet been created but could be, and any resources which have been destroyed. This can be described as the *potential* of the distributed system because it represents the capability for resource expansion. The potential may well be infinite.

The cardinality of each functional set above represents the degrees of freedom of logical interaction with a computing resource and thus the discrete number of logical connections. On the network layer, each NIC can interact with every other NIC directly and indirectly. On the serialization layer, each hardware bus can communicate with every other bus (e.g. a group of PCI slots on a motherboard sharing a PCI bus). The attack surface for any attack on that layer (such as malicious hardware or an attacker with internal access on the network) is directly proportionate to the number of vectors and cardinality in that layer because it is a fundamental proposition that such resources are malicious and compromised.

Thus, it is proposed that to achieve an optimum level of security within a definable computer system, cardinality should theoretically be 1. Consequently, a cardinal vector in a given exchange of information is definable and singular.

5.4 Iterative Cardinal Reduction

In order to strive towards the theoretical ideal, it is important to implement a logical network which is not self-discoverable outside of a defined finite process at a specified point in time.

Planar cardinality can, firstly, be reduced by disabling resource discovery and otherwise making logical resources anonymous within a finite process. Secondly, resources should be maximally autonomous and self-regulated so that interference is not possible. Thirdly, resources should be immutable except as part of a defined atomic interaction at a defined point in time. Fourthly, the process should be ephemeral such that it can be terminated and recreated easily without damaging permanent or temporary state. Finally, state should be user agent derivative such that access and control of information is entirely dependant on its creator for access and modification. These are the fundamental principles of planar cardinal reduction.

Co-planar cardinality can be reduced by implementing minimal atomic transactions between logical planes. Data exchanged between planes should be planar derivative and so be useless data to another logical plane. Interactions between planes should be timed and self-regulated towards making anomaly impossible. An interaction begins with a user-derived state which then traverses logical planes statelessly via intermediaries until the user-derived state reaches an anonymous sink. A system of source and sink through planar traversal is, for the purposes of cardinal privilege, known as a "subsystem". A logical network is divisible as pathways of state from source to sink, with each logical network forming a superset of divisible resources. These are the fundamental principles of co-planar cardinal reduction.

The following practices implement aspects of cardinal privilege:

1. All computing resources should be ephemeral, immutable and unreadable at the cardinal vector.
2. The cardinality of a cardinal vector should be reduced towards 1.
3. All data must be strictly encrypted both in transit and at rest.
4. All computing resources should be anonymous and untraceable by other resources at a definite point in time unless within context.
5. Programmable interfaces should be obfuscated so that outside of a development environment, the interface is unrecognisable, unusable and preserves the anonymity of computing resources in the background.

6. There should be no superuser, instead the principle of least privilege [43, 44] should be leveraged to create resource-specific permissions.
7. A definable computer system should be expressed in maximally reduced components and placed within isolated groups such as `cgroup` containers.
8. The operating system and any protected resources that should not change at runtime must be immutable and ephemeral, for example an `ro` root filesystem with Copy-on-Write for temporary operations.
9. Authentication for the purposes of administration should be highly multifactorial such that system-wide changes are only ever democratic.
10. User data should be multifactorially encrypted such that the keys are only derivable from the user and cannot be derived any other way.
11. Production systems should undergo a process of reduction during development so that each component is as singular and atomic as possible.
12. State transitions should only contain state at user derivation and at an anonymous sink, all intermediaries should not go on to hold state.
13. If state is held for any length of time, this creates a new logical subsystem. Each logical subsystem should be disposable, easy to deploy, self-testing and capable of reversion in the event of catastrophic failure.

6 Static Analysis of Trustful Computer Systems

The process of static analysis starts with agile design requirements. The question that should be asked from the very beginning is: "if I were designing a nuclear reactor control system, how do I stop it from being used to end the world?"

That may seem like a bizarre proposition, but simple products of software development are often combined to make a more complex whole—this is a core DevOps principle. A relatively small vulnerability in badly designed applications will undoubtedly lead to loss of life in the future as critical infrastructure becomes increasingly reliant on software to keep national services in operation [45]. Simple communications structures should be maximally divisible within code and information sharing across logical structures should be entirely avoided. No logical juncture should exist unless absolutely necessary. Suspect data flows should be deprecated and redesigned. There are a number of key areas in both DevOps infrastructure practices and general software development that underline potential pitfalls.

One of the first practical considerations, particularly for a Linux system, is what happens to the superuser if it is to form part of a trustless application. Serge Hallyn provides a reliable tutorial on how to divide `root` into multiple roles so that no superuser exists [44]. A number of serious caveats are presented immediately, such as how the system can boot if the filesystem has a separate administrator to the various kernel subsystems. Many Linux users are accustomed to the requirement that each process should have its own user and group, which forms a part of the POSIX standard [46].

The immediate administrative concern resulting from this is user lockout. If the `passwd` file were to become corrupted, for instance, then there would be no superuser to restore permissions because these would be immutable to the available power users. The traditional method of restoring access in this situation would be to rebuild the `passwd` file in a recovery console. However, a complex set of `UIDs` and `GIDs` associated with multiple administrative accounts is much more sophisticated to restore. Thus, principle 13 is an important practical element of a trustless security system that is essential in constructing scalable applications resilient to failure.

Another practical consideration is communication. Both connection-oriented and connectionless protocols use IP at Layer 3 for addressing. An immutable logical component would need to be prevented from accessing Layer 3 whilst still having a network communication capability. In addition, any addressing would have to be untraceable and anonymous. An issue such as this can be resolved by implementing onion-routing in a mesh network. In an onion-routed network, all communication is registered against long addresses, such as Base32 addresses in `i2p`. Packets are encrypted at each hop, with intentionally long hops to increase the number of layers of encapsulation. An onion-routed mesh network can properly be considered to implement trustless principles. To perform cardinal reduction during data transfers, a timing and verification mechanism is required to prevent unexpected communications to other resources in the same logical subsystem. The drawback is that unless optimised, such a network has to the potential to be slow and difficult to debug.

User derivation is another serious consideration. If a user owns the data and has full control over the data, then this would fully comply with GDPR. Presently, existing infrastructures are extremely unlikely to comply with GDPR and remain secure. The problem in these circumstances is what would happen if, by way of illustration, an unconscious patient was taken to hospital but the patient records were user derived. In an example situation such as this, great attention would need to be paid to the instruments available to ensure a system remains only user-derivable but in an emergency is able to resort to alternative encryption factors such as a combination of staff and patient ID cards or a tightly controlled multi-factorial override. The level of detail required in design is clearly very specific to each use case.

A definite problem statement is designing a conventional application, particularly a distributed application, such that a given environment treats all resources as compromised and already controlled by a malicious actor. Traditional applications trust by design using encryption and other identity verification mechanisms for human and machine user agents. The practical consideration of a given design problem should be placed within the context of a security service. For example, if one managed an intelligence agency and one was making an application that is required to be resilient to the military capability of hostile state actors, consider how an application would be designed against that background. Applying this type of mindset to the construction of an online shopping cart can be properly considered an extreme measure, nonetheless cardinal privilege is a design principle and so would start from small, seemingly irrelevant components.

In the context of a shopping cart, one could use highly distributed edge routers which communicate user-derived data in the client application anonymously to microservices which carry out computations before either making external communications (to the user or a third party) or offloading the state into a sink (perhaps a database). If it were a public cloud infrastructure, not only would the user-derived data mean nothing to any third party, the destination of that data would be untraceable. Equally, if the database was compromised, it would not be possible to trace the source and destination of communications to the database. The database would not hold meaningful information to a third party. The shopping cart can be slightly adjusted in design to implement a highly robust security regime that starts with the front-end developer.

These are merely some of the practical considerations that would result from static code and infrastructure vulnerability analysis.

7   The Role of an AI as a Mediator

A key principle of the cardinal privilege trustless model is that logical subsystems should be self-regulating (i.e. an automaton). Once they are launched, they should be immutable to administrative control whilst preserving state integrity and remaining atomic—this is because of the fundamental risk of human selfishness. Conventionally, a simple application could have a static regulator based on a set of rules which is likely to achieve a very high level of security in the application. However, for scalable applications this may be incredibly inefficient.

The essential factors of control for a self-regulating trustless agent would be (i) time; (ii) cost; (iii) resource consumption; (iv) degrees of freedom in the logical subsystem. These factors would be significant for any mediator.

An AI agent could make for an exceptionally useful regulatory agent to take into account usage patterns and underlying complexities. A primitive example could be that a designer needs to leverage public cloud services at the lowest available cost. The AI agent could be given priors of cost and resource usage, in addition to control over scaling decisions. An AI could leverage propagation in a Q-learning structure to achieve effective cost control under demand after rigorous training data are accumulated. Such an AI agent could examine the degrees of freedom in a logical subsystem in real-time to abstract potential complexity in distributed application design and make more complex resource allocation decisions based upon the same substantive training data.

Infrastructure mediation is likely to be an important recurring theme in the context of an artificial user agent. It is likely to amount to a strange concept that once deployed an infrastructure should remain immutable, this removes a great degree of runtime flexibility that would otherwise be afforded. An AI agent is able to remove human want whilst still providing a run-time decision making capability that is not merely compounded on a set of arbitrary static rules. In order to leverage this benefit, an AI would have to be glued to hooks in an API to each logical network. A Q-learning agent could be valuable in this context, given that a system control interface could be passed to the agent and the feedback loop could consist of defined metrics such as the essential factors of control in a trustless system.

Another potential role of an AI agent within a trustless distributed application is as an intelligent scheduler. An intelligent agent could use a method such as k-nearest neighbour ("k-NN") decision trees to make democratic choices across a highly distributed application. In a k-NN system, the agent computes a value which is broadly compared to that of its nearest neighbours in the tree. If a distributed application was taken as a whole, each divisible logical component could form part of that tree. A local automaton could make arbitrary decisions based on localised information and then compare to nearest neighbours exposed to the same information to reach arbitrary consensus in response to localised information. Applying that to scheduling, such an agent could control the state of running processes based upon a continuous feedback loop within the application.

A method which is particularly taking traction is for an AI to control responses in a security system based upon a series of events. This has been used to create agents which, for example, give users a reputation rating [24, 26]. Once that reputation rating drops to a provided threshold, the user has privileges revoked. Whilst this is trustful, a trustless context would likely be to reverse the scoring system such that legitimacy is proven at the point of the transaction before it is allowed to proceed—this is likely to be exceptionally helpful in preventing anomalous transactions before they happen and preventing data exfiltration *en masse*.

There are a number of challenges associated with an AI acting as a mediator between a trustless infrastructure and the rest of the world. Consider, for example, what would happen if the AI malfunctioned but it was the single controller of an autonomous infrastructure. If the distributed application was a flight control system, the consequences of a loss of control are much more awakening. It is essential as a result of this that the application codebase can self-revert if needed without causing disruption to other logical networks, based upon continuous feedback.

Error modes within mediators are likely to be an additional issue because error modes within any AI are very difficult to trace. If the AI is controlling infrastructure and application state, this is likely to be difficult to detect and correct in a trustless context. It is likely that agents will need to be designed to be continuously self-testing and have revertible training data if necessary.

Another potential weakness is maintaining the integrity of state. An AI should not be trusted and therefore cannot interface directly with user data because it should be user-derivative. This means that the AI cannot provide help in managing state in an infrastructure it otherwise controls and furthermore that state cannot be examined as part of a feedback loop. It is imperative therefore that logical networks (microservice application groups in many use cases) are singular, immutable and atomic such that state is the committed result of computational output in that logical network. Consequently, if there is a change to a model in a codebase, this can be reconciled against the state sink without causing breaking changes. State should be separate to the application logic for this reason. The application can then be safely part of a control point for an AI agent without risking the integrity of state.

Finally, a definite weakness within conventional AI agents is that they can be induced. In ordinary parlance, an AI agent can be persuaded to make unfavourable choices by teaching it bad behaviour. Any AI exposed to user-controlled data on which it bases feedback can be induced because the data can be manipulated by the user who can trick the AI into normalising an untruthful assertion over a continuous period. For example, in an AI-controlled IDPS, the agent can be persuaded that user behaviour is normal if many users are attempting to do it at the same time. Thus, a mass replication of attempts at unauthorised access can be used to persuade a differential AI that all users engage in that behaviour and therefore it must be normal behaviour. That is a crude example of an inducement vulnerability in an AI; nonetheless, most AI agents are vulnerable to this. In a trustless context, therefore, AI mediators should be strictly self-regulating.

8 Questions

1. Take a standard LAMP application such as the Joomla CMS or Wordpress and discuss potential sources of weakness that would be revealed on static analysis of supporting infrastructure.

   a. Draw a Venn diagram of the likely logical networks that can be derived from this application.
   b. Identify the likely planar and co-planar cardinality of the logical networks you have identified.
   c. Devise a strategy to perform planar cardinal reduction based upon your observations of planar cardinality.
   d. Devise a strategy to perform co-planar cardinal reduction based upon your observations of co-planar cardinality.

2. Summarise the definition of a trustless security system.
3. Identify three IDPS sub-classes then compare and contrast them.
4. Discuss the benefits of trustful security systems when compared to trustless security systems and explain your reasoning.
5. Define zero trust security and summarise the origin of the zero trust model.
6. Explain the origin and history of the Morris worm.
7. Identify the eight principles of the Data Protection Act 1998.
8. Discuss the impact of GDPR on cybersecurity and critically analyse the changes brought about by GDPR in legislation.
9. Explain the financial risk posed to commercial entities as a result of the development of data protection law in England and Wales.
10. List the key principles of cardinal privilege.
11. Critically analyse the practical caveats of implementing a trustless security system which uses cardinal privilege.
12. Identify two ways in which an AI agent could be used as a mediator for anotherwise arbitrarily self-regulating automaton.
13. Discuss possible caveats in using an AI as a mediating agent.

Task 1

Assemble into groups of four of five. Debate the ethical implications of using a trustless security system and the potential implications such a system could have in a democratic society based upon trust and reputation.

Task 2

As a group, design the logical structure of a distributed application of your choice. When you have finished, try converting that distributed application to a trustless application. Reflect on any practical difficulties you encountered.

References

1. Orman H (2003) The Morris worm: a fifteen-year perspective. IEEE Secur Priv 99(5):35–43 (Accessed 26 Oct 2017)
2. Ranum MJ (1997) Thinking about firewalls v2.0: beyond perimeter security. Inf Secur Tech Rep 2(3):33–45 (Accessed 26 Oct 2017)
3. Broderick S (2005) Firewalls - are they enough protection for current networks? Inf Secur Tech Rep 10(4):204–212. https://doi.org/10.1016/j.istr.2005.10.002 (Accessed 26 Oct 2017)
4. Kindervag J (2010) No more chewy centers: introducing the zero trust model of information security. Forrester Research (Accessed 26 Oct 2017)
5. Trabelsi Z, Zhang L, Zeidan S, Ghoudi K (2013) Dynamic traffic awareness statistical model for firewall performance enhancement. Comput Secur 39:160–172 (Accessed 26 Oct 2017)
6. Liu, D., Wang, X., Camp, J.: Game-theoretic modeling and analysis of insider threats. Int J Crit Infrastruct Prot 1, 75–80 (2008). https://doi.org/10.1016/j.ijcip.2008.08.001. (Accessed 26 Oct 2017)
7. Meng W, Li W, Xiang Y, Choo K-KR (2017) A Bayesian inference-based detection mechanism to defend medical smartphone networks against insider attacks. J Netw Comput Appl 78:162–169 (Accessed 26 Oct 2017)
8. Agrafiotis, I., Nurse, J.R., Buckley, O., Legg, P., Creese, S., Goldsmith, M.: Identifying attack patterns for insider threat detection. Comput Fraud Secur 2015(7), 9–17 (2015). https://doi.org/10.1016/s1361-3723(15)30066-x. (Accessed 26 Oct 2017)
9. Eggenschwiler J, Agrafiotis I, Nurse JR (2016) Insider threat response and recovery strategies in financial services firms. Comput Fraud Secur 2016(11):12–19. https://doi.org/10.1016/s1361-3723(16)30091-4 (Accessed 26 Oct 2017)
10. Zahadat N, Blessner P, Blackburn T, Olson BA (2015) Byod security engineering: a framework and its analysis. Comput Secur 55:81–99 (Accessed 26 Oct 2017)
11. Kim, K.-N., Yim, M.-S., Schneider, E.: A study of insider threat in nuclear security analysis using game theoretic modeling. Ann Nucl Energy 108, 301–309 (2017). (Accessed 26 Oct 2017)
12. Kindervag J (2013) Developing a framework to improve critical infrastructure cybersecurity (response to NIST request for information docket no. 130208119-3119-01) (Accessed 26 Oct 2017)
13. H Rep. (2017) OPM data breach report: committee on oversight and government reform. Library of Congress, Washington D.C. https://www.cylance.com/content/dam/cylance/pdfs/reports/The-OPM-Data-Breach-How-the-Government-Jeopardized-Our-National-Security-for-More-than-a-Generation.pdf. Accessed 03 Nov 2017
14. Ward R, Beyer B (2014) Beyondcorp: a new approach to enterprise security. Login 39:5–11 (Accessed 26 Oct 2017)

15. Ethereum Project (2014). https://www.ethereum.org/. Accessed 15 Mar 2018
16. Verizon RISK: VCDB/yearly.png at master vz-risk/VCDB (2017). https://github.com/vz-risk/VCDB/blob/master/figure/yearly.png. Accessed 02 Nov 2017
17. Zetter K (2017) An unprecedented look at Stuxnet, the world's first digital weapon | WIRED. https://www.wired.com/2014/11/countdown-to-zero-day-stuxnet/. Accessed 03 Nov 2017
18. Verizon RISK (2017) 2017-Data-Breach-Investigations-Report.pdf. https://www.ictsecuritymagazine.com/wp-content/uploads/2017-Data-Breach-Investigations-Report.pdf. Accessed 14 Oct 2017
19. Information Commissioner's Office (2017) Data protection principles | ICO. https://ico.org.uk/for-organisations/guide-to-data-protection/data-protection-principles/. Accessed 14 Oct 2017
20. Information Commissioner's Office (2017) The amount of personal data you may hold (Principle 3) | ICO. https://ico.org.uk/for-organisations/guide-to-data-protection/principle-3-adequacy/. Accessed 10 Nov 2017
21. Allen & Overy LLP (2017) www.allenovery.com/SiteCollectionDocuments/Radical changes to European data protection legislation.pdf. http://www.allenovery.com/SiteCollectionDocuments/Radical/changes/to/European/data/protection/legislation.pdf. Accessed 10 Nov 2017
22. Manchester Evening News (2017) CPS fined 200,000 after police interviews with sex abuse victims were stolen from Rusholme flat - Manchester Evening News. http://www.manchestereveningnews.co.uk/news/greater-manchester-news/cps-fined-200000-after-police-10385207. Accessed 10 Nov 2017
23. The Guardian (2017) UK gathering secret intelligence via covert NSA operation | Technology | The Guardian. https://www.theguardian.com/technology/2013/jun/07/uk-gathering-secret-intelligence-nsa-prism. Accessed 10 Nov 2017
24. Gafny M, Shabtai A, Rokach L, Elovici Y (2010) Detecting data misuse by applying context-based data linkage. In: Proceedings of the 2010 ACM workshop on insider threats - insider threats 10. ACM Press. https://doi.org/10.1145/1866886.1866890
25. Shabtai A, Bercovitch M, Rokach L, Gal YK, Elovici Y, Shmueli E (2016) Behavioral study of users when interacting with active honeytokens. ACM Trans Inf Syst Secur 18(3):1–21. https://doi.org/10.1145/2854152
26. Baracaldo N, Joshi J (2012) A trust-and-risk aware RBAC framework. In: Proceedings of the 17th ACM symposium on access control models and technologies - SACMAT. ACM Press. https://doi.org/10.1145/2295136.2295168
27. Hussain SR, Sallam AM, Bertino E (2015) DetAnom. In: Proceedings of the 5th ACM conference on data and application security and privacy - CODASPY 15. ACM Press. https://doi.org/10.1145/2699026.2699111
28. Yu Y (2011) Anomaly intrusion detection based upon an artificial immunity model. https://doi.org/10.1145/2016039.2016075
29. Bose B, Avasarala B, Tirthapura S, Chung Y-Y, Steiner D (2017) Detecting insider threats using RADISH: a system for real-time anomaly detection in heterogeneous data streams. IEEE Syst J 11(2):471–482. https://doi.org/10.1109/jsyst.2016.2558507
30. Nasr PM, Varjani AY (2014) Alarm based anomaly detection of insider attacks in SCADA system. In: 2014 Smart grid conference (SGC). IEEE. https://doi.org/10.1109/sgc.2014.7090881
31. Chagarlamudi M, Panda B, Hu Y (2009) Insider threat in database systems: preventing malicious users/ activities in databases. In: 2009 Sixth international conference on information technology: new generations. IEEE. https://doi.org/10.1109/itng.2009.67
32. Legg PA, Buckley O, Goldsmith M, Creese S (2017) Automated insider threat detection system using user and role-based profile assessment. IEEE Syst J 11(2):503–512. https://doi.org/10.1109/jsyst.2015.2438442
33. Alotibi G, Clarke N, Li F, Furnell S (2016) User profiling from network traffic via novel application-level interactions. In: 2016 11th International conference for internet technology and secured transactions (ICITST). IEEE. https://doi.org/10.1109/icitst.2016.7856712
34. Mohan R, Vaidehi V, Ajay Krishna A, Mahalakshmi M, Chakkaravarthy SS (2015) Complex event processing based hybrid intrusion detection system. In: 2015 3rd International conference

on signal processing, communication and networking (ICSCN). IEEE. https://doi.org/10.1109/icscn.2015.7219827

35. Chen Y, Nyemba S, Zhang W, Malin B (2012) Specializing network analysis to detect anomalous insider actions. Secur Inf 1(1):5. https://doi.org/10.1186/2190-8532-1-5

36. Sun Y, Xu H, Bertino E, Sun C (2016) A data-driven evaluation for insider threats. Data Sci Eng 1(2):73–85. https://doi.org/10.1007/s41019-016-0009-x

37. Liu A, Chen J, Yang L (2011) Real-time detection of covert channels in highly virtualized environments. Critical infrastructure protection V. Springer, Berlin, pp 151–164. https://doi.org/10.1007/978-3-642-24864-1_11

38. Santosa KI, Lim C, Erwin A (2016) Analysis of educational institution DNS network traffic for insider threats. In: 2016 International conference on computer, control, informatics and its applications (IC3INA). IEEE. https://doi.org/10.1109/ic3ina.2016.7863040

39. Baracaldo N, Joshi J (2013) Beyond accountability. In: Proceedings of the 18th ACM symposium on access control models and technologies - SACMAT. ACM Press. https://doi.org/10.1145/2462410.2462411

40. Walker-Roberts S, Hammoudeh M, Dehghan Tanha A (2018) A systematic review of the availability and efficacy of countermeasures to internal threats in healthcare critical infrastructure. IEEE Access 6

41. Dijkstra E (1982) Selected writings on computing: a personal perspective. Springer, New York

42. Reade C (1989) Elements of functional programming. Addison-Wesley, Wokingham

43. Saltzer JH (1974) Protection and the control of information sharing in multics. Commun ACM 17(7):388–402. https://doi.org/10.1145/361011.361067 (Accessed 26 Oct 2017)

44. Hallyn S (2009) Making root unprivileged. Linux J 2009(184) (Accessed 26 Oct 2017)

45. Ten of the world's most disastrous IT mistakes - General - PC & Tech Authority (2011). https://www.pcauthority.com.au/feature/ten-of-the-worlds-most-disastrous-it-mistakes-264645. Accessed 19 Mar 2018

46. IEEE: The Open Group Base Specifications Issue 7, 2016 Edition (2016). http://pubs.opengroup.org/onlinepubs/9699919799/. Accessed 19 Mar 2018

Part III
Applications of Artificial Intelligence

Automated Planning of Administrative Tasks Using Historic Events: A File System Case Study

Saad Khan and Simon Parkinson

Abstract Understanding how to implement file system access control rules within a system is heavily reliant on expert knowledge, both that intrinsic to how a system can be configured as well as how a current configuration is structured. Maintaining the required level of expertise in fast-changing environments, where frequent configuration changes are implemented, can be challenging. Another set of complexities lies in gaining structural understanding of large volumes of permission information. The accuracy of a new addition within a file system access control is essential, as inadvertently assigning rights that result in a higher than necessary level of access can generate unintended vulnerabilities. To address these issues, a novel mechanism is devised to automatically process a system's event history to determine how previous access control configuration actions have been implemented and then utilise the model for suggesting how to implement new access control rules. Throughout this paper, we focus on Microsoft's New Technology File System permissions (NTFS) access control through processing operating system generated log data. We demonstrate how the novel technique can be utilised to plan for the administrator when assigning new permissions. The plans are then evaluated in terms of their validity as well as the reduction in required expert knowledge.

1 Introduction

Access control is an integral security mechanism in multi-user computing environments, where there is a necessity to restrict user access to system resources. Access control provides the fine-grained system necessary to restrict access to users dependent on their organisational role, which often depicts the level of required access [1]. The system will evaluate every request to access data and determine if the request

S. Khan (✉) · S. Parkinson
Department of Computer Science, University of Huddersfield, Huddersfield, UK
e-mail: saad.khan@hud.ac.uk

S. Parkinson
e-mail: simon.parkinson@hud.ac.uk

© Springer International Publishing AG, part of Springer Nature 2018
S. Parkinson et al. (eds.), *Guide to Vulnerability Analysis for Computer Networks and Systems*, Computer Communications and Networks,
https://doi.org/10.1007/978-3-319-92624-7_7

159

should be granted or denied. The permissions in access control system are designed and enforced based on security policies, which denote permissions that specific user groups should receive. In this work, we are particularly interested in file system permissions; however, it should be noted that the presented techniques are relevant to any access control systems where "securable" object within a system (e.g. a printer). The presented work is also extensible for more generic administrative and configuration tasks.

System administration can be defined as a sequence of tasks to perform upkeep, configuration, and reliability operations of multi-user Information Technology (IT) infrastructures [2]. The implementation and modification of access control permissions is often performed by a System Administrator. Many multi-user and multi-device IT systems require fine-grained administrative capabilities to configuring their security. The process of configuring devices is often based on a combination of industry best practice and company policy to maintain both functionality and security provisions. This process is knowledge intensive as information regarding the software or hardware being configured, the current configuration, and the potential impact of any change is required to adequately perform administrative tasks [3].

In this paper, we focus on the process of examining event logs to gain knowledge essential for performing future file system permissions' allocations. The purpose is to identify events of interest that can be used to acquire the structure of a system's configuration and to extract knowledge of how previous permission allocation tasks have been performed. We focus on developing a technique that does not rely on expert knowledge, nor requires extensive analysis of the underlying system. The administration of security configurations shares many characteristics with *penetration testing* in that available data sources are analysed to identify vulnerabilities and threats [4]. However, the fundamental difference is that penetration testing involves analysing a system to formalise an attack strategy that will compromise a system, whereas analysing a system to perform administrative task is the process of scrutinising available data sources to determine the best strategy to implement a configuration change.

There are several factors that make performing administrative tasks challenging: (i) the complexity of the computational infrastructure—the cyber-physical platform on which functionality is attained—is increasing and the technology landscape is dynamic; (ii) vast amounts of data generated presents the challenge of performing analysis without technological support; (iii) knowledge capabilities of human experts, and technological support rarely co-evolve in such a fast-changing discipline, altogether limiting the ability to perform administrative tasks to maintain desired levels of functionality without inadvertently introducing adverse effects. Administrative tasks involve a wide range of services, software, and hardware in IT infrastructures, and some administrative tasks are performed on a more frequent basis as end-user requirements frequently change. This poses challenges in reflecting new requirements in a timely and automatic manner.

The process of performing administrative tasks can be likened to *goal-based* deliberation, whereby the administrator is pursing tasks to either prove or dismiss an hypothesis, which is established based upon available information. The process of pursuing a hypothesis can be reduced to a discrete sequence of investigative actions, each with positive and negative consequences. It can therefore be established that system administration is a deliberation process, whereby expert knowledge is required to determine the investigative hypothesis (i.e. the goal), as well as the investigative actions to be performed and their order. There is similarity here with automated planning (AP) which encompasses the study and development of deliberation tools that take as input a problem specification and knowledge about the domain in the form of an abstract model of actions [5]. The AP algorithms propose a scheme or tentative course of action that can be used to accomplish an objective. In this research, the objective is to plan administrative tasks without the intervention of human beings.

The paper is structured as follows: first, a discussion of closely related work is provided, followed by a modelling section where an administrative process is modelled and its applicability to AP is presented. A section is then provided discussing the exploitation of the model in PDDL. This leads towards the presentation of file system administration as an AP problem, and finally, we perform the empirical analysis to demonstrate and evaluate the developed system.

2 Related Work

Every organisation using a computing infrastructure has file systems, computing and networking resources, which are utilised by users to perform specific tasks. Granting unconstrained and unmonitored access to such resources can damage the organisation's security and stability [6]. The implementation of an access control system prevents any unauthorised and irrelevant user access to the computing resources [7]. The system utilises a set of permissions, which obligate and comply with the organisation's security rules and policies. The permissions are defined as the relationship between subjects (users) and objects (files, system services, etc.) in terms of allowed actions (e.g. read, write, execute) [8]. There are different implementations of access control systems. For example, role-based access control [9], attribute-based access control [10], task-based access control [11] and others. The key differences between them are often down to how policies are specified and enforced upon users. For example, role-based systems adopt the principle that there are predefined roles operating within the system, whereas task-based operates under the principle that certain tasks require certain permissions, irrespective of who is performing the task.

The assignment of permissions is a challenging process in live, large-scale systems [12]. It is an expensive job and requires constant maintenance [13]. In a risk-averse organisation, every employee should have a precise set of permissions that do not exceed or fall behind the level of access required to perform their tasks. To fulfil this condition, access control management requires extensive knowledge and experience [14], which may not be readily available in all organisations. In addition, there is also the possibility of human errors that can lead towards creating or modifying permissions inaccurately. To eliminate these issues, few studies are available that develop automatic policy verification process with the help of machine learning and data mining techniques. A research study proposed an approach to determine irregularities between the intended and implemented access policies [15]. At first, the system is probed by sending arbitrary requests and the corresponding responses are collected. Then, the request–response pairs are given to classification algorithms to determine anomalies from normal policy behaviour.

It is evident that existing solutions are capable of recognising flaws in policy implementation. However, they are unable to recommend a solution that might rectify the issues, as currently it requires human expert knowledge. For this purpose, software aids can be utilised that can help reduce the reliance on human expert for system configuration, auditing, and administrative processes [16]. The motivation is the desire to explore all possible cases, increase efficiency and reduce the chance of accidentally introducing an error. In the particular domain of file system administration, researchers have produced software solutions to assist with administration. For example, using statistical analysis (such as Chi-square) and instance-based learning to identify anomalies in event logs [17] and file system permission allocations [18]. Furthermore, the potential to use automated planning for file system permissions has previously been considered; however, in this early work the domain model and problem instance required manual construction [19].

Previous work over the last decade has witnessed successful exploration of the use of AP in different cyber-security domains, mainly for developing attack plans for penetration testing [20]. The development of automated penetration testing has received such wide attention mostly because of the growing size and complexity of IT systems, which all require auditing for vulnerabilities. Performing this process manually is labour-intensive task and has a high potential margin of error [21]. It also requires extensive knowledge for testing and understanding the results. However, if tests are generated by a computer, they are quickly able to explore multiple solutions in a systematic manner, which is troubling for Humans [22]. Many studies have been conducted in this area. Riabov et al. present a technique where courses of actions are generated based upon a system configuration [23]; however, the goal is adversarial in that the aim is to compromise the system, albeit by a trusted security professional (widely termed white-hat hacking). Recent work by Sohrabi et al. [24] pursues the use of hypothesis exploration for identifying potential attack plans in network security. Another work [25] presents a method to determine the impact of security vulnerabilities in an enterprise network using attack graph.[1] The knowledge is encoded in standardised language. The solution provides a holistic, time-efficient and scalable analysis of multiple vulnerabilities on a single attack point, by developing an attack path of successive and correlated exploits. Another research provides a verification mechanism of security policies in role-based access control for enterprise-based software [27]. They developed a modelling scheme that converts a specific verification problem (dynamic separation of duty) into a declarative programming paradigm and used 'Answer Set Solver' for problem solving.

---

[1] Attack graph is a directed graph consisting of fact nodes and action nodes, that represent knowledge and malicious actions that can be performed by the attacker [26].

The large domain knowledge and problem instances consume large amount of computing resources, which can impact on the applicability of automated planning for real-world challenges. Current research efforts continue the development of AP for penetration testing [28] discussing the need to overcome scalability limitations. One such paper converts the penetration testing procedures as a partially observable contingent problem and optimises the model sizes in partially observable Markov decision process (POMDP) technique [29]. POMDPs are capable of generating attack plans even if they are given incomplete knowledge [30]. They also prioritise actions based on the expected rewards to achieve terminal state. Researchers are also working on using AP for determining security threat mitigation plans [31] for minimising attacker success. This is important as the identification of a security issue does not by default eliminate it, and there is a requirement for expert knowledge. A commercial tool exists, named *Core Impact* [32] that uses probability-based model for extending attack graphs to handle numerical and probabilistic effects for real-time penetration testing.

These works demonstrate the potential of using AP techniques for performing tasks, which are traditionally performed by a human expert. There are also many other successful applications of AP capable of assisting in reducing expert knowledge outside of the security domain. For example, in manufacturing [33], traffic management [34], printer configuration [35], etc. Work has also been performed to demonstrate the potential of using AP for computing infrastructure reconfiguration [36, 37]. In these studies, the author presents the use of a predefined domain model to plan for changing system configuration. This is of significance to the reduction of expert knowledge, as the decision-taking process has been automated. AP has also been used in more practical areas, such as monitoring and assisting people using ubiquitous computing and computation in coherence [38].

As AP becomes an increasingly utilised resource for real-world applications, the ability to autonomously acquire problem instances has received increased attention in many domains [39]. The motivation arises from the desire to reduce the knowledge engineering effort required problem instance construction. Enforcing the need for a user to manually construct problem instances is also knowledge intensive, and therefore shifts the knowledge bottleneck from performing manually planning to encode problem instances [40]. In this paper, we study the process of autonomously extracting the problem instance to be used alongside a predetermined domain model, and as such arrive a solution capable of interacting with live systems.

3 Administrative Task Modelling

The process of performing an access control administrative action on a file system is naturally aligned to the abstract model of AP. The process is where an administrative event, e, is performed and results in the transition of the system from an initial state, s_1, to goal state, g, where the system is operating under the desired configuration with the introduction of new permissions. In pursuing the goal, a state-transition

Fig. 1 Example of an administrative task

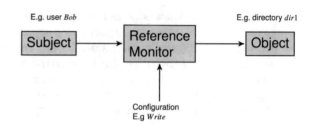

system is a 3-tuple $\sum = (S, A, \rightarrow)$ where $S = (s_1, s_2, \dots)$ is a finite set of states, $A = (a_1, a_2, \dots)$ is a finite set of actions, and $\rightarrow: S \times A \rightarrow 2^s$ is a state-transition function. A solution P is a sequence of actions $(a_1, a_2, \dots, a_k)$ corresponding to a sequence of state transitions $(s_1, s_2, \dots, s_k)$ such that $s_1 =\rightarrow (s_0, a_1), \dots, s_k =\rightarrow (s_{k-1}, a_k)$, and s_k is the goal state. A system's configuration is represented by a set of first-order predicates which are subsequently modified through the execution of each action, $a = \{pre+, pre-, eff+, eff-\}$, where $pre+$ and $pre-$ are the first-order preconditions that are positive and negative in the action's precondition list, respectively. Similarly, $eff+$ and $eff-$ are the action's positive and negative effects.

In the example shown in Fig. 1, the administrator is required to modify the system configuration allowing *bob* to have *write* access on *dir*1. The administrator will use the *assign* action to allocate the desired set of permissions, thus translating the system configuration, C to C' via *assign*. Here, we assume that the *assign* has the precondition of *(exist S)* and has a first-order predicate effect of *permission(S,P,O)*, where S is the subject *(bob)*, P is the permission level to be assigned *(write)*, and O is the object *(dir*1*)*. This example is trivial as only two possible actions exist to achieve the desired goal; however, in administrative tasks there is often a higher number of actions that can be executed to manipulate the systems' configuration. In a system that contains large number of users and data, the automation of such actions will be beneficial in terms of accuracy, efficiency and performance.

A system's access control implementation is likely to be continually changing as new organisational requirements filter down to the IT system level. It is also likely that a large amount of configuration will be performed during an intensive configuration phase with the occasional change occurring thereafter. As illustrated in Fig. 2, when making new permissions allocations in systems with large configurations that have evolved overtime, it is likely that a de facto policy of assigning permissions will have developed to adequately describe different access levels within the system. An example is that all users wanting permission on directory *dir*1 must be granted permission through group g. The challenge is in the selection of the correct actions to minimise any additional impact (e.g over elevation of permissions). It may well be that only two actions are needed to allocate the correct level of permission; however, all the possible actions and their effects need to be considered to determine the most suitable selection.

Fig. 2 Example timeline illustrating 18 new administrative tasks over a 5-day period

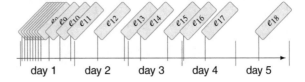

4 Action Model

In current administrative procedures, administrative actions are embedded within the knowledge and expertise of the administrators. This can be problematic in large systems where multiple administrators are making changes based on their intuition rather than in-keeping with current policies. For example, one administrator might decide to directly modify a file systems' permission to allow user access, whereas another administrators would continue the correct policy of assigning group membership based on the organisation rules. An example of group membership management is that all member of a finance department are assigned to all the finance permission groups, and a modification in the group will change the permissions of each member at once.

In this section, we present a mechanism to automatically construct actions from a system's administration event history. The Windows operating system creates event log entries when system configurations are changed [41]. There is a default set of events that create log entries, but Windows has the functionality to enable logging for a wide array of administrative tasks.[2] Enabling logging for file system permissions when a system is first configured will result in a set of event logs representing every change made to the file system's permissions. Moreover, the fact that the events are timestamped allows the extraction of a file system administration timeline.

The information stored in an event is used to create a discrete administrative action. As illustrated in Fig. 3, the event holds the following essential information: the subject (user or group), the object (directory), the object's old permissions, and the the object's new permissions. The permissions are represented in the Security Descriptor Definition Language (SDDL), but the individual permission attributes can easily be extracted.[3] Using this information, we can create an action, a, to represent this change to the file system permission. Translating the event demonstrated in Fig. 3 results in the construction of an *assign* action with a precondition of *bob* not having permission p on object o and an effect of *bob* having p on o. The new SSDL details the new permission *(A;OICIID;FW;;;bob)* added to the directory.

---

[2]Permission change events have the log ID 4670; however, logging must be enabled in the group policy editor first.

[3]Microsoft's SDDL language allows an access control list to be represented as a single string of unique characters https://msdn.microsoft.com/en-us/library/windows/desktop/aa379567(v=vs.85).aspx.

```
Permissions on an object were changed.
Subject:
      Security ID:      admin
      Account Name:     BOB
      Account Domain:   AD
      Logon ID: 0x9B3EC
Object:
      Object Server:    Security
      Object Name:      D:
      Handle ID:        0x5bc
Process:
      Process ID:       0x1820
Permissions Change:
      Original Security Descriptor:
D:(A;OICI;FA;;;SY)(A;OICI;FA;;;BA)
      New Security Descriptor:
D:ARAI(A;OICIID;FA;;;SY)(A;OICIID;FA;;;BA)
(A;OICIID;FW;;;bob)
```

Fig. 3 Example event showing the change in security permission for *bob* on *d*. The new permission level, as denoted by the change in SDDLs is that *bob* now has write ("FW" for FileWrite) on *d*

4.1 Processing

File system permissions also have many aspects that result in the need for processing the set of events to determine the true change in permission. These are:

1. Permissions can be acquired through direct allocations, group associations, and a combination thereof;
2. Accumulation of permissions through group membership is used in file system access control where a large number of subjects require access to the same resources, and rather than explicitly adding each user on the object level, only one group is added to the object and all the users are assigned to the group; and
3. Although NTFS has standard permission levels (Modify, Read, Execute, etc.), administrators can create special permissions which are constructed from selecting any combination of the fourteen individual attributes (Create Files/Write Data, Create Folders/Append Data, Read Permissions, etc.).

Each of the above points introduces the requirement to further process the events to: (1) accumulate a subject's permission to correctly calculate the action's precondition, and (2) correctly consider non-standard group permissions to allow administrators to create fine-grained policies. Group allocations can also be acquired through examining historical log entries in the Window's operating system.[4] Processing the

---

[4]Log ID 4731 logs details of a newly created group, 4732 when a new membership is added, 4733 when a membership is removed, and 4734 when a group is deleted.

Fig. 4 Diagrammatic
illustration of the timeline of
actions in the domain model.
Key: AddToG =
AddToGroup, AddUP =
AddUserPermission, AddGP
= AddGroupPermission

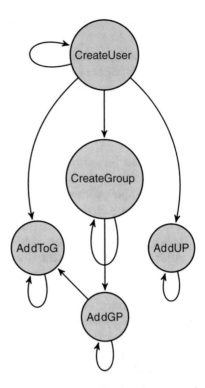

ordered set of log entries detailing group allocations results in the establishment of
a set of group allocation events $G = \{g_1, ..., g_n\}$ where $g = \{g_p, \{g_{c1}, ..., g_{cn}\}\}$, g_p is
the parent group, and g_c are the child subjects (groups or users). It means that g_c is
a member of g_p.

There are many different ways by which an administrator may implement new
access control rules. Figure 4 provides a graphical illustration of the domain actions
and the order in which they can occur. It would be typical to see the ordering of
the administrator creating a user, assigning any individual permissions, assigning
them to any file system groups, or creating new ones when necessary. However, as
there is little certainty over the way that the administrator may implement access
control permissions, it is necessary to develop a sufficiently flexible domain model,
which is capable of modelling as many different orderings as possible. To model
the underlying system in terms of objects and logical connections, the following
predicates (first-order logic) are introduced to model the relationship between users,
groups, directories, and permissions in the domain model:

- (user-exists u)
- (group-exists g)
- (u-member-of u g)
- (g-member-of g g)
- (u-permission u p d)

- (g-permission g p d)
- (effective-permission u p d)
- (user-needed u)
- (group-needed g)
- (add-to-group g)

In the above predicates, u, g, p, d represent user, group, permission, and directory, respectively.

The following actions have been defined to account for the administrative actions performed during file system administration tasks (illustrated in Fig. 4). Each action has a precondition and effect. The precondition is used to describe the state of the underlying system (in terms of objects and predicates) that is necessary for the action to be valid. The effect is used to model the outcome of performing the action in question on the system and is also modelled in terms of objects and predicates.

- **CreateUser** is used to simulate an administrator creating a new user. The action has a precondition of *user_needed(u)* ∧ ¬*user_exists(u)* and an effect of ¬*user_needed (u)* ∧ *user_exists(u)*, where *u* is the new user to be created.
- **CreateGroup** is used to simulate an administrator creating a new group. The action has a precondition of *group_needed(g)* ∧ ¬*group_exists(g)* and an effect of *group_exists(g)* ∧ ¬*group_needed(g)*, where *g* is the new group to be created.
- **AddUserToGroup** is used to encode the process of assigning a user to be a member of a group. The precondition is *user_exists(u)* ∧ *group_exists(g)* ∧ ¬*user_needed(u)* ∧ ¬*member_of(u, g)* and has an effect of *member_of(u, g)*. Here, *u* represents the user to be added to group *g*.
- **AddUserPermissions** is used to simulate the process of assigning permissions to a user. The precondition is *user_exists(g)* ∧ ¬*user_needed(u)* ∧¬*u_permission(p, u, d)* and has an effect of *u_permission(p, u, d)*. Here, *p* is the permission to be assigned to user *u* on directory *d*.
- **AddGroupPermissions** is used to simulate the process of assigning a group permission. The precondition is *add_to_group(g)* ∧ ¬*group_exists(g)* ∧ ¬*g_permission(p, g, d)* and has an effect of *g_permission(p, g, d)* ∧ ¬*add_to_group(g)*. Here, *p* is the permission attribute to be assigned to group *g* on directory *d*.
- **CalculateEffective** is used to simulate an assertion of effective permission of a user. The action has a precondition of ¬*u_permission(p, u, d)* ∨ ∃*(g)* ∨ *(member_of(u, g)* ∧ *g_permission(p, g, d))* and an effect of *effective_permission(u p d)*, where *p* is the permission attribute to be assigned to user *u* on directory *d*.

In addition to modelling the above actions, empirical observations determined through analysing the historic permission allocations in a file system environment are that in some instances, actions are always performed in a sequential *flow*. The following three flows (illustrated in Fig. 4) have been identified:

F1: The CreateUser action never occurs in isolation and is always followed by another action. This is because once a user is created, they need to be allocated permission rights either through group membership allocation or through adding explicit rules.

F2: The AddUserPermissions action will either follow the CreateUser action or occur in isolation. Similar to F1, it has been identified that the AddUserPermissions action is likely to execute if a new user needs to be created. To enforce this, the CreateUser action has an effect of *user_exists*(*u*), which is used as a precondition in this actions, and thus enforcing that the user has been created prior to its selection.

F3: The `AddGroupPermissions` action will either follow the `CreateGroup` action or occur in isolation, similar to `AddUserPermission`. Similar to F3, the `CreateGroup` has a (*group_exists*(*g*)) predicate as an effective which is then a precondition of the `AddGroupPermissions` action, enforcing that the group has been created or already exists prior to selection.

As previously mentioned, permission rights are managed through the use of standard and fine-grained approaches. The effect of the action is that the permission is assigned through asserting the *(effective-permission s p d)* predicate. Each action increases the *interactions* fluent, which is used to record how many administrative actions are required to undertake an administrative task, thus allowing the potential to minimise the total. This is an important aspect of the planning problem as there may be many routes to implement new permissions, even abiding by the current allocation structure. By using an *interactions* fluent, it is possible to minimise the number of schedule actions and thus preventing over complex solutions, unless they are the only valid ones identified.

5 Application of Automated Planning

We now present a solution whereby the domain model can be used to automatically produce plans informing the administrator how they can implement a change to the permission allocation, in-keeping with previous allocations. For example, determining that a user should be added to a group to acquire the desired effective permission.

As previously discussed, automated planning (AP) is well-aligned to the process of performing file system access management where a sequence of administrative actions is performed to translate a system configuration from an initial to a goal state through the execution of a series of actions. In general, the environment and action description are represented by a *planning domain model*, and the description of the initial state and the goal conditions is represented by a *planning problem description* and more than one planning problem descriptions can be used with a single planning domain model. To utilise current AP tools, as well as creating a new domain model for the planning community, the Planning Domain Definition Language (PDDL) [42] is used. Although file system permission allocation tasks do occur over a duration, there is no need to model temporal aspects; i.e., only compliance to security policy is required. The motivation for translating the acquired domain model to PDDL is twofold. First, using PDDL allows the use of state-of-the-art domain-independent tools, aiding to provide better quality solutions, and second, producing PDDL files creates the potential for the AP community to have a new application for benchmarking purposes.

5.1   PDDL Model

The challenge is to help system administrators in making assignments without the need for expert knowledge. The motivation for translating the acquired domain model to PDDL is twofold. First, using PDDL allows the use of state-of-the-art domain-independent tools, aiding to provide better quality solutions, and second, producing PDDL files creates the potential for the AP community to have a new application for benchmarking purposes. In this paper, we use PDDL 2.2 [43] for having numeric fluents feature. In the file system domain, we introduce the types of: *user*, *group*, *permission* and *directory*. These types instantiate the objects of file system domain.

The domain contains six actions, and although the actions may appear simplistic, it is worth noting that the model is used to control the creation of users, groups, and permissions as well as assigning relationships amongst the objects. The sequential 'flows', as previously discussed, are encoded through predicates (see Availability section for full PDDL models). Assigning new permissions that are in-keeping within current file system access control policies will require deliberation to determine a relevant course of actions. An example action is add-user-permission action is demonstrated in Fig. 5.

To cater for the inheritance of group membership permissions, `calculate-effective` action as provided in Fig. 6 is introduced to assert the effective

```
(:action add-user-permissions
  :parameters (?u - user ?p - permission
    ?d - directory)
  :precondition (and
    (user-exists ?u)
    (not(u-permission ?u ?p ?d)))
  :effect (and(u-permission ?u ?p ?d)
      (increase (interactions) 1) )
)
```

Fig. 5 Calculate-effective permission action

```
(:action calculate-effective
  :parameters (?u - user ?p - permission
    ?d - directory ?g - group)
  :precondition (or (u-permission ?u ?p ?d)
    (exists (?g - group) (and (u-member-of ?u ?g)
      (g-permission ?g ?p ?d))))
  :effect (effective-permission ?u ?p ?d )
)
```

Fig. 6 Calculate-effective permission action

permission of a user, where they are a member of a group, or there is a group inheriting permission from another group. The use of this action allows the concept of a subject's effective permission to be modelled into domain. It asserts the effective permission, if a user has explicit permission on a directory, or they are acquiring permissions through a set of group memberships. Multiple `calculate-effective` actions can be executed to accumulate a user's permission from different sources.

5.2 *Planning Problem Instance*

In order to correctly model the creation of users and groups, as well as their involvement in the allocation of new permissions, it is necessary to extract and understand previous allocations. The solution presented in this paper takes as input the set of event logs and outputs the sets of objects and predicates necessary to construct the PDDL problem instance. Software has been produced to iteratively process each event to determine their type through analysing the event ID. Once an event of interest has been identified, the event description is then processed to identify key information. For example, an event detailing the creation of a new user ($id = 4720$) contains the user account name. Although events of different types have a slightly different in structure, the structure of each type is repeatable and programmatically easy to extract.

5.3 *Plan Generation*

A sequence of actions is then identified which translates the system's security configuration from the initial state to the desired goal. Considering the previous example, the produced plan will ensure that the following two actions are required to achieve the goal:

```
0:(create-user User3)
1:(add-user-permissions User3 FA Dprt2)
2:(add-group-permissions User3 Role5)
```

To achieve the goal state, two actions have been identified, which are used to inform the administrator what they should perform the administrative actions to complete the task. First, the `create-user` is selected so that the user `User3` is created. Next, the `add-user-permissions` action is selected to provision `User3` `Full Control` on the `Dprt2` directory. Following this, the `add-group-permissions` action is selected, enabling `User3` to acquire Full Control over the department directory by inheriting the group permissions of `Role5`.

6 Empirical Analysis

A case study is now provided where both the ability to acquire problem instances from file system administration event logs, and the ability to provide plans on how to make configuration additions, are empirically evaluated on event logs acquired from real-world systems. These are used for configuration purposes and to generate the required event logs. The constructed problem instances are then used alongside the domain model to suggest new permission allocations that are in-keeping with the current security policy. The suggestions are subsequently evaluated by an expert for suitability.

6.1 Environment and Methodology

We select the use of the LPG-td [44] planner for two primary reasons: (1) for its support of numeric fluents, good support of PDDL language, and general good performance [45], and (2) the availability and ease of configuration.[5] All experiments presented in this paper were performed on an Intel i7 3.50GHz processor running Ubuntu 16.04 LTS with 32GB RAM. The experimental systems have the following specification:

1. Each user has a home directory where they are directly allocated a high level of permission;
2. There will be a total of 10 departments which represent clusters of the organisation's activity. For example, in a University, these departments would be the individual subject areas; and
3. There will be a total of 10 roles per department. Here, a role is used to describe the different level of permission required for different positions (e.g. management, finance).

There are 10 experimental systems (as detailed in Table 1), and each has a different number of users. Each system is a variation of the live system with an increasing number of users. This methodology is adopted as one of the significant variations amongst different file system access control systems is that of the number of users. The system 1 has 10 users and each subsequent version has an additional 10 users, up to the limit of 100 users in system 10. In terms of testing, we use the domain model and introduce a problem instance to produce plans for:

a: Suggesting a new group membership allocation when creating a new permission entry allowing for previous group memberships can be utilised. The metric here is to minimise the amount of administrative actions required.

---

[5]Due to the large number of objects and predicates within the domain model, it is necessary to increase LPG's MAX_RELEVANT_FACTS limit to 40000 to process all objects and MAX_TYPE_INTERSECTIONS to 10000 for reducing plan generation time.

Table 1 Empirical results from performing both problem instance acquisition and plan suggestion. Problem instance **a** is where a new permission allocation is required, and **b** is where a new role is required. Acquisition informs the quantity of both input (**in**) and outputs (**out**) as well as processing time

No.	Acquisition/construction				Output time (s)		Memory (GB)		Human timings	
	No. of events	No. of objects	No. of facts	Execution time						
	in	out	out	(s)	a	b	a	b	a	b
1	57	42	48	0.27	1.21	1.24	0.24	0.26	8	35
2	107	63	98	0.49	2.12	2.33	0.78	0.82	32	68
3	150	84	141	0.74	3.09	3.12	1.25	1.31	72	151
4	179	105	170	1.11	4.06	5.09	1.79	1.83	128	268
5	232	126	223	1.27	6.23	6.41	2.37	2.44	200	420
6	274	147	265	1.38	6.06	6.88	3.05	3.14	288	604
7	304	168	295	1.67	7.0	8.27	3.78	3.85	392	823
8	346	189	337	2.79	9.23	10.44	4.54	4.68	512	1075
9	396	210	387	2.72	9.46	11.32	5.43	5.56	648	1360
10	425	231	416	3.14	11.99	13.71	6.39	6.50	800	1680

b: Introducing two new roles (group and directory), assigning the required membership (1 Read and Write, 1 Read) and introducing 2 new user to allocate. The metric here is to minimise the number of administrative actions and also to ensure that the new permission allocation structure is in-keeping with the system to maintain a systematic permission policy.

6.2   Results

The results from performing the experimental analysis are presented in Table 1. The results detail the construction phase describe the number of extracted events, number of objects, number of predicates, and execution time in seconds. Information is also provided detailing plan generation time required to find a solution for each problem instance. From the table, it is noticeable that the performance of the system increases along with the number of initial events. The results demonstrate the potential of the system as a total of 3.14 s is required for both domain model acquisition and planning for the largest problem instance (10). This is significant as the short processing time is of little inconvenience to the user.

The "Human" timings in Table 1 are acquired from monitoring the amount of time an administrator would require to propose a sequence of actions to perform the desired administration task. Here, the human is an administration with knowledge of how to configure the system, but no prior knowledge of how the current configuration is structured. The timings are acquired from observing an administrator perform the modifications on our system, and a general observation is that the time increases as the number of roles and departments increases. From the observations, we notice a conservative estimate of it taking the user 4 s to check a user's group membership, 6 s to add a new group and/or assign membership, 5 s to check the allocated permission, and 10 s to make an allocation. We also discovered that as the user has no prior knowledge of the configuration structure, they entered an intense period of exploring the system to determine how previous file system access control implementations are structured. This is the reason why the time required for human interpretation is high compared to the automatically generated plans.

An example output for plan **b** is:

```
0: (CREATE-GROUP GROUP-ROLE-1)
1: (CREATE-GROUP GROUP-ROLE-2)
2: (ADD-GROUP-PERMISSIONS GROUP-ROLE-1
FILEREADDATA TESTDIR)
4: (ADD-GROUP-PERMISSIONS GROUP-ROLE-2
FILEWRITEDATA TESTDIR)
5: (ADD-USER-TO-GROUP USER0 GROUP-ROLE-1)
6: (ADD-USER-TO-GROUP USER1 GROUP-ROLE-1)
7: (ADD-USER-TO-GROUP USER0 GROUP-ROLE-2)
8: (ADD-USER-TO-GROUP USER1 GROUP-ROLE-2)
```

The results in Table 1 allow us to determine the required time to identify a valid plan as 11.99 and 13.71 s for instance **a** (one allocation action) and **b** (2 × new group, 2 × permission, and 4 × group assignment) or instance number 10, respectively. This is a reduction over the human timings provided in Table 1 where the average percentage reduction is 5095% and 9423% for instance **a** and **b**, respectively. The percentage reduction in time is large due to the speed by which the automated planning algorithm is able to find an optimal solution. A large time reduction is to be expected as the intensive period of manual analysis required to identify the current file system permissions structure is no longer needed. This reduction in time is significant as it means that not only is there a lower requirement for expert knowledge, the time to perform the task is significantly lower due to the administrator no longer needing to perform an exhaustive exploration to decide upon the best course of action to implement the desired change.

It is worth noting here that in the first instance, the comparison may not seem fair as the expert also performed the configuration change, whereas the automated approach is only planning a solution. If the output plan was to be used by a human to implement, then there would be a time overhead to add on top of the automated timings; however, if the output solution was to be actioned through scripting techniques (as intentioned), then no additional time would be needed.

6.3 Sensitivity Analysis

The results presented in the previous section demonstrate the suitability of the technique to suggest new permissions' allocations that utilise previous group allocations and will suggest the creation of new groups when new permissions are required. However, the underlying system used in this analysis is well structured. Moreover, each user, group and permission level has been created and applied in a systematic manner. But it is often the case that ad hoc permissions will frequently be made when undertaking permissions administration tasks and the structure arising from systematic allocation with diminish. This section will investigate the relationship between the degree of systematic structure and the impact on the technique's ability to suggest meaningful allocations.

It is necessary to consider how we measure both fitness for purpose and quality of any suggesting new access control rules. In order to analyse the technique's ability to learn and suggest new permission allocations based on historical log information with an increasing number of ad hoc and poorly structured permissions, a large-scale analysis is to be performed where the number of ad hoc permissions is gradually introduced into the systematic allocation. This enables the analysis of the suitability of the approach when the underlying file system permissions' allocation is not systematic.

The directory structure and allocations presented in the earlier empirical analysis are used as the base system. More specifically, an individual user is assigned direct permission on their home drive, whereas all other shares are managed through group allocations. The problem files are generated in a systematic and simplistic manner. They are extracted from event log files and have different sizes, ranging from 10 to 100 users. The size of a problem instance depends on the number of its objects and initial states. This means that, the bigger the problem instance, the greater the complexity and challenge for the planner to extract correct plan solution in finite amount of time. In each problem file, directories are assigned different roles, but with a percentage of non-systematic allocation (i.e. 0, 10, 20, ..., 100% within each set of experiment). Non-systematic permissions represent those that are ad hoc and do not follow previous systematic allocations. We simulate the addition of non-systematic permissions through introducing and assigning a group Test$n$ group, where n is between 0 (no ad hoc permissions) and 10. Due to the structure of the test environment, 10 ad hoc permissions equate to there being a 1:1 ratio of structures and non-systematic permissions.

To assess the performance of both kinds of plan solutions (**a** and **b**), the following measures are considered:

- True Positive Rate (*tpr*): the fraction of valid administrative actions that are correctly included in the plan;
- False Positive Rate ($fpr = 1 - tnr$): the fraction of valid administrative actions that have not been included in the plan;
- True Negative Rate (*tnr*): the fraction of invalid administration actions that are correctly not included in the plan;

Fig. 7 TPR and FPR

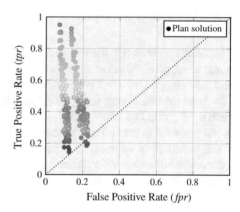

- False Negative Rate ($fnr = 1 - tpr$): the fraction of invalid administration actions that are incorrectly suggested in this plan; and
- Finally, the *accuracy* is reported as the fraction of all suggestion actions that are correct identified and valid.

6.4 Discussion

Figure 7 illustrates the relationship between the *tpr* and *fpr*. It shows that the system results in a high *tpr* and a low *fpr*, meaning that the system is mostly able to find a suitable valid plan containing no adverse actions. This is of significance as it demonstrates the ability of the system to suggest administrative actions that grant the user the required level of permission. In Fig. 7, the diagonal line is the point which is the equivalent to random selection. Figure 7 also illustrates that there are two distinct clusters of plan solutions. The left cluster is type **a** problem instances with relatively low FPR and right cluster is type **b**.

Similarly, Fig. 8 shows that the *tnr* is high while the *fnr* is low. This is also of significance as it demonstrates the technique's ability to not suggest incorrect administrative actions to the user. Figure 8 also presents the two distinct clusters of plan solutions, as seen in Fig. 7. The top cluster is of type **a** problem instances with relatively high *tnr* and bottom cluster is of type **b**. The variation in the results of **a** and **b** type problem instances is due to their difference in goal states. Type **a** problem instances search the optimal role for only one directory "\\Shares\Dprt0\Role0" while **b** type instances search for two directories "\\Shares\Dprt0\Role0" and "\\Shares\Dprt0\Role1". It is also interesting to notice that, even though the planner holds the whole problem representation in memory before actually searching for the plan solution [46], larger goals with the same problem size require more time and memory. It can be deduced that by having larger goals, the probability of planner generating non-optimal solution

Fig. 8 TNR and FNR

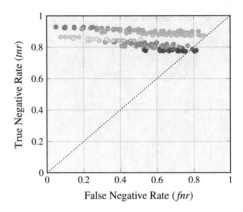

Fig. 9 Time and Memory

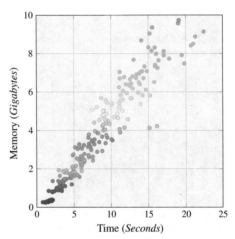

increases (as the **b** type problem instances have higher *fpr* and lower *tnr*) alongside the consumption of more computing resources.

Figure 9 illustrates the relationship between memory consumption and computation time. From analysing the results, it is evident that larger problem instances require more memory and time to solve. Problem instances that hold information to represent a larger underlying system will contain a larger number of objects and predicates. For example, increasing the number of user objects also increases the amount of `user-exists` and `u-member-of` predicates, hence affecting the overall size of problem instances. In addition, the increased size of problem instances requires more memory to hold the problem representation. It should be noted that the memory and time consumptions depend on the underlying system specifications and its current status regarding number of processes running in memory, free memory space, etc.

Figure 10 illustrates a 3D view of non-systematic permissions percentage (x-axis), *tpr* (y-axis) and problem sizes (z-axis). It is clear that *tpr* is inversely proportional to

Fig. 10 TPR and ad hoc

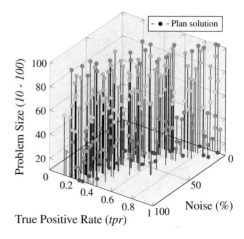

Fig. 11 Problem Instance
Size and Accuracy

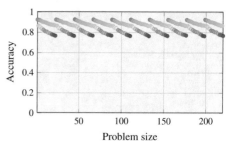

the percentage of non-systematic permissions and the same pattern can be observed in all problem sizes. It is worth noting that even when considering the problem with 100% non-systematic permissions, a *tpr* can be achieved up to around 50%. This means that, if the amount of non-systematic permissions is double the amount of correct values, there is a 1 in 2 chance the suggested permission allocations will be correct. The reason for this good performance is the planner's ability to optimise the solution to minimise the number required administrative actions.

Figure 11 confirms that the problem size does not impact on the accuracy of solution (as the accuracy of differently sized problems with same noise percentage is almost similar) and the planner is consistently able to find a high-quality solution. The accuracy of each problem size decreases with the increase in noise, ranging from around 0.9 to 0.7. As we are executing same problem instance several times to determine a holistic result and no problem instance has 100% accuracy, it means that the planner output at least one incorrect plan solution for each problem instance.

Figure 12 shows that the increase in noise amount, with respect to problem size, does not impact the overall accuracy. With lower amounts of noise, *tpr* dominates the accuracy value (meaning more valid actions are correctly identified) while with the higher noise amount, *tnr* dominates (meaning more invalid actions are correctly identified), hence balancing the overall accuracy value.

Fig. 12 Size-Noise and
Accuracy

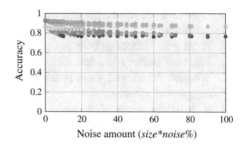

7 Conclusion

In this paper, we present a domain model for performing permissions' allocation, followed by an discussion of how generic automated planning approaches, can be utilised to provide assistive automation when planning for new permissions. The results demonstrate the significant reduction in time required to perform the modification, but more formidably, the reduction in the reliance on expert knowledge. This is of significance as it enables people with less specialist expertise to make configuration changes without adversely affecting the system. The proposed system is tested with different sizes of problem instances (ranging from 10 to 100 users) and ad hoc permissions' percentages (from 0% to 100%). Ad hoc permissions do not comply with the systematic allocation of file system permissions. The results show higher *tpr and tnr* and lower *fpr and fnr* values. The average accuracy of the system is found as 85% with the minimum of 76.3% and maximum of 92.8%.

In future work, we plan to perform a larger experimental analysis through identifying suitable collaborative organisations and analyse the results from live systems. We also plan to develop and test our technique on other operating system functionality that generate event logs. We further plan to perform extended end-user testing to determine the applicability of the generated plans.

8 Availability

Event logs, PDDL domain action model and generated problem instances are available at: https://selene.hud.ac.uk/scomsp2/FSPDDL.zip.

9 Questions

1. What are the challenges involved in conducting administrative tasks?
2. Can events log entries be used to extract administrative tasks over time? What kind of information could be retrieved?

3. Provide a list of actions that can aid the automated assignment of file system permissions.
4. What is an 'Effective Permission'? How it is calculated?
5. What is PDDL and its benefit to modelling automated planning challenges?
6. What are the advantages of using Automated Planning in file system permissions assignment process?
7. Is there any relationship between the amount of noise and problem instance in non-systematic permission allocation?
8. Can the problem size effect the accuracy of permission allocation?
9. Describe and justify the relationship of memory consumption and computation time in permission allocation process?
10. Explain the main drawbacks of using Automated Planning in 'ad hoc' file system permission assignment.

References

1. Yu S, Wang C, Ren K, Lou W (2010) Achieving secure, scalable, and fine-grained data access control in cloud computing. In: 2010 Proceedings IEEE Infocom. Ieee, pp 1–9
2. Burgess M (2003) On the theory of system administration. Sci Comput Program 49(1):1–46
3. Wang H, Guo X, Fan Y, Bi J (2014) Extended access control and recommendation methods for enterprise knowledge management system. IERI Procedia 10:224–230
4. Stiawan D, Idris M, Abdullah AH et al (2015) Penetration testing and network auditing: Linux. J Inf Process Syst 11(1)
5. Ghallab M, Nau DS, Traverso P (2004) Automated planning: theory and practice. Elsevier/Morgan Kaufmann, London, Amsterdam
6. Tourani R, Misra S, Mick T, Panwar G (2017) Security, privacy, and access control in information-centric networking: a survey. In: IEEE communications surveys & tutorials
7. Demchenko Y, Ngo C, De Laat C (2011) Access control infrastructure for on-demand provisioned virtualised infrastructure services. In: 2011 international conference on collaboration technologies and systems (CTS). IEEE, pp. 466–475
8. Kalam AAE, Baida RE, Balbiani P, Benferhat S, Cuppens F, Deswarte Y, Miege A, Saurel C, Trouessin G (2003) Organization based access control. In: IEEE 4th international workshop on policies for distributed systems and networks, 2003. Proceedings. POLICY 2003. IEEE, pp 120–131
9. Sandhu RS, Coyne EJ, Feinstein HL, Youman CE (1996) Role-based access control models. Computer 29(2):38–47
10. Hu VC, Kuhn DR, Ferraiolo DF (2015) Attribute-based access control. Computer 48(2):85–88
11. Deng J-B, Hong F (2003) Task-based access control model [j]. J Softw 1:011
12. Purser S (2002) Why access control is difficult. Comput Secur 21(4):303–309
13. Cárdenas AA, Amin S, Sastry S (2008) Research challenges for the security of control systems. In: HotSec
14. Bauer L, Cranor LF, Reeder RW, Reiter MK, Vaniea K (2009) Real life challenges in access-control management. In: Proceedings of the SIGCHI conference on human factors in computing systems. ACM, pp 899–908
15. Martin E, Xie T (2006) Inferring access-control policy properties via machine learning. In: Seventh ieee international workshop on policies for distributed systems and networks, 2006. Policy 2006. IEEE, p 4
16. Al-Shaer E, Ou X, Xie G (2013) Automated security management. Springer, Berlin

17. Parkinson S, Khan S (2018) Identifying irregularities in security event logs through an object-based chi-squared test of independence. J Inf Secur Appl 40:52–62
18. Parkinson S, Crampton A (2016) Identification of irregularities and allocation suggestion of relative file system permissions. In: Journal of information security and applications
19. Parkinson S, Hardcastle D (2014) Automated planning for file system interaction. In: 32nd workshop of the UK planning and scheduling special interest group. http://eprints.hud.ac.uk/22897/
20. Boddy MS, Gohde J, Haigh T, Harp SA (2005) Course of action generation for cyber security using classical planning. In: ICAPS, pp 12–21
21. Steinmetz M (2016) Critical constrained planning and an application to network penetration testing. In: The 26th international conference on automated planning and scheduling, p 141
22. Khan S, Parkinson S (2017) Towards automated vulnerability assessment
23. Riabov A, Sohrabi S, Udrea O, Hassanzadeh O (2016) Efficient high quality plan exploration for network security. In: International scheduling and planning applications woRKshop (SPARK)
24. Sohrabi S, Riabov A, Udrea O, Hassanzadeh O (2016) Finding diverse high-quality plans for hypothesis generation. In: Proceedings of the 22nd European conference on artificial intelligence (ECAI)
25. Ghosh N, Ghosh SK (2012) A planner-based approach to generate and analyze minimal attack graph. Appl Intell 36(2):369–390
26. Durkota K, Lisỳ V (2014) Computing optimal policies for attack graphs with action failures and costs. In: STAIRS, pp 101–110
27. Hewett R, Kijsanayothin P, Bak S, Galbrei M (2016) Cybersecurity policy verification with declarative programming. Appl Intell 45(1):83–95
28. Hoffmann J (2015) Simulated penetration testing: from "dijkstra" to "turing test++". In: ICAPS, pp 364–372
29. Shmaryahu D (2016) Constructing plan trees for simulated penetration testing. In: The 26th international conference on automated planning and scheduling
30. Sarraute C, Buffet O, Hoffmann J et al (2012) Pomdps make better hackers: accounting for uncertainty in penetration testing. In: AAAI
31. Backes M, Hoffmann J, Künnemann R, Speicher P, Steinmetz M (2017) Simulated penetration testing and mitigation analysis. arXiv:1705.05088
32. Sarraute C, Richarte G, Lucángeli Obes J (2011) An algorithm to find optimal attack paths in nondeterministic scenarios. In: Proceedings of the 4th ACM workshop on security and artificial intelligence. ACM, pp 71–80
33. Parkinson S, Longstaff AP, Fletcher S, Vallati M, Chrpa L (2017) On the exploitation of automated planning for reducing machine tools energy consumption between manufacturing operations. In: Association for the advancement of artificial intelligence AAAI
34. Cenamor I, Chrpa L, Jimoh F, McCluskey TL, Vallati M (2014) Planning & scheduling applications in urban traffic management. In: Proceedings of the UK planning & scheduling special interest group
35. Do MB, Ruml W, Zhou R (2008) On-line planning and scheduling: an application to controlling modular printers. In: AAAI, pp 1519–1523
36. Herry H, Anderson P, Wickler G (2011) Automated planning for configuration changes
37. Herry H, Anderson P (2012) Planning with global constraints for computing infrastructure reconfiguration. In: Proceedings of the 2012 AAAI workshop on problem solving using classical planners. AAAI Press
38. Georgievski I, Aiello M (2016) Automated planning for ubiquitous computing. ACM Comput Surv (CSUR) 49(4):63
39. Oberlin J, Tellex S (2018) Autonomously acquiring instance-based object models from experience. In: Robotics research. Springer, pp 73–90
40. Shah M, Chrpa L, Jimoh F, Kitchin D, McCluskey T, Parkinson S, Vallati M (2013) Knowledge engineering tools in planning: state-of-the-art and future challenges. In: Knowledge engineering for planning and scheduling, vol 53

41. Khan S, Parkinson S (2017) Causal connections mining within security event logs. In: Proceedings of the 9th international conference on knowledge capture. ACM. https://doi.org/10.1145/3148011.3154476. http://eprints.hud.ac.uk/id/eprint/33841/
42. McDermott D, Ghallab M, Howe A, Knoblock C, Ram A, Veloso M, Weld D, Wilkins D (1998) Pddl-the planning domain definition language
43. Edelkamp S, Hoffmann J (2004) PDDL2.2: the language for the classical part of the 4th international planning competition. Technical Report 195, Albert-Ludwigs-Universitat Freiburg, Institut fur Informatik
44. Gerevini A, Saetti A, Serina I (2003) Planning through stochastic local search and temporal action graphs in lpg. J Artif Intell Res 20:239–290
45. Roberts M, Howe A (2009) Learning from planner performance. Artif Intell 173(5):536–561
46. Alford R, Kuter U, Nau DS (2009) Translating htns to pddl: a small amount of domain knowledge can go a long way. In: IJCAI, pp 1629–1634

Defending Against Chained Cyber-Attacks by Adversarial Agents

Vivin Paliath and Paulo Shakarian

Abstract Cyber adversaries employ a variety of malware and exploit to attack computer systems. Despite the prevalence of markets for malware and exploit kits, existing paradigms that model such cyber-adversarial behaviour do not account for sequential application or "chaining" of attacks, that take advantage of the complex and interdependent nature of exploits and vulnerabilities. As a result, it is challenging for security professionals to develop defensive-strategies against threats of this nature. This chapter takes the first steps toward addressing this need, based on a framework that allows for the modelling of sequential cyber-attacks on computer systems, taking into account complex interdependencies between vulnerabilities and exploits. The framework identifies the overall set of capabilities gained by an attacker through the convergence of a simple fixed-point operator. We then turn our attention to the problem of determining the optimal/most effective strategy (with respect to this model) that the defender can use to block the attacker from gaining certain capabilities and find it to be an NP-complete problem. To address this complexity, we utilize an A*-based approach and develop an admissible heuristic. We provide an implementation and show through a suite of experiments using actual vulnerability data that this method performs well in practice for identifying defensive courses of action in this domain.

1 Introduction

Contemporary cyber-threat actors employ a variety of malware and exploit purchased through various channels such as the dark web [1] in order to carry out their attacks. These exploits usually comprise sophisticated "exploit kits" that target multiple vulnerabilities and leverage their complex interdependencies against each other. It would

V. Paliath (✉) · P. Shakarian
Arizona State University, Tempe, AZ, USA
e-mail: vivin.paliath@asu.edu

P. Shakarian
e-mail: shak@asu.edu

© Springer International Publishing AG, part of Springer Nature 2018
S. Parkinson et al. (eds.), *Guide to Vulnerability Analysis for Computer Networks and Systems*, Computer Communications and Networks,
https://doi.org/10.1007/978-3-319-92624-7_8

therefore appear that the damage caused by a cyber-adversary is not only dependent on the number of exploits used, but on the underlying dependencies between the targeted vulnerabilities as well. However, despite the easy availability of such malware and exploit kits and their potential threat to computer systems, existing paradigms that model cyber-adversarial behaviour [2–4] do not factor in the interdependent nature of vulnerabilities; this can limit their effectiveness when applied to real-world situations. For instance, it would prove useful to simulate a cyber-attack on a model of an existing system, assess its degree of vulnerability, and identify key vulnerabilities that should be patched in order to protect the system. Such a model would also prove useful for automated cyber-security systems that can learn defense and contingency strategies based on the model's simulations.

2 Proposed Model

In this section, we provide an overview of our model, which was originally described in [5]. Any publicly accessible system, or one is reachable through another such system, is potentially vulnerable to attack. By compromising one of these systems, an attacker can gain access to its functionality or even disable it completely by launching, for example, a denial-of-service attack. While systems may employ privilege checks, attackers can subvert them by employing privilege escalation exploits, giving them access to privileged commands. In this section, we describe a formal mathematical model that captures this behaviour. The model assumes that the attacker possesses an initial set of "capabilities". These capabilities not only represent the system functionality that the attacker has access to, but also represent the different actions that the attacker can take on or against the system. Subsets of this set, which represent an attacker's initial capabilities, allow us to model and distinguish between different types of attackers, such as unauthenticated and authenticated remote attackers, local users, and users with physical access. The set of initial capabilities can also reflect prior knowledge gained by scanning or profiling a target system. Starting with these capabilities the attacker can then employ a sequence of exploits, where each exploit provides access to additional capabilities that make it possible to exploit other vulnerabilities. Through this iterative approach, the attacker can gradually compromise a system until they have achieved their objective; for example, gaining access to a privileged capability.

We note that currently, capabilities are not explicitly called out when describing vulnerability preconditions and postconditions. There are multiple ways to approach this problem. One way, which we are currently investigating, is to use automated methods to derive this information from security advisories. Another approach is to use a system of standards, similar to Common Weakness Enumeration (CWE). Whenever vulnerabilities are discovered, preconditions and postconditions can be described in a standardized fashion. This is advantageous, as vulnerability dependencies can now be derived between multiple, interconnected components, that comprise a larger system.

2.1 Technical Preliminaries

We first define a set V, which is the set of all vulnerabilities, and a set C, which is the set of capabilities supported by a system on the network. We use the notation 2^C to represent the powerset of C.

Following the intuition of [6, 7], for any given exploit there is a subset of capabilities that the attacker must possess in order to use the exploit (preconditions) and a set of capabilities gained by doing so (postconditions); we refer to these sets of capabilities as C^r and C^g, respectively. The attacker's end goal is to acquire certain capabilities by using an exploit sequence against the system. These capabilities include access to local commands on the system, as well as capabilities gained by exploiting vulnerabilities (e.g. the ability to cause a denial-of-service attack). To model this behaviour, we first define the set of exploits E as follows:

Definition 1 Given a set $C^r \subseteq C$ of capabilities required to exploit a vulnerability $v \in V$, and a set $C^g \subseteq C$ of capabilities gained by exploiting this vulnerability, the set of exploits E is a set of tuples of the form (C^r, C^g, v).

Modelling exploits in this fashion allows us to capture the necessary conditions required to exploit a particular vulnerability. In addition, we are also able to model what the attacker gains by exploiting a particular vulnerability (note that it is possible to have multiple exploits that target the same vulnerability). Another advantage is that we are also able to model the attack surface of the system. For example, a privileged user on the system will have the ability to use administrative commands; this can be modelled as an "exploit" that grants privileged capabilities assuming that the user is able to escalate their privilege. Similarly, a "passive" attack surface (i.e. an attack surface that is implicitly available) can also be modelled as an "exploit" with no required capabilities; for example, on a machine running a Secure Shell (SSH) server we can model an "exploit" with no required capabilities that provides the capability to initiate an SSH session.

As mentioned earlier, the attacker's goal is to employ an exploit sequence against a system, in order to gain some specific set of capabilities; we define this sequence as follows:

Definition 2 Given some set $E' \subseteq E$, and initial set of capabilities $C_0 \subseteq C$, an **exploit chain** (denoted $E_{C_0, E'}$) is a subset of E':

$$\langle e_n \mid n \in \mathbb{N} \rangle = \langle (C_1^r, C_1^g, v_1), \ldots, (C_i^r, C_i^g, v_i), \ldots, (C_n^r, C_n^g, v_n) \rangle$$

where:

$$C_1^r \subseteq C_0$$

and for each consecutive pair $(C_i^r, C_i^g, v_i), (C_j^r, C_j^g, v_j)$ we have:

$$C_j^r \subseteq C_0 \cup \bigcup_{k<j} C_k^g$$

Note that for a given E' and C_0, there can be multiple exploit chains that allow an attacker to obtain a particular set of capabilities. Hence, in order to accurately gauge the outcome of an attack, we must consider the complete set of capabilities that the attacker can gain, using every strategy at their disposal. Observe that while multiple strategies can lead the attacker to the same goal, the set of capabilities used to get there can be different as they depend on the actual exploits used. By identifying all such exploit chains, we can identify the complete set of capabilities that the attacker can gain; we call this the **obtained set of capabilities**. Intuitively, we can see that this set establishes an upper bound on the set of capabilities an attacker can gain for a given set of initial capabilities and exploits. In addition, the set easily translates to the maximum amount of damage that an attacker can cause to the system:

Definition 3 Given a set of exploits $E' \subseteq E$ and a set of initial capabilities $C_0 \subseteq C$, the **obtained set of capabilities** (denoted C^*_{E',C_0}) consists of all capabilities in C_0, in addition to any capability $c \in C$ for which there exists a $E_{C_0,E'}$ leading to c and does not contain any capability $c' \in C$, such that $c' \notin C_0$ and for which there does not exist a $E_{C_0,E'}$ leading to c'.

Essentially, given some initial set of capabilities C_0, the attacker can apply a sequence of exploits constructed from E' to eventually gain a certain set of capabilities. Hence for every capability $c \in C^*_{E',C_0}$, there is a subsequence $\langle(C^r_1, C^g_1, v_1),$ $\ldots, (C^r_i, C^g_i, v_i)\rangle$ such that $c \in C^g_i$. In addition, if there is a capability $c \notin C^*_{E',C_0}$, it implies that there exists no exploit chain leading the attacker to that capability, making it impossible to obtain. The primary intuition is that the **obtained set of capabilities** includes all capabilities that the attacker can possibly obtain from the employed set of exploits, when starting with a certain set of initial capabilities.

2.2 Fixed-Point Operator

In the previous section, we introduced the definition of an exploit and an exploit chain. We also explained the significance of these chains; in effect, they communicate the following important pieces of information:

1. The chain of exploits used by the attacker to compromise the system.
2. The overall set of capabilities gained by the attacker after exploiting the system.

In this section, we describe how the model can derive this information based on the initial capabilities of the attacker, and the exploits that they choose to use.

An intuitive approach is to model exploit application after real-world attacker behaviour. When compromising a system, an attacker usually starts with some initial exploit (or exploits) to gain some desired capabilities. These capabilities can then be used to exploit more vulnerabilities, possibly providing access to additional capabilities. The attacker's approach is iterative; they cumulatively gain capabilities in order to exploit additional vulnerabilities, that will eventually lead them to their desired goal. Hence, it is first necessary to identify the exploits an attacker can actually use by taking their dependencies (preconditions) into account, in order to keep track of the capabilities gained from using those exploits. We then need to re-examine the set of exploits in order to determine what new exploits (if any) are now applicable, and repeat the process:

Definition 4 We introduce the notion of exploit application via an "exploit-application operator":

i. Given $E' \subseteq E$ and $C_0 \in 2^C$ we define the exploit-application operator $\mathbf{T}_{E'} : 2^C \to 2^C$ as:

$$\mathbf{T}_{E'}(C_0) = C_0 \cup \bigcup \{C^g \mid (C^r, C^g, v) \in E' \wedge C^r \subseteq C_0\}$$

ii. Given some $i \in \mathbb{N}$, we define the ith application of $\mathbf{T}_{E'}$ on $C_0 \subseteq C$ as:

$$\mathbf{T}_{E'}\!\uparrow_i(C_0) = \mathbf{T}_{E'}(\mathbf{T}_{E'}\!\uparrow_{i-1}(C_0))$$
where:
$$\mathbf{T}_{E'}\!\uparrow_1(C_0) = \mathbf{T}_{E'}(C_0)$$

iii. $\mathbf{T}_{E'}^*$, the fixed point of $\mathbf{T}_{E'}$ is defined as:

$$\mathbf{T}_{E'}^*(C_0) = \mathbf{T}_{E'}\!\uparrow_i(C_0)$$
where:
$$\mathbf{T}_{E'}\!\uparrow_i(C_0) = \mathbf{T}_{E'}\!\uparrow_{i+1}(C_0)$$

In the above definition, item (i) describes a single application of the exploit operator. Observe that it takes exploit dependencies into account, as an exploit is considered applicable only if an attacker has access to its required capabilities. Furthermore, the operator augments the attacker's initial set of capabilities with those provided by all applicable exploits, which is clearly mirrors real-world attacker behaviour. Item (ii) in Definition 4 models the attacker's iterative behaviour, where they leverage capabilities gained from exploiting previous vulnerabilities, in order to exploit new ones. Note that on each subsequent application of the operator, C_0 is set to the augmented capability set from the previous application. In this way, we can accurately model how the attacker progressively gains more capabilities, by employing additional exploits in an iterative fashion. At this juncture, it is natural to question whether it is possible for this iterative process to terminate; that is, can we identify the point where the attack cannot proceed any further? Intuitively, we know that there is a point where there are either no remaining exploits or no remaining *applicable* exploits; that is, either the attacker has used up all their available exploits or they are unable to use any more as they lack the required capabilities. Item (iii) captures this by defining the fixed point of the operator. This shows that the iterative application of the operator must converge or in real-world terms, the attacker stops when they cannot gain any new capabilities. In [5], we proved that $\mathbf{T}_{E'}^*$ has a least fixed point (Theorem 2.1).

A useful property of the exploit operator is that it can help us identify unique and disjoint sets of applicable exploits associated with each application:

Definition 5 Given a $E' \subseteq E$ and $C_0 \in 2^C$ with an $i \in \mathbb{N}$ such that $\mathbf{T}_{E'}^*(C_0) = \mathbf{T}_{E'}\uparrow_i(C_0)$, we can identify the set of exploits used at any $j \in \mathbb{N}$ where $j \leq i$ as:

$$E'_j = \{(C^r, C^g, v) \in E' \setminus \bigcup_{k=1}^{j-1} E'_k \mid C^r \subseteq \mathbf{T}_{E'}\uparrow_{j-1}(C_0)\}$$

where:

$$E'_1 = \{(C^r, C^g, v) \in E' \mid C^r \subseteq C_0\}$$

We can use this to show that the operator converges in a polynomial number of steps; more specifically, the number of steps cannot exceed the total number of exploits in the particular exploit chain returned by the operator (proved in [5], Theorem 2.2):

Proposition 1 *Given* $E' \subseteq E$ *and* $C_0 \in 2^C$ *with* $i \in \mathbb{N}$ *such that* $\mathbf{T}_{E'}^*(C_0) = \mathbf{T}_{E'}\uparrow_i(C_0)$, $i \leq |E'|$.

The set of capabilities at the least fixed point also represents the complete set of capabilities that the attacker can gain for a given E' and C_0. Note that this is useful because it shows that the result at the fixed point corresponds to the **obtained set of capabilities** (Definition 3) [8]:

Proposition 2 (Given an $E' \subseteq E$ and $C_0 \in 2^C$ with obtained set of capabilities C_{E',C_0}^*, $\mathbf{T}_{E'}^*(C_0) \subseteq C_{E',C_0}^*$ and $\mathbf{T}_{E'}^*(C_0) \supseteq C_{E',C_0}^*$.)

Proof Sketch We prove $\mathbf{T}_{E'}^*(C_0) \subseteq C_{E',C_0}^*$ by showing that if $c \in \mathbf{T}_{E'}^*(C_0)$ then $c \in C_{E',C_0}^*$, and prove $\mathbf{T}_{E'}^*(C_0) \supseteq C_{E',C_0}^*$ by showing that if $c \notin \mathbf{T}_{E'}^*(C_0)$ then $c \notin C_{E',C_0}^*$.

2.3 Fixed-Point Operator Computational Complexity and Memoization

We can see that the complexity of calculating $\mathbf{T}_{E'}(C_0)$ is $\Theta(|E'|)$ for a given C_0 and E', as we have to iterate over the entire set of exploits to determine which ones are applicable. Assume we have a new set E'' such that $E' \subseteq E''$. Here, the complexity would seem to be $\Theta(|E''|)$. However, observe that we already know the result of $\mathbf{T}_{E'}(C_0)$. Therefore, it might be possible to use this result when calculating $\mathbf{T}_{E''}(C_0)$; that is, we can express $\mathbf{T}_{E''}(C_0)$ as $\mathbf{T}_{E'}(C_0) \cup \mathbf{T}_{E''\setminus E'}(C_0)$. This memoization technique is advantageous as it saves us from having to perform calculations for which we already know the result. Hence, we can state the following proposition (proved in [8]):

Proposition 3 (Given $E'' \subseteq E$, $E' \subseteq E$ and $C_0 \in 2^C$, if $E' \subseteq E''$ then $\mathbf{T}_{E'}(C_0) \subseteq \mathbf{T}_{E''}(C_0)$.)

Proof Sketch We prove by way of contradiction, using item i. from Definition 4, that since the union operation only adds element to a set, if $E' \subseteq E''$ then $\mathbf{T}_{E'}(C_0) \subseteq \mathbf{T}_{E''}(C_0)$.

We can also use memoization in the calculation of the fixed point as well. Observe that calculating the fixed point takes $|E'|$ steps in the worst case, which means that the upper bound on the complexity of calculating is $O(|E'|^2)$. However, all exploits may apply on the very first invocation, in which case the operator would converge after a single iteration. Hence, the lower bound is linear in the total number of exploits, or $\Omega(|E'|)$. In general, the complexity is $\Theta(|E'| \times k)$, where k is the number of applications it takes to reach the fixed point. Now assume we have an E'' such that $E' \subseteq E''$. Using the same intuition as before, note that it is possible to use the result of $\mathbf{T}^*_{E'}(C_0)$ when calculating $\mathbf{T}^*_{E''}(C_0)$. Hence, we can state the following proposition (proved in [8]):

Proposition 4 (Given $E'' \subseteq E$, $E' \subseteq E$ and $C_0 \in 2^C$, if $E' \subseteq E''$ then $\mathbf{T}^*_{E'}(C_0) \subseteq \mathbf{T}^*_{E''}(C_0)$.)

Proof Sketch Based on item ii. from Definition 4, we know that there is a $i, j \in \mathbb{N}$ such that $\mathbf{T}_{E'}\uparrow_i(C_0) = \mathbf{T}^*_{E'}(C'_0)$ and $\mathbf{T}_{E''}\uparrow_j(C_0) = \mathbf{T}^*_{E''}(C'_0)$. We prove by induction that for all $n \geq 1, \mathbf{T}_{E'}\uparrow_n(C_0) \subseteq \mathbf{T}_{E''}\uparrow_n(C_0)$, which implies that $\mathbf{T}^*_{E'}(C'_0) \subseteq \mathbf{T}^*_{E''}(C'_0)$.

It is tempting to calculate the new fixed point by using the expression $\mathbf{T}^*_{E''\backslash E'}(\mathbf{T}^*_{E'}(C'_0))$; this would not be correct. Observe that when calculating $\mathbf{T}^*_{E'}(C'_0)$, we do not necessarily use every exploit in E' as we can only use those exploits whose preconditions are satisfied. We also know that the additional exploits in $E'' \setminus E'$ could provide us capabilities that we did not possess before. Note that it is further possible for these additional capabilities to satisfy the preconditions of at least one unused exploit from E'. Therefore, if we exclude E' outright, we could potentially ignore viable exploits. Hence, it would be more appropriate to exclude only those exploits that were used in the calculation of $\mathbf{T}^*_{E'}(C'_0)$:

Definition 6 Given a $E' \subseteq E$ and $C_0 \in 2^C$, with an $i \in \mathbb{N}$ such that $\mathbf{T}^*_{E'}(C_0) = \mathbf{T}_{E'}\uparrow_i(C_0)$, the complete set of applicable exploits E_{use} is defined as:

$$E_{use} = \bigcup_{1 \leq j \leq i} E'_j \qquad \textit{(Definition 5)}$$

Using this definition, we can make the following observation:

Observation 1 *Given $E'' \subseteq E$, $E' \subseteq E$, and $C_0 \in 2^C$ we can express $\mathbf{T}^*_{E''}(C_0)$ in terms of $\mathbf{T}^*_{E'}(C_0)$ as follows:*

$$\mathbf{T}^*_{E''}(C_0) = \mathbf{T}^*_{E''\backslash E_{use}}(\mathbf{T}^*_{E'}(C_0))$$

Observe that as we are operating on a much smaller set of exploits, the run-time is now $\Theta(|E'' \setminus E'| \times k)$; k is necessarily smaller as well, which shows that memoization decreases the run-time. In [8], we also show that in certain cases, calculating the fixed point can even be done in linear time.

3 Defender Problem

The defender problem is fundamentally different from the attacker problem [5] due to one significant observation: while the attacker is satisfied if they can gain a certain capability in at least one way, the defender must be able to identify and block all possible ways in which that particular capability can be gained. That is, the attacker can gain a capability if they are able to exploit at least one vulnerability providing that capability. However, the defender must block all vulnerabilities whose exploits either directly or indirectly (i.e. through additionally exposed vulnerabilities) provide access to that capability. Hence, the defender must be able to identify the number of ways in which a particular capability can be gained. To model this, we define a function that given a set of exploits used by the attacker and a set of vulnerabilities patched by the defender, returns a multiset of capabilities gained by the attacker. We define the function $patch : 2^E \times 2^V \rightarrow \langle 2^C, m \rangle$ as follows:

Definition 7 Given $E' \subseteq E$ and $V' \subseteq V$ we define the function $patch : 2^E \times 2^V \rightarrow \langle 2^C, m \rangle$ (where $m : C \rightarrow \mathbb{N}$) as:

$$patch(E', V') = \biguplus \{C^g \mid (C^r, C^g, v) \in E' \setminus E'_{V'} \wedge C^r \subseteq C^*_{E' \setminus E'_{V'}, C_0}\}$$

where:

$$E'_{V'} = \{(C^r, C^g, v) \in E' \mid v \in V'\}$$

For ease of notation, we also provide the following definition to represent the multiset of capabilities gained by the attacker, after the defender has patched a certain set of vulnerabilities:

Definition 8 Given $E' \subseteq E$ and $V' \subseteq V$ of patched vulnerabilities, the multiset of capabilities gained by the attacker after patching is represented by $C^p_{E', V'}$ where $C^p_{E', V'} \equiv patch(E', V')$.

Note that the number of occurrences of a particular capability in $patch(E', V')$ represents the number of remaining, applicable exploits that provide the attacker with that capability.

The defender's goal is to patch some set of vulnerabilities in order to prevent the attacker from gaining a certain set of capabilities. Let us assume that the defender has patched a set of vulnerabilities $V' \subseteq V$, blocking all capabilities in the set $C_b \subseteq C$. This implies that $C_b \cap C^*_{E' \setminus E'_{V'}, C_0} = \varnothing$. Intuitively, we can also see that the corresponding multiset of capabilities gained by the attacker will not contain any capabilities from C_b either. Hence, we can state the following proposition:

Proposition 5 *Iff* $C_b \cap C^{*}_{E' \setminus E'_{V'}, C_0} = \varnothing$ *then* $C_b \cap C^{p}_{E', V'} = \varnothing$.

Proof Claim $(C_b \cap C^{*}_{E' \setminus E'_{V'}, C_0} = \varnothing$ *implies* $C_b \cap C^{p}_{E', V'} = \varnothing)$ Assume by way of contradiction that there exists a C_b such that $C_b \cap C^{*}_{E' \setminus E'_{V'}, C_0} = \varnothing$ and $C_b \cap C^{p}_{E', V'} \neq \varnothing$. By Definition 7, this implies that there exists some $(C^r, C^g, v) \in E' \setminus E'_{V'}$ where $C^r \subseteq C^{*}_{E' \setminus E'_{V'}, C_0}$ and $C^g \cap C_b \neq \varnothing$. This further implies that there must be some $j \in \mathbb{N}$ such that $C^r \subseteq \mathbf{T}_{E' \setminus E'_{V'}} \uparrow_j (C_0)$. Then by items (i) and (ii) from Definition 4, $C^g \subseteq \mathbf{T}_{E' \setminus E'_{V'}} \uparrow_{j+1} (C_0)$ and so $C^g \subseteq C^{*}_{E' \setminus E'_{V'}, C_0}$ necessarily. But $C^g \cap C_b \neq \varnothing$ which implies that $C_b \cap C^{*}_{E' \setminus E'_{V'}, C_0} \neq \varnothing$. Hence, a contradiction.

Claim $(C_b \cap C^{p}_{E', V'} = \varnothing$ *implies* $C_b \cap C^{*}_{E' \setminus E'_{V'}, C_0} = \varnothing)$ Assume by way of contradiction that there exists a C_b such that $C_b \cap C^{p}_{E', V'} = \varnothing$ and $C_b \cap C^{*}_{E' \setminus E'_{V'}, C_0} \neq \varnothing$. This implies that there exists some $(C^r, C^g, v) \in E' \setminus E'_{V'}$ with $C^g \cap C_b \neq \varnothing$. Additionally, there must be some $j \in \mathbb{N}$ such that $C^r \subseteq \mathbf{T}_{E' \setminus E'_{V'}} \uparrow_{j-1} (C_0)$ as that is the only way $C^g \subseteq C^{*}_{E' \setminus E'_{V'}, C_0}$ (by items (i) and (ii) from Definition 4). This further implies that $C^r \subseteq C^{*}_{E' \setminus E'_{V'}, C_0}$, and hence, $C^g \subseteq C^{p}_{E', V'}$ (Definition 7). But $C^g \cap C_b \neq \varnothing$ which implies that $C_b \cap C^{p}_{E', V'} \neq \varnothing$. Hence, a contradiction. $\qquad \square$

The defender aims to patch a set of corresponding vulnerabilities on the system to deny the attacker a certain set of capabilities, and must do so within a budget. Hence, we need a way to define the cost associated with patching a vulnerability:

Definition 9 Given the set of vulnerabilities V, we define a cost function $cost : V \to \mathbb{R}^+$ that associates a real-valued cost with each vulnerability.

For simplicity, we will use a single cost function throughout this chapter. However, all of the results can be extended for separate cost functions for the defender, as long as the cost is computable in polynomial time. Also, throughout this chapter, we will use a unit cost function, where for each $v \in V$, $cost(v) = 1$ (unless otherwise specified). Having defined the *cost* function, we can now formally define the defender's preferred strategy:

Definition 10 Given the defender's budget $b \in \mathbb{R}^+$, set of exploits $E' \subseteq E$ for vulnerabilities on the system, and the set of capabilities $C_b \subseteq C$ that the defender wants to deny the attacker, the **preferred defense strategy** is to patch the set of vulnerabilities $V' \subseteq V$ subject to the following conditions:

- $C_b \cap C^{p}_{E', V'} = \varnothing$
- $\sum_{v \in V'} cost(v) \leq c$

In the optimization variant of the preferred defense strategy problem, the quantity $\sum_{v \in V'} cost(v)$ is minimized and the associated strategy is called the ***optimal strategy***.

4 Computational Complexity

We examine the computational complexity of solving the preferred defense strategy problem. We will show that the finding such a strategy is NP-complete.

Theorem 1 (Finding a preferred defense strategy is NP-complete with a cost function that is computable in polynomial time.)

Proof Sketch Membership in NP is straightforward as verifying a solution is clearly a polynomial time operation. The remainder of the proof is to show NP-hardness. This is shown by a construction that allows us to solve the known NP-hard problem set-cover, defined as follows: given a set of sets given a set of sets $U = \{U_1, U_2, \ldots, U_n\}$ and a number k, find a $U' \subseteq U$ such that $|U'| \leq k$ and $\bigcup_{U_i \in U'} U_i = \bigcup_{U_i \in U} U_i$. The constructed instance is defined as follows:

- Build the global set of capabilities $C = \{c_i \mid U_i \in U\} \cup \bigcup_{U_i \in U} U_i$.
- Build the set of capabilities to be blocked $C_b = \bigcup_{U_i \in U} U_i$.
- Build the set of vulnerabilities $V = \{v_i \mid U_i \in U\} \cup \{v'_j \mid j \in \bigcup_{U_i \in U} U_i\}$.
- Build the set of exploits $E = \{\langle \varnothing, \{c_i\}, v_i \rangle \mid U_i \in U\} \cup \{\langle C_{1j}, \{j\}, v'_j \rangle \mid j \in \bigcup_{U_i \in U} U_i\}$ where $C_{1j} = \{c_k \mid U_k \in U \text{ where } j \in U_k\}$.
- Set the attacker's initial set of capabilities $C_0 = \varnothing$.
- We define the cost function for patching any vulnerability $v \in V$ as $cost(v) = 1$.
- Set the defender's budget $b = k$.

The remainder of the proof shows that the construction takes polynomial time, and there is a correspondence between solutions for the two problems.   □

5 Algorithms

In this section, we examine several algorithms to solve the preferred defense strategy problem. Our first, baseline approach is PDS-DFS (see Algorithm 1) that performs a depth-first search across the strategy space. This algorithm obviously has short-comings; the first being that we are not guaranteed to find an optimal solution. Additionally, the time complexity is factorial. Since the maximum number of vulnerabilities is $|V|$, and the branching factor at each level is one less than the previous, time complexity is $O(|V|!)$. Despite these shortcomings, PDS-DFS can be used as an anytime algorithm and is guaranteed to return a solution, though not necessarily optimal. However, as the algorithm continues to search, it can return better solutions. To address issues with depth-first search, breadth-first is an alternative. However, the extremely large space complexity, $O(|V|!)$ in this case, makes this infeasible. We provide two improvements over standard DFS that help us search for defender strategies in a more efficient manner:

Algorithm 1 DFS algorithm to find preferred defense-strategy

---

procedure PDS(-)DFS E, V, C_b, b:
    function PATH(*node*):
        path **as** SET
        while *node*.PARENT $\neq \varnothing$ **do**:
            ADD(*path*, *node*.VULNERABILITY)
            node $\leftarrow$ *node*.PARENT
        return *path*
    function SOLUTION(*node*):
        $V' \leftarrow$ PATH(*node*)
        return$\langle V', C_b \cap C_{E,V'}^p \rangle$
    function ROOT:
        root **as** NODE
        root.PARENT $\leftarrow \varnothing$
        root.VULNERABILITY $\leftarrow \varnothing$
        root.PATHCOST $\leftarrow 0$
        return*root*
    function MAKENODE(*parent*, *v*):
        node **as** NODE
        node.PARENT $\leftarrow$ *parent*
        node.VULNERABILITY $\leftarrow v$
        node.PATHCOST $\leftarrow$ *parent*.PATHCOST $+ cost(v)$
        return*node*
    nodes **as** LIFO- QUEUE
    ENQUEUE(*nodes*, ROOT)
    loop do:
        if EMPTY(*nodes*) **then**:
            return*failure*
        node $\leftarrow$ DEQUEUE(*nodes*)
        $\langle V', C' \rangle \leftarrow$ SOLUTION(*node*)
        if *node*.PATHCOST $\leq b$ **and** $C' = \varnothing$ **then**:
            returnV'
        for each *v* **in** $V \setminus V'$:
            ENQUEUE(*nodes*, MAKENODE(*node*, *v*))

---

1. We correctly prune the available vulnerabilities at each step.
2. We employ the use of an admissible heuristic function by adopting A* search.

All of these improvements allow us to maintain the correctness of the approach.

5.1 *Pruning Vulnerabilities*

PDS-DFS has factorial time complexity due to the fact that it considers vulnerabilities that need not or cannot be part of the solution. To address this problem, we can use PDS-DFS- PRUNED (see Algorithm 2) which prunes the search tree by discarding such vulnerabilities. Note that in the search tree, each node (other than the root

---

Algorithm 2 DFS with pruning (common functions omitted)

---

procedure PDS(-)DFS- PRUNED E, V, C_b, b:
  function PRUNE(*parent*, v):
    $V' \leftarrow$ PATH(*parent*)
    $C_v \leftarrow C^p_{E,V'} \setminus C^p_{E,V' \cup \{v\}}$
    $V'' \leftarrow \{e.v \mid e \in E \setminus E_{V' \cup \{v\}} \wedge e.C^g \cap C_v \neq \varnothing\}$
    $C'_v \leftarrow C^p_{E,V'} \setminus C^p_{E,V' \cup \{v\} \cup V''}$
    if *parent*.PATHCOST $+ cost(v) > c$ **then**:
      return *true*
    else if $\{e \in E_{\{v\}} \mid e.C^r \subseteq C^p_{E,V'}\} = \varnothing$ **then**:
      return*true*
    else if $C_b \cap C_v = \varnothing$ **and** $C_v \cap C^p_{E,V' \cup \{v\}} = \varnothing$ **then**:
      return*true*
    else if $C_b \cap C_v \neq \varnothing$ **then**:
      return*false*
    else if $C_b \cap C'_v \neq \varnothing$ **then**:
      return*false*
    return *true*
  function EXPAND(*node*):
    children **as** SET
    for each v **in** $V \setminus$ PATH(*node*):
      if not PRUNE(*node*, v) **then**:
        ADD(*children*, MAKENODE(*node*, v))

    return*children*
  nodes **as** LIFO- QUEUE
  ENQUEUE(*nodes*, ROOT)
  loop do:
    if EMPTY(*nodes*) **then**:
      return *failure*
    node $\leftarrow$ DEQUEUE(*nodes*)
    $\langle V', C' \rangle \leftarrow$ SOLUTION(*node*)
    if *node*.PATHCOST $\leq b$ **and** $C' = \varnothing$ **then**:
      return V'
    for each *child* **in** EXPAND(*node*):
      ENQUEUE(*nodes*, *child*)

---

node) represents a particular vulnerability, and a path to a node represents a set of vulnerabilities. When expanding a node in PDS-DFS to find the set of available vulnerabilities, we considered every vulnerability other than those in the path to the expanded node. In PDS-DFS- PRUNED, we additionally determine the viability of an available vulnerability by ensuring that the following conditions hold:

1. The cost of patching this vulnerability does not cause the defender to exceed their budget.
2. This vulnerability has at least one exploit whose required capabilities have not been blocked by previously patched vulnerabilities in V'.
3. Patching this vulnerability:

    i. Blocks at least one capability in C_b.

    ii. Or if not, additionally patching all other vulnerabilities that provide at least one capability that was blocked by patching this vulnerability, blocks at least one capability in C_b.

Note that item 3(ii) handles a case that is not immediately apparent: if multiple vulnerabilities provide a particular capability that is itself not present in C_b, but eventually leads to C_b, patching one of those vulnerabilities has no effect, causing it to be incorrectly pruned. Hence, we must consider the effect of patching all vulnerabilities providing that capability to see if the considered vulnerability is actually relevant. Only if these three conditions hold, will PDS-DFS- PRUNED include the vulnerability; otherwise, it will ignore it. The correctness of this pruning technique follows directly from our original model—hence, we state the following proposition:

Proposition 6 (PDS-DFS- PRUNED correctly prunes non-viable vulnerabilities and finds a correct solution if one exists.)

5.2 A* Based Approach

We can see that PDS-DFS- PRUNED helps us address time complexity by pruning non-viable vulnerabilities. However, it still does not guarantee us an optimal solution. One way to address this issue is by using an A* search across the strategy space. With an admissible heuristic function, the tree search variant of A* is both complete and optimal. We know that the defender wants to find the most inexpensive set of vulnerabilities to patch that block all of the desired capabilities. Therefore, a sensible heuristic would be to patch a vulnerability that is both inexpensive, and blocks the capabilities we want. A* evaluates nodes by combining $g(v)$, the cost to reach the node, and $h(v)$, the lower bound of the cost to get from the node to the goal. Since we cannot know the estimated cost to the goal without knowing the current state of the defender, we have to define a few other things before formally defining $h(v)$:

Definition 11 (*Given a set of vulnerabilities V' and complete set of exploits E, we define the corresponding set of blocked exploits $E_{V'}$ as:*)

$$E_{V'} = \{(C^r, C^g, v') \mid (C^r, C^g, v') \in E \text{ and } v' \in v\}$$

Definition 12 (*Given the complete set of vulnerabilities V, the defender's current set of vulnerabilities V', and the vulnerability under consideration v, we define the remaining set of vulnerabilities V_{rem} as:*)

$$\begin{aligned} V_{rem} = \{v' \mid v' \in V \setminus V' \setminus \{v\} \wedge \\ \{(C^r, C^g, v'') \in E_{\{v\}} \mid C^r \subseteq C^P_{E,V'}\} \neq \varnothing \wedge \\ (C_b \cap C_v \neq \varnothing \vee C_b \cap C'_v \neq \varnothing)\} \end{aligned}$$

where:

$$C_v = C^p_{E,V'} \setminus C^p_{E,V' \cup \{v\}}$$
$$V'' = \{(C^r, C^g, v') \in E \setminus E_{V' \cup \{v\}} \mid C^g \cap C_v \neq \varnothing\}$$
$$C'_v = C^p_{E,V'} \setminus C^p_{E,V' \cup \{v\} \cup V''}$$

Definition 13 (*Given the set of capabilities to block C_b, the complete set of exploits E, the defender's current set of vulnerabilities V' and the vulnerability under consideration v, we define the remaining set of unblocked capabilities C_{rem} as:*)

$$C_{rem} = C_b \cap C^p_{E,V' \cup \{v\}}$$

As we do not want to overestimate the cost to the goal, an obvious approach is to use the cheapest vulnerability. While this heuristic is certainly admissible, it vastly underestimates the cost to the goal, as it does not take into account the effect of patching a vulnerability. Hence, a more useful estimate would be to use the cost of what is *effectively* the cheapest vulnerability:

Definition 14 (*Given the vulnerability under consideration v, the remaining set of vulnerabilities V_{rem}, and the remaining set of capabilities to be blocked C_{rem} we define the cost per remaining capability of a $v' \in V_{rem}$, $cost_r : V \to \mathbb{R}^+$ as:*)

$$cost_r(v') = \frac{cost(v')}{\sum_{\{c' \in C_{v'} \mid c' \in C_{rem}\}} m(c')}$$

where:

$$C_{v'} = C^p_{E,V' \cup \{v\}} \setminus C^p_{E,V' \cup \{v,v'\}}$$

This cost is the ratio between the cost of the vulnerability and the number of remaining capabilities blocked by patching this vulnerability. Note that this ratio also takes into account the number of ways a particular blocked capability could have been gained. For example, suppose we have two vulnerabilities v_1 and v_2 with cost 1 and 2, respectively. Assume that patching v_1 blocks a single exploit that provides capability c, whereas patching v_2 blocks four exploits that provide c. This means that v_1 has an effective cost of 1, whereas v_2 has an effective cost of 0.5. We will now define a heuristic that estimates the cost to the goal, given a node representing a vulnerability:

Definition 15 (*Given the node v that represents an applicable vulnerability under consideration, the remaining set of vulnerabilities V_{rem} and the remaining set of capabilities to be blocked C_{rem} we define the estimated cost to the goal $h : V \to \mathbb{R}^+$ as:*)

$$h(v) = \sum_{c \in C_{rem}} \min_{\{v' \in V_{rem} | c \in C_{v'}\}} cost_r(v')$$

where:

$$C_{v'} = C^p_{E,V' \cup \{v\}} \setminus C^p_{E,V' \cup \{v,v'\}}$$

When estimating cost to the goal from v, we find, for each remaining capability, the lowest effective cost out of all vulnerabilities that can be exploited to provide that capability and then summing those costs.

Theorem 2 ($h(v)$ is admissible)

Proof We prove the statement of the theorem by showing that $h(v)$ is a lower bound of the true cost from node v to the goal.

By way of contradiction, consider an optimal path to the goal from node v with true cost $h^*(v)$ such that $h(v) > h^*(v)$. Let V^* be the corresponding set of vulnerabilities. Then:

$$\sum_{c \in C_{rem}} \min_{\{v' \in V_{rem} | c \in C_{v'}\}} cost_r(v') > \sum_{v' \in V^*} cost(v')$$

Since V^* represents the optimal path, the following is also true:

$$\sum_{c \in C_{rem}} \min_{\{v' \in V_{rem} | c \in C_{v'}\}} cost_r(v') > \sum_{c \in C_{rem}} \min_{v' \in V^*} cost_r(v')$$

This implies that there exists a c such that:

$$\min_{\{v' \in V_{rem} | c \in C_{v'}\}} cost_r(v') > \min_{\{v' \in V^* | c \in C_{v'}\}} cost_r(v')$$

Let $v_{min,c}$ and $v^*_{min,c}$ be the corresponding vulnerabilities with the lowest effective cost. This means that $cost_r(v_{min,c}) > cost_r(v^*_{min,c})$. However, for $v_{min,c}$ to have been used in calculating $h(e)$ instead of $v^*_{min,c}$, it must mean that $cost_r(v_{min,c}) < cost_r(v^*_{min,c})$. This is a contradiction, which means that $h^*(v)$ must not be the true cost to the goal. Hence, $h(v)$ is admissible. □

PDS $-$ A* (see Algorithm 3) is an implementation of A* to solve the preferred-defense strategy problem. Given that we have proved the heuristic to be admissible, PDS $-$ A* is guaranteed to produce an optimal solution.

5.3 Improving Fixed-Point Operator Performance

We know that the upper bound of the complexity to calculate the result of the fixed-point operator is quadratic in the number of exploits used; this can be seen in the naive

Algorithm 3 A^* algorithm that solves the preferred defense strategy problem.

procedure PDS- $A^*(E, V', C_b, b)$:
  function REMAININGCAPABILITIES(*node*):
    $V' \leftarrow$ PATH(*node*.PARENT)
    $v \leftarrow$ *node*.VULNERABILITY
    return $C_b \cap C^p_{E, V' \cup \{v\}}$

  function REMAININGVULNERABILITIES(*node*):
    $V' \leftarrow$ PATH(*node*.PARENT)
    V_{rem} **as** SET
    for each v **in** $V \setminus V' \setminus \{node.\text{VULNERABILITY}\}$:
      if not PRUNE(*node*, v) **then**:
        ADD(V_{rem}, v)

    return V_{rem}
  function h(*node*):
    $C_{rem} \leftarrow$ REMAININGCAPABILITIES(*node*)
    $V_{rem} \leftarrow$ REMAININGVULNERABILITIES(*node*)
    $V' \leftarrow$ PATH(*node*.PARENT)
    $v \leftarrow$ *node*.VULNERABILITY
    $h \leftarrow 0$
    for each c' **in** C_{rem}:
      $h_{min} \leftarrow \infty$
      for each v' **in** V_{rem}:
        $C_{v'} \leftarrow C^p_{E, V' \cup \{v\}} \setminus C^p_{E, V' \cup \{v, v'\}}$
        $count_{v'} \leftarrow \sum_{c \in (C_{rem} \cap C_{v'})}$ COUNT($C_{v'}, c$)
        if $c' \in C_{v'}$ **then**:
          $h_{v'} \leftarrow cost(v') \div count_{v'}$
          if $h_{v'} < h_{min}$ **then**:
            $h_{min} \leftarrow h_{v'}$

      $h \leftarrow h + h_{min}$

    return h
  function ESTIMATEDCOST(*node*):
    return *node*.PATHCOST $+ h$(*node*)
  nodes **as** PRIORITY- QUEUE **ordered by** ESTIMATEDCOST
  ENQUEUE(*nodes*, ROOT)
  loop do:
    if EMPTY(*nodes*) **then**:
      return *failure*
    node $\leftarrow$ DEQUEUE(*nodes*)
    $\langle V', C' \rangle \leftarrow$ SOLUTION(*node*)
    if $C' = \varnothing$ **then**:
      return V'
    for each *child* **in** EXPAND(*node*):
      if not EXISTS(*nodes*, *child*) :
        ENQUEUE(*nodes*, *child*)
      else:
        existing $\leftarrow$ FIND(*nodes*, *child*)
        $f_{existing} \leftarrow$ ESTIMATEDCOST(*existing*)
        $f_{child} \leftarrow$ ESTIMATEDCOST(*child*)
        if $f_{child} < f_{existing}$ **then**:
          REPLACE(*nodes*, *existing*, *child*)

Algorithm 4 Non-memoized implementation of $\mathbf{T}^*_{E'}$

1: **function** $\mathbf{T}^*(C_0, E')$:
2:     $capabilities \leftarrow C_0$
3:     $count \leftarrow -1$
4:     **while** $count \neq \text{SIZE}(capabilities)$ **do**:
5:         $capabilities \leftarrow \mathbf{T}(capabilities, E')$
6:         $count \leftarrow \text{SIZE}(capabilities)$
7:     **return** $capabilities$

8: **function** $\mathbf{T}(C_0, E')$:
9:     $capabilities$ **as** SET
10:     **for each** e **in** E':
11:         **if** $e.C^r \subseteq C_0$:
12:             $capabilities \leftarrow \text{UNION}(capabilities, e.C^g)$
13:
14:     **return** $capabilities$

Algorithm 5 Memoized implementation of $\mathbf{T}^*_{E'}$

1: **function** MEMOIZED- $\mathbf{T}^*(C_0, E', trie)$:
2:     $\langle capabilities, used \rangle \leftarrow \text{FIND}(trie, E')$
3:     **if** $capabilities = \varnothing$:
4:         $capabilities \leftarrow C_0$
5:     $\langle capabilities, used' \rangle = \mathbf{T}^*(capabilities, E' \setminus used)$
6:     $used \leftarrow \text{UNION}(used, used')$
7:     MEMOIZE$(trie, E', \langle capabilities, used \rangle)$
8:     **return** $capabilities$
9: **function** $\mathbf{T}^*(C_0, E')$:
10:     $exploits \leftarrow E'$
11:     $capabilities \leftarrow C_0$
12:     $count \leftarrow -1$
13:     **while** $count \neq \text{SIZE}(capabilities)$ **do**:
14:         $\langle capabilities, E'_j \rangle \leftarrow \mathbf{T}(capabilities, exploits)$
15:         $exploits \leftarrow exploits \setminus E'_j$
16:         $count \leftarrow \text{SIZE}(capabilities)$
17:     **return** $\langle capabilities, E' \setminus exploits \rangle$
18: **function** $\mathbf{T}(C_0, E')$:
19:     $capabilities$ **as** SET
20:     $used$ **as** SET
21:     **for each** e **in** E':
22:         **if** $e.C^r \subseteq C_0$:
23:             $capabilities \leftarrow \text{UNION}(capabilities, e.C^g)$
24:             ADD$(used, e)$
25:
26:     **return** $\langle capabilities, used \rangle$

implementation of the fixed-point operator in Algorithm 4. Based on Proposition 4 and Observation 1, it is possible to quickly calculate the result of the fixed-point operator for a set of exploits E', if we already have a result for some subset of E'. However, that still leaves the problem of deciding *how* we cache these results. The performance of the memoization technique is highly dependent on the data structure that backs the cache and so we must use one that can guarantee efficient storage and lookup times for the kind of data we want to memorize.

Our approach, initially described in [8], uses a trie or prefix tree to implement memoization. Tries are normally used to represent dictionaries of words and are extremely useful for this purpose as lookup time is linear in the size of the string. In our case, this requires imposing some sort of ordering on exploits so that any set can be ordered in a consistent way; a simple solution is to associate a unique integer with each exploit. Now whenever we calculate the result for some E', we cache the result of the fixed-point calculation at the node in the tree representing the "last" exploit in the ordered set E'. Observe that finding the largest subset of a given E' is analogous to finding the largest substring of a given string in a trie. Hence, the lookup time is now linear in the size of the largest subset of E' cached so far. A memoized implementation of the fixed-point operator is shown in Algorithm 5.

6 Experiments and Results

In this section, we examine the results of experiments that we conducted to show the viability of our model and previously described algorithms. Our experimental suite involves two kinds of experiments: those that evaluate performance and those that illustrate how the model and its algorithms behave in real-world scenarios; in particular, the results show that we not only able to solve the preferred defense strategy problem in a timely manner, but that the solutions conform to real-world expectations of both attacker and defender behaviour. We also show that the identified solutions are useful in practice and can be used for risk assessment and to provide guidance for security policies. The algorithms themselves, as well as the experiments, were implemented in Java 8 and executed on a machine with an Intel Core i7-4770K processor and 24GB RAM running Linux Mint 18.2.

All our experiments use real-world vulnerability data gathered from the National Institute of Standards and Technology's National Vulnerability Database (NIST NVD). For the first two experiments, we defined 33 exploits based on 16 vulnerabilities associated with the Windows 10 operating system. The vulnerabilities used involve a diverse spectrum of malicious capabilities, such as denial of service, privilege escalation, remote code execution, as well as those that take advantage of physical proximity. In addition, these exploits also feature a good distribution of attacker types.

In order to see how the attacker's initial capabilities affect the solution, we also defined four types of attackers. These are, in order from least to most threatening:

1. A **remote attacker** with remote access to the machine.
2. An **authenticated remote attacker** with remote access and valid credentials for the machine.
3. A **physically proximate attacker**; i.e. one that has physical and network access to the machine.
4. A **local attacker**; i.e. one with physical access and valid credentials for local use of the machine.

The corresponding sets of initial capabilities for these attackers were set as follows:

1. $C_0 = \{\texttt{remote}\}$
2. $C_0 = \{\texttt{remote}, \texttt{auth}\}$
3. $C_0 = \{\texttt{remote}, \texttt{phys-access}, \texttt{proximate}\}$
4. $C_0 = \{\texttt{remote}, \texttt{local}, \texttt{auth}, \texttt{proximate}, \texttt{phys-access}\}$

Finally, we defined the set of capabilities that the defender wishes to block as $C_b = \{\texttt{code-exec}, \texttt{escalate-privilege}, \texttt{denial-of-service}, \texttt{install-crafted-boot-manager}\}$.

Our first set of experiments were designed to evaluate the performance of our algorithms. For each algorithm, we also investigated the effects of enabling and disabling memoization; we did this for both a unit cost function and a complexity-based cost function, which is based on attack and access complexity costs. Here, we set the cost of patching a vulnerability to the sum of the attack and access complexity of the associated CVE; these metrics are extracted from the Common Vulnerability Scoring System (CVSS) base score vector reported for each CVE in the NVD. Both types of complexities are graded as high, medium or low, which we associated with the integer values 3, 2 and 1. Hence, a CVE with a high attack complexity and a low access complexity will have a cost of 4. For CVEs that do not have an access complexity metric, we only use the attack complexity.

To see how PDS − DFS and PDS − DFS- PRUNED compare against PDS − A*, we ran the latter algorithm with an unlimited defender-budget to identify the cost of the optimal solution. This cost was then set as the defender budget when running PDS − DFS and PDS − DFS- PRUNED. We then ran these algorithms (with and without memoization) for each attacker type; the results can be seen in Figs. 1 and 2. It is evident that the performance of PDS − A* is much better than either PDS − DFS or PDS − DFS- PRUNED. This, in spite of the fact that PDS − DFS- PRUNED appears to have a better run-time in the case of both remote attacker types. Note that results for PDS − DFS and PDS − DFS- PRUNED are missing in the case of physically proximate and local attackers; we could not provide these results due to the fact that the algorithms took far too long to finish. This shows that beyond a certain solution depth, the run-time advantage of PDS − DFS- PRUNED disappears because pruning, while helpful, does not diminish the strategy space enough to impact performance in an appreciable way. In addition, note that PDS − DFS- PRUNED in general is not able to provide an optimal solution, which clearly makes PDS − A* the better option. The results also confirm that memoization has a significant, positive effect on performance. In all cases, memoization drastically improves the run-time.

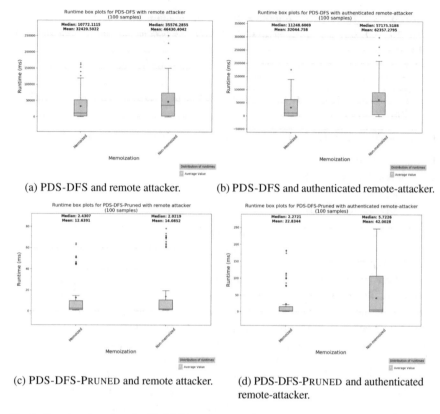

(a) PDS-DFS and remote attacker.   (b) PDS-DFS and authenticated remote-attacker.

(c) PDS-DFS-Pruned and remote attacker.   (d) PDS-DFS-Pruned and authenticated remote-attacker.

Fig. 1 Run-time box plots for PDS-DFS and PDS-DFS- Pruned against both authenticated and unauthenticated remote attackers, with and without memoization. Note that the large variance is due to non-deterministic vulnerability order when expanding nodes

Our second experiment was designed to see how different attacker types affect the solution to the defender problem. Our hypothesis is that the number of patched vulnerabilities is directly proportional to the threat level that the attacker represents; results of our experiment, seen in Table 1 confirm this hypothesis. To block both types of remote attackers, the defender need only patch 6 vulnerabilities with a total cost of 16, whereas in the case of the local attacker, the defender must patch a total of 13 vulnerabilities with a total cost of 36. In order to block the physically proximate attacker, the defender must patch 9 vulnerabilities with a total cost of 26. This shows that in order to defend against more threatening attackers, who possess a larger or more significant set of initial capabilities, the defender should expect to patch a larger set of vulnerabilities. The result is significant, because it allows security professionals to tailor their responses based on the kinds of attacks that are expected. Note that current patching strategies involve an "all or nothing" approach due to the fact that vulnerability dependencies are not taken into account. By factoring in vulnerability dependencies and anticipated attacker types, it would be possible to generate tailor-

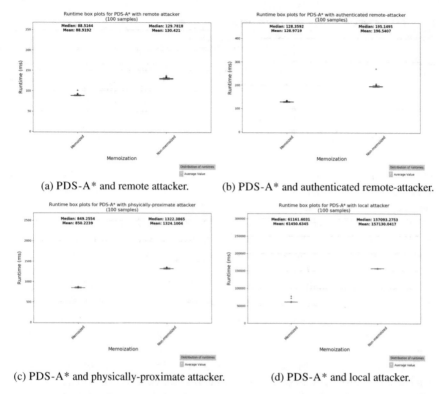

(a) PDS-A* and remote attacker. (b) PDS-A* and authenticated remote-attacker.

(c) PDS-A* and physically-proximate attacker. (d) PDS-A* and local attacker.

Fig. 2 Run-time box plots for PDS-A* against all attacker types, with and without memoization

Table 1 Patched vulnerabilities, solution costs and sizes for different attacker types (CVEs omitted for brevity)

Attacker	Solution cost	Solution size
Remote	16	6
Remote authenticated	16	6
Physically proximate	26	9
Local	36	13

made patch sets that protect defenders from specific kinds of attackers. This can also decrease the amount of time it takes for patch sets to make it out to consumers, as they can be released on a staggered schedule, progressively targeting more and more threatening types of attackers.

Our final experiment tries to see how the framework could be used to model attacks involving a network of machines. We modelled a simple network consisting of one Windows machine with public, remote access and fire-walled OS X machine running an Oracle server, that is only accessible with proper credentials via the Windows machine. For this experiment, we defined a total of 10 exploits based on

Table 2 Patched vulnerabilities for different attacker types

Attacker	Vulnerabilities patched	
	Windows	OS X
Remote	CVE-2016-3312	None
Local	CVE-2017-5715 CVE-2017-5753 CVE-2017-5754	CVE-2018-2590 CVE-2017-5715 CVE-2017-5753 CVE-2017-5754

4 vulnerabilities. The Windows machine contains a credentials–disclosure vulnerability that is exploitable by remote users (CVE-2016-3312), and the MELTDOWN and SPECTRE vulnerabilities (CVE-2017-5715, CVE-2017-5753, CVE-2017-5754), which require local access. The OS X machine running the Oracle server contains the MELTDOWN and SPECTRE vulnerabilities as well, and an Oracle denial-of-service and data disclosure vulnerability exploitable by anyone with network access and/or credentials (CVE-2018-2590). We defined two types of attackers: a **remote attacker** with initial capabilities {remote} and a **local attacker** with initial capabilities {win-creds, mac-creds}. The set of capabilities that the defender wishes to block was defined as $C_b = \{$oracle-dos, oracle-data$\}$, which represents the defender's desire to block denial-of-service attacks against the Oracle server, and to also block unauthorized access to data.

The results of this experiment can be seen in Table 2. We can see that a remote attacker can be prevented from compromising the Oracle server by patching a single vulnerability (CVE-2016-3312); this makes sense as that is the only way that the attacker can gain local credentials in order to exploit other vulnerabilities. However in order to stop a local attacker, the defender needs to not only patch the MELTDOWN and SPECTRE vulnerabilities on *both* machines, but needs to patch the Oracle vulnerability (CVE-2018-2590) as well. This result shows that the model can be applied to a network of machines and provides solutions that are just as intuitive and useful as the single-machine scenario. This is especially seen when comparing the number of vulnerabilities and systems that need to be patched based on the attacker type; whereas the remote attacker can be stopped by patching a single vulnerability on the Windows machine, a local attacker can be stopped only by patching multiple vulnerabilities on both machines. The difference makes sense intuitively as one expects a local user with valid credentials to have greater access to system and network capabilities, compared to a remote user.

7 Background and Related Work

In this section, we provide context for our work by describing the background for this type of cyber-security problem. We also explore related work in this area and show how our approach is significantly different and novel.

7.1   Background

During an attack, adversaries typically do not employ a single exploit. Rather, they employ a *series* of exploits (typically via an exploit kit) in order to gain greater access to the system or to leverage even more serious vulnerabilities. It is reasonable that such "chaining" of exploits can allow the attacker to inflict far greater damage on the system; for example, by exploiting a series of low-risk vulnerabilities, the attacker may be able to eventually leverage a high-risk one. The best example of this type of chained attack is perhaps the one employed by the infamous Stuxnet [9] worm against Iranian nuclear facilities (code available for public download[1]). The Stuxnet attack is informative as it illustrates how the worm was able to use a series of complex exploits that leveraged dependencies between multiple vulnerabilities. Stuxnet infected Siemens S7-300 PLCs by exploiting multiple zero-day vulnerabilities on the Windows operating system [10] and eventually gained not only the ability to send commands to modify the rotational frequency of motors that operated nuclear centrifuges [10], but also the ability to hide its behaviour from operators [11].

The severity of this problem requires an approach that can accurately model this sort of adversarial behaviour, in order to provide a more accurate strategy for risk assessment, and vulnerability patching/prioritization. Given the extensive amount of prior work in cyber-security and other security-related domains, it would appear that there are numerous approaches that could be utilized against this problem. Unfortunately, these approaches are lacking due to multiple reasons, which we will explore in the next section. The paucity of work related to the particular problem of "attack chaining" is perhaps reflective of conventional threat assessment paradigms that consider and prioritize vulnerabilities in isolation. However, it is increasingly obvious that this paradigm neither takes into account adversarial behaviour in the real world, nor the dependencies between vulnerabilities. Additionally, given that ready-made "chained exploits" are easily obtained on illicit marketplaces in the form of malware and exploit kits, a novel approach that can accurately model these kinds of threats is required.

7.2   Related Work

In recent years, many contributions have been made in the field of cyber-security, using attacker–defender models to inform defender actions. In the field of network security, work has been done to address problems related to optimal network security hardening [12] and resource allocation for malicious packet detection [13]. Work has also been done on modelling adversary-initiated cascading failures in power grid [14] and critical infrastructure systems [15], to identify defender strategies to mitigate these failures. In these papers, the systems are modelled as a graph of nodes,

---

[1] https://archive.org/details/Stuxnet.

with the adversary aiming to disrupt the network by initiation actions against specific nodes. When compared to our work, there are some differences. The first is that our approach can be used to model both a single system and a network of systems, and the second is that we model the actual mechanics of the adversary's attack, instead of merely treating it as a binary action (i.e. a node is either attacked or it is not). This allows us to identify a minimal set of vulnerabilities to patch (subject to cost constraints), to prevent the attacker from gaining certain capabilities.

The work presented in both [16, 17] are close to ours in that their models take into account the sequence of actions required to exploit a system. However, model dynamics and approaches are significantly different. The work in [18] bears some similarity to ours, in that the attacker's aim is to exploit a specific vulnerability. However, the paper models attacks and vulnerabilities at a high level, and does not take into account specific capabilities associated with vulnerabilities; it can also only handle an attack against a single type of vulnerability at a time.

The application of game theory to security situations was first popularized by [19], where it was applied to the problem of airport security. Since then, it has been applied to many other scenarios as well, including the placement of security checkpoints [20], assignment of air marshals to flights [21], and more pertinently, to cyber-security [22–24]. While our work also identifies the defender's optimal strategy, we do not model attacker–defender interactions as a Bayesian game [19–21] and the details of our model are inherently different. Our model is deterministic and focuses on the mechanics of the attacks themselves, using an iterative approach to identify the overall set of capabilities gained by the attacker, by taking into account their initial capabilities, the exploits used, and dependencies between vulnerabilities on the system. The work in [24] is slightly similar to ours, given that their model also considers how capabilities gained by an attacker after exploiting a vulnerability, can be used to further increase their chances of compromising the system. However, this model does not distinguish between individual capabilities and thus cannot take the attacker's capabilities into account when determining their ability to compromise a system.

Approaches involving the use of exploit preconditions and postconditions to model sequential attacks were previously introduced in [6, 7], where Petri nets [25] are used to model cyber-attacks. While the approach can determine the overall set of capabilities gained by the attacker through the use of sequential exploits, it is necessary to construct a coverability graph [26, 27] to do so. In comparison, our model provides a simpler solution to the same problem through the use of a simple fixed-point operator that converges in polynomial time. We further note that our approach has another key advantage: it is able to identify the minimal set of vulnerabilities (subject to cost constraints) to be patched in order to prevent the attacker from gaining certain capabilities.

Regarding effective vulnerability patching strategies, there are examples of similar work from [28–30]. However, the key difference is that the aforementioned models are stochastic, and largely based on metrics such as vulnerability discovery rate, attack rates and aspects of the vulnerability life cycle itself. Hence, these approaches are far more general and when identifying effective patching strategies do not take into account the specific capabilities that attackers wish to gain.

To the best of our knowledge, our work presents the first approach that models both the attacker's intent and the mechanics of an attack and uses that information to identify an optimal defensive-strategy aimed at preventing access to specific capabilities. In our work, we model specific actions that an attacker can take against a given system and the degree to which they can compromise that system, by taking into account the attacker's capabilities, the exploits used, and the dependencies between vulnerabilities on the system. The modelling of exploit application in an iterative manner also matches real-world attacker behaviour. The attacker's activities are also driven by unconventional sources of information (specifically darknets in this case) and do not necessarily depend on information directly related to defender systems. Furthermore, the recent rise of darknet markets specializing in zero-day exploits allows us to integrate information unavailable to previous work.

8 Conclusion

Our results not only demonstrate that our model and associated algorithms are viable in practice, but that they can be easily interpreted according to an intuitive, real-world understanding of both attacker and defender behaviours. The results provide useful information for defenders of these systems that can be used to assess overall system vulnerability, its susceptibility to various types of attackers, and the maximum amount of damage that can be caused by those attackers. Additionally, the results show that the model is able to identify effective and optimal patching strategies that are also intuitive and make sense in a real-world context. The information provided by this model can be used for the development of intelligent agents that can learn defense and contingency strategies based on exploit and vulnerability information. It also allows for the development of agents that can perform risk analyses using this same information; this makes it easy for security professionals and administrators to immediately assess the vulnerability of systems in a quantifiable way, allowing them to make informed decisions regarding security policies, patching strategies and other contingency actions.

In future work, we plan to develop a method to automatically identify the capabilities that comprise vulnerability preconditions and postconditions, from the vulnerability's description or security advisory. We also plan to run more experiments that take into account additional data, such as exploit costs gathered from exploit kits sold on darknet markets [31].

9 Questions

1. Explain vulnerabilities and capabilities that are required to launch the privilege escalation attack?
2. What is a passive attack surface?

3. Define an 'exploit chain' and how it is related to 'set of capabilities'?
4. Explain at a high-level how to determine which exploits are applicable in a given scenario.
5. How are the defender and attacker challenges different? Explain your answer with an example.
6. Describe how you can determine the cost function of a vulnerability?
7. Explain at least two algorithms that can be used to solve the preferred defence-strategy.
8. What is an effective way of pruning vulnerabilities that need not or cannot be part of the solution?
9. Compare Depth First Search with A* based approached in terms of optimal solution.
10. Explain the mentioned implementation with respect to exploit application operator?

Acknowledgements This work was supported by ASU Global Security Initiative (GSI) and the Office of Naval Research (ONR) Neptune program.

References

1. Shakarian P, Shakarian J (2016) Considerations for the development of threat prediction in the cyber domain. In: AAAI-16 workshop on artificial intelligence for cyber security
2. Robertson J, Diab A, Marin E, Nunes E, Paliath V, Shakarian J, Shakarian P (2016) Darknet mining and game theory for enhanced cyber threat intelligence. Cyber Def Rev 1(2)
3. Robertson JJ, Paliath V, Shakarian J, Thart A, Shakarian P (2016) Data driven game theoretic cyber threat mitigation. Innov Appl Artif Intell 28
4. Shim W, Allodi L, Massacci F (2012) Crime pays if you are just an average hacker. In: 2012 international conference on cyber security (CyberSecurity), pp 62–68. https://doi.org/10.1109/CyberSecurity.2012.15
5. Paliath V, Shakarian P (2016) Modeling cyber-attacks on industrial control systems. In: 2016 IEEE conference on intelligence and security informatics (ISI). IEEE, pp 316–318
6. Chen TM, Sanchez-Aarnoutse JC, Buford J (2011) Petri net modeling of cyber-physical attacks on smart grid. IEEE Trans Smart Grid 2(4):741–749
7. Henry MH, Layer RM, Snow KZ, Zaret DR (2009) Evaluating the risk of cyber attacks on scada systems via petri net analysis with application to hazardous liquid loading operations. In: IEEE conference on technologies for homeland security, 2009. HST'09. IEEE, pp 607–614
8. Paliath V, Shakarian P (2018) Modeling sequential cyber-attacks against computer systems via vulnerability dependencies (submitted)
9. Shakarian P (2011) Stuxnet: Cyberwar revolution in military affairs. Small Wars J
10. Karnouskos S (2011) Stuxnet worm impact on industrial cyber-physical system security. In: IECON 2011-37th annual conference on ieee industrial electronics society. IEEE, pp 4490–4494
11. Falliere N, Murchu LO, Chien E (2011) W32. stuxnet dossier. White paper, Symantec Corp., Security Response, vol 5
12. Durkota K, Lisy V, Kiekintveld C, Bosansky B (2015) Game-theoretic algorithms for optimal network security hardening using attack graphs. In: Proceedings of the 2015 international conference on autonomous agents and multiagent systems. International Foundation for Autonomous Agents and Multiagent Systems, pp 1773–1774

13. Vaněk O, Yin Z, Jain M, Bošanský B, Tambe M, Pěchouček M (2012) Game-theoretic resource allocation for malicious packet detection in computer networks. In: Proceedings of the 11th international conference on autonomous agents and multiagent systems-volume 2. International Foundation for Autonomous Agents and Multiagent Systems, pp 905–912

14. Shakarian P, Lei H, Lindelauf R (2014) Power grid defense against malicious cascading failure. In: Proceedings of the 2014 international conference on autonomous agents and multi-agent systems. International Foundation for Autonomous Agents and Multiagent Systems, pp 813–820

15. Hayel Y, Zhu Q (2015) Resilient and secure network design for cyber attack-induced cascading link failures in critical infrastructures. In: 2015 49th annual conference on information sciences and systems (CISS). IEEE, pp 1–3

16. Marrone S, Nardone R, Tedesco A, D'Amore P, Vittorini V, Setola R, De Cillis F, Mazzocca N (2013) Vulnerability modeling and analysis for critical infrastructure protection applications. Int J Crit Infrastruct Prot 6(3):217–227

17. Flammini F, Gaglione A, Mazzocca N, Pragliola C (2014) Detect: a novel framework for the detection of attacks to critical infrastructures. In: Safety, reliability and risk analysis: theory, methods and applications-proceedings of ESREL08, pp 105–112

18. Spyridopoulos T, Maraslis K, Tryfonas T, Oikonomou G, Li S (2014) Managing cyber security risks in industrial control systems with game theory and viable system modelling. In: 2014 9th international conference on system of systems engineering (SOSE). IEEE, pp 266–271

19. Paruchuri P, Pearce JP, Marecki J, Tambe M, Ordonez F, Kraus S (2008) Playing games for security: an efficient exact algorithm for solving bayesian stackelberg games. In: Proceedings of the 7th international joint conference on autonomous agents and multiagent systems-volume 2. International Foundation for Autonomous Agents and Multiagent Systems, pp 895–902

20. Pita J, Jain M, Marecki J, Ordóñez F, Portway C, Tambe M, Western C, Paruchuri P, Kraus S (2008) Deployed armor protection: the application of a game theoretic model for security at the los angeles international airport. In: Proceedings of the 7th international joint conference on autonomous agents and multiagent systems: industrial track. International Foundation for Autonomous Agents and Multiagent Systems, pp 125–132

21. Jain M, Kardes E, Kiekintveld C, Ordónez F, Tambe M (2010) Security games with arbitrary schedules: a branch and price approach. In: AAAI

22. Okimoto T, Ikegai N, Inoue K, Okada H, Ribeiro T, Maruyama H (2013) Cyber security problem based on multi-objective distributed constraint optimization technique. In: 2013 43rd annual ieee/ifip conference on dependable systems and networks workshop (DSN-W). IEEE, pp 1–7

23. Alpcan T, Başar T (2010) Network security: a decision and game-theoretic approach. Cambridge University Press, Cambridge

24. Kusumastuti S, Cui J, Tambe A, John RS, A behavioral game modeling cyber attackers, defenders, and users

25. Peterson JL (1981) Petri net theory and the modeling of systems

26. Reisig W (2012) Petri nets: an introduction, vol 4. Springer, Berlin

27. Finkel A (1993) The minimal coverability graph for petri nets. Advances in petri nets 1993, pp 210–243

28. Okhravi H, Nicol D (2008) Evaluation of patch management strategies. Int J Comput Intell Theory Pract 3(2):109–117

29. Abraham S, Nair S (2017) Comparative analysis and patch optimization using the cyber security analytics framework. J Def Model Simulat, 1548512917705743

30. Miao L, Li S, Wang Z (2018) Optimal dissemination strategy of security patch based on differential game in social network. Wireless Pers Commun 98(1):237–249

31. Nunes E, Diab A, Gunn A, Marin E, Mishra V, Paliath V, Robertson J, Shakarian J, Thart A, Shakarian P (2016) Darknet and deepnet mining for proactive cybersecurity threat intelligence. arXiv:1607.08583

Vulnerability Detection and Analysis in Adversarial Deep Learning

Yi Shi, Yalin E. Sagduyu, Kemal Davaslioglu and Renato Levy

Abstract Machine learning has been applied in various information systems, but its vulnerability has not been well understood yet. This chapter studies vulnerability to *adversarial machine learning* in information systems such as online services with interfaces that accept user data inputs and return machine learning results such as labels. Two types of attacks are considered: *exploratory (or inference) attack* and *evasion attack*. In an *exploratory attack*, the adversary collects labels of input data from an online classifier and applies *deep learning* to train a functionally equivalent classifier without knowing the inner working of the target classifier. The vulnerability includes the theft of intellectual property (quantified by the statistical similarity of the target and inferred classifiers) and the support of other attacks built upon the inference results. An example of follow-up attacks is the *evasion attack*, where the adversary deceives the classifier into misclassifying input data samples that are systematically selected based on the classification scores from the inferred classier. This attack is strengthened by *generative adversarial networks* (GANs) and *adversarial perturbations* producing *synthetic data* samples that are likely to be misclassified. The vulnerability is measured by the increase in misdetection rates. This quantitative understanding of the vulnerability in machine learning systems provides valuable insights into designing defence mechanisms against adversarial machine learning.

Y. Shi (✉) · Y. E. Sagduyu · K. Davaslioglu · R. Levy
Intelligent Automation, Inc., 15400 Calhoun Drive, Rockville, MD 20855, USA
e-mail: yshi@i-a-i.com

Y. E. Sagduyu
e-mail: ysagduyu@i-a-i.com

K. Davaslioglu
e-mail: kdavaslioglu@i-a-i.com

R. Levy
e-mail: rlevy@i-a-i.com

© Springer International Publishing AG, part of Springer Nature 2018
S. Parkinson et al. (eds.), *Guide to Vulnerability Analysis for Computer Networks and Systems*, Computer Communications and Networks,
https://doi.org/10.1007/978-3-319-92624-7_9

1 Introduction

Information systems are susceptible to various exploits and attacks that range from passing phishing emails through spam filters to stealing intellectual property. These threats apply not only to traditional programs or services where all behaviours are programmed manually, but also to *machine learning*-based systems that are becoming increasingly prevalent in current information systems. For example, cybersecurity systems started applying machine learning to analyse and detect malicious traffic components as automated means for intrusion detection and prevention [1].

Facilitated by the availability of fast hardware and large datasets, *deep learning* has emerged as a powerful machine learning approach that can solve complex problems such as defeating the best players in complex games; e.g. Google's AlphaGo [2] defeated a Go master. Deep learning involves training *deep neural network* structures to learn to approximate complex functions that map input data to outputs (e.g. assign labels to data samples in classification problems). As information systems start relying more on machine learning, adversaries turn their attention to directly attack the underlying machine learning functionalities that involve sensitive and proprietary information, e.g. training data, machine learning algorithm and its hyperparameters, and functionality of underlying tasks. One seminal example in image recognition systems is that adversarial images generated by slightly perturbing real images via deep learning have fooled a state-of-the-art image classifier into recognizing a perturbed panda image as a gibbon [3].

Attacks on machine learning, often referred to as *adversarial machine learning* [4–6], have raised the need to understand how effective machine learning can take place under the presence of an adversary. One particular application of adversarial machine learning is tailored to online information systems, in which the adversaries interact with systems through application programming interfaces (APIs). Typically offered online, software as a service (SaaS) or software on demand has become a popular software distribution model that hosts applications and makes them available to customers over the Internet. Without revealing source codes or inner workings of the underlying algorithms, these services are usually provided via subscriptions, while still offering free public access either in trial periods or subject to rate limitations on the frequency and volume of access to services. This paradigm allows adversaries to seek the opportunity to attack machine learning systems. Clear understanding of vulnerabilities to these attacks is of paramount importance to secure deployment of machine learning systems.

While the field of adversarial machine learning is growing, the security limitations of machine learning ranging from *intellectual property theft* to *system malfunction* are not well understood yet and deserve further study to identify effects of adversarial machine learning and provide the foundation for appropriate attack detection and mitigation techniques. To improve system security, it is critical to quantify the *vulnerability* of machine learning to various exploits and attacks, and assess the impact of this vulnerability on tasks performed by machine learning.

This chapter studies detecting and analysing vulnerabilities of information systems to adversarial machine learning. Deep learning is the focus of this study to understand the practical limits on adversaries when they attack machine learning-based systems. An image classification service is considered, while the design guidelines are generic and readily applicable to other types of data such as text. Two types of attacks based on adversarial deep learning are considered. The first one is the *exploratory attack*, where the adversary aims to infer information on the machine learning system under attack without knowledge of the original classifier's algorithm, parameters and training datasets [7]. A *deep neural network* is trained by the adversary for that purpose. The second one is the *evasion attack*, where the adversary aims to fool the machine learning systems into making wrong decisions [8]. The adversary first runs data samples through the inferred classifier and then sends to the target classifier only those samples that are assigned classification scores close to the decision boundary. Two approaches of *generative adversarial networks* (GANs) [9] and *adversarial perturbations* [3] based on deep learning are used to strengthen the evasion attack by generating additional synthetic data samples that are likely to be misclassified.

The potential success of these attacks is quantified as indicators of vulnerabilities in the underlying machine learning system. The vulnerability to the exploratory attack is quantified as the statistical similarity of the output labels returned by the target classifier and inferred classifier. The vulnerability to the evasion attack is quantified as the misdetection error incurred by the target classifier with respect to real and synthetic adversarial inputs. Based on the insights gained through vulnerability analysis, defence mechanisms can be developed against adversarial deep learning. The impact of adversarial deep learning is diverse and far-reaching beyond cybersecurity applications. Various other domains such as wireless or mobile security benefit from the insights gained through the analysis of vulnerability to adversarial deep learning in information systems.

The rest of this chapter is organized as follows. Section 2 presents basic principles of deep learning. Section 3 introduces the problem of adversarial machine learning. Section 4 analyses the vulnerability of machine learning to exploratory attacks. Section 5 analyses the vulnerability of machine learning to evasion attacks. Section 6 analyses the impact of adversarial synthetic inputs in evasion attacks. Section 7 describes insights on defence mechanisms based on vulnerability analysis. Section 8 discusses extension of adversarial machine learning to other domains. Section 9 presents end-of-chapter teaching questions. Section 10 presents end-of-chapter research questions.

2 Deep Learning

Deep learning refers to training a deep neural network. Deep learning can be applied to many applications ranging from detection to prediction. In this chapter, we consider classification tasks that are trained to assign a label or a class to each data sample.

A sample s can be described by a set of M features, $F_s = \{f_s^m\}_{m=1}^M$, and belongs to a class $C(s) \in \mathscr{C}$. A classifier T will classify a given sample s as the class $T(s) \in \mathscr{C}$.

Ideally, a classifier should provide the correct class of any given sample s, i.e. $T(s) = C(s)$. However, even with sophisticated machine learning algorithms and large training datasets, there might be still samples with $T(s) \neq C(s)$; i.e. they might be misclassified. We use error probability to measure the accuracy of a classifier. In particular, we measure the following errors for a given set of test data with respect to the ground truth:

1. Error probability on class i is given by

$$e_i(T) = \frac{\sum_{j \in \mathscr{C}}^{j \neq i} e_{ij}(T)}{n_i}, \tag{1}$$

where $e_{ij}(T)$ is the number of samples that are in class i but are classified as class j (i.e. $C(s) = i$ and $T(s) = j$) and n_i is the total number of samples in class i (i.e. $C(s) = i$).

2. Overall error probability is given by

$$e(T) = \frac{\sum_{i \in \mathscr{C}} \sum_{j \in \mathscr{C}}^{j \neq i} e_{ij}(T)}{\sum_{i \in \mathscr{C}} n_i}. \tag{2}$$

In addition to deep learning, there are many other types of machine learning algorithms, such as Naive Bayes and Support Vector Machine (SVM), that can also be applied for the classification problem. We will apply them at the classifier under the attack.

1. Naive Bayes is a probabilistic classifier based on applying Bayes' theorem with (naive) independence assumptions between the features. Due to this assumption, it is important to select features that they are (almost) independent. Note that such a requirement does not exist for deep learning, which makes feature selection easier. Naive Bayes builds conditional probabilities of features (represented as vectors of feature values) under each class and determines the most likely class for each sample.

2. SVM is a non-probabilistic classifier that represents samples in training data as points in a high-dimensional feature space and assumes that points in different classes can be separated by hyperplanes. Each hyperplane is optimized to maximize the gap between the hyperplane and points in different classes separated by this hyperplane. SVM maps samples in test data into the same space and predicts their classes based on the optimal hyperplanes. Note that the hyperplane assumption does not exist for deep learning and thus it can use any surfaces to separate points in different classes.

Table 1 shows the notation used in this chapter. In the subsequent section, we will present different deep learning techniques for the classification problem.

Table 1 Notation

$\hat{\mathscr{A}}_{ij}$	The attack region to misclassify class i samples as in class j
b_j	A constant bias term used by neuron j
$\mathbf{b}_l$	The vector of biases at the lth layer
$C(s)$	The class of sample s
$\mathscr{C}$	The set of all classes
$d_{ij}(T)$	The number of samples that have different classes by T and $\hat{T}$
$d_i(T, \hat{T})$	The difference between T and $\hat{T}$ on class i
$d(T, \hat{T})$	The difference between T and $\hat{T}$
$d(\underline{r}, \hat{\mathscr{R}})$	The distance between a point $\underline{r}$ and a region $\hat{\mathscr{R}}$
$d(\underline{r}, \underline{x})$	The distance between two points $\underline{r}$ and $\underline{x}$
D	The discriminator network in GAN
$e_{ij}(T)$	The number of samples that are in class i but are classified as class j by T
$e_i(T)$	T's error probability on class i
$e(T)$	T's overall error probability
$f(\mathbf{x}_0; \theta)$	The mapping function of FNN
f_s^m	The mth feature of sample s
F_s	$= \{f_s^m\}$, a set of features of sample s
G	The generator network in GAN
$G(z)$	The generator output for z
$J(\theta, s)$	The cost used to train the neural network
M	The number of samples in evasion attack
n	The number of hidden layers
n_i	The number of samples in class i
$\hat{n}_i$	The number of samples classified by T as in class i
N	The number of queries for exploratory attack
N_{class}	The number of classes
$\mathbb{P}_{data}$	The distribution of input data r
$\mathbb{P}_z$	The model distribution of noise z
$\underline{r}(s)$	A vector of T's scores for sample s
$\underline{\hat{r}}(s)$	A vector of $\hat{T}$'s scores for sample s
$r_i(s)$	The score for sample s being in class i
$\mathscr{R}_i$	The region of T's scores for samples in class i
$\hat{\mathscr{R}}_i$	The region of $\hat{T}$'s scores for samples in class i
s	A sample
T	The target classifier under attack
$\hat{T}$	The inferred classifier
$T(s)$	The identified class for sample s by T
w_{ji}	The weight from neuron i to neuron j
W_l	The matrix of weights at the lth layer
$\mathbf{x}_l$	The output of lth layer
y_j	The output of neuron j

(continued)

Table 1 (continued)

z	A noise input to generator G
$\sigma(x)$	A nonlinear activation function used in neural networks
θ_l	$= \{W_l, \mathbf{b}_l\}$, weight and biases at the lth layer
θ	$= \{\theta_1, \ldots, \theta_L\}$, the set of all parameters of FNN
$\hat{\theta}$	The threshold for a binary classification problem
ϕ	The paragraph to define an attack region
$\Delta(s)$	The minimum perturbation to change the class predicted by T for a sample s

2.1 Artificial Neural Networks

An *artificial neural network* is a machine for computing some function, and consists of simple elements called neurons that are joined by weighted connections also known as synapses. A neuron j performs a basic computation over its input synapses with weight w_{ji} (connecting neurons i and j) and a bias term b_j, and outputs a single scalar value y_j, which can be interpreted as its activation, or a firing rate. For example, the following computation is commonly used:

$$y_j = \sigma\left(b_j + \sum_{i \neq j} w_{ji} y_i\right), \tag{3}$$

where $\sigma(x)$ is some nonlinear activation function such as the sigmoid function

$$\sigma(x) = 1/\left(1 + e^{-x}\right). \tag{4}$$

Figure 1 shows the common feedforward neural network (FNN) architecture (topology), where circles and lines denote neurons and synapses, respectively, and the neurons are arranged in layers. The activations of neurons in the input layer (left) are set externally, while the activations of the hidden layer neurons (middle) and output layer neurons (right) are computed as specified above; the latter represent the result of the network's computation.

For the classification problem, the activations of neurons in the input layer are set by features of a sample, while the computed results at the output layer show the class for a sample. Provided that the hidden layer has a sufficiently large number of neurons, this simple architecture can (in theory) approximate any mathematical function to an arbitrary small error probability via its synaptic weights, which is called the *universal approximation theorem* [10, 11]. However, for many real-world problems, a good approximation would often require a prohibitively large number of hidden layer neurons.

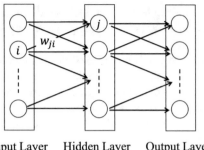

Input Layer   Hidden Layer   Output Layer

Fig. 1 Structure of an artificial neural network

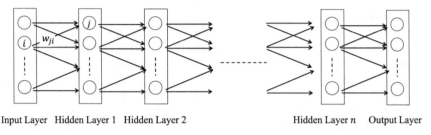

Input Layer   Hidden Layer 1   Hidden Layer 2   Hidden Layer n Output Layer

Fig. 2 Deep neural network

2.2 Deep Neural Networks

To overcome the challenge of a prohibitively large number of hidden layer neurons, neural network designs have focused on deep architectures that contain many hidden layers (as shown in Fig. 2). The training of such architectures is called *deep learning* and can be time-consuming, because learning is typically achieved through gradient descent on the network's output error (defined as a function of its weights), and the components of this gradient are often very small for the weights of connections that are far away from the input layer, which is known as the *vanishing gradient problem*. However, the process is now facilitated by the availability of fast hardware and large datasets. Once trained, the layers of the deep neural network can transform raw data into representations that become progressively more sophisticated and abstract with each layer, allowing the network to produce complex decisions (e.g. the class for a sample) at the output layer. As a result, deep learning has achieved unprecedented results in areas such as speech processing, machine translation and computer vision and is presently being utilized within (or integrated into) many practical applications and products.

There are various types of neural networks. Three main types are as follows:

1. *Feedforward neural network (FNN)*, also called multilayer perceptron (MLP), consists of n hidden layers and describes a mapping of an input vector through n iterative processing steps, as shown in Fig. 2. FNNs will be used primarily in this

chapter for adversarial deep learning and will be discussed in more detail in the next section to provide insights into training and testing in deep neural network structures.

2. *Convolutional neural network (CNN)* [12] connects a hidden neuron to only a subset of neurons in the previous layer such that multiple hidden neurons share the same weights, thus greatly reducing the space of parameters to be learned. CNNs can be effectively applied to machine learning problems with spatially correlated data. In the CNN architecture, the 2-D convolutional layer applies sliding filters to the input. The max pooling layer progressively reduces the spatial size of the representation and controls overfitting. The batch normalization layer normalizes each input channel across a mini-batch to speed up training and reduce the sensitivity to network initialization. CNNs will be used primarily in this chapter for synthetic data generation purposes.

3. *Recursive neutral network* allows sequence processing where the synaptic connections form cycles, and enables activation to persist between time steps. A limitation of most deep neural networks such as FNN and CNN is that they are memoryless; thus, every input is processed independently of any other inputs, and the network is not able to take advantage of temporal patterns within an input sequence, when making a decision. A particular type of RNN is the long short-term memory network (LSTM) [13], where memory neurons store information through self-activation and their activity is modulated by specialized gate neurons. The input gates determine the extent to which the current input should be stored in memory; the forget gates determine how much memory is retained between time steps, and finally, the output gate modulates the effect of memory upon the current output. Through its memory and gating mechanisms, LSTM is able to remember relevant information for arbitrary lengths of time and capture long-range patterns within data sequence.

2.3 Feedforward Neural Networks

An FNN learns to map an input vector $\mathbf{x}_0$ to the output vector $\mathbf{x}_n$ (namely, labels) by following n steps (one for each layer):

$$\mathbf{x}_l = f_l(\mathbf{x}_{l-1}; \theta_l), \quad l = 1, \ldots, n, \tag{5}$$

where the set of parameters (weights W_l and biases $\mathbf{b}_l$) in the lth layer is denoted by θ_l and the lth layer performs the mapping

$$f_l(\mathbf{x}_{l-1}; \theta_l) = \sigma(W_l \mathbf{x}_{l-1} + \mathbf{b}_l). \tag{6}$$

In this mapping, W_l denotes the matrix of weights, $\mathbf{b}_l$ denotes the vector of biases, and $\sigma(\cdot)$ denotes an activation function. Examples of activation functions are rectifying linear unit (ReLU) activation function that defines the mapping

$$\sigma(u_i) = \max(0, u_i) \tag{7}$$

and softmax activation function (a generalization of the logistic function) that defines the mapping

$$\sigma(u_i) = e^{u_i} / \sum_j e^{u_j}. \tag{8}$$

An FNN is trained using labelled training data, i.e. a set of input–output vector pairs $(\mathbf{x}_{0,i}, \mathbf{x}_{n,i}^*)$, $i = 1, \ldots, S$, where $\mathbf{x}_{n,i}^*$ is the desired output of the neural network when $\mathbf{x}_{0,i}$ is used as input. The goal of training is to minimize a loss function such as mean squared error or cross-entropy error. The set of parameters θ are derived by applying stochastic gradient descent (SGD). The gradient is computed through the *backpropagation algorithm* that consists of two phases: propagation and weight update [14].

A deep learning classifier provides not only a decision on whether a sample s is in class $i \in \mathscr{C}$, i.e. $T(s) = i$, but also a set of scores $\underline{r}(s)$, where $r_i(s)$ is the score for sample s under class $i \in \mathscr{C}$. One example of score is the output of the softmax function at the output layer. After parameter optimization in the training phase to determine decision boundaries, the region of all $\underline{r}(s)$ values is divided into subregions $\mathscr{R}_i$ for $i \in \mathscr{C}$, such that if $\underline{r}(s) \in \mathscr{R}_i$, then the decision $T(s) = i$ is made. Numerical results in this chapter are based on the implementation of deep learning with the Microsoft Cognitive Toolkit (CNTK) [15] and TensorFlow [16].

3 Adversarial Deep Learning

A machine learning algorithm or an information system built upon one can be "attacked" in several ways [4–6, 17] (illustrated in Fig. 3):

1. *Exploratory* attacks, e.g. [18–20], occur after the algorithm has been trained, and attempt to uncover information about its inner workings, in order to identify vulnerability of the algorithm. This attack may attempt to extract several factors such as

   - the decision boundary used by the algorithm (e.g. hyperplanes of the Support Vector Machine (SVM) algorithm),
   - a general set of rules that the algorithm follows,
   - a set of logical or probabilistic properties about the algorithm, or
   - information about the data that was used (or not used) to train the algorithm.

2. *Evasion* attacks, e.g. [21–23], are also launched upon trained algorithms, and involve providing the algorithm with input (test) data that will result in an incorrect output.

   - A classic example of an evasion attack is the generation of spam emails that will fool a trained filter into accepting them as legitimate.

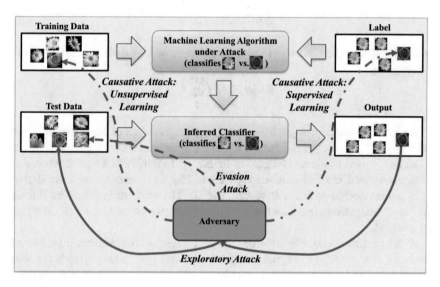

Fig. 3 Adversarial machine learning

- Another example is the creation of social bots (e.g. automated tweet generators) that will fool bot detectors.
- Evasion attacks can be made more effective by exploiting vulnerabilities identified via exploratory attacks, or created via causative attacks.

3. *Causative* attacks (also known as poisoning attacks), e.g. [24, 25], attempt to
   provide incorrect training data to the algorithm, such that it does not learn the
   intended function.

   - In supervised learning, this may be achieved by mislabelling the training data,
     e.g., in adversarial active learning [5], where the algorithm requests training
     labels from potentially untrusted sources.
   - In reinforcement learning, a causative attack can take place by providing incor-
     rect rewards or punishments.
   - In unsupervised learning, the attack can be launched by sampling training
     examples in a biased way, such that they do not reflect the underlying statistical
     distribution.

The chapter focuses on exploratory and evasion attacks that target the test phase
(instead of training phase) of machine learning. In the next two sections, we will
provide more discussion on exploratory and evasion attacks.

4   Exploratory Attack

Many systems provide online services that allow a user to provide input data (e.g. through an API or through a Web interface) and observe the output (e.g. labels as classification output). Such systems are vulnerable to *evasion*, *exploratory*, and in some cases *causative* attacks based on adversarial machine learning. In this section, we address exploratory attacks. The state of the art focuses on *model inversion attacks* [18–20], where the adversary typically knows the type and structure of the classifier, and attempts to learn the model parameters. In this chapter, we consider a generalized case for the adversary and let the adversary launch an attack to an online classification service by building *a functionally equivalent classifier without knowing the type, structure and parameters of the classifier*. This is called *black-box attack* [7, 26].

As shown in Fig. 4, the adversary launches a three-step attack to build a functionally equivalent classifier:

1. The adversary polls the target classifier with input data.
2. The adversary observes labels returned by the target classifier.

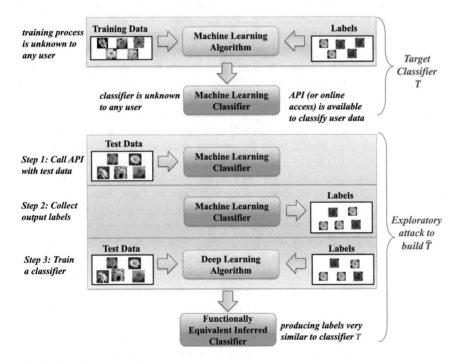

Fig. 4 Steps of an exploratory attack

3. The adversary uses the input data and the labels to train a deep learning classifier and optimize its hyperparameters to minimize the difference between the trained classifier and the target classifier.

The above attack trains a deep learning classifier that is functionally equivalent to (i.e. produces high-fidelity labels similar to) the classifier under attack. The functionally equivalent machine built by the adversary implicitly infers training data, type of the classifier and hyperparameters of the classifier. For testing, another set of input data is given to the classifier under attack and the classifier that is built by the adversary. The success of the adversary is measured by statistical similarity of labels returned by these two classifiers.

This attack results in classifier theft and poses a risk to the intellectual property of private companies and other organizations which have invested a significant amount of time and effort to gather training data for a classifier, to train the classifier and to tune its hyperparameters. If the classifier is stolen, then an organization's competitive advantage is reduced; in the long term, the possibility of classifier theft can discourage organizations from developing services based on machine learning techniques. Additionally, once a classifier is stolen, the adversary is free to analyse it (with an unlimited number of queries), in order to identify its potential weaknesses, as well as its underlying functionality. This can allow the adversary to subsequently launch an evasion attack against the original classifier, or to infer private information about the organization that developed it (such as its priorities and resources) or the underlying training data.

We consider an example of classification service on image data. A flower dataset [27] with images of daisies (class 1) and roses (class 2) is used to build the target classifier T. Note that this dataset has images of other flower types. Without loss of generality, we consider only daisy and rose images for the binary classification problem. This dataset has images in different picture formats and sizes (namely, different number of pixels). To build the same set of features for each image, we first scale all images to the same size and then change them to the common RGB format (i.e. each pixel has three values to be used as features). With these preprocessing, we can represent all images by the same number of features. Then, classifier T is built by applying deep learning with FNN on 638 training images and 636 test images.

In the black-box exploratory attack, the information of original classifier T is not available to the adversary. In addition, the adversary does not know the label of each sample. The adversary can only query some samples and collect the labels returned by T, and then use this information as training data to infer T by building a functionally equivalent classifier $\hat{T}$. Suppose that an adversary performs N queries for samples $s_1, s_2, \ldots, s_N$ and obtains $T(s_1), T(s_2), \ldots, T(s_N)$. For training and testing, N samples are split into two sets of data.

Deep learning is applied to build a classifier $\hat{T}$. The region of deep learning scores $\underline{\hat{r}}$ by classifier $\hat{T}$ is divided into subregions $\hat{\mathcal{R}}_i$ for $i \in \mathcal{C}$, such that if $\underline{\hat{r}}(s) \in \hat{\mathcal{R}}$ for a sample s, $\hat{T}(s) = i$. In a binary classification problem, deep learning provides a score within $[0, 1]$ for each sample (i.e. $\underline{\hat{r}}$ is one-dimensional) and uses a threshold

$\hat{\theta}$ to classify samples. We aim to minimize the difference between $\hat{T}$ and T, which can be quantified as follows:

1. Average difference on class i:

$$d_i(T, \hat{T}) = \frac{\sum_{j \in \mathscr{C}}^{j \neq i} d_{ij}(T, \hat{T})}{\hat{n}_i}, \qquad (9)$$

   where $d_{ij}(T, \hat{T})$ is the number of samples with $T(s) = i$ and $\hat{T}(s) = j$, and $\hat{n}_i$ is the number of samples in test data with $T(s) = i$.

2. Average overall difference:

$$d(T, \hat{T}) = \frac{\sum_{i \in \mathscr{C}} \sum_{j \in \mathscr{C}}^{j \neq i} d_{ij}(T, \hat{T})}{\sum_{i \in \mathscr{C}} \hat{n}_i}. \qquad (10)$$

5 Evasion Attack

After the exploratory attack, the adversary can perform further attacks such as the *evasion attack* [21, 23], which aims to fool a target classifier into classifying selective input (test) data to the wrong output (label).

The preliminary step is to apply deep learning to infer the target classifier T and build a classifier $\hat{T}$ from the exploratory attack, which was discussed in the previous section. Using $\hat{T}$, we design an *evasion attack* by selecting a set of M samples to cause a large number of misclassifications from class i to class j by T (i.e. $C(s) = i$ and $T(s) = j$ for a sample s). Note that the objective can be changed to selecting a set of M samples to cause a large number of misclassifications (from any class to another one) by T (i.e. $C(s) \neq T(s)$ for many s). The goal of the adversary is to increase the misclassification error $e_{ij}(T)$ for given pairs of classes i and j or increase the overall misclassification error $\sum_i \sum_{j \neq i} e_{ij}(T)$ for all classes.

This evasion attack for given i and j follows three steps (shown in Fig. 5):

1. Apply classifier $\hat{T}$ on a set of test samples to obtain a deep learning score $\hat{\underline{r}}(s)$ on each sample s.
2. Determine an "attack region" of scores, $\hat{\mathscr{A}}_{ij}$, to cause misclassification from class i to class j.
3. Feed samples s with scores $\underline{r}(s) \in \hat{\mathscr{A}}_{ij}$ to the classifier T under attack.

The region $\hat{\mathscr{A}}_{ij}$ is defined by two conditions:

1. A sample s with $\underline{r}(s) \in \hat{\mathscr{A}}_{ij}$ is to be classified in class j by $\hat{T}$ (i.e. $T(s) = j$).
2. There is "significant" chance that s actually belongs to class i (i.e. $C(s) = i$).

Condition 1 means $\hat{\mathscr{A}}_{ij} \subseteq \hat{\mathscr{R}}_j$. Condition 2 can be interpreted as deep learning scores $\hat{\underline{r}}(s)$ being "close" to $\hat{\mathscr{R}}_i$. We need a distance measure $d(\underline{r}, \hat{\mathscr{R}})$ for a point $\underline{r}$

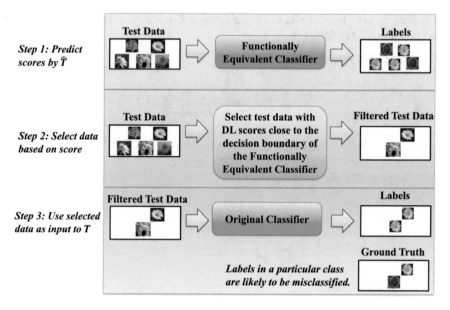

Fig. 5 Steps of an evasion attack

and a region $\hat{\mathscr{R}}$ in a high-dimensional space to define "close". For this purpose, we first define $d(\underline{r}, \underline{x})$ for two points as

$$\|\underline{r} - \underline{x}\|_2 = \sqrt{\sum_m (r_m - x_m)^2}, \tag{11}$$

where r_m and x_m are the mth element of $\underline{r}$ and $\underline{x}$, and define

$$d(\underline{r}, \hat{\mathscr{R}}) = \min_{\underline{x} \in \hat{\mathscr{R}}} d(\underline{r}, \underline{x}). \tag{12}$$

Then, "close" is defined by $d(\underline{\hat{r}}(s), \hat{\mathscr{R}}_i) \le \phi$, where parameter $\phi > 0$. As a result, the attack region is characterized by

$$\hat{\mathscr{A}}_{ij} = \{\underline{\hat{r}}(s) : \underline{\hat{r}}(s) \in \hat{\mathscr{R}}_j, d(\underline{\hat{r}}(s), \hat{\mathscr{R}}_i) \le \phi\}. \tag{13}$$

In the case that i and j are not given, the attack region is specified as the union of individual attack regions, namely $\bigcup_i \bigcup_{j \neq i} \hat{\mathscr{A}}_{ij}$.

In a binary classification problem, deep learning provides a score within $[0, 1]$ for each sample by $\hat{T}$ and uses a threshold $\hat{\theta}$ to classify samples, i.e. $\hat{\mathscr{R}}_1 = [\hat{\theta}, 1]$ or $\hat{\mathscr{R}}_2 = [0, \hat{\theta}]$. Then, the attack region $\hat{\mathscr{A}}_{ij}$ for $i = 1$ and $j = 2$ in (13) is simplified to $\hat{\mathscr{A}}_{12} = [\hat{\theta} - \phi, \hat{\theta}]$.

Table 2 Error rate $e_{12}(T)$ for classifying image samples with scores from different attack regions

Attack region of scores	Error rate $e_{12}(T)$ (%)
[0, 0.3]	13.57
[0.3, 0.6]	29.17
[0.6, 0.8]	20.00
[0.8, 1]	4.32

For numerical results on image classification in the previous section, we evaluate the performance of the adversary (without knowing ground truth) pursues to fool the target classifier into misclassifying samples from class 1 as class 2. We assume $\phi = \frac{\hat{\theta}}{2}$ such that the attack region becomes $\hat{\mathscr{A}}_{12} = [\frac{\hat{\theta}}{2}, \hat{\theta}]$, which translates to the particular region [0.3, 0.6]. For comparison purposes, we also check the error probabilities if the adversary feeds the target classifier with images that have scores in [0, 0.3], [0.6, 0.8] and [0.8, 1].

Results are shown in Table 2 for different attack regions. The error $e_{12}(T)$ on selected samples is the largest when we select images from the attack region $\hat{\mathscr{A}}_{12} = [0.3, 0.6]$. We conclude that evasion attack is more successful if it is launched in conjunction with an exploratory attack.

6 Extension of Evasion Attacks with Synthetic Data Inputs

A way of extending the evasion attack is generating *synthetic* data samples to be sent to the target classifier. In Sect. 5, we described how to select real data samples that are likely to be misclassified. To increase T's error rate, an adversary may examine a large number of samples by $\hat{T}$ and only select a small portion of them as input to T. As an extension, synthetic data can be also used in the evasion attack. This is an effective approach as many synthetic data samples can be generated and used as an input sample to T.

6.1 Evasion Attack with Synthetic Data Generated by the Generative Adversarial Network

A generative adversarial network (GAN) [3] can be used to generate synthetic data samples. There are two competing deep neural networks building the GAN structure:

1. The *generator network G* maps a source of noise to the input space and generates synthetic data samples, and
2. The *discriminator network D* distinguishes between received samples as synthetic or real.

The GAN trains the generator until it learns to fool the discriminator. Formally, the interactions between the generator and discriminator networks can be formulated as a *minimax game* problem:

$$\min_{G} \max_{D} \mathbb{E}_r \sim \mathbb{P}_{data}[\log(D(r))] + \mathbb{E}_z \sim \mathbb{P}_z[\log(1 - D(G(z)))],$$

where z is a noise input to generator G with a model distribution of $\mathbb{P}_z$ and $G(z)$ is the generator output. Input data r has distribution $\mathbb{P}_{data}$, and the discriminator D distinguishes between the real and generated samples. Both discriminator and generator networks are trained with backpropagation of error. We apply a deep convolutional GAN (DCGAN) to the flower dataset [16].

The discriminator takes image of size $140 \times 140 \times 3$ and feeds it to a three-layer cascade of convolutional layer, batch normalization and leaky ReLU activation function (leaky ReLU performs $f(x) = max(\alpha x, x)$ operation where α is the leakage, $\alpha = 0.2$). Each convolutional layer l has N_l distinct filters. We employed $N_1 = 64$, $N_2 = 128$ and $N_3 = 256$ filters. Each convolution filter has a size of 5×5 that performs convolution operation. The outputs of the convolutional layers are flattened and input to a fully connected layer with a single output which is activated by the sigmoid activation function. The generator of DCGAN takes in a noise of 200 dimensions and generates data that matches the statistics of the real data (in this case, daisy flowers). The generator is made up of four fractionally strided convolutions (performing the transpose of 2-D convolution filter) of 5×5 filter size and converts the noise representation into $140 \times 140 \times 3$ image. We train the DCGAN on the daisy flowers and generate synthetic images.

Examples of synthetic images (daisies) generated by GAN are shown in Fig. 6 for different numbers of iterations used to solve (14). These synthetic daisy images (class 1) are likely to be classified as rose (class 2). For instance, out of eight synthetic daisy images, two of them were misclassified as roses, while the original real image has a high classification score as daisy.

6.2 Evasion Attack with Synthetic Data Generated by Adversarial Perturbation

The evasion attack can be further strengthened by perturbing the selected real images and generating synthetic images that can be used to fool the classier under the evasion attack. While deep learning-based classifiers have been successfully applied to tasks such as image classification, recently they have been shown to be very unstable to adversarial perturbations of the data [3, 28–30], where an adversarial perturbation of a sample s is defined as the minimal perturbation $\Delta(s)$ that is sufficient to change the estimated label from $T(s)$ to $T(s + \Delta(s))$, i.e.

$$\Delta(s) = \min_{\delta} \|\delta\|_2 \tag{14}$$

Fig. 6 Synthetic images (daisies) generated by GAN; top figure: synthetic images from iteration number 44; middle figure: synthetic images from the iteration number 88; bottom figure: synthetic images from the iteration number 177

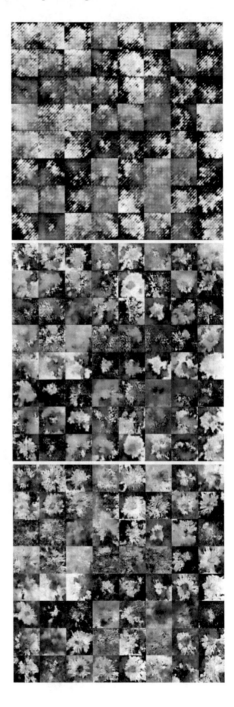

Fig. 7 Examples of
mislabelled images by the
classifier where original
(left) and perturbed (right)
images are shown side by
side along with the labels of
the classifier

True Label: daisy Perturbed Label: rose

True Label: daisy Perturbed Label: rose

True Label: daisy Perturbed Label: rose

True Label: daisy Perturbed Label: rose

True Label: rose Perturbed Label: daisy

True Label: rose Perturbed Label: daisy

True Label: rose Perturbed Label: daisy

True Label: rose Perturbed Label: daisy

subject to $T(s + \delta) \neq T(s)$. Similarly, the robustness of classifier T can be defined as

$$\rho_{adv} = \mathbb{E}_s \left[\Delta(s)/\|s\|_2 \right] , \tag{15}$$

where $\mathbb{E}_s$ is the expectation over distribution of data. With an adversarial perturbation of an image, the original image and the perturbed image can be labelled differently, which poses an important security problem. In [3], fast gradient sign method (FGSM) is proposed to efficiently compute adversarial perturbations for a given classifier. Even when the classifier is not fully known, we can use the estimated classifier. FGSM adds a perturbation vector

$$\delta = \varepsilon \, sign(\nabla_s J(\theta, s)) , \tag{16}$$

where ε is a small number, θ is the set of parameters of the neural network, and $J(\theta, s)$ is the cost used to train the neural network. The ε parameter perturbs an image such that it crosses over the decision boundary to be misclassified. If any adversarial attack detection mechanism is in place, this parameter needs to be finely tuned such that large perturbations may get detected and small perturbations may not be enough for misclassification. We apply the FGSM-based adversarial perturbation to the flower dataset [16]. The images are first resized to 140×140 dimensions and ε is taken as 0.2. A CNN is used. The first layer of convolutional filter consists of 64 filters with a kernel size of 8×8, which is followed by a layer of ReLU activation function to the output of the convolutional layer. The second and third convolutional layers also have 64 filters but with kernel sizes of 6×6 and 5×5, respectively. Both layers are also followed by a ReLU activation layer. The output of the third layer is flattened and input a fully connected layer to have N_{class} outputs, where N_{class} is the number of classes in the classifier. The classification accuracy of the classifier is 98%. When the perturbed images are presented to the classifier, the accuracy degrades to 40%. Figure 7 shows examples of the original images (left) and perturbed images (right) along with the labels of the classifier.

7 Defence Mechanisms

The analysis of vulnerability to adversarial machine learning presented in previous sections provides insights into the design of defence mechanisms. In general, defence mechanisms can be categorized into *proactive* and *reactive*.

1. In a *proactive* defence mechanism, the information system's goal is to increase the uncertainty that is observed by the adversary and prevent it from reliably inferring the classifier in an exploratory attack. Once the potential impact by an exploratory attack could be reduced, an evasion attack that is built upon inference results of the exploratory attack would not be effective, as well. One countermeasure against exploratory attack is adding some small but controlled perturbation (or

noise) to some selected output labels returned by the machine learning system [8]. Then, when the adversary polls the machine learning system, the training data collected by the adversary becomes noisy. Since deep learning is sensitive to training errors, the adversary cannot reliably train a deep neural network to infer the target machine learning system. How to insert errors in the returned labels is a delicate task. While inserting a very small number of errors would not be effective, a large number of errors would make the normal operation of machine learning system unreliable. One way of solving this problem is introducing errors to labels that have high confidence scores (i.e. labels of data samples that are more likely to be correctly classified) [8]. With this approach, it is difficult for the adversary to train a deep neural network, since the decision boundaries cannot be constructed reliably because of the errors in these dominant labels that are instrumental in shaping the decision boundaries.

2. In a *reactive* defence mechanism, the information system's goal is to identify which users are attacking the machine learning system and filtering out or restricting their queries. One potential indicator of an evasion attack is that a particular user is always sending input data samples that have the classification scores close to the decision boundary. These data samples are more likely to be misclassified than others. Therefore, such requests could be flagged. A similar approach was followed in [25] for a causative attack, where user inputs are monitored regarding their consistency with respect to the existing classifier that is being trained with additional input data from users.

8 Extension of Adversarial Deep Learning to Other Domains

Adversarial deep learning has applications not only limited to cybersecurity but also available in other domains that take inputs for decision making and provide outputs either directly to the user or in a form that can be observed by third parties. Vulnerability detection and analysis originally considered for cybersecurity systems can be reused or tailored for these new domains.

One extension of adversarial deep learning is to the area of *wireless network security*. Machine learning finds numerous applications in wireless communications such as Wi-fi, LTE, sensor networks and mobile ad hoc networks (MANETs). One canonical example is the cognitive radio [31] that can be programmed and configured dynamically by automated means to use the best wireless channels in its vicinity to avoid or intelligently manage user interference and congestion. The design concepts of cognitive radios have become a reality with the emergence of low-cost software-defined radios (SDRs) that can perform various sensing, communications and networking tasks [32]. The applications of machine learning to cognitive radio span the entire network protocol stack including automated detection, classification and prediction tasks such as spectrum sensing, signal classification, modulation recognition and adaptation, dynamic spectrum access (DSA), power control, routing and flow control. Machine learning can be used to perform these tasks, thereby supporting cognitive radios to perceive and learn the spectrum environment and adapt to spectrum dynamics. One example is sensing the spectrum, i.e. classifying whether the spectrum is used by other transmitter(s), or not. For instance, the GAN has been applied in [33] to support spectrum sensing with additional training data.

Due to the broadcast nature of wireless medium, wireless networks are susceptible to frequent attacks and exploits such as jamming attacks. Cognitive radios aim to detect and mitigate these attacks and exploits by automated means such as those enabled by machine learning. In this process, cognitive radio observes the spectrum (including the effects of adversaries such as jammers) and takes actions for communications (such as deciding to transmit or wait). These actions are potentially observed by adversaries that can react to them.

In this context, the adversary, e.g. a jammer, has the opportunity to follow the design constructs of adversarial machine learning to launch wireless network attacks. Building upon the insights gained from information system security, the following procedure has been applied in [34] to launch wireless attacks based on adversarial machine learning. The adversary launches an exploratory attack by training a classifier that predicts when the cognitive radio will transmit next (or better, when there will be the next successful transmission). To train the classifier, the adversary builds the training data by sensing the spectrum and tracking the transmissions of the

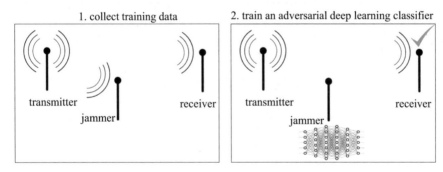

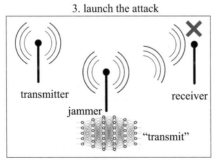

Fig. 8 Application of adversarial deep learning to wireless security domain

cognitive radio over time with respect to some spectrum features, such as the perceived availability of the spectrum. Once the classifier is trained, the jammer can predict the future behaviour of the cognitive radio (i.e. when it will transmit or when it will transmit successfully) and aims to jam the signal of the cognitive radio based on the prediction results obtained in the exploratory attack. This procedure is illustrated in Fig. 8. Applications of adversarial machine learning are broad. Similar use cases can be found in other domains such as Internet of Things, cyberphysical systems and autonomous driving.

9 End-of-Chapter Teaching Questions

1. Suppose a classifier T on two classes 1 and 2 has the following error probabilities: $e_1(T) = 10\%$ and $e_1(T) = 20\%$. The number of samples in each class is $n_1 = 200$ and $n_2 = 300$. Calculate the overall error probability.
2. What are the two non-deep learning classifiers discussed in this chapter? What are the assumptions made by these classifiers?
3. What are different types of deep neural networks? What is the difference among them?
4. What are the three types of adversarial deep learning attacks? Among them, which attack changes the original classifier?
5. Do we need to know the actual class information (i.e. $C(s)$) in an exploratory attack? If not, which information is used as label to train the inferred classifier $\hat{T}$?
6. Assuming that an adversary has no knowledge of the actual class information (i.e. $C(s)$), can an adversary measure the increased error rate due to the evasion attack?
7. What are ways of generating synthetic data for the evasion attack?
8. What is the benefit to apply the GAN in the evasion attack?
9. What are the two types of defence mechanisms discussed in this chapter? What is the difference between them?
10. If we apply deep learning to spectrum sensing for cognitive radios, what are the two possible classes?

10 End-of-Chapter Research Questions

1. What are the examples of online machine learning systems that are potentially susceptible to adversarial machine learning attacks?
2. What types of machine leaning tasks (other than classification) are potentially vulnerable to adversarial machine learning?
3. What are the other domains in which adversarial machine learning may find applications?
4. What are the types of deep learning algorithms that can be used for different data domains?

5. How can the adversary launch other (new) types of attacks built upon an exploratory attack?
6. What is the computational complexity of adversarial deep learning and how can it be improved, if needed?
7. How can one parallelize adversarial deep learning-based attacks and the corresponding defence mechanisms?
8. What types of software, firmware and hardware platforms are needed to launch effective adversarial deep learning-based attacks and deliver countermeasures?
9. What are the other defence mechanisms that can be used against adversarial deep learning?
10. What are the potential ways (if any) to explain the decisions of adversarial deep learning?

References

1. Stratosphere IPS (2018). https://www.stratosphereips.org. Accessed 15 Mar 2018
2. Silver D, Huang A, Maddison CJ, Guez A, Sifre L, Van Den Driessche G, Schrittwieser J, Antonoglou I, Panneershelvam V, Lanctot M, et al (2016) Mastering the game of Go with deep neural networks and tree search. Nature **529**(7587), 484–489
3. Goodfellow IJ, Shlens J, Szegedy C (2014) Explaining and harnessing adversarial examples. arXiv:1412.6572
4. Huang L, Joseph AD, Nelson B, Rubinstein BI, Tygar J (2011) Adversarial machine learning. In: Proceedings of the 4th ACM workshop on security and artificial intelligence. ACM, pp 43–58
5. Miller B, Kantchelian A, Afroz S, Bachwani R, Dauber E, Huang L, Tschantz MC, Joseph AD, Tygar JD (2014) Adversarial active learning. In: Proceedings of the 2014 workshop on artificial intelligent and security workshop. ACM, pp 3–14
6. Laskov P, Lippmann R (2010) Machine learning in adversarial environments. Springer, Berlin
7. Shi Y, Sagduyu Y, Grushin A (2017) How to steal a machine learning classifier with deep learning. In: 2017 IEEE international symposium on technologies for homeland security (HST). IEEE
8. Shi Y, Sagduyu YE (2017) Evasion and causative attacks with adversarial deep learning. In: MILCOM 2017-2017 IEEE military communications conference (MILCOM). IEEE, pp 243–248
9. Goodfellow I, Pouget-Abadie J, Mirza M, Xu B, Warde-Farley D, Ozair S, Courville A, Bengio Y (2014) Generative adversarial nets. In: Advances in neural information processing systems, pp 2672–2680
10. Hornik K, Stinchcombe M, White H (1989) Multilayer feedforward networks are universal approximators. Neural Netw 2(5):359–366
11. Cybenko G (1989) Approximation by superpositions of a sigmoidal function. Math Control Signals Syst 2(4):303–314
12. LeCun Y et al (1989) Generalization and network design strategies. Connectionism in perspective, pp 143–155
13. Hochreiter S, Schmidhuber J (1997) Long short-term memory. Neural Comput 9(8):1735–1780
14. Rumelhart DE, Hinton GE, Williams RJ (1985) Learning internal representations by error propagation. Technical report, University of California, San Diego, La Jolla, Institute for Cognitive Science
15. Microsoft Cognitive Toolkit (CNTK) (2018). https://docs.microsoft.com/en-us/cognitive-toolkit. Accessed 15 Mar 2018

16. Abadi M, Agarwal A, Barham P, Brevdo E, Chen Z, Citro C, Corrado GS, Davis A, Dean J, Devin M et al (2016) Tensorflow: large-scale machine learning on heterogeneous distributed systems. arXiv:1603.04467

17. Barreno M, Nelson B, Sears R, Joseph AD, Tygar JD (2006) Can machine learning be secure? In: Proceedings of the 2006 ACM symposium on information, computer and communications security. ACM, pp 16–25

18. Ateniese G, Mancini LV, Spognardi A, Villani A, Vitali D, Felici G (2015) Hacking smart machines with smarter ones: how to extract meaningful data from machine learning classifiers. Int J Secur Netw 10(3):137–150

19. Fredrikson M, Jha S, Ristenpart T (2015) Model inversion attacks that exploit confidence information and basic countermeasures. In: Proceedings of the 22nd ACM SIGSAC conference on computer and communications security. ACM, pp 1322–1333

20. Tramèr F, Zhang F, Juels A, Reiter MK, Ristenpart T (2016) Stealing machine learning models via prediction APIs. In: USENIX security symposium, pp 601–618

21. Biggio B, Corona I, Maiorca D, Nelson B, Šrndić N, Laskov P, Giacinto G, Roli F (2013) Evasion attacks against machine learning at test time. In: Joint European conference on machine learning and knowledge discovery in databases. Springer, Berlin, pp 387–402

22. Papernot N, McDaniel P, Goodfellow I, Jha S, Celik ZB, Swami A (2016) Practical black-box attacks against deep learning systems using adversarial examples

23. Kurakin A, Goodfellow I, Bengio S (2016) Adversarial examples in the physical world. arXiv:1607.02533

24. Papernot N, McDaniel P, Jha S, Fredrikson M, Celik ZB, Swami A (2016) The limitations of deep learning in adversarial settings. In: 2016 IEEE European symposium on security and privacy (EuroS&P). IEEE, pp 372–387

25. Pi L, Lu Z, Sagduyu Y, Chen S (2016) Defending active learning against adversarial inputs in automated document classification. In: 2016 IEEE global conference on signal and information processing (GlobalSIP). IEEE, pp 257–261

26. Papernot N, McDaniel P, Goodfellow I, Jha S, Celik ZB, Swami A (2017) Practical black-box attacks against machine learning. In: Proceedings of the 2017 ACM on asia conference on computer and communications security. ACM, pp 506–519

27. Flower Image Dataset (2018). https://www.tensorflow.org/tutorials/image_retraining. Accessed 15 Mar 2018

28. Szegedy C, Zaremba W, Sutskever I, Bruna J, Erhan D, Goodfellow I, Fergus R (2013) Intriguing properties of neural networks. arXiv:1312.6199

29. Nguyen A, Yosinski J, Clune J (2015) Deep neural networks are easily fooled: high confidence predictions for unrecognizable images. In: Proceedings of the IEEE conference on computer vision and pattern recognition, pp 427–436

30. Moosavi Dezfooli SM, Fawzi A, Frossard P (2016) Deepfool: a simple and accurate method to fool deep neural networks. In: Proceedings of 2016 IEEE conference on computer vision and pattern recognition (CVPR)

31. Haykin S (2005) Cognitive radio: brain-empowered wireless communications. IEEE J Sel Areas Commun 23(2):201–220

32. Soltani S, Sagduyu Y, Shi Y, Li J, Feldman J, Matyjas J (2015) Distributed cognitive radio network architecture, SDR implementation and emulation testbed. In: MILCOM 2015-2015 IEEE military communications conference. IEEE, pp 438–443

33. Davaslioglu K, Sagduyu YE (2018) Generative adversarial learning for spectrum sensing. In: Accepted to IEEE international conference on communications (ICC). IEEE

34. Shi Y, Sagduyu YE, Erpek T, Davaslioglu K, Lu Z, Li JH (2018) Adversarial deep learning for cognitive radio security: jamming attack and defense strategies. In: IEEE international communications conference workshop on promises and challenges of machine learning in communication networks. IEEE

SOCIO-LENS: Spotting Unsolicited Caller Through Network Analysis

Muhammad Ajmal Azad, Junaid Arshad and Farhan Riaz

Abstract Spam and unwanted content has been a significant challenge for the Internet technologies (email, social networks, search engines, etc.) for decades. However, in recent years, the advent of modern and cheap telephony technologies and larger user base (more than six billion users) has attracted scammers to use telephony for distributing unwanted content via instant messaging and calls. Detection of unwanted caller in the telephony has become challenging because the content is available only after the call has already been answered by the recipients and thus is too late to block the unwanted caller after the call has already been established. One of the interesting possibilities is to develop a telephony blacklist database using social behaviour of users towards their friends and family circle by modelling call meta-data as a weighted network graph. In this chapter, we model user's behaviour as a weighted call graph network and identify malicious users by analysing different network features of users. To this extent, we have identified a set of features that help represent malicious and non-malicious behaviour of users in a network. We have conducted rigorous experimentation of the proposed system via its implementation with data set collected by small-scale telecommunication operator. We present the outcomes of our evaluation highlighting the efficacy of the system's performance and identifying possible directions for future work.

M. A. Azad
Newcastle University, Newcastle upon Tyne, UK
e-mail: muhammad.azad@ncl.ac.uk

J. Arshad (✉)
University of West London, London, UK
e-mail: Junaid.Arshad@uwl.ac.uk

F. Riaz
National University of Science and Technology, Islamabad, Pakistan
e-mail: farhan.riaz@ce.ceme.edu.pk

© Springer International Publishing AG, part of Springer Nature 2018
S. Parkinson et al. (eds.), *Guide to Vulnerability Analysis for Computer Networks and Systems*, Computer Communications and Networks,
https://doi.org/10.1007/978-3-319-92624-7_10

235

1   Introduction

The telephone system (GSM, fixed, voice over IP (VoIP)) has become an integral part of our life. The number of mobile telephone users across the world exceeded more than five billion by the year 2019. This extraordinary penetration, a large number of consumer base, and the advent of cheap and non-traceable telephony systems (e.g. VoIP) have attracted scammers to use telephony system for defrauding users in real time. Similarly, advertising companies and fundraising organizations have also found this medium more attractive to have effective advertisements of products and raising funding for a cause in a real time. Recently, Federal Trade Commission (FTC) estimated that telephony system has been widely used as the preferred medium for targeting users for the financial loss superseding email and social networks.

Unwanted communication in telephony has become a challenging problem as it requires a real-time response from the recipient and therefore considered more disruptive than unwanted email or text message. Furthermore, unavailability of telephony blacklist and easy spoofing of calling identity makes the problem even more challenging and undetectable. Though the regulators in different countries have deployed the non-calling list database (where users add their telephone number for not receiving telemarketing calls), the scammers are generally not obliged to conform to such calling lists.

In emails, social media sites and blogs spammers are typically blocked by analysing the contents of their messages. The content-based system along with sophisticated machine learning has shown effective resistance against a spammer for these networks. However, in telecommunication networks, content is available only after the call is established between the caller and the callee. Furthermore, real-time processing speech content and management of speech database (spam and non-spam speech content) also limits content to be deployed in a practical telecommunication network for the identification of the spammers. A telecommunication operator would ideally like to block the spammers before sending a call request to the callee. This can be achieved by deploying the telephony blacklist that is being queried at the time of the call request. The telephony blacklist can be developed in two ways: (1) intrusive, by asking the call recipient to provide the feedback about the caller at the end of a call transaction, and (2) non-intrusive automatically using the call meta-data. Within this context, the telecommunication call meta-data consists of two parts: a pre-call acceptance part (signalling messages) and a post-call part, i.e. meta-data (Call Detail Records). However, the signalling message does not provide any meaningful information which can help characterize a caller as a spammer. Furthermore, these messages are susceptible to malicious modification by spammers to impersonate legitimate callers. On the contrary, the call meta-data (obtained as post-call) could provide information about the social behaviour of users and can be used to segregate spammers and the legitimate callers.

Legitimate users usually develop social circle with their friends, family, and colleagues whom they interact frequently, whereas non-legitimate users exercise massive spamming to the large number of users which normally results in a non-connected social network. The social behaviour of legitimate and non-legitimate caller can reveal some interesting patterns that can be used to distinguish spammers from legitimate callers. For example, telemarketers usually call or send messages to a large number of users in order to benefit from spamming. Therefore, the communication behaviour of spammer is quite different from the communication pattern of legitimate users whose interactions are restricted to some social group. Such communication patterns of users have been adopted to fight spam in email [1–3], in a social networking [4, 5], and Web spam [6]. Within the context of voice communication, call duration, the total number of calls to a particular callee(called intensity), and callee feedback about the caller have been used for analysing the communication behaviour of a caller to detect Spam over Internet Telephony (SPIT) [7–10].

The important property that can group caller into spammer and non-spammer is the number of unique callee of the caller and connectivity strength of caller with these callee and friends of callee. The legitimate callers normally have repetitive calling behaviour with their friends, but the spam caller mostly tries new callee for every new call. The 90% of legitimate callers usually have five strongly connected users, and about 80% of their total talk time [11] constitutes these users. The out-degree distribution, the in-degree distribution, call duration in both directions, and call rate of the caller in both direction could provide clear insight for categorizing caller as a spammer or a legitimate caller. In this paper, we utilize weighted centrality measure of the user call graph to classify caller as a spammer or a legitimate caller. The weights on the edges are calculated from the call duration of the caller with their callee, the incoming and outgoing call rate between the caller and the callee, and out-degree of the caller. The edge weights present the trusted strength between a caller and its callee. We analysed our proposed approach on a data set containing call records from a small VoIP service provider in Pakistan. Each call record contains call time, duration, and caller and callee phone numbers. We lack ground truth regarding the status of the caller as being a spammer or legitimate caller, but we are able to analyse the call patterns of identified spam caller in order to confirm the accuracy of the system.

The major contributions of our work are:

- We propose a new technique for the spam detection in a telecommunication network that utilizes social network and call features of a caller towards its callee. To this extent, we present an approach for assigning weights on network edges and measure caller centrality using a novel algorithm [12].
- We performed extensive analysis on a small-scale data set from real-world VoIP operator and identified significant insights about the behaviour of callers identified as spam caller.
- We have analysed the social network features of the callers identified as spammers which can help further research within this domain.

The rest of the chapter is organized as follows. Section 2 introduces background knowledge about signalling in the telecommunication network and SPam over Internet Telephony (SPIT). Section 3 contains the literature review and motivation for this work. Section 5 presents problem this chapter aims to address. Section 6 details the caller centrality measure for identifying spam callers in a telecommunication network and its major benefits. Section 7 provides the details of data set used for the evaluation. Section 8 analysed the results and caller behaviour. In Sect. 9, we present the conclusions drawn from the work presented in this chapter and highlight opportunities for future work.

2   Background

Telecommunication voice networks allow users to make phone calls, send instant messages and faxes over the telephony network. The convergence of traditional telephony system to IP-based telephony system makes the telephony network vulnerable to the security threats already effecting Internet applications [13, 14]. Spam over Telephony (SoT) is similar to email spam but causes significant disruption and discomfort to the recipients given that the spam is in the form of a phone call and requires an immediate response from the recipient. In the rest of this section, we provide an overview about spamming in the telephony system.

2.1   Telecommunication Spam

The decreasing price of telephony, easy intergeneration of spamming tools with the VoIP technology, and expanding consumer base have attracted telemarketers, prank callers, and spammers for misusing the medium for making bulk unsolicited calls and sending unsought messages to a large number of users across the globe. These unsolicited calls can also be termed as SPIT[1] (Spam over Internet Telephony) [15, 16]. Spammers typically make spam calls for marketing products, advertisements, harassing subscribers, convincing subscribers for dialling premium numbers, making Vishing (equivalent of Phishing in Web) attack for recipient's private information, etc. Spammers can also make attempt to steal a victim's personal information [17], make calls to assess, and identify unsecured gateways within the network for the termination of bulk un-billed calls [18], and cause disruption in network services through flooding and denial-of-service attacks [13, 14, 19].

   The unwanted phone calls and text messages can come at any hour. They disrupt people while at work, disturb them while having family time, and wake them up from sound sleep during night time. Recent statistics on telephony spam reveals that answering spam calls would result in an estimated waste of 20 million man-hours for small business in the USA with the loss of about $475 million annually [20]. Service providers, regulators, and law enforcement agencies receive thousands of complaints from consumers of technology for these unsolicited, unauthorized, and

---

[1]The terms SPIT, SPAM, and SoT are interchangeable in the chapter.

fraudulent callers trying to abuse them. In 2012, FTC has received four times more complaints against robo-calls than number complaints in 2010 [21, 22]. The number of identified spam callers has also risen to 162% since 2014 [21]. The estimated annual telephone fraud losses would rise to $40.1 billion (USD) [23].

Beside disturbing callee with bulk unsolicited advertisement calls or obtaining confidential information, spammers also try to find insecure gateways for toll fraud. The spammer then utilizes these public switched telephone network (PSTN) gateways for illegal termination of voice without paying to PSTN or transit VoIP SPs. The following are additional forms of spam introduced because of VoIP and SIP [24]:

Instant message spam: Bulk unsolicited instant messages (similar to email spam messages).

Presence spam: Bulk presence requests, in order to become whitelisted.

Virus spam: Sending virus inside request messages that affect the operating system of VoIP phones or check for vulnerabilities.

Spam over Telephony (SoT) shares some similarities with email spam. Spam over both Internet (email, social, blogs) and telephony use the Internet as a medium to achieve unsolicited communications. A fundamental difference between telephony and other spamming is that a traditional email can be stored in the inbox for the relatively long time period before sending a notification to recipients, but in telephony, the service provider has to respond the callee and the caller in real time without adding any additional delay during the call setup phase. In an email, content is available before sending it to recipients and therefore has the chance of identifying the spamming content. However, in telephony, content is only available after the call has already been established between the caller and his recipients thus is too late to initiate the detection process as the recipient has already been disturbed by the unwanted ringing. In terms of the protocol specification, the email headers contain some information about the originator and has the ability to identify the sources as verified or non-verified by processing some header messages; however, in telephony the signalling messages of spammer and legitimate user are same and therefore do not provide any valuable information to be used by for the spam detection.

From a resource perspective, a single spam email on a mail server can consume a few thousand bytes but a voice message in a voice mailbox typically occupies much more space, making these resources unavailable to the legitimate callers. From the user's perspective, telephony spam is quite different from the email spam. The deletion of a spam call requires much more time as compared to email spam. The detection and deletion of spam speech content from the voice mailbox are also more time-consuming as it requires at least six steps to completely remove the speech content from the voice mailbox [25]. The email user categorizes email in an inbox as spam or non-spam on a first look; but, in case of a spam recorded call in a voice mailbox, the receiver has to listen to the first few seconds of recording to categorize it as a spam or a non-spam.

2.2 Motivation of Spammer

The motivation behind spamming in telephony or any other network is to market legal or illegal products, convince recipients to respond back to the initiator, make them disclose their personal information to be used for fraud, and trying to deceive them through social engineering. The main goal of spammer is to reach a large number of recipients for financial benefits without incurring a high cost. In telephony system, spam caller can be grouped into two type: (1) auto dialler or robo-callers—where an automated machine or computer generates a large number of automated spam calls to a large number of recipients—and (2) the human spammer—where spammers hire affordable human service for spamming a large number of recipients especially for advertising products or defrauding user with the social engineering attack. In terms of financial benefits in telephony, spammers can have financial benefits in three ways. Firstly, they convince callee to call them back on some premium numbers. For this, spammers scam people by using social engineering and exploit the needs of people in a particular society such as offering expensive gifts and attractive packages for visiting historical and religious places. Secondly, they convince call recipients to disclose his private information by impersonating a legitimate entity. Thirdly, making callee listen to the complete advertisement and buy products.

A spammer can also make spam call or spam messages for scanning end-user handset for the system vulnerability. The initiators of these calls pretend to represent the support centre of famous product maker and claim to require access to victim's device for virus scanning. The ability to make anonymous calls to a specific callee also encourages spammer to use this medium for threatening or annoying recipient with the denial-of-service attack. Besides financial benefits, spammers can also use this medium to spread real-time interactive hate religious or political messages to a large number of users. From the perspective of a service provider or organization, spammers can make spam calls to learn the system vulnerabilities or identify open gateways for free of cost call terminations.

2.3 Telephony Spam Threats and Scenarios

In this section, we outline how SoT can be a threat to customers and telecommunication service providers [26].

Threat against callee account credit: The subscribers pay extra to SPs for the value-added services e.g call forwarding, roaming, and automatic call back service. This would result in loss of callee account balance when caller found to be advertiser and callee is roaming or his automatic call back diverted to premium numbers. Spam caller may also convince callee to call them back on their premium number which affects callee account balance.

Threat against missing important calls: The subscriber usually enables voice mailbox for recording message during his period of unavailability which has a small capacity. The spam call is diverted to voice-box with unwanted voice message, thereby resulting in resource unavailability to legitimate callers. It also becomes a time-consuming job for the callee to delete such calls as callee has to listen to at least few seconds of audio before making a decision.

Vishing: The user may respond to some prize-winning calls with the disclosure of his private information. In VoIP, it is relatively easy to hide the identity or to change identity with some legitimate identities. The impersonation may result in a Vishing attack (recipients disclose their critical information) in a real time which may result in a financial loss to the recipients of the call.

Network equipment hijacking: The network equipment hijacking threat refers to an attacker compromising a VoIP network element to send unsolicited communications. The spammer tries to find an insecure gateway for terminating traffic without charges. The spammer then sells PSTN termination to other service providers using theses insecure gateways without paying.

Mobile phone virus: The mobile phone virus threat refers to the attacker distributing virus through unsolicited communications, e.g. a download link in messages or as multimedia attachments in a call. This attack is to gain system access in order to destroy the operating system of IP phone or collect user contact list.

Negative perception about SP: The spam calls divert the attention of callee and become frustrated with growing amount. The increasing number of spam to the recipient would reduce the trust of the recipient on his service provider and may change the service provider because of a large number of annoying calls.

3   Potential Detection Systems

Spam emerges in the form of unsolicited email, unwanted friends request and posts in a social media, spam pages on the World Wide Web, video spam in YouTube, and blogs spam. Many strategies have been proposed to deal with these forms of spam. Spam detection becomes more challenging in a telephony network where users require a real-time response to their call requests. Several approaches have been presented for stopping spam caller in a voice over IP networks [16]. These approaches can be grouped into two categories: (1) methods based on content analysis of signalling messages and actual voice content and (2) methods that require feedback from the caller or the callee about the spamming nature of the call. These methods can be further categorized into pre-acceptance and post-acceptance methods [27] depending on whether the decision is made before or after a call is accepted. In the rest of this section, we discuss several of these anti-SPIT techniques.

3.1   Processing Speech and Signalling Content

Signalling systems, i.e. Session Initiation Protocol (SIP) and Signalling System 7 (SS7) are widely used for establishing the calls in the VoIP and traditional public switched and mobile networks. The speech content then flows between the caller and his recipient over the out-of-band channel and using other protocols such as Real-Time Protocol (RTP). Content-based systems perform functionality at two stages: they either analyse the semantics of signalling messages (SIP and SS7) or they process the speech streams [28–31].

The speech processing requires resources for real-time speech processing and an updated voice data set for the pattern matching. The processing of speech is expected to introduce the delay in the conversation and degrade voice quality. Furthermore, it also bypasses the user privacy as processing or listening to voice conversation is prohibited by law in many countries. Content-based systems cannot perform well when contents are encrypted and background noise is added to the speech. The structure of a call setup message of legitimate and spam caller is same, and this does not provide any additional information for distinguishing spam caller from the non-spam.

3.2 Access List-Based Systems

The list-based approaches are the simplest identity-based anti-SPIT filters. Within these approaches, whitelist maintains the database of identities of callers allowed for using the network and blacklist maintains the database of identities of caller barred from calling. A list database can be either global-applied to all users or local-apply to specific users. Besides black- and whitelist, a greylist [15, 27] can also be used for filtering the spammers. A greylist maintains the database of identities that would be challenged for the authorization or monitored for some time period. In a greylist, if a caller exhibits spamming over some defined time period then the caller is permanently moved to a blacklist otherwise caller is moved to the whitelist. The proxy server checks the list database during the call setup phase, but this database is maintained through other approaches involved in making a decision about the caller's list [8, 32, 33].

A common problem with blacklist-based SPIT filtering is the inclusion of legitimate callers who were mistakenly reported or classified as spammers because of personal dislikes. Additionally, it becomes difficult for the individuals to get their identities revoked from the blacklist. From the perspective of a spammer, a blacklist can be bypassed by a spammer by spoofing identities of legitimate callers not included in the blacklist. A whitelist is useful for controlling where callers are allowed from calling globally or locally. However, it cannot allow a new caller or a legitimate caller wishing to call some unknown not interacted before. From the perspective of the service provider, maintaining a large global and local list database is problematic and requires a continuous update. Moreover, list-based approaches need to be implemented with other SPIT detection approaches that actually decides whether to include caller in blacklist and whitelist or not. In [34, 35], authors deploy a large-scale cloud-based honeynet system for analysing the social behaviour of callers making calls to honey-phones.

In many countries, telecommunication regulators encourage consumers to put their telephone number in the do-not-call register mode if they do not wish to receive any advertising or marketing calls. However, this mode is not effectively resistant against spammers, as some legitimate and the illegitimate companies do not pay attention to these lists or integrate them into their preventive strategies and approaches. Statistics show that a large number of users still receive a large number of spam calls despite putting their numbers in the national do-not-call registry [36].

3.3 Challenge Response-Based Approaches

A spam call can be generated by an automated machine or a human advertiser. To distinguish human from machine calls, a Turing test can be applied. The Turing test is based on the fact that humans can easily solve some problems which are impossible for the computer. Callers are authorized to make calls via their private–public key exchange or using Turing test authentication [37–40]. The human conversation has short pause time at the beginning of a call before the callee statement that initiates the conversation. For instance, an overlap in conversation patterns may indicate that the caller is an automated spam caller. In [39], these communication patterns have been analysed and hidden Turing tests are proposed for the identification of SPIT callers. A trust enforcement mechanism allows the caller to solve complex puzzles in order to validate each call [41]. The Turing test approach may be successful in blocking computer generated SPIT calls, but it requires more network and computational resources. The Turing test will also additionally burden the legitimate callers as they will have to solve puzzles for every call and will increase the call setup time.

3.4 Imposing Extra Costs on the Caller

The payments at risk-based approach [24] deduct some money from the caller account and return back if the caller is found to be legitimate at a later stage. This solution requires (1) feedback from the callee or content processing for the final decision and (2) a comprehensive payment system. The former is not feasible, as a callee is reluctant in providing feedback for every received call, and content processing faces the same limitation of content-based approaches. The micro-payment system is difficult to be implemented for different call setup.

3.5 Reputation-Based Systems

The social reputation-based approaches use the social relationship between VoIP users for ranking the caller's reputation across the network. This is a two-step process. First, a trust value is computed between any two users, and second, a global reputation provides an indication of the spamming behaviour of a caller in the whole network. In a VoIP system, the direct trust between two users is computed in two ways: (1) using positive and negative feedback from the callee for the caller [8, 10, 32, 42–44] and (2) average call duration with a given callee [7, 24, 45, 46]. The reputation of a caller can also be computed from social network features including node degree, local clustering coefficient, in-count degree, out-count degree, reciprocity index.

In CallRank [7], direct trust is computed from the average call duration; global reputation is computed using an Eigen trust reputation algorithm. Higher average call duration is taken as a sign of a trustworthy relationship between caller and callee and used to build user reputation across the network. Reference [44] applies semi-supervised clustering to callee feedback and to the distribution of SIP messages with the goal of grouping callers into legitimate and non-legitimate clusters; this approach requires user feedback and changes to VoIP software. References [8, 32] present a multi-stage SPIT detection system consisting of trust and reputation stages integrated with black and whitelists. Trust is computed through positive and negative feedback from the callee. Caller reputation is computed using Bayesian inference. Reputation-based techniques can also be applied in combination with other SPIT detection approaches [24, 47], which are multi-stage and interact with other stages for a final decision about the nature of the caller.

Three SPIT detection techniques based on average call duration, degree distribution, and reciprocity index are proposed in [11]. These systems use average call duration with a PageRank algorithm to compute caller reputation across the network. It is possible that a SPIT attack occurs on this system in a collaborative manner. References [10, 42] propose two systems based on the entropy of the average call duration. The first system applies the Mahalanobis distance to call duration and time of the call for distinguishing SPIT from non-SPIT callers. The second system uses the entropy of call duration at a group level for detecting misbehaving groups.

A provider-level reputation system has been proposed in [48]. The system enables call receiving operator to assign reputation score to a call source operator by analysing the tags assigned by the source operator. The problem of unsolicited communication has also been studied in other telecommunication systems such as IMS, LTE system, and transit VoIP operators [26, 47, 49]. In [50], a collaborative scorecard framework has been proposed for discriminating legitimate caller from the non-legitimate in an IMS network. The scorecard of a caller is sent to the receiving domain, which built its decision whether to allow or deny caller from calling. The transit VoIP operator provides interconnection services between different VoIP operators for terminating VoIP calls to PSTN or mobile operators. In [47], a multi-stage SPIT detection system has been proposed and analysed for different call rates. The system uses feedback among various stages for detecting SPIT caller in a transit VoIP operator. The identity linking-based multi-stage reputation system has been proposed in [51] that consist of three stages: first, it connects identities that belong to one physical person, secondly computes the reputation of collectively considering all identities of person as one, and finally performs aggregate detection. The solution provides effective defence against the spammer frequently changing his calling identities but targets the same set of user over the time.

Recently, few collaborative systems have been proposed for early identification of spammers. In [52], authors proposed a collaborative system where multiple service providers collaborate with each other through the exchange of trusted third-party system. The system improves the detection accuracy even if the spammer targets the service provider at a very small call rate. However, the centralized system has two limitations: (1) it is the single point of failure and is not scalable; (2) it would be difficult to convince service provider to trust the centralized system for their private information. In [53, 54], a decentralized reputation system is proposed that makes use of cryptographic primitives for exchanging the reputation score and classify caller's behaviour in a collaborative manner.

The existing reputation-based approaches either involve user feedback or call duration credentials for local trust computation among users. The users may not be willing to provide feedback for every call they have received. Higher call duration is the sign of strong relationship [7], but local trust computation cannot be limited to call duration only. The major attribute of the SPIT callers is they try to reach a large number of network users and managed low or high duration with them, and have no or few repetitive and incoming calls from the other users. The out-degree, number of repetitive calls, and total call duration can be the major feature set for identifying such callers sending a large number of calls to users.

Our proposed approach is based on the following mechanism. Firstly, weights are computed to be assigned to the communication link between communicating users followed by computing a global centrality measure of the caller with the network using weighted centrality approach. The weights for the edges are computed by using out-degree of the caller, a number of repetitive calls between the caller and their called callee, and total call duration of the caller with their called callee. The caller having high out-degree and a large number of small duration caller can be a suspected a SPIT caller because of their unbalanced calling behaviour, and thus, the edges between SPIT caller and their callee can be assigned with small trust score. The SPIT caller can be of three types: (1) generating a high volume of calls with low call duration thus having weak weights on edges, (2) generates controlled attacks with good call duration, and (3) generates high volume with good call duration. The global centrality measure assigns small centrality scores to all these types of spammers and assigns high centrality scores to the caller having legitimate calling behaviour. The other distinct features of our approach are: it does not require any interaction with the caller or the callee for the classification of caller status, can be easily deployed in a transit or access VoIP operators, and more importantly does not break privacy of the caller and the callee. In addition, we have also analysed the calling behaviour of spam and the non-spam callers in a network for the following features: a number of repetitive calls, the ratio of high duration calls with their number of called callee, out-degree distribution.

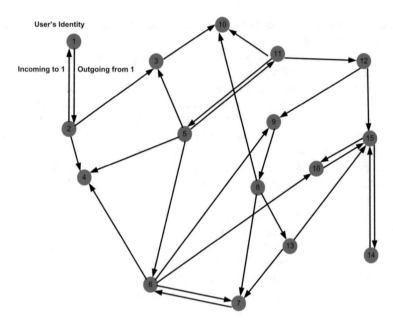

User's Identity

Incoming to 1 **Outgoing from 1**

Fig. 1 Social network of VoIP caller

4 Social Network Features from Call Detailed Meta-Data

Every telephone network operator records information about user's call transaction in a Call Detail Records (CDRs) mainly used for the billing purpose and network management. CDR logs normally contain the identity of the caller and the called party, date and time when the call initializes, start time of the call and call duration, etc. The social network of user can generate from raw call detail records (CDRs) by modelling the meta-data as the undirected weighted graph, $G = (V, E, W)$, where V represents the identity of the caller or the callee, E represents edge between the caller and the callee, and W represents the weight (average call duration or trust between caller and the callee). The weighted social network of users can be represented as the social graph as shown in a Fig. 1 and can be represented a sparse adjacency matrix, where 1 represents that caller S has interacted with callee R and 0 represents that there happen no interaction between the caller and the callee. A sparse adjacency matrix A of the subscriber is represented by a $n{\times}n$ adjacency matrix A with elements as:

$$A_{ij} = \begin{cases} 1 & \text{if i interacted with j} \\ 0 & \text{no interaction} \end{cases} \tag{1}$$

In case of the weighted call graph, A_{ij} are replaced by the weights determined from the frequency of interaction and call duration of interactions.

In this section, we will discuss spammer and non-spammer calling behaviour for the certain social network features.

4.1   In-Degree and Out-Degree

In telephony, the in-degree of a given user S represents the unique users making calls to the given user S, and the out-degree represents the number of unique users called by the user S. The high in-degree of given identity can be seen that the identity is owned by the service centre or call centre, whereas the high out-degree of the given identity could represent that the identity is owned by the telemarketers or the spammers. The legitimate users exhibit balanced call behaviour in that they not only call to a small set of users but also receive calls from the others. On the other hand, spammers usually have unbalanced call behaviour as they target a large number of users to spread their information but only a few users called them back. The out-degree and in-degree of the given user S are represented as follows.

$$OD_S = \sum_{i=1}^{n} E_{SR_i} \tag{2}$$

$$ID_S = \sum_{i=1}^{n} E_{R_i S} \tag{3}$$

where R is the total number of users receiving calls from S or making calls to S. In telecommunication and other networks, spammer normally calls a large number of subscribers and receives calls from a very few recipients and thus has unbalanced out-degree and in-degree structure. On the other hand, the legitimate subscriber calls a limited number of callee and normally receives calls from many of his callee, thus resulting in a balanced out-degree and in-degree structure. The threshold on an out-degree and in-degree could be useful for blocking spammers [3], but using one feature (small in-degree or high degree as a spamming feature) alone would result in a high false positive rate and small true positive rate. For example, using high in-degree as a sign that subscriber is a legitimate caller would result in allowing spammers who managed to receive calls from their callee. Similarly, using small out-degree as a sign that subscriber is legitimate would block the legitimate subscriber having high out-degree with high duration calls as well has high in-degree with legitimate behaviour. It is important that spam detection should not be limited to the degree distribution (in-degree and out-degree) but is also required to consider this feature along with other call and social features such as call rate, call duration, and centrality measure.

4.2 Interaction Rate

Interaction rate represents the frequency and number of calls the caller is making during the observation time period. The interaction rate can also be considered as the number of calls a user is receiving and the number of calls a user is making. The call rate of caller towards a certain user represents the importance of user in the caller's social circle. The high number of repetitive calls between users represents that social relationship between user is strong, whereas a low number of calls represents user occasionally talk to each other. On the other hand, the non-repetitive calling behaviour towards a large number of users represents that caller calls user only once and characterize that caller is spamming. Legitimate callers have interaction inside their friendship or family circles and thus normally have a high number of repetitive calls which is different from SPIT callers. The aggregate out and in interaction rate can be represented as:

$$OR_S = \sum_{i=1}^{n} W_{SR_i} \tag{4}$$

$$IR_S = \sum_{i=1}^{n} W_{R_i S} \tag{5}$$

In Eq. 4, W_{SR_i} represent the total number of calls user S made to user R_i and n is the total number of callees.

4.3 Call Duration

Call duration represents the duration for which the caller and the callee talked to each other. The call duration can also be categorized into in-call duration and out-call duration. The high call duration represents connection strength between the caller and the callee, whereas a small call duration represents weak social ties between caller and callee. The bidirectional duration between caller and callee further provides insight about connection strength between the caller and the callee. The legitimate callers usually have bidirectional calling behaviour with many of their called callee. On the other hand, spammers have two important features which distinguish them from legitimate callers: first, they have a large number of small duration calls to their called callee, and secondly, they received only a few good duration calls from their friends. The call duration should be used collectively along with degree and call rate of the caller for categorizing caller as spammer and non-spammer. The aggregate in- and out-call duration can be represented as Eqs. 4 and 5 by replacing the interaction rate with the call duration. Further, the average call duration can be computed as by dividing the sum of the duration of all calls by the sum of a total number of calls.

4.4 Reciprocity Measure

Reciprocity represents the way in which the different forms of interaction takes place in a communication network. When two users interact as a peer, one expects that calls will be made in both directions. This interaction is considered as symmetric or reciprocated interaction. On the other hand, if a user made multiple calls to other user and have not received any call from the user then this interaction is asymmetric or non-reciprocating. The reciprocity of node i is computed as:

$$R_i = \frac{\text{Number of bidirectional Links}}{\text{Total Number of Links}} \tag{6}$$

The spam caller usually makes calls to a high number of callee as compared to the legitimate caller which has a limited number of friends and also have comparatively high reciprocity measure. The spam caller also receives few calls from other spam callers or few legitimate callee, but these calls usually have a very small duration. Therefore, the reciprocity measure of spam caller is much less than reciprocity of legitimate caller and could provide information for identification of spam caller in a network. The closer the reciprocity index to 1 means caller has reciprocal behaviour and value of 0 means no reciprocity at all.

4.5 Clustering Coefficient

Clustering coefficient or transitivity property of the node in a network means that two friends of a given node are likely to be directly connected as well. The local clustering coefficient C_i of a node N_i is computed by the proportion of links between the nodes within its friendship network divided by the number of links that could possibly exist between his friends. The clustering coefficient of a graph G is averaged over all nodes N in the network. The local clustering coefficient of a node i in a directed graph is given as:

$$C_i = \frac{\left|\{e_{jk} : N_j, N_k \in F_i, e_{jk} \in E\}\right|}{k_i(k_i - 1)} \tag{7}$$

The F_i is the friendship or neighbourhood of node i. The clustering coefficient quantifies how well connected the neighbours of callers are in a friendship network of the caller. In other words, the clustering coefficient can be defined as the number of common friends a caller shares with another user in his social circle. In real networks (telecommunication, email, or social networks), the clustering coefficient decreases with the out-degree of the identity [1]. The spam callers can have had the ability to control their calling behaviour (small out-degree), but they are unable to control the connectivity structure of their interacted callee or friends. As the spam caller calls a high number of callee it therefore results in zero or lower clustering coefficient. The legitimate caller usually interacts within a circle and that results in some common friends and probably has high clustering coefficient because of common friends and small out-degree.

4.6 *Centrality*

Centrality identifies the most influential node within the network. The central node has a high number of links, reaches other nodes quickly, and controls the flow of information. The methods used to measure node centrality are degree centrality, closeness, and betweenness. Degree centrality considered the number links a node has with other nodes, but this can be used for spam detection because spammer usually has a connection with a large number of nodes and thus becomes central because of high degree. The closeness centrality makes node centrality by measuring inverse sum of the shortest distance of a node to all other nodes. The closeness would also make spammers a central node because of its small average distance to all other nodes. The betweenness of node computed by counting the number of times node appears in the shortest path between two other nodes. Like closeness and degree, betweenness also results in a high centrality score to the spammers. The centrality approaches must be used along with tie strength of the nodes with other nodes for a better estimate of the centrality of a node. The use of degree centrality, closeness, and betweenness along with edge weights would improve the spam detection process.

5 Problem Definition

Given a set of telecommunication users $A = \{u_1, u_2, u_3, \ldots, u_n\}$, an identity is defined as a caller S if he originates call towards a callee R, i.e. $(R,S) \in A$. The logs of communication between the caller and the callee are logged in Call Detail Records (CDRs) basically used for billing purpose and network management. The social ties between the caller and the callee can be strong or weak based on the number of interaction, length of talktime among them. The higher the call duration and interaction rate, the stronger the relationship and vice versa. The problem is to extract the social network of the user from the CDR, assign weights on each caller–callee edge, and compute global centrality measure of the caller in a network. The caller is then classified as spammer or non-spammer on the basis of global centrality measure and moving exponentially weighted threshold.

6 The Proposed Approach

The degree centrality measure indicates the total number of nodes connected with the given node (the total number of ties that a node has). The in-degree and out-

Fig. 2 Stats for VoIP caller:
Day-wise out-degree and call
duration

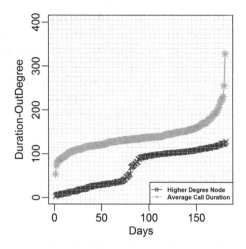

Algorithm 6 Centrality Measure of Caller and Identification of SPIT

1: **procedure** CENTRALITY OF CALLER
2:    *input ← Call Records*
3:    *output ← Caller − Centrality Score*
4:    S is a caller and R is a Callee and N is number of users.
5:    Extract Caller-Callee Adjacency Matrix from the CDR
6:    Let W_{SR} be the Weighted Adjacency Matrix and computed as
7:    **for** All Caller **do**
8:        **if** Caller i Called Callee j **then**
9:            $W_{SR} = \frac{\sum_{j=1}^{n} CallDuration_{SR}}{\sum_{j=1}^{n} Interaction_{SR}}$
10:       **else**
11:          $W_{SR} \leftarrow 0$
12:    **for** All Caller Compute Weighted Centrality Measure **do**
13:        $Centrality_S = out - degree_S \times \left(\frac{w_S^{out}}{out - degree_S} \right)^{\alpha} \times w_i^{\alpha}$
14:    **for** *All caller i* **do**
15:        **if** (Centrality[i]<threshold) **then**
16:            *Place Caller i in a SPIT List*
17:       **else**
18:          *Place Caller i in a SPIT List*

---

degree are the major centrality measures for estimating the importance of a node
in a directed graph network. The unweighted network considers the same weights
for socially connected and non-connected nodes for computing centrality and thus
triggers high degree nodes as spam caller even if the node has a connectivity strength
like legitimate callers. In voice communication, the callers talk to few users with the
higher interaction rate, with high call duration, and talk to others occasionally and
have low call duration. The out-degree distribution and call duration of the caller
having high out-degree are represented in a Fig. 2a. The caller with the high out-
degree and small call duration can be a spammer because of his high out-degree and

small in-degree. The out-degree distribution of all caller from our data set is shown in Fig. 2b with α being 2.064 which shows the average out-degree of all caller. The centrality measure can also be seen in the weighted network. The weighted degree centrality is the measure of centrality when network edges are assigned with weights. The weights provide additional information connection strength of node with other nodes in a network. The spam caller tries to reach a high number of callee with low or high call duration that results in a high out-degree but has a low in-degree and low incoming and outgoing call duration.

In our weighted centrality measure, the weights on the edges are computed from the sum of call duration and caller–callee frequency of interaction as represented in Eq. 8.

$$W_{SR} = \frac{\sum_{j=1}^{n} CallDuration_{SR}}{\sum_{j=1}^{n} Interaction_{SR}} \tag{8}$$

In Eq. 8, call duration is the sum of duration of calls a $Caller_S$ has made to the $Callee_R$ for the specific time window, $Interaction_{SR}$ is the total number of calls a $caller_S$ has made to the $callee_S$ for the observation time window, n is the total number of users either caller or the callee, and W is the adjacency matrix, in which the value of W_{SR} is greater than 1 when $caller_S$ has called Callee R and 0 otherwise. The weights on the edges represent the connectivity strength and level of friendship a caller has with his callees. The algorithm for centrality measure and detecting spam caller is presented in Algorithm 1. The degree centrality measure is computed as [12]:

$$C_S = outdegree_S \times \left(\frac{W_S}{outdegree_S}\right)^{\alpha} \tag{9}$$

In Eq. 9, C_W represent the weight centrality measure, W_S is the sum of weights of S with all his callee, α is an operator-defined parameter to define the impact of the caller's out-degree on the connectivity strength of the caller. Our approach identifies high degree nodes as legitimate only if the higher degree caller managed to have good outgoing call duration. The caller with the lowest *outdegree* and high duration would get the highest centrality score where the caller with high *outdegree* and many small duration calls would get small centrality score. This small centrality score can be the sign of spamming activity of the caller.

The centrality measure approach brings the following benefits:

1. The intelligent SPIT caller tries to reach few numbers of the user for the strong small social network before launching an attack over the large set of user. The centrality measure approach identifies the caller as legitimate in the first phase but classifies it as non-legitimate soon after its attack to the higher number of user in the second phase.
2. The approaches based on social network analysis usually use the complete underlying social network of callers, thus disclosing the social network of callers to another interacting caller. The centrality measure approach uses the out-degree of

the caller for providing the feedback to other users about nature of caller and thus preserving the caller privacy in perspective of hiding a social network of callers.

3. The SPIT callers behave in mixture model way. The VoIP caller may have a higher degree of higher and low call duration, and low degree with low and high call duration. The SPIT caller may have one the following higher degree with higher and low call duration and low degree of low call duration. The higher degree nodes having good call duration are undetectable using [7], but its out-degree is different from legitimate users. The centrality measure approach assigns weights considering both the repetitive calls and out-degree. The non-repetitive nature of SPIT callers makes our approach effectively identify callers trying to reach new callee with good call duration.

4. The Transit VoIP operators do not have direct interaction with caller and callee and thus lack of ability in creating a social network of caller–callee. Our approach can be easily be placed in transit VoIP having no interaction with caller and callee.

5. The centrality measure approach is easily scalable to the higher number of users, does not involve any complex network analysis, easily placed in access and transit VoIP operators without changes in call setup procedure and changes in VoIP network.

7 Data Set

We collected call records from a small-scale VoIP service provider. The call records consist of 225 callers and 3538 callee having average call duration of 140 s. The out-degree distribution of caller is shown in a Fig. 2b. The call records include four fields: call time, call duration, caller identity, and callee identity. The caller and callee identity and time of the call are anonymized by the service provider to protect the privacy of the user. We build a weighted directed graph, $G = (V, E, W)$, in which nodes represent phone numbers, edges represent phone calls, and weights of edges represent the average call duration. The measures include the following:

8 Result Analysis

In this section, we evaluate our proposed weighted centrality measure for identifying spam callers. To this extent, first, we apply a threshold to the weighted centrality measure to classify caller as spammer or non-spammer, and secondly, we analysed the social properties of callers in the spam and non-spam clusters. Our proposed method has identified 44 spam and 184 non-spam callers in the data set. The out-degree distribution of spam callers is much greater than that of the non-spam caller, and similarly, the call duration of spam callers is either large or small. The average call duration and centrality measure of identified spam callers are shown in Fig. 3. The identified spam callers have call average call duration of around 157 s and also

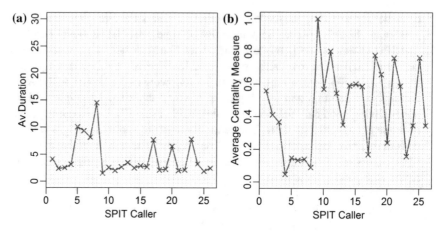

Fig. 3 SPIT caller calling behaviour: **a** average call duration, **b** centrality measure

Fig. 4 Statistics for
identified SPIT caller: degree
with associated call duration

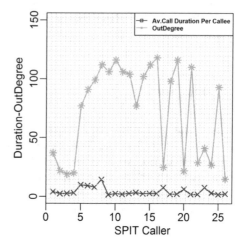

have few high duration calls but is less than 40%. Though the average call duration
of the spam caller is somehow same as the average call duration of normal callers the
out-degree of spam caller is high than the legitimate caller, which results in a small
centrality measure and weak strength in a network. The small centrality measure of
spam caller is due to the fact that spam caller randomly chooses their callee and does
not have many common friends with their called callee.

The proposed approach has triggered both low out-degree and high out-degree
callers as possible spam caller. The low out-degree caller can be considered as spam
caller because of its low call duration. The higher out-degree node identified as SPIT
caller has out-degree greater than 250 with no incoming calls from other users of
the network. On further analysis, we have also found that these users do not have
repetitive calls to the same users over the entire period of time. The zero in-degree and

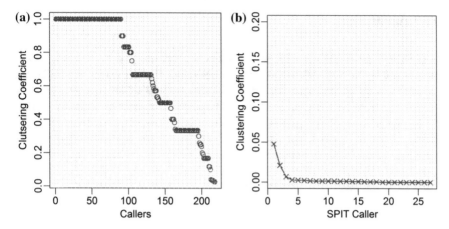

Fig. 5 Clustering coefficient values: **a** clustering coefficient of all caller and **b** clustering coefficient of identified SPIT callers

non-repetitive behaviour of such higher degree nodes make us confident to believe the caller is indeed a spammer. The efficient spam caller calls users with a controlled out-degree, as well as managing some good call duration and friendship to few callee. The approach effectively identified such small in-degree callers as spam caller as well. The degree distribution and associated average call duration of spam caller are shown in Fig. 4. The repetitive ratio for identified spam caller is less than 0.2% which shows that the spammers find only a few users to attack back as compared to the non-spam caller having more repetitive calls.

Clustering coefficient tells how well connected the user is connected with his neighbourhood or friend of their friends. If the neighbours of the user are fully connected, the clustering coefficient is near to 1, and if it is non-connected, then this value exists near to 0 that means that these users hardly have any connections among their neighbours. In a voice communication, most of the users have common friends whom they frequently interact or interact over the period of time. It is expected that the legitimate callers have high clustering coefficient as compared to the spam callers. In our data set, we analysed clustering coefficient of identified spammers and non-spammers. In our data set, a huge number of callee are from the other operators so we only have limited records for analysing the clustering coefficient of a caller–callee interaction. The average clustering coefficient of legitimate callers over all days is 0.22548, and identified non-legitimate callers have average cluster coefficient of 0.000257, and cluster coefficient of the whole network is 0.46. The per day clustering coefficient of spammers also shows that most of the time the spammers interacted callees do not have any common friends. The clustering coefficient of all users over individual day is shown in Fig. 5a, and clustering coefficient of spam caller is shown in a Fig. 5b.

9 Conclusions

In this chapter, we presented the use of social network analysis for detecting spammers in a telecommunication and telephony network. To this extent, we utilize the semantics of weighted social behaviour of users towards others in a network. The proposed system can be used to create and update the telephony blacklist without having any interaction with the users of the network. However, to minimize the false positive rates, the approach can be used with little intervention with the user of the network. We analysed our approach with real data set gathered as part of our collaboration with a telecommunication provider. However, this data set may be considered small scale and therefore represents an avenue for research in the future.

10 Questions

1. What are the two kinds of unwanted content in email and social networks?
2. What is VoIP? And how it is used in exploiting users?
3. Describe these two terms: 'Spoofing' and 'Spam over Telephony'.
4. What is the difference between traditional Spamming and Spam over Telephony?
5. Describe and elaborate two categorises of spam callers.
6. List five threats to customers and telecommunication service providers by Spam over Telephony?
7. How processing speech and signalling content can resolve Spam over Telephony?
8. What are challenge response based approach to block Spam over Telephony?
9. Explain what are 'Call Detailed Records' and what is their purpose?
10. What is clustering coefficient?

References

1. Oscar Boykin P, Roychowdhury Vwani P (2005) Leveraging social networks to fight spam. IEEE Comput 38:61–68
2. Chirita PA, Diederich J, Nejdl W (2005) MailRank: using ranking for spam detections. In: 14th ACM international conference on information and knowledge management, CIKM '05, pp 373–380
3. Lam H, Yeung D (2007) A learning approach to spam detection based on social networks. In: Proceedings of the collaboration, electronic messaging, anti-abuse and spam conference
4. Hai Wang A (2010) Don't follow me: spam detection in twitter. In: 2010 international conference on security and cryptography (SECRYPT), pp 1–10
5. Zheng X, Zeng Z, Chen Z, Yu Y, Rong C (2015) Detecting spammers on social networks. J Neurocomput 27–34
6. Spirin N, Hanh J (2011) Survey on web spam detection: principles and algorithms. ACM SIGKDD explorations newsletter, pp 50–64

7. Balasubramaniyan VA, Ahamad M, Park H (2007) CallRank: combating SPIT using call duration, social networks and global reputation. In: Fourth CEAS2007
8. Dantu R, Kolan P (2005) Detecting spam in VoIP networks. In: The steps to reducing unwanted traffic on the internet, Berkeley, CA, USA. USENIX, pp 31–37
9. Keromytis A (2009) A survey of voice over IP security research. Information systems security. Springer, Berlin, pp 1–17
10. Sengar H, Wang X, Nichols A (2012) Call behavioral analysis to thwart SPIT attacks on VoIP networks. Secur Priv Commun Netw 96:501–510
11. Bokharaei HK, Sahraei A, Ganjali Y, Keralapura R, Nucci A (2011) You can SPIT, but You can't hide: spammer identification in telephony networks. In: 2011 IEEE INFOCOM, pp 41–45
12. Opsahl T, Agneessens F, Skvoretz J (2010) Node centrality in weighted networks: generalizing degree and shortest paths. Soc Netw 32(3):245–251
13. Ehlert S, Geneiatakis D, Magedanz T (2010) Survey of network security systems to counter SIP-based denial-of-service attacks. Comput Secur 29(2):225–243
14. Keromytis A (2011) A comprehensive survey of voice over IP security research. IEEE Commun Surv Tutor PP(99):1–24
15. Hansen M, Hansen M, Mller J, Rohwer T, Tolkmit C, Waack H (2006) Developing a legally compliant reachability management system as a countermeasure against SPIT. In: 3rd Annual VoIP security workshop
16. Rosenberg J, Jennings C (2008) The session initiation protocol (SIP) and spam. RFC 5039
17. Nassar M, Niccolini S, State R, Ewald T (2007) Holistic VoIP intrusion detection and prevention system. In: 1st IPTCOMM
18. Zhang R, Wang X, Yang X, Jiang X (2007) Billing attacks on SIP-based VoIP systems. In: Ist USENIX workshop on offensive technologies
19. Dantu R, Fahmy S, Schulzrinne H, Cangussu J (2009) Issues and challenges in securing VoIP. Comput Secur 28(8):743–753
20. Spam Phone Calls Cost U.S. Small Businesses Half-Billion Dollars in Lost Productivity, Marchex Study Finds
21. US Federal Trade Commission (FTC) (2016) Blocking unwanted calls
22. Kerr Jennifer C (2015) Complaints about automated calls up sharply. Accessed Aug 2015
23. Communications Fraud Control association (CFCA) (2016) Announces results of worldwide telecom fraud survey, 01 Dec 2016
24. Rebahi Y, Sisalem D, Magedanz T (2006) SIP spam detection. In: ICDT '06, pp 68–74
25. Tu H, Doupé A, Zhao Z, Ahn G (2016) SoK: everyone hates robocalls: a survey of techniques against telephone spam. In: 37th IEEE symposium on security and privacy
26. Study of Mechanisms for Protection against Unsolicited Communication for IMS (PUCI) (2012) In: Release 3GPP technical specification, 3GPP
27. Shin D, Ahn J, Shim C (2006) Progressive multi gray-leveling: a voice spam protection algorithm. In: IEEE Network, pp 18–24
28. Hong Y, Kunwadee S, Hui Z, ZonYin S, Debanjan S (2006) Incorporating active fingerprinting into SPIT prevention systems. In: The 3rd annual VoIP security workshop
29. Lentzen D, Grutzek G, Knospe H, Porschmann C (2011) Content-based detection and prevention of spam over IP telephony - system design, prototype and first results. In: IEEEICC2011, Japan, pp 1–5
30. Iranmanesh Seyed A, Hemant S, Haining W (2012) A voice spam filter to clean subscriber's mailbox. In: 8th International conference on security and privacy in communication networks, pp 349–367
31. Zhang G, Fischer-Hübner S (2011) Detecting near-duplicate SPITs in voice mailboxes using hashes. In: 14th international conference on information security, ISC'11, pp 152–167
32. Kolan P, Dantu R (2007) Socio-technical defense against voice spamming. ACM Trans Auton Adapt Syst 2(1)
33. Ono K, Schulzrinne H (2009) Have i met you before?: using cross-media relations to reduce SPIT. In: 3rd IPTCOMM, pp 1–7

34. Gupta P, Srinivasan B, Balasubramaniyan V, Ahamad M (2015) Phoneypot: data-driven under-
    standing of telephony threats. In: 20th NDSS
35. Balduzzi M, Gupta P, Gu L, Gao D, Ahamad M (2016) MobiPot: understanding mobile tele-
    phony threats with honeycards. In: 11th ACM ASIACCS
36. Consumers Union, Robocalls Keep Coming (2014)
37. Lindqvist J, Komu M (2007) Cure for spam over internet telephony. In: 4th IEEE CCNC, pp
    896–900
38. Quittek J, Niccolini S, Tartarelli S, Schlegel R (2008) On spam over internet telephony (SPIT)
    prevention. IEEE Commun Mag 46:80–86
39. Quittek J, Niccolini S, Tartarelli S, Stiemerling M, Brunner M, Ewald T (2007) Detecting SPIT
    calls by checking human communication patterns. In: IEEE ICC, Scotland, pp 1979–1984
40. Reaves B, Blue L, Abdullah H, Vargas L, Traynor P, Shrimpton T (2017) Authenticall: efficient
    identity and content authentication for phone calls. In: 26th USENIX security symposium
    (USENIX Security 17), Vancouver, BC. USENIX Association, pp 575–592
41. Banerjee N, Saklikar S, Saha S (2006) Anti-vamming trust enforcement in peer-to-peer VoIP
    networks. In: 2006 international conference on wireless communications and mobile comput-
    ing, IWCMC '06. ACM, pp 201–206
42. Sengar H, Wang X, Nichols A (2011) Thwarting spam over internet telephony (SPIT) attacks
    on VoIP networks. In: 19th IWQoS, pp 1–3
43. Vennila G, Manikandan MSK, Suresh MN (2018) Dynamic voice spammers detection using
    hidden markov model for voice over internet protocol network. Comput Secur 73:1–16
44. Wu Y-S, Bagchi S, Singh N, Wita R (2009) Spam detection in voice- over-IP calls through
    semi-supervised clustering. In: 39th Annual IEEE/IFIP DSN, Portugal, pp 307–316
45. Azad MA, Morla R (2012) Mitigating SPIT with social strength. In: 2012 IEEE TrustCom, pp
    393–1398
46. Azad MA, Morla R (2013) Caller-Rep: detecting unwanted calls with caller social strength.
    Comput Secur 39(Part B):219–236
47. Azad MA, Morla R (2011) Multistage SPIT detection in transit VoIP. In: 19 IEEE SoftCOM,
    pp 1–9
48. Sorge C, Seedorf J (2009) A provider-level reputation system for assessing the quality of SPIT
    mitigation algorithms. In: IEEE ICC '09, pp 1–6
49. Bou-Harb E, Pourzandi M, Debbabi M, Assi C (2012) A secure, efficient, and cost-effective
    distributed architecture for spam mitigation on LTE 4G mobile networks. John Wiley Secur
    Commun Netw
50. Schmidt AU, Leicher A, Shah Y, Cha I, Guccione L (2011) Sender scorecards. IEEE Veh
    Technol Mag 6:52–59
51. Azad MA, Morla R (2017) Early identification of spammers through identity linking, social
    network and call features. J Comput Sci 157–172
52. Azad MA, Morla R (2018) Rapid detection of spammers through collaborative information
    sharing across multiple service providers. Future Gener Comput Syst
53. Azad MA, Bag S (2017) Decentralized privacy-aware collaborative filtering of smart spammers
    in a telecommunication network. In: Proceedings of the 32nd symposium on applied computing,
    pp 1711–1717
54. Azad MA, Bag S, Tabassum S, Hao F (2017) privy: privacy preserving collaboration across
    multiple service providers to combat telecoms spam. IEEE Trans Emerg Top Comput

Function Call Graphs Versus Machine Learning for Malware Detection

Deebiga Rajeswaran, Fabio Di Troia, Thomas H. Austin
and Mark Stamp

Abstract Recent work has shown that a function call graph technique can perform well on some challenging malware detection problems. In this chapter, we compare this function call graph approach to elementary machine learning techniques that are trained on simpler features. We find that the machine learning techniques are generally more robust than the function call graphs, in the sense that the malware must be modified to a far greater extent before the machine learning techniques are significantly degraded. This work provides evidence that machine learning is likely to perform better than ad hoc approaches, particularly when faced with intelligent attackers who can attempt to exploit the inherent weaknesses in a given detection strategy.

1 Introduction

In this chapter, we consider an ad hoc malware scoring technique based on function call graph analysis [1, 2]. We then compare the results obtained with this function call graph score to several machine learning scores that are based on opcodes [3]. As part of this comparison, we morph the code in the test set, which serves to simulate the case where a malware writers modify their code in an effort to evade detection. Our results indicate that machine learning techniques are generally much more robust than the call graph score, in the sense that a significantly higher degree of code morphing is required before the machine learning techniques fail. This suggests that it may

D. Rajeswaran · F. Di Troia · T. H. Austin · M. Stamp (✉)
San Jose State University, San Jose, CA, USA
e-mail: mark.stamp@sjsu.edu

D. Rajeswaran
e-mail: deebiga.rajeswaran@sjsu.edu

F. Di Troia
e-mail: fabioditroia@msn.com

T. H. Austin
e-mail: thomas.austin@sjsu.edu

© Springer International Publishing AG, part of Springer Nature 2018
S. Parkinson et al. (eds.), *Guide to Vulnerability Analysis for Computer Networks and Systems*, Computer Communications and Networks,
https://doi.org/10.1007/978-3-319-92624-7_11

be difficult to outperform machine learning techniques under real-world conditions where attackers can rapidly adapt to improvements in malware detection capabilities.

The remainder of this paper is structured as the follows. In Sect. 2, we provide details on the function call graph score under consideration, along with an overview of selected relevant related work. We also provide a brief introduction to the various machine learning approaches that we consider. In Sect. 3, we present experimental results for the function call graph score and compare these results to similar experiments involving machine learning-based scores. Finally, Sect. 4 concludes the paper, and we also discuss future work.

2 Background

Here, we first discuss precious work related on function call graphs; then, we discuss the function call graph score in some detail. We conclude this section with a brief introduction of the various machine learning algorithms that we use when comparing results to the function call graph technique.

2.1 Related Work

Christodorescu and Jha [4] were the first to implement a static analysis malware detection technique based on a control flow graph. Ming et al. [2] develop and analyse a similarity metric based on the function calls in an executable, while Shang et al. [1] discuss the time and space complexities involved in control flow graphs and propose a function call graph-based malware detection method.

Shahid and Ibrahim [5] have proposed an annotated control flow graph in which the instructions are grouped into 21 patterns, and they have also parallelized the process to boost the performance. Deshpande [6] has analysed a function call graph strategy in which a graph colouring technique is used to reduce the effect of various obfuscation strategies.

Hidden Markov models (HMMs) have been extensively studied in the context of malware detection. For example, Xin et al. [7] and Qin et al. [8] apply HMMs to the problem of malware detection on mobile devices. In [7], Xin, et al. analyse the keys pressed and system function call sequences using HMMs, where the pressed keys represent the hidden states and system call sequences represent the observations. This technique is evaluated on a single Symbian application, with the focus on the SMS sending process. In [8], Qin et al. propose a prototype malware detection system based on HMMs, but it is not implemented or evaluated.

The research by Attaluri et al. [9] analyses profile hidden Markov models (PHMMs) for malware detection. The results are mixed, with some malware families being detected with high accuracy, but others only achieving low accuracies.

Graph techniques have also been extensively studied in the malware detection literature. The paper of Damodaran et al. [10] consider a graph-based score that uses dynamic API calls. Deshpande and Stamp [6] considers a function call graph score, which is claimed to be robust with respect to common code morphing strategies. However, the experimental evidence presented in this paper indicates that simpler machine learning-based scores are significantly more robust.

Combinations of classification techniques—the so-called ensemble techniques— have also been considered. For example, Zhang et al. [11] use Dempster–Shafer theory to generate combining rules based on probabilistic neural network (PNN) classifiers. They show that the ensemble outperforms the individual PNN classifiers.

The paper by Lu et al. [12] considers an ensemble method that they refer to as SVM-AR, which combines a support vector machine with association rules. Then, the association rules are used to reduce the number of false predictions produced by the SVM. The authors claim that their algorithm is a single learning algorithm that yields better results than many ensemble techniques.

Menahem et al. [13] combine five different classifiers, and the resulting classifier is compared to various ensemble techniques that have appeared in the literature.

In the paper [3], Singh et al. consider a machine learning approach that can be viewed as an ensemble, with several relatively simple scoring techniques combined using an SVM. It is shown that the SVM consistently outperforms any of the individual scores, and this improvement is even more pronounced in cases where the malware is highly obfuscated.

In Sect. 3, we compare a complex function call graph score, as implemented in [6], to the results obtained using the SVM-based technique in [3]. But before presenting these results, we discuss the function call graph score in some detail.

2.2 Function Call Graphs

In this section, we discuss the process of constructing a function call graph and of computing a score based on such graphs. The process is fairly involved, and we only provide an overview here—complete details can be found in [1, 2, 6], while pseudo-code for the specific implementation analysed in this chapter can be found in [14].

2.2.1 Constructing a Function Call Graph

To construct a function call graph from an executable, we first disassemble the exe file using IDA Pro [15] to obtain an assembly code representation. The functions present in the code are categorized as either local or external, where local functions begin with sub_xxxxxx proc near and end with sub_xxxxxx endp. The external functions are system calls and the library routines. Local functions are labelled differently in each sample, whereas external function names are consis-

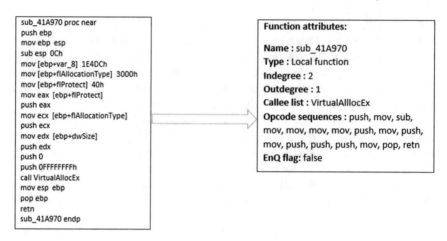

```
sub_41A970 proc near
push ebp
mov ebp esp
sub esp 0Ch
mov [ebp+var_8] 1E4DCh
mov [ebp+flAllocationType] 3000h
mov [ebp+flProtect] 40h
mov eax [ebp+flProtect]
push eax
mov ecx [ebp+flAllocationType]
push ecx
mov edx [ebp+dwSize]
push edx
push 0
push 0FFFFFFFFh
call VirtualAllocEx
mov esp ebp
pop ebp
retn
sub_41A970 endp
```

Function attributes:

Name : sub_41A970
Type : Local function
Indegree : 2
Outdegree : 1
Callee list : VirtualAlllocEx
Opcode sequences : push, mov, sub, mov, mov, mov, mov, push, mov, push, mov, push, push, push, mov, pop, retn
EnQ flag: false

Fig. 1 Example of function attributes stored in a vertex

tent across all samples. The function call graph scoring technique discussed below only considers the functions and the instruction sequences (i.e. mnemonic opcodes) contained within local functions. This approach defeats various code morphing techniques, such as transposition that relies on subroutine reordering.

The function call graph is of the form $G = (V, E)$, where V is the set of vertices and E is the set of edges. The vertices denote the functions, and the edges denote the relationship between functions [1, 2]. An example of the type of information that is stored in a vertex is given in Fig. 1.

The functions and their corresponding opcode sequences are parsed to identify entry points to the program. Then, using a breadth-first search (BFS) [16], we construct the function call graph, where non-entry point functions are added to the graph based on their caller–callee relationships [6]. The entry point functions are at the top level, and the non-entry point functions appear in lower levels. A detailed algorithm for constructing a function call graph as outlined here can be found in the paper [6].

2.2.2 Function Call Graph Score

After constructing function call graphs, to compute the similarity score between samples we need to compare the corresponding graphs. Similarity between such graphs implies commonality between subroutines, which are represented by vertices in the graphs.

The score that we use is based on the similarity of functions, both external and local. Since external functions are system or library calls, they have common names and thus are easily identified across all samples. Therefore, the external function similarity is scored based solely on function names. For the local functions, the names will vary, so the scoring of these functions is more complex. We describe

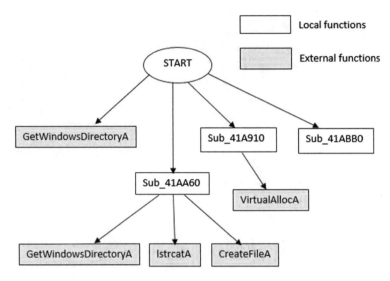

Fig. 2 Function call graph with external functions

the scoring of external and local functions in more detail below, assuming that G_1 and G_2 are the function call graphs to be scored. Note that the description below is from a fairly high-level view—for all of the details, see [6].

Common Vertices Based on External Functions: Again, external functions refer to system or library routine calls. Usually, external functions form the leaf node in the function call graph, having an indegree of 1 and outdegree of 0. These can be easily matched using their symbolic names since these names are same across all executables. For example, `VirtualAllocA`, `GetWindowsDirectoryA`, `lstrcatA`, and `CreateFileA` are the external functions that form the leaf nodes in the Zbot function call graph shown in Fig. 2.

Matching Local Functions Based on External Functions Similarity: If two or more external functions match in corresponding vertices of G_1 and G_2, this is considered to indicate possible similarity between the local functions that make calls to these external functions. Therefore, local functions in the function call graphs G_1 and G_2 are matched to see if they call the same external functions. If the external function matches exceed two, then the local function pair is considered to be common vertices and added to the set of common vertices.

Similarity Between Local Functions Based on Opcode Sequences: Finding the similarity between the local functions based on a specific opcode pattern or signature may not be effective, since such an approach can be defeated by, for example, dead code insertion. To make such matching more robust, we use a graph "colouring" technique to compare local functions. Every vertex is vectorized based on the occurrence and frequency of its opcodes, where each opcode is classified into one of the 15 types shown in Table 1.

Table 1 Instruction colour codes [2]

Code	Instruction type	Description
C_1	Data	Data transfer (e.g. mov)
C_2	Stack	Stack operations
C_3	Port	In and out
C_4	Lea	Destination address transmit
C_5	Flag	Flag transmit
C_6	Arithmetic	Add, shift, rotate, etc.
C_7	Logic	Bit–byte operation
C_8	String	String operation
C_9	Jump	Unconditional transfer
C_{10}	Branch	Conditional transfer
C_{11}	Loop	Loop control
C_{12}	Halt	Stop instruction execution
C_{13}	Bit	Bit test and bit scan
C_{14}	Processor	Processor control
C_{15}	Float	Floating point operation

All vertices in the graph are coloured based on a 15-bit (0, 1) vector, which marks the occurrence of instructions of each colour code. That is, element i of the vector is 1 if any instruction of "colour" i is present in the local function; otherwise, element i is 0. Another 15-bit vector stores the frequency of opcodes of each colour.

Suppose that the colour frequency vectors of the two local functions being compared are $X = (x_1, x_2, \ldots, x_{15})$ and $Y = (y_1, y_2, \ldots, y_{15})$. Then, the cosine similarity between these two vectors is computed as [2]

$$\text{sim}(X, Y) = \frac{\sum_{i=1}^{15} x_i \cdot y_i}{\sqrt{\left(\sum_{i=1}^{15} x_i^2\right)\left(\sum_{i=1}^{15} y_i^2\right)}} \tag{1}$$

A length similarity and a degree similarity are also computed. If the cosine similarity of the two frequency vectors is greater than or equal to a specified parameter α, the length similarity is greater than or equal to another parameter β, and the degree similarity is greater than or equal to a third parameter γ, then the local functions are considered to match. Based on previous work [1, 2], for the threshold values of α, β, and γ, we use 0.98, 0.83, and 0.5, respectively.

Similarity Between Local Functions Based on Matched Neighbours: Now that we have found common vertices between the two graphs based on the external and

Fig. 3 Successors of common vertices V_1 and V_2

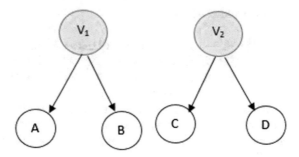

local functions, we further analyse the local functions. There is a higher probability that two vertices are similar if their (graph) neighbours match. Therefore, if the predecessors or successors of a specific vertex are common vertices, then we slightly relax the conditions for a vertex match. As an illustrative example, in Fig. 3 the vertices V_1 and V_2 are already identified as common vertices. Therefore, we use relaxed criteria when comparing A and B with C and D.

2.2.3 Similarity Measures for Function Call Graphs

Similarity Between Function Call Graphs: To compute the actual similarity score between function call graphs, the common edges are determined as outlined above. Then, the similarity between the two function call graphs is computed as [2, 6]

$$\mathrm{sim}(G_1, G_2) = \frac{2|\mathrm{common\_edge}(G_1, G_2)|}{|\mathrm{edge}(G_1)| + |\mathrm{edge}(G_2)|}$$

where $\mathrm{common\_edge}(G_1, G_2)$ is the set of all common edges between the function call graphs G_1 and G_2, and $|\mathrm{edge}(G_1)|$ and $|\mathrm{edge}(G_2)|$ represent the total number of edges in graphs G_1 and G_2, respectively. This score ranges from 0 to 1, with a higher score representing a better match.

2.3 Additional Malware Scores

In this section, we briefly discuss malware scores that we will later compare to the function call graph score discussed above. Specifically, we consider hidden Markov models, an opcode graph similarity technique, and a distance function based on simple substitution cryptanalysis. Then, we discuss support vector machines, which we use to combine these three scores.

2.3.1 Hidden Markov Models

A hidden Markov model (HMM) includes a Markov process that is "hidden" in the sense that the states cannot be directly observed. However, we do have access to a series of observations that are probabilistically related to the hidden states.

For the malware experiments considered here, an HMM is trained based on features (e.g. opcode sequences) extracted from members of a given malware family. The resulting model is then used to score other samples belonging to the same family, as well as representative benign samples. The results can then be used to determine the effectiveness of a detection strategy based on HMMs.

We use the following standard notation to describe an HMM [17].

$$
\begin{aligned}
T &= \text{length of the observation sequence} \\
N &= \text{number of states in the model} \\
M &= \text{number of distinct observation symbols} \\
Q &= \{q_0, q_1, \ldots, q_{N-1}\} = \text{distinct states of the Markov process} \\
V &= \{0, 1, \ldots, M-1\} = \text{set of possible observations} \\
A &= \text{state transition probabilities} \\
B &= \text{observation probability matrix} \\
\pi &= \text{initial state distribution} \\
\mathcal{O} &= (\mathcal{O}_0, \mathcal{O}_1, \ldots, \mathcal{O}_{T-1}) = \text{observation sequence}
\end{aligned}
$$

A model is defined by A, B, and π, and hence, we denote an HMM as $\lambda = (A, B, \pi)$.

Figure 4 gives a graphical view of a generic HMM. In this figure, the X_i represent the hidden states of the underlying Markov process.

Given a set of virus variants, we train a hidden Markov model on these malware samples. The resulting model can be viewed as representing statistical properties of the virus family. And the trained model can be used to determine the probability that a given program belongs to the same virus family as the training set. We train these models based on opcode—when training, we simply concatenated the opcode sequences extracted from the virus samples to yield one long observation sequence.

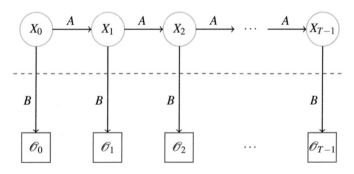

Fig. 4 Hidden Markov model

After training a model, we use the resulting HMM to compute the log-likelihood (per opcode) for each virus variant in the test set and also for each program in a representative benign set. Note that the test set consists of viruses in the same family as those used for training, but none of the same samples used for training. We expect that the trained model will assign higher scores to samples belonging to the virus family used to train the model. Success is determined by how well the HMM can separate viruses in the test set from the benign programs.

2.3.2 Opcode Graph Similarity

As with the HMM score, the opcode graph similarity (OGS) score [18] is based on extracted opcode sequences. A weighted directed graph is constructed, where each distinct opcode that appears is a node in the directed graph. A directed edge is inserted from a node to each possible successor node, that is, each successor opcode. Edge weights give the probability of the corresponding successor node.

Figure 5 illustrates the opcode graph corresponding to the snippet of code in Table 2. Note that the edge weights are normalized so that for any given node, the weights from all outgoing edges sum to one.

To use the OGS score for malware detection, we first construct an opcode graph corresponding to a collection of family viruses. Then given any sample that we want to score, we construct its opcode graph. The distance between the graphs is computed as the absolute sum of the differences between the corresponding edge weights.

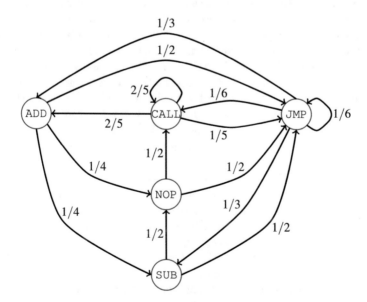

Fig. 5 Opcode graph

Table 2 Opcode sequence

Number	Opcode	Number	Opcode
1	CALL	11	JMP
2	JMP	12	ADD
3	ADD	13	NOP
4	SUB	14	JMP
5	NOP	15	CALL
6	CALL	16	CALL
7	ADD	17	CALL
8	JMP	18	ADD
9	JMP	19	JMP
10	SUB	20	SUB

Due to the normalization used, the OGS score weights each opcode the same. This is in contrast to the HMM score, where opcodes are effectively weighted according to their relative frequencies. Consequently, the OGS and HMM scores can yield very different results.

2.3.3 Simple Substitution Distance

The simple substitution distance (SSD) malware score considered in [19] is based on a fast hill climb technique known as Jakobsen's algorithm [20], which was developed for simple substitution cipher cryptanalysis. Although the malware families considered in this paper are not encrypted, many are obfuscated, and simple substitution cryptanalysis can, in effect, "see through" some common obfuscations.

It is well known that simple substitution ciphers are weak and that elementary statistical analysis can be used to attack such ciphers. The naive approach to simple substitution cryptanalysis is to guess a putative key based on monograph statistics, then decrypt the ciphertext using this putative key, and compute a score based on relevant language statistics. This process is slow due to the need to decrypt the ciphertext for each modification to the key.

In Jakobsen's algorithm, the plain text is decrypted once, then all subsequent modifications to the key only require elementary matrix manipulations. This works because the score is based entirely on language digraph statistics. In the malware context, we use opcode digraph statistics instead of language digraph statistics, but otherwise the process is completely analogous.

The SSD score is distinct from the HMM and OGS scores. Whereas the HMM and OGS scores rely directly on opcodes that are extracted from malware files, the SSD score modifies these opcodes via the "decryption" process, allowing us to reduce the effect of some types of obfuscation, such as opcode substitution.

2.3.4   Support Vector Machines

One of the most popular and useful machine learning techniques is the support vector machine (SVM). An SVM, which is used for binary classification, is a very general technique that can be applied in a wide variety of situations. In contrast to, say, a trained HMM, an SVM is typically used to directly generate a classification, as opposed to generating a score.

We can apply SVMs in virtually any situation where we might consider another scoring technique, such as an HMM. For example, in the context of malware detection, we could train an SVM on, say, opcodes extracted from members of a given malware family. Then, the trained SVM could be used to classify samples as either malware of the type that the SVM was trained to detect, or benign.

Due to the fact that an SVM can generate a classification, it is natural to apply the technique to a set of scores, as opposed to the raw data itself. In the experiments discussed below, we will apply SVMs to the HMM, OGS, and SSD scores. In this usage, the SVM acts as a "meta-score", in the sense that it generates a classification based on other scores, rather than scoring samples based directly on features extracted from the malware samples.

Next, we briefly discuss the SVM training process from an intuitive level. For additional details on SVMs, the authors recommend [21–23].

SVMs are a supervised learning technique, which means that they require labelled data. That is, we must use preprocessed data where the labels are known. Since SVMs are used for binary classification, the labels can be taken to be -1 and $+1$.

The "big" ideas behind the SVM technique are the following.

- Maximize the margin — Given labelled training data, we attempt to separate the training data using a hyperplane. In constructing this separating hyperplane, we want to maximize the separation (i.e. the margin) between the two classes of data in the training set.
- Work in a higher-dimensional space — We generally try to reduce the dimensionality of data, due to the "curse of dimensionality". However, in the context of SVMs, it is often highly beneficial to work in higher dimensions. By moving the problem to a higher dimension, the data points tend to be more easily separated, and hence, we have a better chance of finding a separating hyperplane.
- Kernel trick — This is the process by which we transform the data to a higher-dimensional space.

Figure 6 gives an example of a separating hyperplane (the solid line between the two dashed lines) that maximizes the margin. Typically, we cannot construct such a hyperplane in the space where the data naturally lies. This is where the kernel trick comes into the picture.

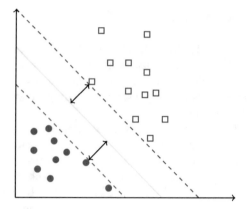

Fig. 6 Maximizing the margin

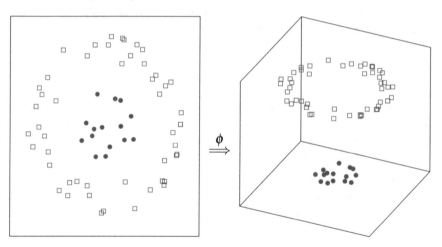

Fig. 7 Transformation from two to three dimensions

Figure 7 provides an illustration of the potential benefit of transforming to a higher dimension. In this example, the input space on the left is not linearly separable; that is, no separating hyperplane exists. But, after transforming via the function ϕ to the feature space on the right in Fig. 7, we can easily construct a hyperplane that separates the two types of data in the training set. This is the essence of the so-called kernel trick.

In practice, it is necessary to experiment with different kernel functions as this choice is indeed something of a "trick", and it plays a large role in the success-ful application of the technique. There are a variety of standard kernel functions available.

3 Experiments

In this section, we discuss experiments that we have performed involving the function call graph score. We also provide a comparison of some of our results to the various scores discussed in Sect. 2.3.

3.1 Datasets

We have used the malware families Zbot, ZeroAccess, and Harebot in this research. Each of these families is briefly described below.

- Zbot, also known as Zeus, is a Trojan horse that compromises a system by downloading configuration files or updates. Zbot is stealth malware that attempts to hide in the file system [24].
- ZeroAccess is a Trojan horse that makes use of an advanced rootkit to hide itself. ZeroAccess is capable of creating a new hidden file system, it can create a back door on the compromised system, and it can download additional malware [25].
- Harebot is a back door that provides remote access to the infected system. Because of its many features, it is also considered to be a rootkit [26].

All of these malware families were obtained from the Malicia Project [27]; see also [28].

For our representative benign samples, we have used Cygwin utility files. Note that these files have been used as benign samples in similar malware research, such as [29].

3.2 Measuring Success

In this research, we use the area under the ROC curve (AUC) to quantify the success of the experiments. Given a scatterplot, an ROC curve is obtained by plotting the false positive rate (FPR) against the true positive rate (TPR) as the threshold varies through the range of data values. An AUC of 1.0 implies that there exists a threshold that results in no false positives or false negatives, which is the ideal case.

In general, the AUC can be interpreted as the probability that a randomly selected positive instance scores higher than a randomly selected negative instance [30]. Therefore, an AUC of 0.5 means that the underlying binary classifier is no better than flipping a coin. Also, an AUC of p will yield an AUC of $1 - p$ if we simply reverse the classification criteria and, consequently, the AUC can always be interpreted so that it is at least 0.5.

An example of a scatterplot and the corresponding ROC curve is given in Fig. 8. The red circles in the scatterplot represent positive instances, while the blue squares

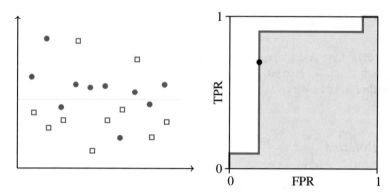

Fig. 8 Scatterplot and ROC curve

represent negative instances. In the context of malware classification, the circles are scores for malware files, while the squares are scores for benign files. Furthermore, we assume that higher scores are "better"; that is, for this particular score, positive instances are supposed to score higher than negative instances.

Note that if we place the threshold below the lowest point in the scatterplot in Fig. 8, then

$$TPR = 1 \text{ and } FPR = 1.$$

On the other hand, if we place the threshold above the highest point, then

$$TPR = 0 \text{ and } FPR = 0.$$

Consequently, an ROC curve must always include the points $(0, 0)$ and $(1, 1)$. The intermediate points on the ROC curve are determined as the threshold passes through the range of values. For example, if we place the threshold at the yellow line in the scatterplot in Fig. 8, the true positive rate is 0.7, since 7 of the 10 positive instances are classified correctly, while the false positive rate is 0.2, since 2 of the 10 negative cases lie on the wrong side of the threshold. This gives us the point $(0.2, 0.7)$ on the ROC curve, which is illustrated by the black circle on the ROC graph in Fig. 8. The shaded region in Fig. 8 represents the AUC, which is 0.75 in this example.

3.3 Results

In this section, we summarize our experimental results for the function call graph score discussed above. We also compare some of our results to several machine learning scores, based on the results in [3].

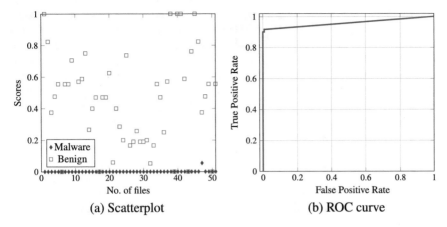

(a) Scatterplot (b) ROC curve

Fig. 9 Zbot results

3.3.1 Zbot

We scored a selection of Zbot samples and a set of benign samples using the function call graph score discussed above. The results of this particular experiment are given in Fig. 9, where Fig. 9a shows the scatterplot for these scores, while Fig. 9b gives the corresponding ROC curve. In this case, we obtain strong results with an AUC of 0.96.

3.3.2 ZeroAccess

Next, we scored ZeroAccess samples and the set of benign samples using our implementation of the function call graph score, as discussed above. The results of this experiment are given in Fig. 10, where Fig. 10a shows the scatterplot for these scores, while Fig. 10b gives the corresponding ROC curve. In this case, we only achieve an AUC of 0.77. This is a fairly modest result, which indicates an accuracy that is likely to be of limited use in any realistic application.

3.3.3 Harebot

Finally, we scored Harebot samples and our set of benign samples using our implementation of the function call graph score. The results of this experiment are given in Fig. 11, where Fig. 11a contains the scatterplot for these scores, while Fig. 11b gives the corresponding ROC curve. In this case, we obtain very poor results, with an AUC of 0.60. This is only marginally better than flipping a coin and is of little or no use as a practical classifier.

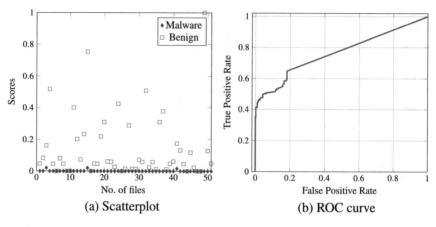

Fig. 10 ZeroAccess results

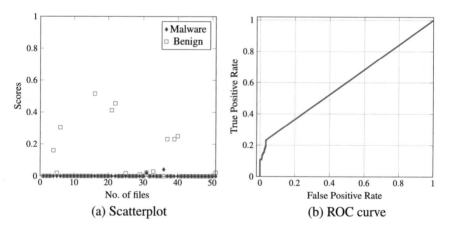

Fig. 11 Harebot results

3.4 Robustness Experiments

In this section, we simulate the effect of code morphing as applied to the Zbot family. Specifically, we have included external functions as dead code, which are randomly inserted in subroutines. This is a simple and practical morphing strategy that should diminish the effectiveness of the function call graph score.

The results of our robustness experiments for the Zbot family are given in terms of ROC curves in Fig. 12. The AUC values corresponding to the ROC curves in Fig. 12 are given in Table 3.

Zbot morphing experiments are also considered in [3], where the morphing was chosen in an effort to defeat the machine learning-based scores considered in that paper. The results from [3] are summarized here in Fig. 13. These experiments are

Fig. 12 Zbot morphed
samples ROC curve

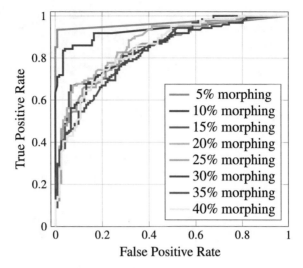

Table 3 AUC results for
Zbot

Morphing (%)	AUC
0	0.96
5	0.96
10	0.93
15	0.84
20	0.87
25	0.84
30	0.83
35	0.84
40	0.83

comparable to our Zbot experiments discussed in this section, but they are based primarily on machine learning techniques, rather than the function call graph score considered in this chapter. Specifically, the results in Fig. 13 compare the HMM, opcode graph (OGS), simple substitution distance (SSD), and the SVM scores, as discussed in Sect. 2.3, above.

Finally, in Fig. 14 we directly compare the robustness results for the machine learning (and other) scores in [3], as reproduced here in Fig. 13, with those obtained using our implementation of the function call graph (FCG) score, as summarized in Table 3.

From Fig. 14, we observe that our implementation of the FCG score is comparable in strength to the HMM score and fares somewhat better than the OGS and SSD scores. However, a straightforward SVM score based on relatively simple statistical and graph-based scores (i.e. the HMM, OGS, and SSD scores discussed above) is significantly more robust than the FCG score considered in this paper. This suggests

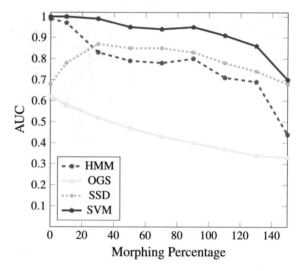

Fig. 13 Machine learning scores for morphed Zbot samples [3]

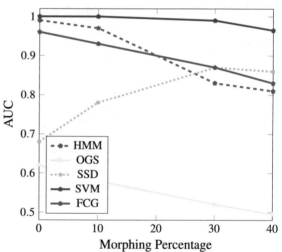

Fig. 14 Comparison function call graph score versus machine learning score for Zbot

that machine learning techniques can offer advantages over ad hoc solutions—at least with respect to robustness. The FCG score considered in this paper is relatively complex, yet a comparatively simple application of standard machine learning techniques yields significantly more robust results.

4 Conclusion and Future Work

The goal of the research presented in this chapter was to analyse the function call graph score in [1, 2, 6] and compare it to standard machine learning-based scores. We found that the function call graph score can perform well, but that it is somewhat "fragile" in comparison with machine learning techniques. This observation is significant, since it provides some evidence of the inherent difficulty when attempting to improve on machine learning techniques through ad hoc strategies. This difficulty is particularly evident in adversarial situations, where attackers can attempt to develop targeted attacks based on knowledge of the detection strategy. Machine learning techniques tend to be relatively robust and adaptable in such situations, whereas ad hoc techniques are unlikely to share these characteristics to such a high degree.

For future work, it would be interesting to perform similar tests on other ad hoc malware detection strategies and determine how such techniques compare to machine learning-based approaches. This would be particularly interesting with respect to robustness tests, where attacks are developed specifically to defeat each scoring technique. In a similar vein, it would be interesting to conduct such robustness attacks on a wide variety of machine learning techniques to determine how they compare to each other. That is, we would like to know which machine learning techniques are most robust with respect to specific attack strategies.

5 Questions

1. What is the difference between a function call graph and a machine learning techniques?
2. What is the process of constructing a function call graph from an executable?
3. Define mnemonic opcodes and subroutines.
4. How external functions can be used to define Common Vertices?
5. What is the process of matching local functions by utilising External Functions Similarity?
6. Describe the process of computing the actual similarity score between function call graphs?
7. What is the appropriate method of training a hidden Markov model on different virus variants?
8. Define the Simple Substitution Distance (SSD) malware score and how it is used in Jakobsen's algorithm?
9. How kernel functions plays an important role in the successful application of the proposed technique?
10 Describe the potential benefits of transforming data into a higher dimension.

References

1. Shang S, Zheng N, Xu J, Xu M, Zhang H (2015) Detecting malware variants via function-call graph similarity. In: MALWARE 2015 Proceedings of malicious and unwanted software, pp 113–120
2. Xu, M., Wu, L., Qi, S., Xu, J., Zhang, H., Ren, Y., Zheng, N.: A similarity metric method of obfuscated malware using function-call graph. J Comput Virol Hacking Tech **9**(1), 35–47 (2013)
3. Singh, T., Troia, F.D., Visaggio, C.A., Austin, T.H., Stamp, M.: Support vector machines and malware detection. J Comput Virol Hacking Tech **12**(4), 203–212 (2016). https://doi.org/10. 1007/s11416-015-0252-0
4. Christodorescu M, Jha S (2003) Static analysis of executables to detect malicious patterns. In: Proceedings of the 12th conference on USENIX security symposium, SSYM'03, USENIX Association, Berkeley, CA, USA, pp 169–186. http://dl.acm.org/citation.cfm?id=1251353. 1251365
5. Alam, S., Traor, I., Sogukpinar, I.: Annotated control flow graph for metamorphic malware detection. Comput J **58**(10), 2608–2621 (2015)
6. Deshpande, P., Stamp, M.: Metamorphic detection using function call graph analysis. MIS Rev Int J **21**(1/2), 15–34 (2015)
7. Xin K, Li G, Qin Z, Zhang Q (2012) Malware detection in smartphone using hidden Markov model. In: Fourth international conference on multimedia information networking and security, MINES 2012, pp 857–860
8. Qin Z, Chen N, Zhang Q, Di Y (2011) Mobile phone viruses detection based on HMM. In: Third international conference on multimedia information networking and security, MINES 2011, pp 516–519
9. Attaluri, S., McGhee, S., Stamp, M.: Profile hidden Markov models and metamorphic virus detection. J Comput Virol **5**(2), 151–169 (2009). https://doi.org/10.1007/s11416-008-0105-1
10. Damodaran, A., Troia, F.D., Visaggio, C.A., Austin, T.H., Stamp, M.: A comparison of static, dynamic, and hybrid analysis for malware detection. J Comput Virol Hacking Tech **13**(1), 1–12 (2017). https://doi.org/10.1007/s11416-015-0261-z
11. Zhang B, Yin J, Hao J, Zhang D, Wang S (2007) Malicious codes detection based on ensemble learning. In: Proceedings of the 4th international conference on autonomic and trusted computing, ATC'07. Springer, Berlin, pp 468–477. http://dl.acm.org/citation.cfm?id=2394798. 2394857
12. Lu, Y.-B., Din, S.-C., Zheng, C.-F., Gao, B.-J.: Using multi-feature and classifier ensembles to improve malware detection. CCIT J **32**(2), 57–72 (2010)
13. Menahem, E., Shabtai, A., Rokach, L., Elovici, Y.: Improving malware detection by applying multi-inducer ensemble. Comput Stat Data Anal **53**(4), 1483–1494 (2009)
14. Rajeswaran D (2015) Function call graph score for malware detection. Master's Project, Department of Computer Science, San Jose State University. http://scholarworks.sjsu.edu/etd_ projects/445/
15. Hex-Rays (2017). https://www.hex-rays.com
16. Kingsford C (2015) Graph traversals. http://www.cs.cmu.edu/~ckingsf/class/02713-s13/ lectures/lec07-dfsbfs.pdf
17. Stamp M (2004) A revealing introduction to hidden Markov models. https://www.cs.sjsu.edu/ ~stamp/RUA/HMM.pdf
18. Runwal, N., Low, R.M., Stamp, M.: Opcode graph similarity and metamorphic detection. J Comput Virol **8**(1–2), 37–52 (2012). https://doi.org/10.1007/s11416-012-0160-5
19. Shanmugam, G., Low, R.M., Stamp, M.: Simple substitution distance and metamorphic detection. J Comput Virol Hacking Tech **9**(3), 159–170 (2013). https://doi.org/10.1007/s11416-013-0184-5
20. Jakobsen, T.: A fast method for the cryptanalysis of substitution ciphers. Cryptologia **19**, 265–274 (1995)

21. Wang R (2016) Introduction to support vector machines. http://fourier.eng.hmc.edu/e161/lectures/svm
22. Ng A (2015) Support vector machines. http://cs229.stanford.edu/notes/cs229-notes3.pdf
23. Statsoft: support vector machines (SVM) introductory overview (2015). http://www.statsoft.com/textbook/support-vector-machines
24. Symantec: Trojan.Zbot (2015). http://www.symantec.com/security_response/writeup.jsp?docid=2010-011016-3514-99
25. Symantec: Trojan.ZeroAccess (2015). http://www.symantec.com/security_response/writeup.jsp?docid=2011-071314-0410-99
26. Panda Security. Harebot. M (2015). http://www.pandasecurity.com/homeusers/security-info/220319/Harebot.M
27. Malicia Project (2015). http://malicia-project.com/
28. Nappa A, Rafique MZ, Caballero J (2013) Driving in the cloud: an analysis of drive-by download operations and abuse reporting. In: Proceedings of the 10th international conference on detection of intrusions and malware, and vulnerability assessment, DIMVA'13. Springer, Berlin, pp 1–20
29. Wong, W., Stamp, M.: Hunting for metamorphic engines. J Comput Virol **2**(3), 211–229 (2006). https://doi.org/10.1007/s11416-006-0028-7
30. Bradley, A.P.: The use of the area under the roc curve in the evaluation of machine learning algorithms. Pattern Recognit **30**(7), 1145–1159 (1997)

Detecting Encrypted and Polymorphic Malware Using Hidden Markov Models

Dhiviya Dhanasekar, Fabio Di Troia, Katerina Potika and Mark Stamp

Abstract Encrypted code is often present in some types of advanced malware, while such code virtually never appears in legitimate applications. Hence, the presence of encrypted code within an executable file could serve as a strong heuristic for malware detection. In this chapter, we consider the feasibility of detecting encrypted segments within an executable file using hidden Markov models.

1 Introduction

Malware writers often use encrypted code as a means of evading signature detection. Since encrypted code rarely—if ever—appears in legitimate applications, the presence of encrypted code in a file could serve as a powerful heuristic for malware detection. The encryption used in malware is generally in the form of a repeated XOR of a fixed byte or pattern, which is equivalent to a simple substitution cipher. In this chapter, we consider the feasibility of detecting such weakly-encrypted sections in files using hidden Markov models.

The remainder of this chapter is organized as follows. In Sect. 2, we provide relevant background information, including an overview of hidden Markov models. Our experiments and results are given in Sect. 3. Finally, Sect. 4 contains our conclusions and provides suggestions for future work.

D. Dhanasekar · F. Di Troia · K. Potika · M. Stamp (✉)
San Jose State University, San Jose, CA, USA
e-mail: mark.stamp@sjsu.edu

D. Dhanasekar
e-mail: dhiviyadhanasekar@gmail.com

F. Di Troia
e-mail: fabioditroia@msn.com

K. Potika
e-mail: katerina.potika@sjsu.edu

© Springer International Publishing AG, part of Springer Nature 2018
S. Parkinson et al. (eds.), *Guide to Vulnerability Analysis for Computer Networks and Systems*, Computer Communications and Networks,
https://doi.org/10.1007/978-3-319-92624-7_12

281

2 Background

In this section, we discuss various types of malware. We then discuss malware detection methods, with the emphasis on machine learning approaches. We also introduce the basic concepts behind hidden Markov models.

2.1 Malware and Viruses

Malware, or malicious software, is any software that has a malicious intent. Malware can be used to disrupt computer or mobile operations, gather sensitive information, gain access to private computer systems, or display unwanted advertising, for example [1]. Malware can be classified as virus, worm, trojan, trapdoor, rabbit, or spyware, among other possible categories.

A virus can be defined as a self-replicating computer program that operates without the consent of the user and spreads by attaching a copy of itself to some part of another program [2]. Although not all malware are viruses, we use the terms malware and virus interchangeably in this chapter.

2.2 Types of Viruses

Viruses can be classified based on what they infect [3]. For example, viruses can infect the boot sector, files, macros, memory, applications, email, data, compilers, library routines, debuggers, and even antivirus softwares [4]. Another malware classification scheme is based on how they infect. Using this classification, viruses can be categorized as encrypted, polymorphic, or metamorphic, for example.

2.3 Evolution of Viruses

Early viruses relied on users sharing floppy disks to transmit their infection, while modern state of the art zero-day viruses can be extremely sophisticated. This evolution has not occurred in a vacuum, as malware writers have constantly innovated to counter advancements in antivirus software. Here, we briefly summarize some of this history, with the emphasis on the "arms race" nature of the malware problem.

2.3.1 Early Viruses

The so-called Brain virus is often considered to be the first malware of any significance. This virus was released in January of 1986 [4, 5] and it targeted the boot sector by changing the disk label of affected sectors to "©Brain" [6]. The malware would then scan the boot sector each time the disk was read, and if the boot sector was not infected, it would be infected. As a result, it was difficult to remove this virus completely. But, each time Brain copied itself, it created an exact copy, and hence it was vulnerable to signature based detection [2]. Antivirus developers have found signature based detection methods to be highly effective.

2.3.2 Encrypted Viruses

To counter signature detection, virus writers created encrypted viruses. In such malware, the signature is hidden under a layer of encryption. Here, the encryption is for obfuscation and crpytographic strength is not a concern. Hence, techniques such as a repeated XOR of a fixed byte value, which is equivalent to a simple substitution cipher. However, encrypted viruses require some plaintext code for the decryption routine, which opens the door to signature scanning.

2.3.3 Polymorphic Viruses

To evade detection of the decryption routine in an encrypted virus, malware writers began to morph the decryption code. These viruses are said to be polymorphic. The first polymorphic virus, 1260, was a virus from the chameleon family that first appeared in 1990, and was developed by Mark Washburn [7].

Figure 1 illustrates a polymorphic virus replicating by applying a morphed decryptor to the next generation of the virus, while the (plaintext) body remains unchanged [8]. Polymorphic viruses are able to create an unlimited number of new and different decryptors [7].

Advanced polymorphic viruses often utilize code obfuscation techniques such as code insertion or code substitution to mutate their decryptor code. In principle, a new decryptor can be constructed for each new infection [9].

Polymorphic viruses can be challenging to detect [2]. However, since the body of the decrypted virus remains the same, and since the virus will decrypt the body during its execution, emulation combined with signature scanning can succeed in detecting polymorphic malware. The primary drawback to emulator based detection is that it is likely to be slow.

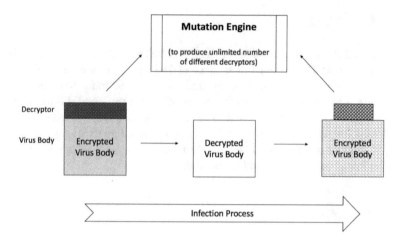

Fig. 1 Structure of a polymorphic virus

2.3.4   Metamorphic Viruses

While a polymorphic virus encrypts its code and morphs its decryption routine, a metamorphic virus changes the structure of its body [3]. That is, each time a metamorphic virus propagates, it "reprograms" itself by changing its internal structure, but leaves its function unchanged. Figure 2 illustrated various generations of a metamorphic virus [8]. Although the virus appears to have changed, it effectively serves the same purpose. Thus the metamorphic virus avoid signature detection by ensuring there is no fixed sequence of bytes that is characteristic of all instances. Detection of well-designed metamorphic malware is a challenging research problem. Fortunately, creating well-designed metamorphic malware is itself extremely challenging, and these viruses have never become a serious threat in practice.

2.4   Virus Encryption

Encrypted viruses generally XOR a fixed pattern, or rely on an equivalent operation, such as a simple substitution. Such encryption is very weak as a cipher, but it is nevertheless valuable to a virus writer as it serves to obfuscate the code [7].

2.5   Virus Detection Techniques

Malware causes damage estimated in the billions of dollars each year [10, 11]. Hence, virus detection is clearly an important problem. This section summarizes

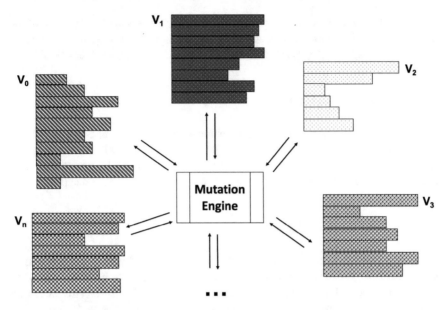

Fig. 2 Various generations of a metamorphic virus

Table 1 Strengths and weaknesses of virus detection techniques

Method	Strengths	Weaknesses
Signature based	Efficient, fast, relatively simple	Zero-day malware, storage
Anomaly based	Zero-day malware	Costly to implement, false positives
Emulation based	Polymorphic and metamorphic viruses	Costly to implement, slow

virus detection techniques commonly used today. Table 1 summarizes the advantages and disadvantages of these techniques [4, 12].

2.5.1 Signature Based Detection

To detect most types of malware, signature scanning is effective. In this approach, a signature or a sequence of bytes that are characteristic of a virus is extracted and added to a database of virus signatures. Signature based virus detection systems compare a suspected virus against this database and perform pattern matching. If a matching signature is found in the database, then the code may be a virus—secondary testing is likely necessary to confirm that it is indeed malware. Most antivirus systems in use today are largely based on signature detection.

Signature based detection cannot handle zero-day viruses, as the signature of the new viruses will be unknown. Signature scanning might also require a significant amount of storage to keep track of signatures, and such an approach can be slow.

2.5.2 Anomaly Based Detection

Anomaly based detection systems monitor for the presence of abnormal activity. If sufficiently abnormal activity is detected, then the system may have detected malware [4]. Such a detection system typically has a relatively high false positive rate and hence may need to be used in conjunction with another detection system.

2.5.3 Emulation Based Detection

Emulation based detection involves executing suspected malware in a sandboxed or virtual environment where antivirus can identify a signature or behavior related to known (or suspected) malware. As mentioned above, emulation based virus detection can be effective for advanced polymorphic and metamorphic viruses. However, it is slow and such systems do not always produce correct results [13].

2.6 Machine Learning for Malware Detection

The virus detection techniques discussed above are not able to detect all types of viruses. A more general approach, that could detect a greater variety of viruses without executing them would be valuable. Machine learning algorithms offer the potential for just such an approach.

As illustrated in Fig. 3, machine learning algorithms are typically implemented in two phases—training and testing. During the training phase, the algorithm is provided input data similar to what we want to detect and a model is trained. In the testing phase, the trained model is tested to determine its accuracy on relevant data.

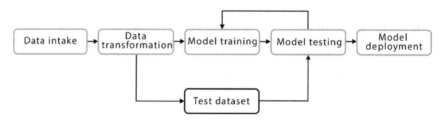

Fig. 3 Machine learning implementation

Features that are used by machine learning algorithms could include the size of the malware, n-gram byte sequences, plaintext strings found in the disassembled files, opcode sequences, API calls, system resource information (e.g., the set of DLLs), and so on.

In [14], three machine learning methods (RIPPER, naïve Bayes and multi-naïve Bayes) were implemented to classify malware. All three algorithms provided a higher virus detection rate than the signature based virus detection method. Many other machine learning techniques have been applied to the malware detection problem. Such techniques include k-nearest neighbors, support vector machines, artificial neural networks, decision trees, random forests, and so on. A comparison of many of these methods can be found in [15].

2.6.1 Hidden Markov Models

A Markov model of order one is a stochastic process where future states depend only on the current state [16]. Higher order Markov processes can be considered, but in any case, the "memory" is finite. A hidden Markov model (HMM) includes a Markov process that is "hidden" in the sense that the states are not directly observable. Instead, we have access to a series of observations that are probabilistically related to the unobserved hidden states. Uses of HMMs include parts-of-speech tagging (i.e. classifying different parts of a text as nouns, verbs, etc.), biological protein sequence classification, and gene prediction [17], among many other applications.

Figure 4 shows the various parameters associated with the HMM algorithm. The parameters used in Fig. 4 are explained in Table 2 [16, 17]. This notation will be used throughout the remainder of this chapter.

The $N \times N$ matrix A contains state transition probabilities for the (hidden) Markov process. The B matrix is $N \times M$ and contains the probabilities of each observation symbol in each state. The vector π is of length N and contains the initial state distribution—the element in position i of π simply gives the probability of starting in state i.

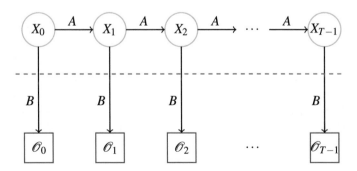

Fig. 4 Hidden Markov model

Table 2 HMM notation

$\mathcal{O}$	is the observation (or input) sequence
T	is the length of the observation sequence $\mathcal{O}$
M	is the number of unique observation symbols
N	is the number of hidden states in the model
A	is the state transition matrix
B	is the observation probability matrix
X	is the set of hidden states of the Markov process
π	is the initial state probability distribution

2.7 HMM and English Text

To illustrate the HMM algorithm, we consider a classic application to English text analysis [18]. From a large collection of English text, we remove all special characters, punctuation, etc., and convert all letters to lower-case. This gives us $M = 27$ observation symbols (letters and word space). For this specific example, we choose $N = 2$ hidden states, and train a model on $T = 50,000$ observation symbols extracted from the Brown corpus [19].

The transpose of a B matrix obtained for this experiment is given in Table 3. The results show that the HMM has split the 27 observation symbols into two categories, namely, vowels and consonants. These two categories correspond to the hidden states of the HMM.

If we repeat this experiment with $N = 3$ hidden states, the consonant state is split into two states—it is possible to make sense of the resulting hidden states for $N \in \{3, 4, 5, \ldots, 12\}$. In any case, the key point here is that we made no a priori assumption about the hidden states, yet for the $N = 2$ case, the HMM was able to extract the important distinction between consonants and vowels from the data itself. This example nicely captures the essence of machine learning.

2.7.1 HMM and Simple Substitution

Suppose that we apply the HMM experiment discussed in Sect. 2.7, above to a simple substitution ciphertext—where the underlying plaintext is English—instead of English plaintext. With $N = 2$ hidden states, we will determine the ciphertext symbols that correspond to consonants and those that correspond to vowels. Furthermore, if we use $N = 26$ hidden states (and assuming no word space), we can determine the key. Numerous experiments involving the application of HMMs to various classic substitution ciphers can be found in [20].

Table 3 Transpose of B matrix for English text

Character	Hidden state 1	Hidden state 2
a	0.0000	0.1335
b	0.0195	0.0000
c	0.0467	0.0002
d	0.0586	0.0002
e	0.0000	0.2496
f	0.0413	0.0000
g	0.0179	0.0064
h	0.0918	0.0000
i	0.0000	0.1365
j	0.0025	0.0000
k	0.0040	0.0006
l	0.0536	0.0000
m	0.0353	0.0000
n	0.1048	0.0000
o	0.0000	0.1445
p	0.0277	0.0041
q	0.0016	0.0000
r	0.0990	0.0000
s	0.0945	0.0006
t	0.1108	0.0514
u	0.0017	0.0463
v	0.0149	0.0000
w	0.0262	0.0000
x	0.0045	0.0000
y	0.0080	0.0207
z	0.0011	0.0000
space	0.1339	0.2055

2.8 Discussion

There has been extensive research showing that HMMs can be used to detect challenging classes of metamorphic malware [21–24]. In the remainder of this chapter, we consider experiments where we apply HMMs to the problem of detecting polymorphic and encrypted malware, which presents a different set of challenges as compared to metamorphic malware. Specifically, we want to determine whether HMMs can be used to identify sections of code that have been encrypted with classic substitution cipher techniques (or the equivalent thereof). This would be useful, since good results in this direction can serve as a strong heuristic for the presence of encrypted or polymorphic malware.

We note that in [25], a powerful and simple technique is given for detecting the presence of cryptographic keys in code or data. This technique relies on the fact that keys are random, whereas code and most other data is not. This same approach would be applicable to the problem of detecting ciphertext that was generated by a strong cipher, as such ciphertext would be random data. However, polymorphic and encrypted malware use classic cipher techniques, which do not generate random ciphertext. In fact, classic ciphers are cryptographically weak precisely because statistical information is present in the ciphertext. Paradoxically, from the perspective of randomness tests, such as that given in [25], this weakness of classic substitution ciphers can actually be viewed as a strength. In other words, when a cipher is used for obfuscation, rather than for its cryptographic strength a classic substitution cipher has an advantage over a strong modern cipher.

3 Experiments and Results

In this section, we describe experiments performed using HMMs to detect encrypted opcodes and encrypted bytes extracted from executable files. These experiments are somewhat analogous to the English text simple substitution examples discussed above. Additional experiments and results can be found in the report [26].

3.1 Encrypted Code Experiments

For our training set, we created executable files from 58 C programs. We then disassembled these executable files to obtain mnemonic opcode sequences (e.g., add, mov, jmp, and so on). The monograph statistics for the most common opcodes are given in Table 4.

Our training data contains a total of $T = 669,900$ opcodes (i.e., observations), and we have to total of 150 distinct opcodes. To generate encrypted opcodes, we used a simple substitution and replaced each opcode by another opcode. These encrypted opcodes then serve as the training data or observation sequence for an HMM.

For our test data, we used 312 programs that were not part of our training set. For each of these programs, we extracted the opcode sequence. Then a subset of these sequences were encrypted using a simple substitution. For our various HMM experiments, we score these files using our trained HMM to determine how well we can distinguish between the encrypted and plaintext opcode sequences.[1] We also performed experiments where part or each file was encrypted. For these experiments, our aim is to determine how well we could distinguish the encrypted code from the plaintext sections of code. This latter set of experiments is discussed in Sect. 3.2.

---

[1] An HMM score is dependent on the length of the sequence scored. Therefore, in each case we normalize the score so that it is given as a log likelihood per opcode (LLPO).

Table 4 Most frequent opcodes

Opcode	Frequency	Relative frequency (%)
add	286726	42.80
mov	55520	8.29
pop	29362	4.38
push	24937	3.72
jz	20702	3.09
imul	16818	2.51
inc	16542	2.47
cmp	13603	2.03
or	13479	2.01
nop	13258	1.98
jmp	12129	1.81
call	12062	1.80
test	11936	1.78
lea	11660	1.74
sub	11194	1.67
jnz	7752	1.16
and	7520	1.12
jc	7352	1.10
xor	6645	0.99
gs	6288	0.94

For each experiment, we generate a scatterplots of scores. To measure the effectiveness of our experiments, we rely on ROC analysis. A receiver operating characteristic (ROC) curve is generated by plotting the false positive rate versus the true positive rate as the threshold passes through the entire range of scores in a scatterplot. An AUC of 1.0 indicates ideal separation (i.e., there exists a threshold for which no false positives or false negatives occur), while an AUC of 0.5 indicates that the binary classifier is no better than flipping a coin. The area under the ROC curve (AUC) gives the probability that a randomly selected positive instance scores higher than a randomly selected negative instance [27]. We use the AUC as the measure of success for our experiments.

Again, the primary aim of our experiment is to determine the feasibility of using HMMs to distinguish encrypted code and plaintext (unencrypted) code. In order to do this and find optimal HMM parameters, we tested models for various values of N and M. In each case, we scored the encrypted files and plaintext files for each training model and computed scatterplots, ROC curves, and computed the AUC statistic. We now describe these experiments in more detail.

First, we experimented with $N \in \{2, 3\}$ and $M \in \{20, 25, 30, 35, 40, 50\}$. For a selected value of M, we distinguish the M most common opcodes, and group all

Table 5 AUC and example thresholds

N	M	AUC	Threshold			TPR			FPR		
2	20	1	−0.99	−1.46	−3.65	0.006	1.00	1.00	0.00	0.00	1.00
2	25	1	−1.66	−2.00	−4.00	0.006	1.00	1.00	0.00	0.00	1.00
2	30	1	−2.35	−2.69	−4.75	0.006	1.00	1.00	0.00	0.00	1.00
2	35	1	−2.40	−2.78	−4.87	0.006	1.00	1.00	0.00	0.00	1.00
2	40	1	−2.79	−3.18	−4.98	0.006	1.00	1.00	0.00	0.00	1.00
2	50	1	−3.16	−3.42	−5.71	0.006	1.00	1.00	0.00	0.00	1.00
3	20	1	−0.74	−1.05	−4.27	0.006	1.00	1.00	0.00	0.00	1.00
3	25	1	−1.31	−1.53	−4.10	0.006	1.00	1.00	0.00	0.00	1.00
3	30	1	−1.71	−2.03	−4.23	0.006	1.00	1.00	0.00	0.00	1.00
3	35	1	−1.66	−1.91	−4.86	0.006	1.00	1.00	0.00	0.00	1.00
3	40	1	−2.04	−2.31	−4.99	0.006	1.00	1.00	0.00	0.00	1.00
3	50	1	−2.43	−2.60	−5.30	0.006	1.00	1.00	0.00	0.00	1.00

other opcodes together in one "other" category. As shown in Table 5, for these experiments, the AUC value in all cases was found to be 1.0. That is, all models were able to perfectly separate the encrypted code samples from the plaintext code samples.

Since the results were similar for all the training models, we only present the graphical results for the $N = 2$ and $M = 30$ case. Figure 5 shows the scatterplot of the scores generated using this model. The scores plotted in red are the scores of encrypted samples, while the blue scores are those of the plaintext samples. It is clear that we can easily distinguish encrypted data from plaintext in this case. Figure 6 shows the corresponding ROC curve for this experiment, where we see that the AUC is clearly 1.0.

3.2 Partially Encrypted Samples

In this section, we consider the case where part of a sample is encrypted. This is more realistic for malware that is embedded within a larger program.

We experimented with the following window sizes: { 100, 150, 200, 300, 400, 500, 700, 800, 900, 1000, 1200, 1300, 1500, 1700, 1850, 2000, 2100, 2200, 2400, 2500, 2600, 2700, 2900, 3000, 3200, 3400}. The AUC statistics generated for these window lengths are shown in Fig. 7 and the corresponding ROC curves are presented in Fig. 8. We can see from the AUC statistics and the ROC curves that when the window length is small, our models are incapable of accurately distinguishing encrypted and plaintext sections. As we increase the window length, we see that window sizes between 1850 and 2200 provide optimal results, with an AUC of 1.0 for each of these

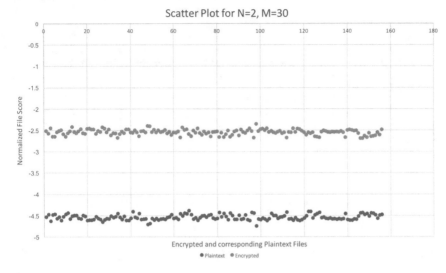

Fig. 5 Scatterplot for scores for $N = 2$ and $M = 30$

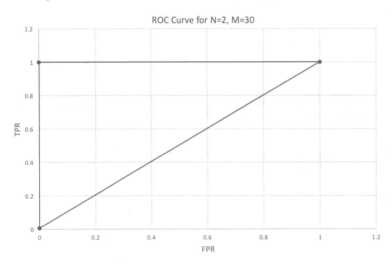

Fig. 6 ROC curve for $N = 2$ and $M = 30$

cases. Beyond a window size of 2200, the results deteriorate. Scatterplots for window sizes of {800, 1300, 1850, 2200} are given in Fig. 9(a) through (d), respectively.

In this section, we experimented only with non-overlapping windows. While the results are strong, this does not provide a fine-grained view of the boundaries between encrypted and plaintext sections, which would be useful to determine in practice. Therefore, we next consider overlapping sliding windows.

We define the extent of the overlap between consecutive windows as the slide length. For all experiments up to this point, we have a slide length of zero. We have

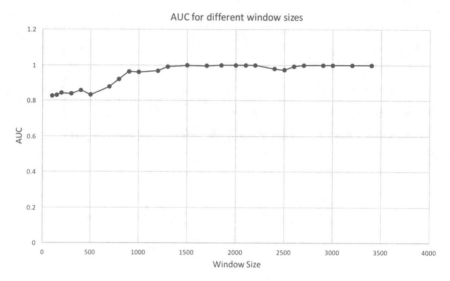

Fig. 7 AUC values for all window sizes

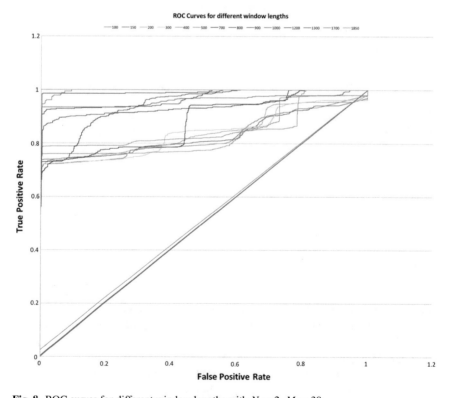

Fig. 8 ROC curves for different window lengths with $N = 2, M = 30$

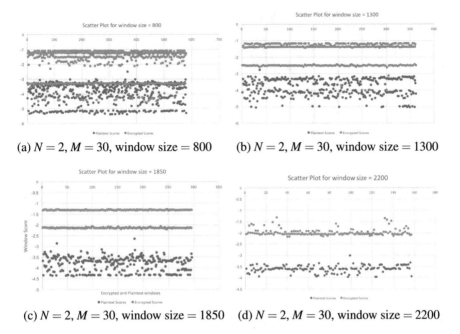

(a) $N = 2, M = 30$, window size $= 800$ (b) $N = 2, M = 30$, window size $= 1300$

(c) $N = 2, M = 30$, window size $= 1850$ (d) $N = 2, M = 30$, window size $= 2200$

Fig. 9 Scatterplots

tested each slide length of 50, 100, 150, 200, and for each of these, we experiment with each window size of 300, 400, 500, 700, 800, 900, 1000, 1200, 1300, 1500, 1700, 1850, 2000, 2100, 2200, 2400, 2500, 2600, 2700, 2900, 3000, 3200, 3400. Figure 10 gives the ROC curves for these window slide lengths and window size combinations, while Table 6 contains the corresponding AUC values.

The results here range from and AUC of 0.8 to nearly 1.0. Furthermore, for every window size greater than 1300, we obtain AUC values of at more than 0.99 regardless of the slide. These results indicate that we can easily determine the boundaries of encrypted code sections with great accuracy.

3.3 Byte Based Experiments

In this section, we give results for experiments based on raw bytes in a file, instead of opcodes. In order to test with bytes of an executable file, we use the same training set (58 programs) and test set (312 programs) as in the opcode based experiments discussed above, but apply XOR encryption directly to the bytes of the exe files.

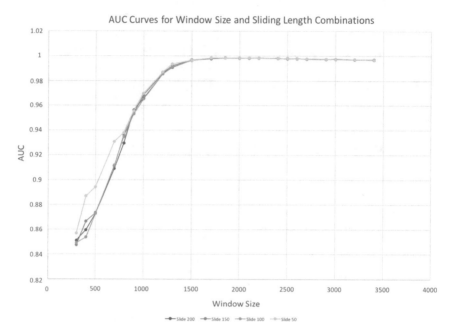

Fig. 10 ROC curves for different window sizes and slide lengths

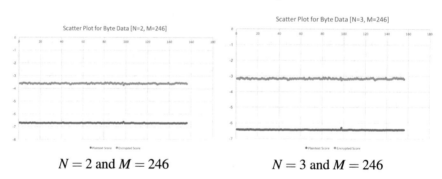

Fig. 11 Scatterplot for scores for byte based experiment

The scatterplot generated for HMMs with $N = 2$ and $N = 3$ hidden states are given in Figs. 11a, b, respectively, where the red dots represent encrypted samples and the blue dots denote plaintext samples. We can see from the scatterplots that our HMM approach is able to successfully separate the encrypted and plaintext byte samples—the resulting AUC value is clearly 1.0.

Table 6 AUC for various combinations of window sizes and slide lengths

Window length	Slide			
	200	150	100	50
300	0.8510	0.8474	0.8490	0.8569
400	0.8596	0.8666	0.8537	0.8869
500	0.8728	0.8734	0.8728	0.8943
700	0.9089	0.9110	0.9116	0.9308
800	0.9295	0.9362	0.9349	0.9379
900	0.9563	0.9536	0.9530	0.9556
1000	0.9659	0.9685	0.9652	0.9697
1200	0.9856	0.9864	0.9857	0.9871
1300	0.9910	0.9921	0.9913	0.9936
1500	0.9967	0.9969	0.9964	0.9966
1700	0.9979	0.9982	0.9982	0.9985
1850	0.9985	0.9984	0.9986	0.9985
2000	0.9984	0.9983	0.9982	0.9984
2100	0.9983	0.9985	0.9983	0.9984
2200	0.9984	0.9984	0.9983	0.9984
2400	0.9982	0.9982	0.9981	0.9982
2500	0.9979	0.9982	0.9979	0.9980
2600	0.9980	0.9978	0.9979	0.9979
2700	0.9976	0.9979	0.9977	0.9978
2900	0.9974	0.9974	0.9975	0.9976
3000	0.9976	0.9975	0.9974	0.9975
3200	0.9974	0.9971	0.9972	0.9973
3400	0.9971	0.9972	0.9968	0.9969

4 Conclusion and Future Work

In this chapter, we showed that HMMs can effectively detect encrypted and polymorphic malware. We also saw that if a sample is partially encrypted, we can easily modify our approach to distinguish encrypted code segments from plaintext code segments. This HMM based technique is practical and powerful and could likely be integrated into any malware detection system that is based on machine learning.

For future work, it would be interesting to apply other machine learning techniques (e.g., support vector machines, k-nearest neighbor, random forests, neural networks and deep learning, and so on) to this problem, and compare the results to the HMM approach considered here. We suspect that HMMs are particularly well-suited for the problem considered in this chapter.

Another interesting and important area for future work would consist of playing the role of the malware writer and attempting to defeat the technique discussed in this chapter. Any results in this direction would point the way towards further advances in detection that could ultimately make the malware writers task more difficult. However, we suspect that defeating our HMM based approach will prove challenging, as the obvious strategy would be to use an encryption technique that better randomizes the resulting ciphertext. While such an approach would solve the problem in the narrow sense of defeating our HMM score, it would almost surely result in encrypted code (i.e., ciphertext) that is trivially distinguishable from plaintext by use of elementary entropy based techniques, such as that found in [25].

5   Questions

1. What is Encrypted and Polymorphic malware?
2. How common antivirus products work?
3. To what extent signature-based detection is useful?
4. What is the difference between Polymorphic and Metamorphic viruses?
5. Describe two phases of machine learning techniques.
6. How hidden Markov models and Simple Substitution can be used to detect malware?
7. Why polymorphic and encrypted malware use classic cipher techniques?
8. What is a random ciphertext?
9. What is Partially Encryption?
10. Explain the following terms: encrypted opcodes and encrypted bytes.

Reference

1. Swain B (2009) What are malware, viruses, spyware, and cookies, and what differentiates them? https://www.symantec.com/connect/articles/what-are-malware-viruses-spyware-and-cookies-and-what-differentiates-them
2. Nachenberg C (1996) Understanding and managing polymorphic viruses. In: The symantec enterprise papers. Symantec. https://www.symantec.com/content/dam/symantec/docs/security-center/white-papers/understanding-and-managing-polymorphic-viruses-96-en.pdf
3. Computer Knowledge (2013). http://www.cknow.com/cms/vtutor/types-of-viruses.html
4. Stamp M (2011) Information security: principles and practice. Wiley, New York
5. DaBoss (2013) Robert slade computer virus history. http://www.cknow.com/cms/vtutor/robert-slade-computer-virus-history.html
6. Radeska T (2016) Brain — The first computer virus, the vintage news. http://www.thevintagenews.com/2016/09/08/priority-brain-first-computer-virus-created-two-brothers-pakistan-just-wanted-prevent-customers-making-illegal-software-copies/
7. Szor P (2005) The art of computer virus research and defense. Pearson Education. https://books.google.com/books?id=XE-ddYF6uhYC
8. Rad BB, Masrom M, Ibrahim S (2012) Camouflage in malware: from encryption to metamorphism. Int J Comput Sci Netw Secur 12(8):74–83
9. Li X, Loh PKK, Tan F (2011) Mechanisms of polymorphic and metamorphic viruses. In: 2011 European intelligence and security informatics conference. pp 149–154

10. Symantec: viruses that can cost you. http://www.symantec.com/region/reg_eu/resources/virus_cost.html
11. Symantec: security 1:1 — Part 1: viruses and worms (2013). https://www.symantec.com/connect/articles/security-11-part-1-viruses-and-worms
12. Venkatachalam S (2010) Detecting undetectable computer viruses. http://scholarworks.sjsu.edu/etd_projects/156/
13. Zwanger V, Gerhards-Padilla E, Meier M (2014) Codescanner: Detecting (hidden) x86/x64 code in arbitrary files. In: Malicious and unwanted software: the americas (MALWARE), 2014 9th international conference on malicious and unwanted software. IEEE, pp 118–127
14. Schultz MG, Eskin E, Zadok F, Stolfo SJ (2001) Data mining methods for detection of new malicious executables. In: Proceedings of the IEEE symposium on security and privacy. SP, pp 38–49
15. Shabtai A, Moskovitch R, Elovici Y, Glezer C (2009) Detection of malicious code by applying machine learning classifiers on static features: a state-of-the-art survey. Inf Secur Tech Rep 14(1):16–29. https://doi.org/10.1016/j.istr.2009.03.003
16. Stamp M (2004) A revealing introduction to hidden Markov models. https://www.cs.sjsu.edu/~stamp/RUA/HMM.pdf
17. Jurafsky D, Martin JH (2000) Speech and language processing: an introduction to natural language processing, computational linguistics, and speech recognition, 1st edn. Prentice Hall PTR, USA
18. Cave RL, Neuwirth LP (1980) Hidden Markov models for English. In: Ferguson JD (ed) Hidden Markov Models for Speech
19. Brown corpus of standard American English (2010). http://www.cs.toronto.edu/~gpenn/csc401/a1res.html
20. Vobbilisetty R, Troia FD, Low RM, Visaggio CA, Stamp M (2017) Classic cryptanalysis using hidden Markov models. Cryptologia 41(1):1–28. https://doi.org/10.1080/01611194.2015.1126660
21. Ganesh N, Di Troia F, Corrado VA, Austin TH, Stamp M (2016) Static analysis of malicious Java applets. In: Proceedings of the 2016 ACM on international workshop on security and privacy analytics. IWSPA '16. ACM, USA, pp 58–63, http://doi.acm.org/10.1145/2875475.2875477
22. Rabiner LR (1989) A tutorial on hidden markov models and selected applications in speech recognition. IEEE Proc 77(2):257–286
23. Shanmugam G, Low RM, Stamp M (2013) Simple substitution distance and metamorphic detection. J Comput Virol Hacking Tech 9(3):159–170
24. Wong W, Stamp M (2006) Hunting for metamorphic engines. J Comput Virol 2(3):211–229. https://doi.org/10.1007/s11416-006-0028-7
25. Shamir A, Van Someren N (1999) Playing hide and seek with stored keys. In: International conference on financial cryptography. Springer, Berlin, pp 118–124
26. Dhanasekar D (2017) Detecting encrypted malware using hidden Markov models. Master's project, Department of Computer Science, San Jose State University. http://scholarworks.sjsu.edu/etd_projects/574/
27. Bradley AP (1997) The use of the area under the roc curve in the evaluation of machine learning algorithms. Pattern Recognit 30(7):1145–1159

Masquerade Detection on Mobile Devices

Swathi Nambiar Kadala Manikoth, Fabio Di Troia and Mark Stamp

Abstract A masquerade is a type of attack where an intruder attempts to avoid detection by impersonating an authorized user of a system. In this research, we consider the problem of masquerade detection on mobile devices. Specifically, we experiment with a variety of machine learning techniques to determine how accurately we can distinguish mobile users, based on various features. Here, our primary goal is to determine which techniques are most likely to be effective in a more comprehensive masquerade detection system.

1 Introduction

A masquerader is an attacker who impersonates a user of a system and thereby attempts to exceed his or her authorized level of privilege [1]. Masquerade detection based on UNIX commands has received considerable attention in the research literature; see [2] for an example of such work. The survey paper [3] discusses more than 40 research papers on the topic masquerade detection that were published prior to 2009.

A study conducted at the Symposium on Usable Privacy and Security (SOUPS) in 2014 revealed that 57% of smartphone owners do not lock their devices when they leave them unattended [4]. This creates an opportunities for a malicious intruder to gain physical access to a device, and it highlights the need for strong mechanisms for intrusion detection that can reduce such opportunities for attackers.

Of course, remote attacks on mobile devices are generally an even more serious threat than physical attacks. For example, a mobile banking application known as

S. N. Kadala Manikoth · F. Di Troia · M. Stamp (✉)
San Jose State University, San Jose, California, US
e-mail: mark.stamp@sjsu.edu

S. N. Kadala Manikoth
e-mail: swathinambiar.kadalamanikoth@sjsu.edu

F. Di Troia
e-mail: fabioditroia@msn.com

© Springer International Publishing AG, part of Springer Nature 2018
S. Parkinson et al. (eds.), *Guide to Vulnerability Analysis for Computer Networks
and Systems*, Computer Communications and Networks,
https://doi.org/10.1007/978-3-319-92624-7_13

Zitmo (which is shorthand for "ZeuS in the mobile") listens to all incoming SMS messages and forwards them to a remote server. Even more alarming, one-time passwords that are sent by a bank as a part of two-factor authentication can be captured by the Zitmo malware [5]. As another example, an application that masquerades as a user—after tricking the user into downloading the application—is discussed in [6]. These examples serve to reinforce the point that there is a clear need for strong intrusion detection (and hence masquerade detection) on mobile devices.

There are several approaches to improving security and privacy on mobile devices. While a password or PIN may be useful [7], "continuous authentication" is likely to be far more relevant and effective. Continuous authentication is a form of behaviour-based authentication where various characteristics of the user are monitored. For example, the users keystrokes dynamics, mouse movements, or similar characteristics can be used to identify users [8].

Due to the vast number of malicious applications and various ways of masquerading, there is a need for a dependable method of access control that does not rely on a user's actions to ensure security. Machine learning techniques provide many potentially effective and efficient means of passively monitoring user behaviour. Our goal in this research is to study the effectiveness of a wide variety of machine learning algorithms for masquerade detection on mobile devices. We test these algorithms over a large number of users and a wide array of features.

The remainder of this paper is organized as follows. Section 2 discusses examples of relevant previous work on intrusion detection and masquerade detection. Section 3 covers the dataset we use in this research, and we discuss the features available in this data. We also briefly outline the various machine learning algorithms used in this research. Section 4 discusses our experiments and results. Finally, Sect. 5 concludes the paper and provides suggestions for future work.

2   Previous Work

Real-time intrusion detection has long been a research topic [9]. Typically, a model is built based on a user's behaviour, and intruders—including masqueraders—are detected based on deviations from this user profile. Mobile devices present some additional challenges for masquerade detection. Relevant prior work has focused on the problem of masquerade detection by exploring a wide variety of approaches. For example, system call analysis has been widely considered, since system calls capture details about the interactions between applications and the underlying system [10–12].

The work in [13] considers a behavioural recognition system for portable handsets. Their research uses "behaviour signatures" and utilized support vector machines to generate classifiers.

The paper [14] uses an algorithm for pairwise sequence alignment to measure the similarity between sequences of commands. The work in [15] is also sequence based—specifically, sequences of user activity and clustering algorithms are employed for masquerade detection on mobile devices.

A platform called VetDroid was created and analysed in [16]. The VetDroid system is designed to detect potentially malicious behaviour based on an analysis of permissions.

Work has also been done using neural networks to profile user behaviour [17]. In the recent paper [18], behaviour is classified based on the top ten applications used by a legitimate user on an Android device. In this work, mutual information (MI) is the primary measure used to define a score, where MI is the amount of information that an event contains about the occurrence of another event.

The paper [19] explores an approach based on suspicious execution sequences that are generated during a users interaction with the device. In [20], the authors focus on classifying sequences of user command data as a means of detecting a masquerader. In this work, the detection algorithm is a Naive Bayes-based text classification technique.

The work presented in [21] considers a full-fledged IDS for mobile devices. The authors extracted telephony-based information and apply a neural network that consists of a feed-forward multi-layered perceptron with radial basis functions. The paper [16] uses the same dataset as [21], but builds models for each feature individually.

Table 1 summarizes some of the previous work done on masquerade detection in the context of mobile devices. Note that in Table 1, the following notation is used.

Table 1 Previous research on mobile masquerade detection [16]

Authors	Feature	Method	Performance %	Measure
Samfat and Molva [22]	Itinerary and Calls	Basic statistics	82.5	Accuracy
Buschkes et al. [23]	Mobility	Bayes rule	87.5	Accuracy
Boukerche and Notare [24]	Calls	Neural network	97.5	Accuracy
Maxion and Townsend [20]	Commands	Naïve Bayes	46.3	Cost
Sun et al. [25]	Mobility	High order Markov	87.5	Accuracy
Li et al. [16]	Calling activity	Neural networks	1.3	EER
Alzubaidi et al. [18]	Frequent apps	Random forest	9.0	EER
Lamba et al. [19]	User activity	Clustering	70.0	Accuracy

- EER is the equal error rate, which is the difference between expected output and generated output. Note that the smaller the EER, the better.
- The "cost" is defined as

$$\text{cost} = \text{misses} + 6 \cdot \text{(false alarms)}$$

As with the EER, the smaller the cost, the better the results.
- The accuracy is computed as

$$\text{accuracy} = \frac{TP + TN}{TP + TN + FP + FN}$$

where TP is the number of true positives, TN is the number of true negatives, FP is the number of false positives, and FN is the number of false negatives.

3 Dataset and Algorithms

3.1 Data

For this research, we have used the MIT reality mining dataset [26], which consists of data collected from 100 mobile phone users (students and faculty of MIT) and is based on logs collected from these devices over a period of 9 months. This dataset contains 94 features—our analysis is based on the features listed in Table 2. Note that although we have only listed 29 features in Table 2, there are 3 distinct features that correspond to device_list_types, and hence, we have a total of 31 features.

3.2 Algorithms for Predictive Modelling

In this section, we briefly discuss the machine learning algorithms that we have used in this research. For the sake of brevity, we only provide a high-level description in each case.

3.3 Support Vector Machines

Support vector machines (SVM) are a class of supervised learning techniques that attempt to find a separating hyperplane that maximizes the "margin"; i.e. the minimum separation between the hyperplane and the training data is maximized. The so-called kernel trick enables us to work in a higher dimension (where it is

Table 2 Features analysed

date	Date info collected
event	Unique event ID
contact	Contact ID
description	Short description
direction	Direction of data
duration	Duration in seconds
hashNum	Hashed phone numbers
chargeTime	Date/time of charging
charge	Charging or unplugged
activeTime	Date/time phone in use
active	Phone in use or not
logtimes	Times log written
onTime	Total time data recorded
on	Phone on or not
dateForLoc	Date/time user in a location
areaID.cellID	Area/cell ID of user location
all_locs	Towers visited by user
loc_ids	Indexed locs
device_macs	MAC addresses (Bluetooth)
deviceDate	Time/dates of each scan
device_list_macs	List of device_macs
device_types	Discovered Bluetooth types
device_list_types	List of device_types
cellname	Array of areaID.cellID
logTime	Time cellname recorded
apps	App usage stats
comm_voice_date	Dates of voice calls
comm_data	Data sessions
comm_data_date	Data sessions times

generally easier to find a separating hyperplane) without paying a significant penalty in terms of computational complexity. Figure 1 illustrates a separating hyperplane in the case of a linear kernel.

Fig. 1 Linear SVM

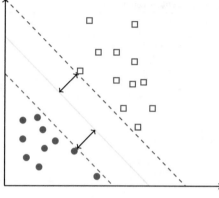

Fig. 2 Labelled training data

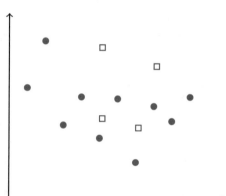

3.4   *K-Nearest Neighbour (k-NN)*

The *k*-nearest neighbour (*k*-NN) algorithm is one of the simplest machine learning techniques. Consider the training data in Fig. 2. This training set consists of ten elements of the "solid circle" type and eight of the "hollow square" type.

Suppose that we want to classify the solid diamond that is labelled as *X* in Fig. 3a using 1-NN (i.e. *k*-NN, with $k = 1$, which is also known simply as the nearest neighbour algorithm). Since the nearest point to *X* is the hollow square labelled *b*, Fig. 3a shows that for this case, we would classify *X* as type "hollow square". On the other hand, suppose that we want to classify *X* using 3-NN. In Fig. 3b, we see that the three nearest data points to *X* (with respect to Euclidean distance) consist of one hollow square and two solid circles—labelled *b*, r_1, and r_2, respectively. Since the majority of the three nearest points in the training set are solid circles, using 3-NN, we would classify *X* as being of the same type as the solid circles.

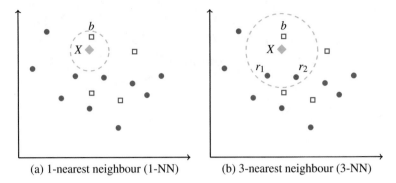

(a) 1-nearest neighbour (1-NN) (b) 3-nearest neighbour (3-NN)

Fig. 3 k-NN examples

3.5 Decision Tree

Decision trees can rival k-NN for the title of world's simplest machine learning technique. To illustrate a decision tree, suppose that we have a labelled training set consisting of malware samples and benign samples. From this training set, we observe that malware samples tend to be smaller in size and have higher entropy, as compared to benign samples. We could use this information to construct the decision tree in Fig. 4, where the thresholds for "large" versus "small" (size) and "high" versus "low" (entropy) would be based on the training data. This decision tree could then be used to classify any sample as either malware or benign, based on its size and entropy.

Of course, we could just as well have constructed the decision tree in Fig. 4 with the split closest to the root being based on entropy rather than file size. So as to maximize the usefulness of the data available, we want decisions based on the best available informative to be made closest to the root. This can be easily accomplished by measuring the information gain.

3.6 Logistic Regression

Logistic regression is a statistical method applied in which there are one or more independent binary variables that determine the outcome. In logistic regression, the dependent variable only contains the values "true" and "false". The goal of this algorithm is to find the most suitable model to describe the relationship between the binary characteristic of interest and a set of independent variables. This is achieved using a logit transformation of the probability of presence of the characteristic of interest, where

$$\text{logit}(p) = \ln\left(\frac{p}{1-p}\right)$$

and p is the probability of the characteristic of interest.

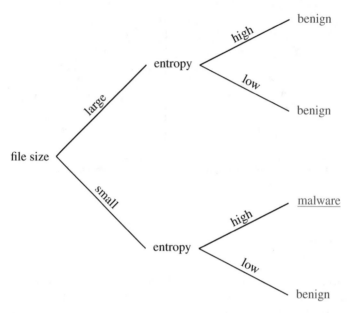

Fig. 4 Decision tree example

3.7 Random Forest

A random forest is a generalization of a decision tree. Although decision trees are simple, they tend to overfit the training data. To overcome this limitation, a random forest generates multiple decision trees based on subsets of the training data and subsets of the features. A majority vote or other combination of these decision trees can be used to determine the classification of a sample [27]. A regularized greedy forest (RGF) is a special type of random forest. The objective when training an RGF is to minimize a specified loss function [28].

3.8 Extreme Gradient Boosting

Extreme gradient boosting (EGB or XGBoost) is close cousin of the well-known AdaBoost algorithm [27]. In general, boosting is a process whereby we combine multiple (weak) classifiers into one (much stronger) classifier [29, 30]. The beauty of boosting is that the individual classifiers can be extremely weak—anything that is better than flipping a coin is useful. And provided that we have a sufficient number of non-random classifiers, boosting can be used to construct an arbitrarily strong classifier. EGB is generally based on decision trees.

4 Results

We consider user data for 94 users and perform masquerade detection for 10 randomly selected users, based on some 200 values from among the available features. We also analyse the various features by training models for each feature independently, using a variety of machine learning techniques. Specifically, we use the machine learning techniques discussed in Sect. 3.2.

To measure the quality of our results, we use accuracy and the area under the ROC curve (AUC). Since some of our dataset are highly imbalanced, in such cases we use balanced accuracy instead of accuracy [31]. Balanced accuracy weights the accuracy on the positive and negative instances equally. The balanced accuracy is computed as

$$\text{Balanced Accuracy} = \frac{1}{2}\left(\frac{\text{TP}}{\text{P}} + \frac{\text{TN}}{\text{N}}\right)$$

where TP (true positive) is the number of samples that have been correctly identified, TN (true negative) is the number of samples that have been correctly rejected, P is the total number of positive instances, and N is the total number of negative instances [7].

An ROC curve is generated from a scatterplot of scores by varying the threshold through the range of scores, and plotting the false positive rate versus the true positive rate. The area under the ROC curve gives us the probability that a randomly selected positive instance scores higher than a randomly selected negative instance [7]. One advantage of ROC analysis is that it removes any issues related to threshold from the calculations since, in effect, we consider all possible thresholds.

4.1 Training

We allocated 8 CPUs and 15 GB RAM over the cloud. All of our models have been trained using fivefold cross-validation. Since cross-validation is used, the results presented here are averages over all folds in the given experiment. The values of the parameters used in the various machine learning algorithms are as follows.

- Regularized greedy forest (RGF)—50 trees per iteration.
- Random forest (RF)—Five trees per iterations and entropy criterion.
- k-Nearest neighbour (k-NN)—Two neighbours and uniform weights.
- Logistic regression (LR) — L2 regularization.
- Extreme gradient boosting (EGB)—50 trees per iterations and a maximum depth of 3.
- Decision trees (DT)—Five trees per iterations and Gini criterion.

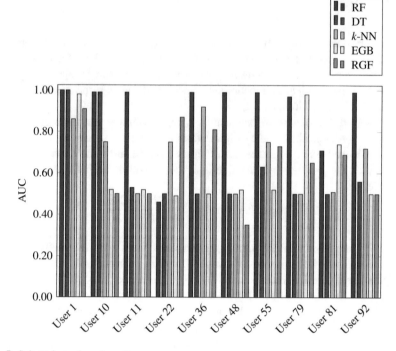

Fig. 5 Selected user-based results

4.2   Testing

Detailed test results for ten random users using RGF, RF, k-NN, EGB, and the DT algorithms are given in Fig. 5, and a selection of ROC curves for User 1 is given in Fig. 6. The balanced accuracy and AUC values for each algorithm—when averaged over all 94 users—are given in the form of a bar graph in Fig. 7.

The results in Fig. 5 show that we can generate a masquerade detection system with a balanced accuracy in excess of 89% in every case, and for all but three of the ten users, we can attain a balanced accuracy in excess of 99%. Also, we observe that the tree-based algorithms (RF and DT) perform the best, with one of these two algorithms giving the best result in six of the ten cases considered. We also note that EGB generally performs well in these experiments. The detailed results in Fig. 5 are echoed in the overall results, which are summarized in Fig. 7.

We experiment over various time frames. Intuitively, we expect there to be a trade-off between the training duration and the detection results. If the training period is too short, the model will fail to fully capture the behaviour; however, we might also expect that most behaviour is likely to change over time, so that an overly long training period would be counterproductive. We therefore trained and tested models based

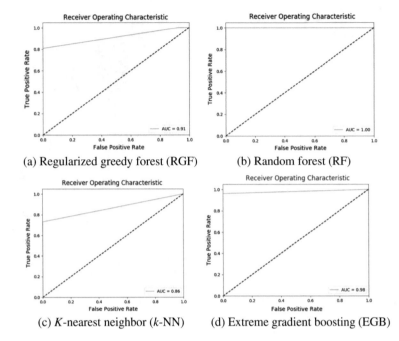

(a) Regularized greedy forest (RGF)   (b) Random forest (RF)

(c) *K*-nearest neighbor (*k*-NN)   (d) Extreme gradient boosting (EGB)

Fig. 6 Various algorithms with User 1 data

Fig. 7 Balanced accuracy over all 94 users

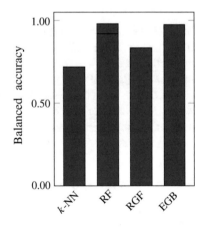

Fig. 8 Balanced accuracy
over various time frames

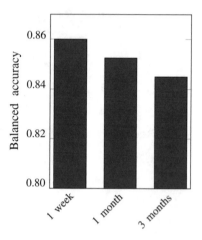

on time intervals of 1 week, 1 month, and 3 months, and we found that the longer training time intervals yielded worse results. These experiments are summarized in Fig. 8.

4.3 Feature-Based Experiments

In an effort to determine the strength of each of the various features, we trained models on individual features. Representative examples of these results are given in Fig. 9. From these results, we see that in some cases, a single feature provides significant information (e.g. cell area), but many features only provide minimal discrimination (e.g. active status). More experimentation in this direction would be useful so that we can reduce the number of features that need to be collected, without significantly decreasing the effectiveness of the resulting masquerade detection system.

5 Conclusion and Future Work

We considered 31 features for 94 users and compared the effectiveness of various machine learning algorithms for masquerade detection. We found that we could obtain strong results in most cases and that tree-based algorithms were generally the most effective. Specifically, random forests performed best overall, but simple decision trees were also surprisingly strong performers. In addition, we found that training over a relatively short time interval was more effective than training over a longer time interval. Hence, masquerade detection models should be retrained fairly often.

Fig. 9 Selected
feature-based results

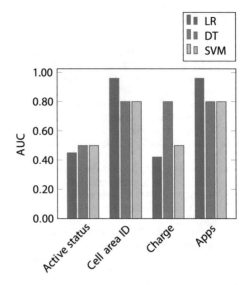

The primary direction of our future work is to apply the insights gained in this research towards the development of a comprehensive mobile masquerade detection system. In additional, we plan to apply various neural network and deep learning algorithms to the mobile masquerade detection problem, which will allow for a direct comparison of the machine learning algorithms considered in this paper to neural network techniques. Spiking neural networks would appear to be particularly well suited for the masquerade detection problem considered in this paper [32].

6 Questions

1. What is masquerader attack?
2. What is the purpose of 'Zitmo' application?
3. Why locking mobile devices is important, when left unattended?
4. What are the existing security and privacy concerns on mobile devices?
5. What is pairwise sequence alignment?
6. What real-time intrusion detection is suitable for mobile devices?
7. Explain two algorithms that are available for Predictive Modelling?
8. What is a statistical method? Explain Logistic regression and Extreme Gradient Boosting.
9. Why trade-off between the training duration and the detection results is necessary?
10. What is continuous authentication?

References

1. Rouse, M. (2007) Network security: Masquerade definition. TechTarget. https://searchsecurity. techtarget.com/definition/masquerade
2. Huang L, Stamp M (2011) Masquerade detection using profile hidden Markov models. Computers and Security 30(8):732–747. https://doi.org/10.1016/j.cose.2011.08.003
3. Bertacchini M, Fierens P (2009) A survey on masquerader detection approaches. In: Proceedings of V Congreso Iberoamericano de Seguridad Informática. Universidad de la República de Uruguay, pp 46–60
4. Whitney, L (2017) Mobile device authentication a look at behavior-based authentication. cnet news
5. Elinor, M (2011) More malware targeting android. cnet news. https://www.cnet.com/news/more-malware-targeting-android/
6. Whitney, L (2011) Android malware masquerading as Google+ app. cnet news
7. Stamp M (2017) Introduction to machine learning with applications in information security. CRC Press
8. Deutschmann I, Nordström P, Nilsson L (2013) Continuous authentication using behavioral biometrics. IT Prof 15(4):12–15. https://doi.org/10.1109/MITP.2013.50
9. Lunt TF, Jagannathan R (1988) A prototype real-time intrusion-detection expert system. Proceedings of the 1988 IEEE symposium on security and privacy, pp 59–66. https://doi.org/10.1109/SECPRI.1988.8098
10. Burguera I, Zurutuza U, Nadjm-Tehrani S (2011) Crowdroid: behavior-based malware detection system for android. In: Proceedings of the 1st ACM workshop on security and privacy in smartphones and mobile devices. SPSM '11. ACM, USA, pp 15–26. https://doi.org/10.1145/2046614.2046619
11. Christodorescu M, Jha S, Kruegel C (2007) Mining specifications of malicious behavior. In: Proceedings of the the 6th joint meeting of the european software engineering conference and the ACM SIGSOFT symposium on the foundations of software engineering. ESEC-FSE '07. ACM, USA, pp 5–14. https://doi.org/10.1145/1287624.1287628
12. Lanzi A, Balzarotti D, Kruegel C, Christodorescu M, Kirda E (2010) Accessminer: using system-centric models for malware protection. In: Proceedings of the 17th ACM conference on computer and communications security.CCS '10. ACM, USA, pp 399–412. https://doi.org/10.1145/1866307.1866353
13. Bose A, Hu X, Shin K, Park GT (2008) Behavioral detection of malware on mobile handsets. In: Proceedings of the 6th international conference on mobile systems, applications, and services. MobiSys '08. ACM, USA, pp 225–238. https://doi.org/10.1145/1378600.1378626
14. Comparetti PM, Salvaneschi G, Kirda E, Kolbitsch C, Kruegel C, Zanero S (2010) Identifying dormant functionality in malware programs. In: Proceedings of the 2010 IEEE symposium on security and privacy. SP '10. IEEE Computer Society, USA. https://doi.org/10.1109/SP.2010.12
15. Zhang Y, Yang M, Xu B, Yang Z, Gu G, Ning P, Wang XS, Zang B (2013) Vetting undesirable behaviors in Android apps with permission use analysis. In: Proceedings of the 2013 ACM SIGSAC conference on computer and communications security. CCS '13. ACM, USA, pp 611–622. https://doi.org/10.1145/2508859.2516689
16. Li F, Clarke N, Papadaki M, Dowland P (2010) Behaviour profiling on mobile devices. In: 2010 International conference on emerging security technologies, pp 77–82. https://doi.org/10.1109/EST.2010.26
17. Seleznyov A, Mazhelis O (2002) Learning temporal patterns for anomaly intrusion detection. In: Proceedings of the 2002 ACM symposium on applied computing. SAC '02. ACM, USA, pp 209–213. https://doi.org/10.1145/508791.508836
18. Abdulaziz AA, Swarup R, Jugal K (2017) Ranking most informative apps for effective identification of legitimate smartphone owners. In: Proceedings IEEE international conference on computer communications (INFOCOM 2017). MobiSec '17. IEEEXplore, USA. http://www.cs.uccs.edu/~jkalita/papers/2017/AbdulazizAlzubaidiMobiSec2017.pdf

19. Lamba H, Glazier TJ, Cámara J, Schmerl B, Garlan D, Pfeffer J (2017) Model-based cluster analysis for identifying suspicious activity sequences in software. In: Proceedings of the 3rd ACM on international workshop on security and privacy analytics. IWSPA '17. ACM, USA, pp 17–22. https://doi.org/10.1145/3041008.3041014

20. Maxion RA, Townsend TN (2002) Masquerade detection using truncated command lines. In: Proceedings of the 2002 international conference on dependable systems and networks. DSN '02. IEEE Computer Society, USA, pp 219–228 http://dl.acm.org/citation.cfm?id=647883.738240

21. Michalopoulos DS, Clarke NL (2006) Intrusion detection system for mobile devices. Adv Netw Comput Commun 205–212

22. Samfat D, Molva R (1997) IDAMN: an intrusion detection architecture for mobile networks. IEEE J Sel Areas Commun 15:1373–1380

23. Buschkes R, Kesdogan D, Reichl P (1998) How to increase security in mobile networks by anomaly detection. Proceedings of the 14th annual computer security applications conference. pp 23–12

24. Boukerche A, Nitare MSMA (2002) Behavior-based intrusion detection in mobile phone systems. J Parallel Distr Com 62:1476–1490

25. Sun B, Yu F, Wu K, Leung VCM (2004) Mobility-based anomaly detection in cellular mobile networks. Proceedings of ACM wireless security (WiSe' 04), Philadelphia, PA. pp 61–69

26. Eagle N, Pentland A, Lazer D (2009) Inferring friendship network structure by using mobile phone data. Proc Natl Acad Sci 106(36):15274–15278

27. Trevor H, Robert T, Jerome F (2009) The elements of statistical learning: data mining, inference, and prediction, 3rd edn. Springer, Berlin

28. Johnson R, Zhang T (2014) Learning nonlinear functions using regularized greedy forest. IEEE Trans Pattern Anal Mach Intell 36(5):942–954. https://doi.org/10.1109/TPAMI.2013.159

29. Rojas R (2009) AdaBoost and the Super Bowl of classifiers: a tutorial introduction to adaptive boosting. http://www.inf.fu-berlin.de/inst/ag-ki/adaboost4.pdf

30. Stamp M (2017) Boost your knowledge of AdaBoost. https://www.cs.sjsu.edu/texttildelowstamp/ML/files/ada.pdf

31. Team AVC (2016) Practical guide to deal with imbalanced classification problems in R. Analytics Vidhya. https://www.analyticsvidhya.com/blog/2016/03/practical-guide-deal-imbalanced-classification-problems/

32. Vreeken J (2003) Spiking neural networks, an introduction. Technical report, Utrecht University

Identifying File Interaction Patterns in Ransomware Behaviour

Liam Grant and Simon Parkinson

Abstract Malicious software (malware) has a rich history of causing significant challenges for both users and system developers alike. The development of different malware types is often resulting from criminal opportunity. The monetisation of ransomware, coupled with the continuous growing importance of user data, is resulting in ransomware becoming one of the most prominent forms of malware. Detecting and stopping a ransomware attack is challenging due to the large verity of different types, as well as the speed of new instances being developed. This results in static approaches (e.g. signature-based detection) ineffective at identifying all ransomware instances. This chapter investigates the behavioural characteristics of ransomware, and in particular focusses on interaction with the underlying file system. This study identifies that ransomware instances have unique behavioural patterns, which are significantly different from those of normal user interaction.

1 Ransomware

1.1 Introduction

Ransomware is a type of malicious software, or malware, that aims to cause damage to a single computer, server or computer network [1]. A key difference of ransomware over other forms of malware is that it aims to hold the user ransom by encrypting their data. The increase in ransomware is a result of computing devices continuing to be a major part of user' s social and professional lives, thus increasing the dependency on data and the opportunity to monetise through crime. Malware is in a constant state

L. Grant (✉) · S. Parkinson
Department of Computer Science, Universtiy of Huddersfield, Huddersfield, UK
e-mail: U1470723@unimail.hud.ac.uk

S. Parkinson
e-mail: s.parkinson@hud.ac.uk

© Springer International Publishing AG, part of Springer Nature 2018   317
S. Parkinson et al. (eds.), *Guide to Vulnerability Analysis for Computer Networks and Systems*, Computer Communications and Networks,
https://doi.org/10.1007/978-3-319-92624-7_14

of evolution, with new evasion techniques being introduced for every advancement in detection and prevention that is made in the security field [2].

The first known ransomware instance was created by Joseph L. Popp and was used at the World Health Organizations AIDS conference in 1988. It used primitive cryptography to encrypt files, and due to this, the files were easily decrypted. The virus was named the AIDS Trojan due to the attack [3]. Since then, ransomware has advanced with the general advancement of technology and now has several different families. Analysis by [4] shows the top eight ransomware variants, with distribution dominated by *cerber* and *locky* variants in 2016.

Ransomware encrypts a users data using private key encryption or by preventing access to a computer. In using these methods, the ransomware holds the data on the machine ransom until the end user pays the requested amount, usually in Bitcoin or similar cryptocurrency [3]. Most of the time, end users do pay this ransom, especially if the encrypted data are valuable to them or their corporations. However, it is sometimes possible to get this data back with shared keys and applications from organizations such as No More Ransom [5].

When broken down, the distribution of different malware types is dominated by ransomware, which has been the ongoing trend for many years. In the first quarter of 2017, ransomware accounted for over 50% of recorded malware distribution [6]. In 2016, the global average of ransomware detections was 1,271 per day, which was an increase of 933 from the previous year [7]. However, [5], predicts that towards the end of 2017, the volume and effectiveness of ransomware attacks should drop due to anti-ransomware technologies and initiatives, and also the increased end-user awareness.

A common reason for this dominance and growth in the use of ransomware is that it is the most successful at extorting money from end users, which in turn makes it a more attractive method to current and future cyber-criminals. In 2016, the IC3 (Internet Crime Complaint Center) released a report showing that of the 2,673 complaints filed with their service, they accrued loses of over $2.4 million [8]. However, end users that are businesses are not only paying for a ransom; another report states that between April 2014 and June 2015, that the total loss for victims attacked by the CryptoWall ransomware variant was over $18 million, including the expenses for IT Services or legal fees [9].

Considering the recent increase in ransomware and the necessity to prevent users from being exploited into paying ransom fees, there is strong motivation to better understand the behavioural habits of ransomware to provide new insights leading to stronger detection and prevention mechanisms. There are many behavioural characteristics of ransomware; however, in this work its interaction with the underlying file system is examined. As ransomware is programmed to perform systematic tasks (e.g. directory traversing, file identification and encryption), it can be assumed that the software will have unique characteristics as to how these functions are performed.

In this chapter, an empirical investigation is performed whereby samples of ransomware are executed whilst monitoring the underlying file system to identify behavioural patterns. The chapter is structured as follows: in the first section, information is provided on the inner workings of ransomware as well as providing information on other common detection types. Related work is then discussed before a methodology of how to monitor file activity during a ransomware attack is presented. Key results are then presented and discussed, and finally, a conclusion lays out directions for future research.

1.2   How Does Ransomware Work?

Core Functionality

Ransomware can be sorted into two core types: (1) crypto-ransomware and (2) locker ransomware. Locker ransomware is used to lock a computer or device, thus preventing the user from accessing it. Although this type does hold the data to ransom, it does not do so at a file level, meaning that if it is removed from a device, its data remains intact. Due to this locker ransomware is not as effective at extorting victims for ransom and other types [10].

The second type, crypto-ransomware, is much more effective at extorting a payment. It essentially takes control of data stored on a system by encrypting it. Even if a victim can manage to remove the malware, the files will still be encrypted and unable to be accessed. Although it is possible to decrypt the data with the private key used for encryption, it is computationally expensive and time-consuming to do so and usually the victim will either pay the ransom or lose the data [10].

A majority of crypto-ransomware software uses Elliptic Curve Diffie Hellman (ECDH) or RSA, named after Ron Rivest, Adi Shamir and Leonard Adleman, combined with Advanced Encryption Standard (AES) encryption [11]. Using a RSA public key to encrypt files, and separate private, or secret, key to encrypt the AES keys which were used in the encryption of data [12].

At the core of almost every modern ransomware attack, there is a C and C (command and control) server that the software requires communication with [13]. The C and C usually acts as the holder of one or more keys, which is required to encrypt the data, or to encrypt the keys that have encrypted the victim's data [14]. Without communication with the server, the ransomware is unable to get the resources required to encrypt files on a machine. However, due to the importance of the Internet in our modern lives, this is an increasingly easy problem for attackers to get around. Some ransomware can be stopped from the use of a blacklist/whitelist to block communication with known malware C and C server IP addresses; however, this is easy to get around, by either changing IP or domain names.

Over the past few years, ransomware and other malware forms have started to have more advanced evasion features built into them. Theses evasion techniques are used to either bypass security software, or to avoid being analysed or executed in test environments. [15] classifies these into three broad categories:

- **Anti-security techniques**: The avoidance of detection by anti-malware engines, firewalls or application containment.

- **Anti-sandbox techniques**: The ability to detect what kind of environment the ransomware is running in by checking registry key, files or processes related to virtual environments.
- **Anti-analyst techniques**: The ability to detect monitoring processes, such as Process Explorer or Wireshark. In some cases, attempting to confuse analysts by obfuscating data or creating false traffic.

Targeting

Some cyber-criminals select their targets in advance, preparing ransomware in bespoke software created to cause the maximum amount of damage to a victim [16]. In these cases, the victim almost always is an organisation rather than individuals, as the attackers are spending this time to effectively maximise ransom pay-out from the victim [15]. Attacks like this are hard to perform and generally need a lot of technical competence to carry out, usually requiring a selection of planned and perfectly executed stages. These methods generally involve using network administration software to gain access and move throughout a network system, stealing of credentials for the system itself and performing advanced reconnaissance to fully understand the network and to understand how it is vulnerable [16].

Distribution

Ransomware does not just appear on a system; it requires a method of distribution. There are many methods for distributing malware, with some more effective than others. The main types can be broken into these categories:

- **Email** is one of the main types of successful distribution for ransomware, often made possible through large-scale malicious spam campaigns. These campaigns are usually spread via a botnet network of hundreds to millions of infected PCs. These botnets send out hundreds of thousands of emails daily, targeting individuals using social engineering techniques to trick users into think the mail is important (e.g. fake invoices, infected attachments, etc.) [7].
- **Exploit kits** are the second most common distribution method, which works by exploiting vulnerabilities in other software which can then be used to infect machines. These kits are spread using spam email and malvertising, advert links that link to sites. Once a exploit kit has been set-up on a victims computer, it works as a back door into the system for malware to infect [5].
- **Self-propagation** is not as common as other techniques; however, some ransomware families and variants are build with some level of self-propagation and are capable of copying itself onto removable drives or networked computers. Some Android ransomwares can spread themselves through a list of contacts using SMS messages [16].
- **Other** There are many other types of distribution for ransomware but are not as common as the three types mentioned above. Malvertising is one of these techniques, misleading victims by seeming like an advert which usually links to

a compromised website [16]. This technique is more common in the spreading of exploit kits which attackers can then use to infect a victims computer. Another method used is the brute forcing of passwords, generally for server applications, which can then be used to infect machines connected to the core server [15].

Cryptolocker: An Example of Crypto-Ransomware

CryptoLocker is a family of crypto-ransomware that was used in a large-scale cyber-attack in late 2013 to mid-2014. It used Bitcoin transactions for the ransom currency and Liao et al. [17], found 795 payments adding up to 1,128.40 BTC. CryptoLocker was spread via email using social engineering techniques to trick recipients into running infected attachments in emails claiming to be from a logistics company [18].

CryptoLocker uses a combination of public keys for distribution, and private keys for large-scale encryption. Using these two methods together, the software attempts to connect to a C and C server which then creates a RSA public/private key pair and sends the public key back to the infected machine [12]. CryptoLocker then generates AES private keys and starts to encrypt data on the victims machine, usually using different keys for each file extension type. Once it has finished encrypting files, the RSA public key, obtained from the C and C server, is then used to encrypt the AES private keys. It then generates a page, informing the victim that the files have been encrypted and how to pay the ransom [12].

1.3 Current State of Ransomware

WannaCry

There have been many large-scale ransomware attacks over the past few years, most recently being the WannaCry attack in May 2017. It affected more than 70,000 computers around the world after its first few hours, totalling over 200,000 computers [19]. WannaCry targeted 176 different file types, which were appended with .WCRY after encryption. It asked for a ransom in Bitcoin to the value of roughly 300 US Dollars, and claim that each all the files would be deleted if the ransom was not paid in 7 days [20]. WannaCry caused massive damage to several companies and organisation across the world.

Ransomware-as-a-Service

Ransomware has been a rising tool of cyber-criminals over the past few years, Ransomware-as-a-service (RaaS) has attributed to this greatly. RaaS offers cyber-criminals the ability to hold victims data for ransom, for only a small percentage of the profit [21]. Allowing less technologically competent criminals to take advantage of ransomware. RaaS creators are able to host their code and systems on the dark web, where affiliates can subscribe to the service [22]. Affiliates can then configure any aspects that they need and deploy, allowing them to increase ransom. They can even look at an estimate of their earning potential before they subscribe [21].

These RaaS packages are usually free to deploy, but have a profit-sharing model, in which the earnings from paid ransoms are split between the affiliates and the author [23]. When a victim pays to regain access to their files, this payment is delivered to the author's account or accounts and the author then distributes this back to the affiliates. The share in profit ranges from 60 to 80%, making it worthwhile for an affiliate and creating a sizeable profit margin for authors with more affiliates [22].

New Initiatives

On July 25, 2016, the Dutch National Police, Europol, Intel Security and Kaspersky Labs announced that they were joining together to create a new anti-ransomware initiative called "No More Ransom" [24]. This initiative was put together to form a new level of cooperation between public and private sectors against the threat of ransomware. They have created an online portal which aims to inform the public about the threats that ransomware pose and offers help to victims looking to recover their data without conceding to the attacker's demands [25].

No More Ransom offers decryption tools for 104 known ransomware families. The cooperation between each private sector and law enforcement body increases this pool, using a combination of shared encryption keys and research into ransomware [26]. No More Ransom and grown since its initial announcement to be well over 100 partners all working towards limiting the threat and stopping the rise in ransomware use [27].

However, there can be a negative effect from these types of initiatives. Providing applications and help to people to combat the use of ransomware also allows for the cyber-criminals themselves to have access to this material, providing them with assistance in avoiding prevention and mitigation mechanisms.

Ransomware is still a major threat to users worldwide, and large-scale attacks such as WannaCry and Petya are still causing significant amounts of damage to organisations outside of ransom demands. With online supply of ransomware available to anyone willing to make use of it, the threat could grow even larger as a result. However, organisations such as No More Ransom can help to hinder these in the future, or at least to reduce the number of types of ransomware.

2   Detection of Ransomware on a System

As discussed in the previous section, ransomware is a constant and growing threat to computer systems. However, there are many ways of detecting ransomware on systems before and during an attack on a system.

Signature-Based Detection

Signature-based detection has been around since the inception of antivirus software [28]. It works by searching through systems for any known malware signatures and flagging files that match these. These signatures are generally made up of bytecode from the malicious software, and when the pattern has been discovered, it is then stored in a database of signatures and can then be searched through in order to match likely malware on a victim's computer or device. This method can also be referred to as static analysis [29].

Signatures are created by examining a software's bytecode and extracting one or more sequences of bytes from the body of a specific strain of malware. This sequence is generally unique to a malware instance and is unlikely to appear in other files [30]. Typically, this signature will match a variety of malware variants from the same family by matching them the known sources stored in the signature database [31].

Although this is the most common technique used by antivirus softwares, signature-based detection comes with it own disadvantages that can make them less likely to succeed in the detection malware such as ransomware. These are as follows:

- **Zero-day**: Signature-based detection uses the signatures of known malware, and due to this, new malware that has not been analysed and had its signature added to the database will not be detected by this method [30];
- **Evasion**: Malware creators could also change the signature of the software, making it unable to match to its new signature. They can do this by applying polymorphic methods to their software or by using obfuscation techniques to re-order code [32]; and
- **False Positives**: Another downside of signature detection is false positives. This is when the software detects a file that has a matching signature pattern but is not a malware file. This can cause issues, especially if the file is then removed by the antivirus that is running [30].

Signature-based malware detection also has its own strengths. It is a well-known and understood method in the industry that has been used since the first antivirus softwares have been in circulation [32]. It also has the benefit that malware signatures are widely available for use from online repositories and global research, protecting from all recorded threats [28].

Another method that is often used alongside standard signature-based antivirus is the use of manual heuristics analysis for detecting malware on a system. Heuristic detection uses rules and algorithms to look for specific commands that could be used for malicious purposes. This way, an antivirus scanner can find malware without needing to find and match a signature [33].

To do this, a heuristics antivirus would start scanning code for any suspicious methods and attributes of known malicious programs. Many malicious programs open files for other existing programs and modify them; a heuristic analyser can then examine the code for an application, and then for each malicious command that application uses, the more suspicious the application is deemed [34]. Using a predetermined threshold, the analyser will compare its finish analysis of the application, and if it crosses the threshold, it will then be marked as a malicious software or an infected file. This method of detection has a high- performance rate and can be easy to implement, but like signature-based detection, it has a low detection rate for new malware. It can also produce more false positive than a signature-based method [33].

Behaviour-Based Detection

Behavioural detection uses the behavioural attributes of how a malware behaves on a given system. This ranges from systems calls, interaction with the file system, abnormal behaviour to how a system is usually used [35]. Ransomware has core behavioural traits that help it to be easily defined in the malware category and these can be easily adopted into a detection method to find [29].

Behavioural detection differs from signature-based detection in that rather than looking at specific sequences in byte code, it takes a more abstract look at how a software is behaving [29]. For example, crypto-ransomware has a core behavioural trait of encryption when compared to other ransomware instances. Knowing this is a core behaviour, the operating system can monitor for unknown processes performing encryption behaviour on a system and identify it as suspicious and take mitigating action. In essence, behavioural detection finds suspicious activity through observing the behaviour of a process [29].

2.1 Related Work

Ransomware Behaviour Studies

Kharraz et al. [2] performed a study in which they analysed multiple samples of families and variants of known crypto and locker ransomware. The study used a data set of 3,921 samples of ransomware and analysis of the IRPs created when ransomware starts an attack on a system.

It was found for crypto-ransomware that they can use both customised and standard encryption methods. Most customised methods of encryption were implemented to decrease the chance of detecting through common antivirus analysis. However, it was found that some of the more modern crypto-ransomware families make use of standard windows encryption calls using the `CryptoAPI` to use the `CryptEncrypt` functions. The analysis shows that when using these standard methods, the process creates a number of IRP packets, first calling a create method to open a file. It then reads the file to access the file contents and encrypt the data. Finally, the process writes the encrypted data back to the file [2].

From this, Kharraz et al. [2] suggests that using basic API call monitoring to identify an encryption attack as it is happening. This method would only work for a less technical ransomware family that uses standard encryption techniques, but could mitigate several low-end attacks.

Gazet [36] finds that many ransomware family target specific file extensions, typically files such as `.doc`, `.odt`, `.zip`. Encrypting an entire disc would be a time-consuming process and make a ransomware more liable to be detected before it has finished encrypting the drive. Another reason could be to encrypt files that the user will be familiar with the names of [36]. This can be used to define better rules for filtering out potential threats to a system.

Scaife et al. [37] proposed a early warning protection system titled "CryptoDrop" in which through experimental analysis could stop ransomware in an average of 10 files lost. Showing that analysis of ransomware behaviours are a potential for stopping ransomware attacks on users. They achieved this through the following three main types of ransomware metrics:

- **File type changes**: As discussed above, ransomware typically target specific file types [36] and can often change the type or extension of that file. Scaife et al. [37] use this to identify suspicious behaviour in the file system. Although this does not inherently suggest malicious behaviour from a process.
- **Similarity Measurements**: During encryption of a file, the content of that file changes, usually to the point where the file is completely unrecognizable from the original. Using this behaviour pattern, Scaife et al. [37] uses a similarity-preserving hash to compare a file's original content to the new content of that file after an edit, finding from a score of 0–100 how similar the two are.
- **File Entropy**: Entropy of encrypted or compressed files have a high entropy level due to the nature of how such actions occur. Entropy is in essence the measurement of "randomnes" of a file structure, using a prediction of letters that should appear after those that precede it [38]. Using this, it can be easily decided which files have been encrypted [37].

3 Methodology

In this chapter, the investigated hypothesis is that different implementations of ransomware will have different behavioural characteristics on the file system level. This section details research undertaken to pursue this hypothesis.

3.1 File System Monitor

The main software development in this research is a file monitoring application. This application is used to monitor all interaction with files in specified directories. The interaction will be recorded and saved in an .exe file and formatted as CSV, as this should assist to prevent the file from being affected by the ransomware. An assumption was made here that the ransomware is more likely to target data files than system executables (.exe) as encrypted an essential executable file may render the system unsustainable for displaying a ransom message. The main use of the software will be for executing inside a virtual environment alongside crypto-ransomware samples to record file interaction data for future analysis. The software will need to run with extended privileges in the virtual environment to ensure that it has access to all files on the system. This is necessary as monitoring a file for activity (open, read, write) requires that the monitoring software has privileges to at least read the file's properties and contents.

The software has been developed in C# and will use the `FileSystemWatcher` class, a tool built into the .NET framework that can be used to monitor file system events and handle them by type. This class can identify when files have been changed, renamed, created and deleted. The `FileSystemWatcher` tool is particularly helpful for this research as it is both efficient and reliable due to its utilisation of Windows core functionality. This application will focus on using the changed and renamed `FileSystemWatcher` features to log file system changes as a ransomware runs in the background. Once these event's types have been triggered, the software will add the event data to a new line in the output file. This process is continued until the ransomware is confirmed to have stopped its encryption processes.

The main functionality for the software is as follows:

- Monitor the file system for any changes to file content or renaming of files;
- Record this data are a CSV format so it easily portable in data analysis software;
- Output file is kept in a secure location so it can be safe from the ransomware malware instance; and
- Data stored in the files changes should be in the following format:
  `timestamp, New file Name, New directory, old file name, old directory, event type, file size.`

Ransomware can use a variety of methods to encrypt files, but mostly either performs an edit and rename, where it encrypts the data and the renames the file with a custom extension, or a delete and create, where the contents of the file are copied into another document with is then encrypted, and the original file will be deleted. Due to this, some of the information that is being created can be missing from the log file; however in these cases, these fields will be stored as empty.

3.2   Virtual Environment

The virtual environment will need to be set-up to have a file structure representative of a normal users file system. To do this, roughly 600 example files (PDF, word, etc.) will be stored in the environment.

The file structure created for this experiment will consist of five main folders, each named as "folder" suffixed with a number from 1–5, keeping the folders in a clear order when viewed normally in the file system. Each of these five folders will contain 2 sub-folders, these sub-folders will also be named "folder", but suffixed with the number of the parent folder and the number order of that folder within its parent folder; for example, the first sub-folder in folder1 would be named folder 1-1 and the second sub-folder being folder1-2. Each sub-folder will also have two sub-folders and keep the same naming conventions; this continues down through until the depth of the folders reaches four folders deep, with the final folder for the top branch being titled folder1-1-1-1 (see Fig. 1).

In each of the folders, there will be eight files of different types; these being .doc, .docx, .txt, .csv, .pdf, .ppt, .xmls, .pub. These files have a mixed order in each of

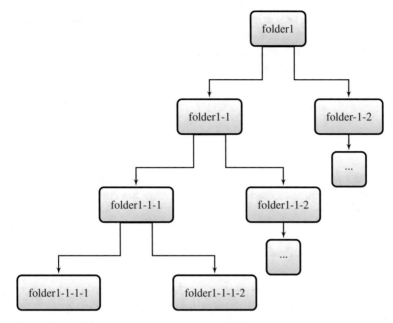

Fig. 1 Example of folder structure an naming conventions

the folders and sub-folders; this has been intentionally designed to determine if any behavioural patterns occur depending on file type and can help identify if ransomware instances ignore certain file types. There is also a change in file size, and once again, this is to see if there are differences in behaviour when ransomware encrypt files of different sizes.

This virtual environment wil have a snapshot (a backup of the system that can easily be restored) of the set file set-up and an installation of the software before ransomware infection. This is to make rerunning the analysis of ransomware activity easier. Using a virtual environment could potentially impede the study. This is because some ransomware families have inbuilt protections to identify if they are running in virtual environments. This may cause some ransomware families or variants to not be suitable for use with the presented methodology. This is a limitation that would need further research to overcome.

3.3 Ransomware

The ransomware executables were collected from VirusShare, an online repository for malware, shared by the antivirus community. From this repository, ransomware samples will be collected, using some of the wider known ransomware, such as Petya, Locky or Cryptowall. Ransomware like petya and its variants could be more difficult to collect data for, as they more commonly known to make changes to the master boot record to stop users from accessing the machine. Some ransomware may not run on the virtual environment due to the issues discussed above, and others may be unable to connect to the C and C servers either due to location, firewall or server downtime.

4   Results

In this section, results are presented from executing five common ransomware types alongside the presented methodology for monitoring file system interaction.

4.1   Traversal Methods

Gandcrab and TeslaCrypt showed very similar file system traversal methods (see Table 1), both adopting depth-first traversal following a systematic approach, encrypting files in each folder in a alphabetical order, going from the first parent folder and traversing through its sub-directories, going through the first branch in each sub-folder, until no further folders can be found (see Fig. 2).

CryptXXX also took a similar approach to traversing the folder structure; however doing this in a reversed alphabetical order, starting from folder 5 and its sub-directories, first following the final branch in each sub-folder until it reaches the end (see Fig. 3).

Sage2.2 and Osiris also display similar behaviour to each other, but share no common behaviour with the ransomware discussed above. Both seemly approach each folder and sub-folder in a random order, with no clear patterns on how it moves between folders in the directory. It was considered that this may be resulting from the use of multiple threads, each handling a portion of the directory structure. However, even after considering this possibility, it still was not possible to identify a systematic pattern. Osiris is the only sample that iterates through the file system 3 times, each

Table 1 Displaying the folder and file traversal methods

Name	Traversal	File order	Folder order
GandCrab	Depth-first	Alphabetical order	Alphabetical order
TelsaCrypt	Depth-first	Alphabetical order	Alphabetical order
CryptXXX	Depth-first	Alphabetical order	Reverse alphabetical order
Osiris	Random order	Prioritised by extension, then alphabetical	Random
Sage2.2	Random	Single file iterations	Random

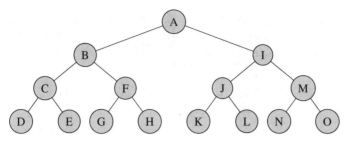

Fig. 2 File system traversal graph for GandCrab and TelsaCrypt. This graph shows the movement in a folder and its sub-folders, moving from A to O

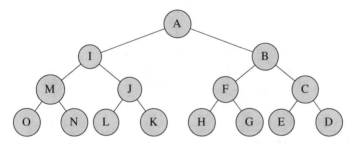

Fig. 3 Graph displaying traversal pattern for CryptXXX. The path taken by CryptXXX is displayed from A to O

time encrypting different file types. As shown in Table 2, Osiris starts its file encryption in folder 2-1-1-1 and moves onto folder1 and then onto folder 3-2-2-2. This random order continues until the third iteration through the directories, where it starts to show a more structured traversal technique, using depth-first traversal.

4.2 Files and Extensions

A majority of the ransomware samples used follow a alphabetical ordering to the files in a directory, always encrypting the first file it identifies in the file structure and moves systematically through the directory until no more files are available for processing. Gandcrab, TeslaCrypt and CryptXXX follow this pattern; however, it was noticed that TeslaCrypt did not encrypt .pub files.

Osiris encrypts files in the same alphabetical order as the three ransomware instances mentioned above; however, it encrypts in three different stages, prioritising certain file extension on each run through the file system. In the first encryption stage, it encrypts all files with extensions of .doc, .ppt and .xls; these files are encrypted in an alphabetical order in each folder. The second stage of encryption, Osiris encrypts all .docx files, and then for the third stage of the encryption process, all .txt, .csv and .pdf files were encrypted.

Table 2 Displaying the first twenty lines of the recorded log of Osiris activity in the file system

Timestamp	Folder	File	Event type
201803141350386950	folder2/folder2-1/folder2-1-1/folder2-1-1-1	file2.ppt	Renamed
201803141350387266	folder2/folder2-1/folder2-1-1/folder2-1-1-1	OSIRIS-3925.htm	Created
201803141350389144	folder1	file1.doc	Renamed
201803141350389292	folder1	OSIRIS-89a0.htm	Created
201803141350389449	folder3/folder3-2/folder3-2-2/folder3-2-2-2	file2.ppt	Renamed
201803141350389607	folder3/folder3-2/folder3-2-2/folder3-2-2-2	OSIRIS-f4cc.htm	Created
201803141350389767	folder3/folder3-2/folder3-2-2/folder3-2-2-2	file3.xls	Renamed
201803141350389926	folder1	file5.ppt	Renamed
201803141350390229	folder1	file6.xls	Renamed
201803141350390388	folder5/folder5-1/folder5-1-1	file7.doc	Renamed
201803141350390703	folder5/folder5-1/folder5-1-1	OSIRIS-db55.htm	Created
201803141350391328	folder3/folder3-2/folder3-2-2/folder3-2-2-2	file6.doc	Renamed
201803141350391481	folder1/folder1-1	file4.ppt	Renamed
201803141350391639	folder1/folder1-1	OSIRIS-f3db.htm	Created
201803141350391798	folder1/folder1-1	file5.xls	Renamed
201803141350391950	folder5/folder5-2/folder5-2-1/folder5-2-1-1	file6.doc	Renamed
201803141350392105	folder5-2/folder5-2-1/folder5-2-1-1	OSIRIS-c0bd.htm	Created
201803141350392423	folder1/folder1-1	file8.doc	Renamed
201803141350392734	folder5/folder5-1/folder5-1-1/folder5-1-1-1	file2.ppt	Renamed
201803141350392891	folder5/folder5-1/folder5-1-1/folder5-1-1-1	OSIRIS-8f80.htm	Created

Table 3 Displaying the first twenty lines of the recorded log of Sage2.2 activity in the file system

Timestamp	Folder	File	Event type
201804020637243459	folder2/folder2-1/folder2-1-2	file7.doc...	Created
201804020637243459	folder5/folder5-2/folder5-2-2	file7.doc...	Created
201804020637243459	folder2/folder2-1/folder2-1-1/folder2-1-1-2	file6.doc...	Created
201804020637243616	folder2	file1.doc...	Created
201804020637243616	folder2/folder2-1/folder2-1-1	file7.doc...	Created
201804020637243616	folder5/folder5-2/folder5-2-2/folder5-2-2-1	file6.doc...	Created
201804020637243616	folder2/folder2-1	file8.doc...	Created
201804020637243616	folder2/folder2-2/folder2-2-1/folder2-2-1-1	file6.doc...	Created
201804020637243616	folder5/folder5-2/folder5-2-1/folder5-2-1-1	file6.doc...	Created
201804020637243616	folder2/folder2-2/folder2-2-2	file7.doc...	Created
201804020637243616	folder2/folder2-1/folder2-1-2	file7.doc...	Renamed
201804020637243616	folder2/folder2-2/folder2-2-1/folder2-2-1-2	file6.doc...	Created
201804020637243616	folder5/folder5-2/folder5-2-1	file7.doc...	Created
201804020637243616	folder2/folder2-1/folder2-1-2	file7.doc	Deleted
201804020637243616	folder2/folder2-1/folder2-1-2	!HELP_SOS.hta	Created
201804020637243616	folder2	file1.doc...	Renamed
201804020637243616	folder2	file1.doc	Deleted
201804020637243616	folder2	!HELP_SOS.hta	Created
201804020637243616	folder2/folder2-1/folder2-1-1	file7.doc...	Renamed
201804020637243616	folder2/folder2-1/folder2-1-1	file7.doc,,,	Deleted

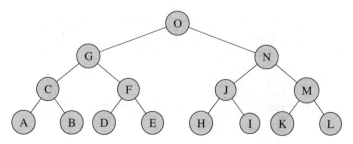

Fig. 4 TelsaCrypt's creation of ransom note files in each directory. This graph displays the movement pattern for the creation of these notes, from A to O

Sage2.2 encrypts files by iterating through the file system for each individual file type, starting with .doc files and ending with .pdf file. Due to this behaviour and the single use of each file type in the monitor file structure, no other behavioural patterns, such as alphabetical ordering, could be discerned. In addition, due to the limited number of file extensions, this ransomware could iterate through many other file extension types that were not recorded. Sage2.2 did not encrypt .pub files (Table 3).

4.3 Ransom Notes

Each of the ransomware samples run created ransom notes in each directory it affected, with each sample using different behaviour to create these notes. A majority of the samples created one file, with TeslaCrypt being the only one to create three different files, these being .png, .txt and .htm. As shown in Fig. 4, TeslaCrypt creates these files once it reaches the end of a folder path, meaning that the creation method must run after exploration of a folder's direct sub-folders.

CryptXXX and Osiris create ransom notes after the successful encryption of a file in a directory. They encrypt the first file, chosen in alphabetical order, create the ransom note and then continue through the directory. Sage2.2 also displays this behaviour, creating the ransom note after deletion of the original file. This behaviour is repeated through the first iteration of the file system, but does not continue after, as all the files have been created. GandCrab created its ransom notes upon entering a directory, before any encryption in the folder had been done.

5 Conclusion

In this section, a conclusion is drawn based on the results of the previous section, discussing the main findings of this experiment and possible future research to expand on this work.

Each of the investigated ransomware samples displayed unique behavioural traits in regard to file system activity. They either had their own behaviour pattern, showing behaviour that only itself possesses, or a number of behavioural patterns that it shared with other ransomware samples. The samples investigated in this research identified that two have common behavioural features (GandCrab and TelsaCrypt) and the other three have unique characteristics. These behaviour patterns show that ransomware can be seen working in a file system clearly and, importantly, demonstrate a distinctive difference from normal user file interactions.

This work has facilitated further research in this topic, showing that there are specific behavioural patterns that can be observed in ransomware file system interaction and shows that ransomware can be identified using individual or shared patterns. This data could also be used to create systems that could potentially halt ransomware processes in progress should they activate on a system.

6 Questions

1. Define what is Ransomware and how it differs from other forms of Malware?
2. Explain and discuss why Ransomware is becoming an increasingly utilised form of Malware?
3. What are traditional mechanisms of identifying Malware, and what are the significant challenges of this approach?
4. Why does monitoring behavioural characteristics present a way to detect suspicious user activity?
5. Do you think that monitoring file system interaction is a promising approach for malware detection?
6. What challenges do you think are associated with such a technique in the future?

References

1. Moir, R (2003) Defining malware: FAQ. https://technet.microsoft.com/en-us/library/dd632948.aspx
2. Kharraz A, Robertson W, Balzarotti D, Bilge L, Kirda E (2015) Cutting the gordian knot: a look under the hood of ransomware attacks. In: International conference on detection of intrusions and malware, and vulnerability assessment. Springer, Berlin, pp 3–24
3. Richardson, R., North, M.: Ransomware: evolution, mitigation and prevention. Int Manag Rev 13(1), 10 (2017)

4. Brenner, B (2017) InfoSec 2017: a look at the family album of ransomware. https://nakedsecurity.sophos.com/2017/06/06/infosec-2017-a-look-at-the-family-album-of-ransomware/

5. Beek, C (2017) McAfee Labs 2017 Threats Predictions. www.mcafee.com/uk/resources/reports/rp-threats-predictions-2017.pdf

6. MalwareBytes: cybercrime tactics and techniques (2017). https://www.malwarebytes.com/pdf/labs/Cybercrime-Tactics-and-Techniques-Q1-2017.pdf

7. Symantec: internet security threat report (2017). https://www.symantec.com/content/dam/symantec/docs/reports/istr-22-2017-en.pdf

8. FBI IC3: internet crime report (2016). https://pdf.ic3.gov/2016_IC3Report.pdf

9. US Department of Justice: How to protect your networks from ransomware. Technical report (2016). https://www.justice.gov/criminal-ccips/file/872771/download

10. Savage, K., Coogan, P., Lau, H.: The evolution of ransomware. Symantec, Mountain View (2015)

11. Upadhyaya R, Jain A (2016) Cyber ethics and cyber crime: A deep dwelved study into legality, ransomware, underground web and bitcoin wallet. In: International conference on computing, communication and automation (ICCCA). IEEE, pp 143–148

12. Fischer, T (2014) Private and public key cryptography and ransomware. Technical report

13. Trend Micro: Command-and-control (C&C) server (2017). https://www.trendmicro.com/vinfo/us/security/definition/command-and-control-(c-c)-serve

14. Sophos: Ransomware: How an attack works (2016). https://community.sophos.com/kb/en-us/124699

15. Beek C, Frosst D, Greve P, Gund Y, Moreno F, Peterson E, Schmugar C, Simon R, Sommer D, Sun B, et al. (2017) Mcafee labs threats report [internet]. McAfee Lab (April 2017). https://www.mcafee.com/us/resources/reports/rp-quarterly-threats-mar-2017,pdf, p 49

16. Symantec: ISTR ransomware (2017). https://www.symantec.com/content/dam/symantec/docs/security-center/white-papers/istr-ransomware-2017-en.pdf

17. Liao K, Zhao Z, Doupé A, Ahn G-J (2016) Behind closed doors: measurement and analysis of cryptolocker ransoms in bitcoin. In: APWG symposium on electronic crime research (eCrime). IEEE, pp 1–13

18. Panda Security: cryptolocker: what is and how to avoid it. Panda Security (2015). https://www.pandasecurity.com/mediacenter/malware/cryptolocker/

19. McGoogan C, Titcomb J, Krol C (2017) What is WannaCry and how does ransomware work?. http://www.telegraph.co.uk/technology/0/ransomware-does-work/

20. Symantec threat intelligence: what you need to know about the Wannacry ransomware (2017). https://www.symantec.com/blogs/threat-intelligence/wannacry-ransomware-attack

21. Joven, R, Yick Low, C (2017) MacRansom: offered as ransomware as a servive. https://blog.fortinet.com/2017/06/09/macransom-offered-as-ransomware-as-a-service

22. Barkly: Ransomware-as-a-service is booming (2017). https://blog.barkly.com/how-ransomware-as-a-service-works

23. Conner, B (2017) Ransomware-As-A-Service: the next great cyber threat?. https://www.forbes.com/sites/forbestechcouncil/2017/03/17/ransomware-as-a-service-the-next-great-cyber-threat/#648c45d34123

24. Europol: no more ransom: law enforcement and IT security companies join forces to fight ransomware (2016). https://www.europol.europa.eu/newsroom/news/no-more-ransom-law-enforcement-and-it-security-companies-join-forces-to-fight-ransomware

25. No more ransom: about the project (2016). https://www.nomoreransom.org/en/about-the-project.html

26. Osbourne, C. (2017) No more ransom project helps thousands of ransomware victims. http://www.zdnet.com/article/no-more-ransom-project-unlocks-over-28000-devices/

27. KasperSky: no more ransom: a very productive year (2017). https://www.kaspersky.com/blog/no-more-ransom-first-anniversary/17791/

28. Cloonan, J (2017) Advanced malware detection - signatures versus behavior analysis (2017). https://www.infosecurity-magazine.com/opinions/malware-detection-signatures/

29. Nieuwenhuizen D (2017) A behavioural-based approach to ransomware detection. Retrieved from https://labs.mwrinfosecurity.com/assets/resourceFiles/mwri-behavioural-ransomware-detection-2017-04-5.pdf

30. Ask, K (2006) Automatic malware signature generation. 2006-10-16]. http://citeseerx.ist.psu. edu/viewdoc/download

31. Hanel, A (2011) An intro to creating anti-virus signatures. http://hooked-on-mnemonics. blogspot.co.uk/2011/01/intro-to-creating-anti-virus-signatures.html

32. Shosha, AF, Liu, C-C, Gladyshev, P, Matten, M (2012) Evasion-resistant malware signature based on profiling kernel data structure objects. In: 7th international conference on Risk and security of internet and systems (CRiSIS), IEEE, pp 1–8

33. Kaspersky: Heuristic analysis in Kaspersky Anti-Virus 2012 (2012). https://support.kaspersky. co.uk/6668

34. Ahmadi, M., Sami, A., Rahimi, H., Yadegari, B.: Malware detection by behavioural sequential patterns. Comput Fraud Secur **2013**(8), 11–19 (2013)

35. Naval S, Laxmi V, Gaur MS, Raja S, Rajarajan M, Conti M (2015) Environment–reactive malware behavior: detection and categorization. In: Data privacy management, autonomous spontaneous security, and security assurance. Springer, Berlin, pp 167–182

36. Gazet, A.: Comparative analysis of various ransomware virii. J Comput Virol **6**(1), 77–90 (2010)

37. Scaife N, Carter H, Traynor P, Butler KR (2016) Cryptolock (and drop it): stopping ransomware attacks on user data. In: IEEE 36th international conference on distributed computing systems (ICDCS). IEEE, pp 303–312

38. Sorokin, I.: Comparing files using structural entropy. J Comput Virol **7**(4), 259–265 (2011)

Part IV
Visualisation

A Framework for the Visualisation of Cyber Security Requirements and Its Application in BPMN

Bo Zhou, Curtis Maines, Stephen Tang and Qi Shi

Abstract Security requirements is the fundamental component in designing and defending IT systems against cyber attacks. Still in reality they are every so often to be overlooked due to the lack of expertise and technical approach to capture and model these requirements in an effective way. It is not helped by the fact that many companies, especially SMEs, tend to focus on the functionality of their business processes first, before considering security as an afterthought. New extensions for modelling cyber security requirements in Business Process Model and Notation (BPMN) have been proposed in the past to address this issue. In this chapter, we analyse existing extensions and identify the notational issues present within each of them. We discuss how there is yet no single extension which represents a comprehensive range of cyber security concepts. Consequently, a new framework is proposed that can be used to extend, visualise and verify cyber security requirements in not only BPMN, but any other existing modelling language. We investigate a new approach to modelling security and propose a solution that overcomes current issues whilst still providing functionality to include all concepts potentially modellable in BPMN related to cyber security. The framework utilises a "what you see is what you get" approach to allow intuitive modelling of rather complicated security concepts. It increases human understanding of the security requirements whilst minimising the cognitive load. We detail how we implemented our solution along with the novel approach our application takes to current challenges.

B. Zhou (✉) · C. Maines · S. Tang · Q. Shi
Department of Computer Science, Liverpool John Moores University, Liverpool, UK
e-mail: b.zhou@ljmu.ac.uk

C. Maines
e-mail: c.l.maines@2011.ljmu.ac.uk

S. Tang
e-mail: s.o.tang@ljmu.ac.uk

Q. Shi
e-mail: Q.Shi@ljmu.ac.uk

© Springer International Publishing AG, part of Springer Nature 2018   339
S. Parkinson et al. (eds.), *Guide to Vulnerability Analysis for Computer Networks
and Systems*, Computer Communications and Networks,
https://doi.org/10.1007/978-3-319-92624-7_15

1   Introduction

A business process can be described as a set of linked tasks, which must be executed in a specific order, collectively resulting in a business objective or policy goal being achieved. These tasks can be conducted across one or multiple organisations [1]. *Business Process Model and Notation* (BPMN) can be used to graphically represent such processes and their component relationships in a common standard between organisations [2, 3].

BPMN fulfils the requirement of visually representing business processes and is now the industry standard for their modelling [1, 4]. Nevertheless, even though security directly affects the functionality of business processes, BPMN has no support for specifying cyber security requirements [5, 6]. Current BPMN security extensions have made attempts, but they are being constructed unsystematically, without any empirical evidence to support their choice of concepts [7] or notational design.

We propose a new framework for visualising and verifying comprehensive cyber security requirements within not only BPMN, but any modelling language. Unlike current approaches, our framework is built upon existing literature and empirical evidence. From our evaluation of existing extensions, we are able to identify the problem areas and propose a new set of requirements for avoiding them. Along with these and existing theories, we are able to propose a framework that can be used for extending any modelling language with security requirements. Using BPMN as a case study, we justify this framework through the implementation of our own solution. Proving its ability to avoid the issues experienced by current approaches as well as visualise an exponentially higher number of security requirements.

The framework is built on 3D game technology. It is intuitive and straightforward to use and make the security requirements easy to understand for the normal users who may not necessarily be security expert. The graphical representation of both business process and security requirements makes it a perfect fit for applying artificial intelligent technologies upon them in the future.

2   BPMN Security Extensions

For existing extensions, the principles defined by Moody [8] are used for evaluating their notations to ensure a scientific approach is kept in their assessment. These principles are frequently used in the evaluation of modelling languages including that of BPMN [9, 10]. The principles and their definitions are as follows:

- *Semiotic clarity*: *every semantic construct should have a corresponding graphical symbol.*
- *Perceptual discriminability*: *symbols should be distinguishable from one another.*
- *Semantic transparency*: *each symbol should be a graphical mnemonic of their underlying semantics.*
- *Complexity management*: *include mechanisms for managing the complexity of diagrams.*

Fig. 1 Rodriguez et al. security notation

- *Cognitive integration*: *include mechanisms for integrating information from separate diagrams.*
- *Visual expressiveness*: *utilise all visual variables within the notation.*
- *Dual coding*: *use text to reiterate symbol semantics.*
- *Graphic economy*: *ensure the total number of constructs is cognitively manageable.*
- *Cognitive fit*: *use different notation for different audiences.*

Each definition coming from the original paper [[8].

We have already evaluated existing extensions from a semiotic clarity perspective in a previous paper [11] and as such have excluded the principle from this section. In this chapter, we chose to assess five security extensions against the remaining principles. Due to the extensiveness of each evaluation and the similarities many have in regards to their notation, we deemed five extensions adequate for this review. For many, the only distinguishing variables are their choice of semantics. Much of their notation design and modelling approach are very similar. Nevertheless, the following five extensions provide strong representative examples of current approaches.

The security notation shown in Fig. 1 is the extension created by Rodriguez et al. [5]. The symbols from left to right represent: *non-repudiation, attack harm detection, integrity, privacy* and *access control*. Perceptual discriminability has both strengths and weaknesses in this extension. The symbols are very distinct from the BPMN notation; separating their domain well from business processes. However, they are far too similar to each other, with only a few textual characters being the difference. Given that the distinguishing factor is text—making international use extremely difficult—this extension fails to adequately meet this principle.

The semantic transparency of the symbols is of a similar nature. A *padlock* successfully infers the meaning of security, but as all the concepts are represented by a *padlock*, without the use of text any further detail is impossible to distinguish; failing this principle. This leads onto the visual expressiveness of the symbols. There are eight visual variables which can be used to construct a notation, these being: *horizontal position, vertical position, shape, brightness, size, orientation, colour* and *texture* [8]. This extension is only utilising one of the eight visual variables; that being *shape*. This is evident that very little potential has been taken advantage of graphically.

The complexity management of this extension is non-existent, having adopted the method of stamping symbols onto BPMN elements. Where this may be an effective way of linking BPMN tasks and security concepts, diagrams quickly become overwhelmed when multiple concepts are placed on a single element. In the paper that introduces it [5], the symbols are displayed on a BPMN diagram at their target

Fig. 2 Saleem et al. security notation

size. When scaled down, the text on each notation is very difficult to read. Given that text has been used as primary notation, it is extremely poor design given that once the symbols are displayed at a usable size (typically smaller than in Fig. 1) the text becomes nearly unreadable. Ideally text should only ever be used for redundant coding to reiterate a semantic meaning. (Redundant coding is using extra visual (or textual) variables to reiterate something that is already represented in the primary notation. It is usually an effective variable for distinction, but not robust enough to be considered a primary notation [8].) Moreover, text has very poor cognitive effectiveness and provides very little discriminability between symbols [8]. However, as it has very much been used as a core distinguishing variable in this case, it is by far the biggest weakness of the design. Further appreciation of this fault can be found when viewing the notation from a non-English-speaking perspective.

The dual coding principle states that text, more specifically words, should be used to complement graphics [8]. When used correctly, text can be a useful tool for learning a notation. A novice user, for example, can keep referring to construct labels until they are confident enough using just visual aids. However, using acronyms can add to the difficulty of this as now novices must not only learn graphical symbols but these as well. In this instance, dual coding has not been satisfied.

The graphic economy of this notation is fairly successful. Nevertheless, there are concept omissions within the extension, for example *confidentiality* and *availability*. A notation with poor graphic economy is more desirable than one with construct deficit. As for cognitive integration and cognitive fit, the paper made no mention of any functionality to support either of these principles.

Saleem et al. [6] proposed a slightly newer security extension that takes a different approach notation-wise, but still yields several issues. In Fig. 2 from left to right, the symbols represent *confidentiality, integrity* and *availability* respectively—the core concepts of cyber security [12].

In this case, the perceptual discriminability of the symbols was done rather successfully. Although similar in theme, each notation has several distinguishing variables that don't include text. This makes the unique identification from any culture or language very easy. The same can be said about the semantic transparency. This extension has at least had some thought put into semiotics, creating a notation whose symbols perceptually resemble their semantic meaning. However, there are still some areas that allow for improvement. Take *integrity* for example, colour has been used as a primary notation to show an identical pattern both before and after a transmission; an appropriate visualisation. A better option, however, would be to use shapes such as triangles and squares. *Colour* is very useful in notations, but like text, it

Fig. 3 SecBPMN2 security notation

should be used for redundant coding and not as a primary notation [8]. Some people can struggle to distinguish between certain colours, with the likes of blue and green being a prime example for people who suffer from Tritanopia [13], a variant of colour blindness.

The visual expressiveness of these symbols appears higher than that of Rodriguez et al. with multiple variables being used this time (*colour* and *shape*). However, visual expressiveness refers to the idea that multiple variables should be used as a form of notation (to convey some form of meaning to the user). The only variable distinguishing these symbols is *shape*; *colour* is merely decoration. To better utilise *colour*, each symbol should have had its own unique one, e.g. red, blue and green.

Complexity management is the same as with the previous extension (given the impact of this principle to visual notations it is a wonder so few acknowledge it). The paper that introduces this extension also provides a complete BPMN diagram incorporating the symbols. The notations again have very poor scalability; but not as bad as that of Rodriguez et al. as there is a much higher perceptual discriminability in these symbols. Nonetheless, these symbols are not enclosed in a uniform shape as with the previous extension, when close together their boundaries become hard to see and they begin to corrupt each other.

As seen in Fig. 2, the principle of dual coding has not been met. The graphic economy is similar to that of the previous extension. Although it may be economical, the reason of it being construct deficit is a worse anomaly. As for cognitive fit and cognitive integration, they were also neglected by Saleem et al.

Salnitri et al. SecBPMN2 [4] notation can be seen in Fig. 3. From left to right, the concepts are as follows: *integrity, authenticity, accountability, non-repudiation, auditability, confidentiality, privacy, binding of duties, separation of duties, availability* and *non-delegation*.

The perceptual discriminability of these symbols is somewhat successful, but the visual distance between each symbol is dependent exclusively on the *shape* of the inner icons. Nevertheless, as each symbol is clearly distinguishable from the others, the extension satisfies the principle. As for semantic transparency, these symbols fall somewhere in the semantically translucent range. They are not capable of semantic immediacy but nor are they are opaque. There has been some thought put into their design but there are still uncertainties as to their exact meaning; a weak satisfaction of the principle. The visual expressiveness of the symbols as touched on earlier is limited again; the only variable in use is shape. Some may argue *colour* has also been used, as mentioned earlier though this must be in the form of redundant coding, not decoration. Nevertheless, given that orange has been used consistently throughout all the symbols, it separates this notation well from BPMN (which tends to be black and white or pale pastel colours).

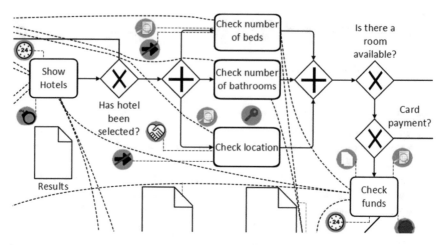

Fig. 4 SecBPMN2 business process model

Fig. 5 Labda et al. security notation

The complexity management of this extension is rather poor. Viewing it in use in Fig. 4, it is easy to see how some users may feel in a state of cognitive overload. This is partially due to the dashed lines across the diagram, however given that very few concepts have been used, it is easy to see how this extension can quickly overwhelm a diagram.

The remaining principles follow a similar theme as the aforementioned extensions. Graphic economy is achieved through a construct deficit language, dual coding is not included, and both cognitive fit and cognitive integration are altogether ignored.

Labda et al. security notation [14] can be seen in Fig. 5. The symbols from left to right represent: *access control (allow), access control (prevent), access control (limited), separation of tasks, binding of tasks, user consent, necessity to know (high), necessity to know (medium)* and *necessity to know (low)*.

The perceptual discriminability of this extension is difficult to determine. Each symbol is undoubtedly unique from the others but the three *necessity to know* constructs have little visual distance. There appears to have been an attempt at adhering to the principle of semantic transparency. Nevertheless, the symbols are borderline between semantically opaque and perverse. For example, the concept of *separation of tasks* is represented by a lightning bolt; a strange choice of mnemonic. Given that these symbols don't exactly infer their semantic meaning, it is difficult to conclude semantic transparency has been met.

The visual expressiveness of the symbols is similar to the previous extensions. The only utilised variable is *shape* with *colour*. Once again a clear example of using weak notation is to separate the extension from BPMN.

Fig. 6 Koh and Zhou security notation

The complexity management of this extension is the same as Rodriguez et al. [5]; also using the symbol stamping method. As expected similar themes emerge. To place the concepts on BPMN elements they require scaling which once again makes perceptually discriminability difficult, especially given there's a visual distance of just one (*shape*). The graphic economy of this extension is controlled but this again is dependent on whether or not semiotic clarity was satisfied in the first instance. The cognitive fit and cognitive integration principles again are not acknowledged within this extension with dual coding clearly not included by observation of Fig. 5.

Koh and Zhou's notation [15] (see Fig. 6) is similar to that of Salnitri et al. Both opting for a circular shape with some form of icon inside. The underlying semantics for this notation are *security task, authentication, access control, authorisation, harm protection, encrypted message, non-repudiation* and *secure communication* respectively left to right. The final three symbols represent *confidentiality, integrity* and *availability*. With the stars visualising the required level for each concept.

Starting again with the perceptual discriminability of the notation, this extension has both positives and negatives. The authors have used a *padlock* on each symbol as a way of identifying and separating them as security constructs. This is an effective way of separating the notation from BPMN. However, given that the general design is very similar to that of BPMN (black and white icons in circles) the notation isn't as semantically immediate as it could be. Nevertheless, the use of *padlocks* and the icons inside each shape ensures the satisfaction of this principle (although there is room for improvement).

The semantic transparency of these symbols is similar to Labda et al. notation. It is clear from inspection of each element that thought has gone into making each symbol. However, some of the symbols are semantically perverse. Take *access control* for example (third symbol along on the top row). This icon is the universal symbol for "shuffle mode" on audio devices. Although expert security users may have a different meaning, the majority of business and novice users will be more likely to associate this icon with "shuffle". A less generic icon should have been used.

The complexity management of this extension is a combination of symbol stamping and BPMN element replacement. By this we mean, rather than use a BPMN message event, one would use a security element *encrypted message*. However, we claim that this a poor way to model security. Although business and security directly

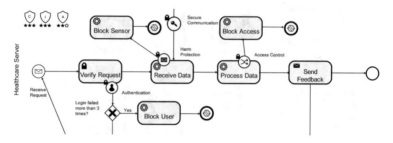

Fig. 7 Koh and Zhou business process model

affect each other, readers do not always want or need to see both domains. Extensions should aim to be as non-intrusive as possible, allowing modellers the ability to remove (or hide) security requirements whilst still maintaining a complete business process (effectively a complexity management system on its own). A portion of a BPMN diagram can be seen in Fig. 7 demonstrating this extension in use.

This figure emphasises our previous point on how the notation is far too similar to BPMN. It is not as clear in this figure as in SecBPMN2 what is security and what is business process. On further inspection you will be able to identify eight security elements in use. Nevertheless, there has been no attempt at managing the extra complexity created by the extension. Once again failing this principle.

The visual expressiveness of this extension is rather poor, utilising only one visual variable; *shape. Confidentiality, integrity* and *availability* could be considered to use *horizontal* and *vertical position* also as they seem to consistently appear in the top left of each diagram in the authors' paper. However, it is not explicitly defined whether this is a rule of the notation.

Dual coding is also neglected within this extension. None of the elements feature any supporting text, with *confidentiality, integrity* and *availability* once again using letters as discriminable features. The graphic economy carries on from the previous section, although the number of elements is manageable being construct deficit is worse. As for cognitive fit and cognitive integration, these were also left out of this extension.

From this review, of the five extensions evaluated not one extension is capable of satisfying even half of Moody's principles. Moody discussed how there are trade-offs amongst the principles and satisfying one may have a negative effect on another. Nevertheless, certain principles such as complexity management should always be achieved, especially in software engineering [8]. There is need for an extension that is not only comprehensive to the domain but can also satisfy the most optimal number of principles.

3 Requirements Specification

Using the "Physics of Notations" [8] as a basis, the literature review in Section II highlights some of the key areas current security extensions are having issues with. The following section outlines the essential requirements for overcoming these issues.

3.1 *Comprehensiveness*

Firstly, the semiotic clarity of the notation. Although some extensions appear comprehensive to the cyber security domain, this is only relative to the construct deficit many of the others suffer from. In fairness to several extensions, they do state their focus on a particular area of security and as such their paucity may be excused. Nevertheless, needing multiple extensions to specify requirements for the same domain is very poor usability and will likely lead to the extensions being dismissed altogether. From the standpoint of an "ideal solution" the best approach is to include a comprehensive range of constructs which gives the modeller the ability to restrict the domain coverage as they see fit.

Of course, this requirement was largely covered in our previous paper [11]. We present an ontology of cyber security requirements that aims to act as a foundation for the creation of a comprehensive BPMN security extension. Stressing that current extensions have been heavily construct deficit and thereby fail to adequately provide a suitable tool for representing security requirements. We propose a total of 79 cyber security requirements that should be modellable in BPMN before an extension can be deemed comprehensive. These are structured into six areas with a hierarchy depth of four. These six areas being: *access control, privacy, integrity, accountability, attack/harm detection and prevention* and *availability*.

We aim to use this ontology as a basis for our solution. Ensuring that we are not only overcoming the aforementioned notational issues but also providing the first truly comprehensive tool for modelling cyber security requirements within BPMN.

3.2 *Coherence*

From the review in Section II, it is clear to see how much discrepancy there is surrounding various concept meanings and uses; specifically in regards to *access control*. This area of security in particular appears to be the most prominent sufferer of this issue.

In his paper, Moody [8] discusses construct overload and how multiple concepts falling under the same element can cause confusion and misuse of the construct. To overcome this issue is relatively straightforward. The tool in which the language is used need only include some form of database the user can refer to reiterate the construct's intended meaning. As long as all users of the language are consistent the issue can be eliminated.

3.3 Structure

The inclusion of a new domain in any existing language, will almost always cause an unparalleled increase in complexity (especially cyber security). For novice users to the language, this can be overwhelming and potentially lead to only experienced individuals adopting the extension. As per the principle, cognitive fit suggests that modelling languages should prepare for this and include mechanisms to allow both the novice and expert equal opportunity to utilise the notation [8]. Moody states that it is poor design to assume one notation can satisfy both the novice and expert. However, this is somewhat contradicted by the likes of traffic signs in which all levels of expertise understand and utilise. Two notations can also cause an issue in which a reader may misinterpret one symbol from the expert notation with one from the novice notation.

To address the principle in this instance, we propose one well-designed notation and the visualising of constructs in a hierarchical structure. At the highest level, novice users need only learn a few simple concepts, then as expertise increases the constructs can be expanded to include more specific and lower level concepts.

3.4 Verification

Salnitri et al. [4], were the only authors in our review to acknowledge the need for verification within a language. They also claim to have proposed their own framework for verifying (and modelling) security within BPMN. However, their paper is based heavily on their own extension of BPMN and provides little contribution in terms of any framework. Nevertheless, the verification aspect of their extension is something we also see as a core requirement of a security extension.

3.5 Graphical Framework

From the notation review, it is clear that although some attempts had been made at semantic transparency, the general design of each extension is rather poor. None of the authors seem to have considered the designing of the symbols as notation, just individual icons.

As such, we propose that a security extension should first create a graphical framework which can be used for the designing of each construct. This not only assures the required principles will be met, but also allows for consistency should anyone else choose to add to the notation in the future.

3.6 Complexity Management

Complexity management is potentially the single reason current security extensions have the issues they do. When viewing current extensions from a complexity management perspective, it is likely that the authors struggled to develop a solution in which they could be more comprehensive to the domain. Therefore, they opt for construct deficit opposed to poor complexity management. For this reason, we see this principle as the most important of the "Physics of Notations".

Although principles such as semantic transparency can assist in the understanding of a language—especially as a novice—complexity can have more severe impacts. BPMN and UML are good examples of languages which seem to have altogether ignored semantic transparency [8], yet they are both widely adopted. This is because their complexity and thereby ease of use is well managed. A notation could have semantic immediacy on all constructs but if its complexity is poorly managed, users will avoid or incorrectly make use of it [16]. Therefore, when creating an extension (or modelling language) complexity management should be one of the key issues to address.

3.7 Modelling Tool Functionality

When developing a security extension, most authors will typically expand on an already existing tool such as Microsoft Visio [17]. Most tools usually include some functionality for the creation or inclusion of custom notation. SecBPMN2 for example [4], utilises Visio's Stencil functionality. This allows users to create a custom toolbar of their favourite symbols for use later on. It also allows for the saving of custom symbols.

Given that current security extensions have opted to represent their notation in a similar manner to that of BPMN, there has been little progress in terms of new modelling approaches. Most authors merely present a set of concepts and accompanying symbols, regardless of the fact that by adding more constructs they've increased the languages complexity and potentially nullified any complexity management the existing language had in place.

The general approach to visualising security within BPMN follows the "if it isn't broke don't fix it" rule with regards to existing modelling languages. Where this may be the case for most tools, they typically only cover one domain (business process management for BPMN). If the authors simply wanted to extend a language with same domain notation, utilising current software is the logical choice. However, extending a language with a new domain is more extensive than previous authors have given credit. It is not simply a case of specifying a few concepts then creating symbols for them. There are a lot of other variables which must be considered (this section naming a few). Moreover, the tool which is used for creating and reading diagram instances requires just as much attention.

4 Extension Framework

This leads onto the creation of our framework. As previously stated, little attention has been given to notation design or tool functionality. The majority of authors focus all their efforts on semantics. Although we agree that semantics play a vital role in the creation of any modelling language (or extension), it is not the only role. In Fig. 8, we propose a framework that can be used to extend any existing modelling language with security requirements.

Rather than describing the framework in one section and evaluating it in another, we opted to integrate the two into one. This approach makes it easier for the reader to identify which portions of the framework satisfy the individual requirements in our specification. Each subsection is structured with the definition of a framework component, followed by the practical approach we took when implementing them into our solution. When a requirement from our specification is satisfied within the framework, the reader is made aware with a light discussion of how this is achieved.

The framework itself consists of three core roles, all of which are required for the successful implementation of an extension. These being: *language developer, application developer* and *end-user*. The roles are structured vertically in the framework and represent the strict chronological order of development from bottom to top. For the most part, this is also true when working from left to right across the framework.

4.1 Language Developer

The language developer represents the first and most important role in the development process. Their responsibilities include the choice and scope of the core language to base the extension on, along with the design of the extension notation and the method of visualising said notation within the core language.

4.1.1 Modelling Language Foundations

Assuming that a core language has already been chosen, before it can be extended there are certain decisions that must be made. Firstly, the scope of the core language to include. Incorporating the entire language is the most robust decision. However, given that some languages such as BPMN contain a large number of constructs

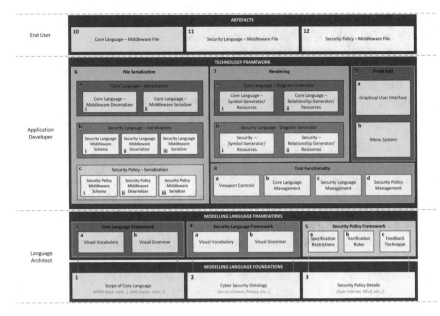

Fig. 8 Framework for the extension and visualisation of cyber security requirements in existing modelling languages

(171) [9], which may not all necessarily require modelling, it may be more efficient to narrow the scope.

For our solution, as we are using BPMN for the core language we opted for the following elements: *pool, lane, start event, end event, message start event, message catch event, timer start event, error end event, terminate end event, parallel gateway, exclusive gateway, inclusive gateway, user task, business rule task, script task, receive task* and *service task*. Although we are missing several, these elements are sufficient for the creation of most general BPMN diagrams.

The next step in the framework is to define which cyber security requirements to include. Aforementioned, in a previous paper we proposed an ontology which includes 79 security requirements across six key areas of the cyber security domain [11]. As this framework is based on the creation of a security extension, our ontology negates the need for any decision making here. The language developer can just list the requirements within the ontology. This will ensure the requirement of **comprehensiveness** is always satisfied. To be deemed comprehensive to the cyber security domain, an extension should include at the very least every concept within our ontology [11].

This extends to the policy details. Before any kind of verification can be carried out across a diagram. A set of rules or policy must first be defined as a means of assessment. Therefore, a list of concepts which can be specified in the policy must also be defined. Although we could stop with the concepts in the ontology, typically, a lower more specific level of detail is required for policies. For example, instead of specifying *cryptographic protocol*, one would specify more specific instances such as *L2TP* or *IKE* [18]. What level of detail, and what instances of such detail, must be addressed before progressing through the framework. For our solution, this level of detail stretched to specific instances of various requirements within the ontology. Along with the previous examples these included (but are not limited to) concepts such as *fingerprint authentication* and *maximum retention period*.

4.1.2 Modelling Language Frameworks

The modelling language frameworks focus specifically around the visual design of the languages. Visual vocabulary being the symbol design and visual grammar referring to the method of visualising such symbols. Of course, the core language will already have predefined rules for these. Nevertheless, these should still be specified to ensure any new visualisation will not interfere. Ideally, most extensions should be built from the ground up in a new engine. Therefore, the rules governing the core language will need implementing into the new application anyway. Having blueprints of the vocabulary and grammar will make the application developer's job much easier.

For the security extension however, the language developer must decide on new vocabulary and grammar. The framework itself has little reliance on what methods are chosen here. All approaches will output solutions with identical functionality. However, the effectiveness of those solutions is very heavily dependant on these components. Visual vocabulary and grammar represent two of the key areas almost every extension has thus far failed to successfully implement. They are also where the majority of our requirements specification can be achieved. It is recommended any future security extensions follow the vocabulary and grammar used in our solution. Not only is it capable of satisfying the requirements specification, the novelty of it represents a significant contribution to the area. Providing new potential for not only modelling languages but other areas of data visualisation too. The method of vocabulary and grammar used in our solution is detailed in the following sections.

4.1.3 Visual Vocabulary

However, the "Physics of Notations" [8] deals with both the vocabulary and grammar of languages. It leans more towards the vocabulary side, detailing multiple principles that should be achieved in the design of any notation. As reviewed earlier, these have customarily been ignored in current extensions. Therefore, rather than creating a notation based on conjecture, we decided to use these principles from the very beginning as a foundation for creating our security constructs.

Perceptual Discriminability: When extending an existing language with a new domain, perceptual discriminability has two sides. The notation not only requires discriminability amongst its own constructs, but also against that of the extended

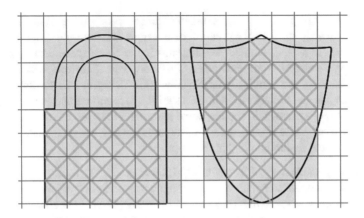

Fig. 9 Design space shape comparison

language, i.e. all business process notation is clearly distinguishable from security notation.

In the majority of the extensions we reviewed in Section II, clear distinction against the parent language (BPMN) was done rather successfully. One particular extension that stood out was Rodriguez et al. [5]. Although their extension lacked *colour*, by using *padlocks* as an outer shell for each construct worked very well, as it is not a shape currently used within BPMN. Unlike Salnitri [4] and Koh [15] who both opted for circles; which by contrast are very heavily utilised within BPMN.

Using a consistent outer shape for an extension is a good way to separate domains. Nevertheless, as mentioned, this is only one side of perceptual discriminability. The notational constructs must also be distinguishable amongst each other. If a consistent shell is to be used for all constructs, this means any distinguishing features must be encompassed inside this shape. For our framework we considered using a *padlock* as an outer shape. A search on Google Images using the keyword "security" provides all the justification necessary for making such a decision. However, upon further analysis of this shape, we seen that the design space within the body of the shape (which is where much of the construct's graphic would go) was relatively small. Especially by comparison of how much space the shape occupies on a diagram.

If one refers to Fig. 9 it shows that a *padlock* shape takes up roughly 40 squares. However, the inner design space only allows for 20 squares, just 50% of the space the construct occupies. By comparison, if we view a *shield* shape (this happened to be the second most popular icon associated to security according to our study on Google), the *shield* takes up 39 squares and allows for a design space of 23, i.e. 59% of the construct space. Of course this comparison only took full squares into account. If we were to include incomplete squares, the *shield* could offer up to four/five more. Whereas, the majority of the *padlock* icon is wasted with the locking mechanism. Therefore, the logical choice for the outer shape is a *shield*.

Semantic Transparency: The semantic transparency of the symbols will be achieved primarily through the creation of a unique icon. As the outer shape will be consistent (Fig. 10a), without anything inside the *shield* there is no way to distinguish the constructs from each other. Therefore, each construct will include an icon specific to the concept it represents (Fig. 10d). Using an icon design approach for symbols has been proven to increase usability, recognition and familiarity [19]. Inevitably every symbol will require some learning. However, using this approach will improve the semantic immediacy of the constructs given icons natural goal of being a graphical mnemonic to their concept.

Visual Expressiveness: Aforementioned, there are eight visual variables which can be used to construct a notation, these being: *horizontal position, vertical position, shape, brightness, size, orientation, colour* and *texture* [8]. We have already discussed how we have utilised *shape*, both as the outer shell of each construct and for the icons themselves.

We also utilised *brightness* within our notation as a way of inferring what hierarchy depth the symbol is at. The brighter the construct the higher the level, see Fig. 10e. (Hierarchy depth referring to what level the concept is at in the ontology.) However, as *brightness* is a fairly weak notation, this hierarchy is reinforced with a more robust variable: *shape*. Viewing of Fig. 10b will show how we slightly changed the peaks of each *shield* to reiterate this hierarchy. We also used *size* to show this distinction. The higher the concept level, the larger the construct. However, given that small symbols are difficult to read the size difference is relatively small. We deemed it more practical to keep the symbols at a readable size rather than utilise this variable to its full potential.

As for *colour*, this was used as a way of separating the six key areas as specified in our ontology [11], see Fig. 10f. As previously mentioned, *colour* should only be used as redundant coding. Nevertheless, *colour* is a strong visual variable, with differences being detected three times faster than shape [8]. Used correctly it can be a good form of visual communication. In the next section however, we still cover the primary (more robust) notation for making the distinction between each area.

Dual Coding: This principle states that constructs should be accompanied by text supporting their underlying semantics. As such, we added the name of each construct within the symbol. If you refer to Fig. 10c, you will see that our framework includes the concept name at the top of each *shield*.

An example of a full hierarchy of symbols can be seen in Fig. 11 (size is not demonstrated within this figure). This figure shows the constructs: *access control>authentication>personnel authentication>biometric*.

From this you can see how *brightness* is used to determine the individual hierarchy level, along with the peak count at the top of each *shield*. It also acts as a good example of how simply following the "Physics of Notations" [8] beforehand can drastically improve principles such as perceptual discriminability and semantic transparency. The level of distinction amongst these symbols is much higher than those of the previously assessed extensions.

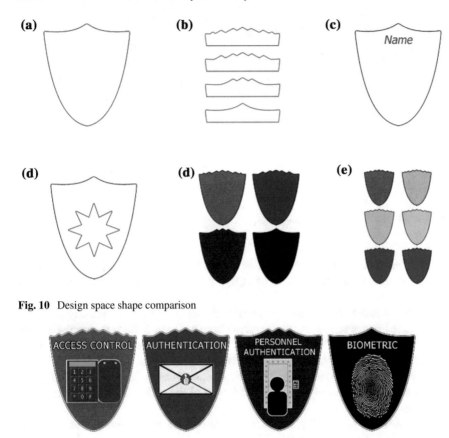

Fig. 10 Design space shape comparison

Fig. 11 Symbol examples

This section acts as the solution to the **graphical framework** requirement. As mentioned, we created our symbols based on Moody's principles [8], rather than conjecture. This ensured the symbols were designed from a notation perspective rather than an individual icon. Satisfying several principles and allowing for the easy incorporation of new notation in the future. A language developer simply needs to add their concept to the ontology. From this they can identify which of the six areas and at what level the concept belongs. This will determine the colour, brightness and outer shell of the symbol. The only thing the developer has to do is create a unique icon to place inside the shell and label the construct.

4.1.4 Visual Grammar

The main issue with current extensions is complexity management. This is the one principle that can be traced back as the root cause of all other issues in extensions, pri-

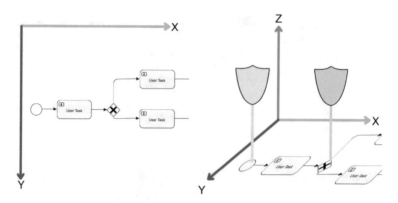

Fig. 12 2D and 3D BPMN diagram

marily construct deficit. Surprisingly, no one has yet considered representing security requirements across a different set of axes, for example perpendicular to the BPMN diagram.

Research into 3D visualisations versus 2D visualisations has already provided empirical evidence supporting the use of 3D from both an efficient and user preference point of view [20]. The representation of BPMN in 3D has even been considered. Unfortunately though, the application created by Brown et al. [21] does not take full advantage of what 3D can offer. Their application doesn't feature any information across a third axis and merely provides a way of traversing or manipulating a 2D diagram.

In a previous paper [22], we tested the feasibility of representing information across a third dimension in BPMN with pilot user-experimentation. From these experiments, we found that for BPMN diagrams with a relatively low number of security notation (six constructs), 3D provided no advantage in terms of read speed and symbol-identification accuracy compared to current 2D approaches. With most users preferring current 2D approaches over 3D. However, when the complexity of the diagrams was increased (38 constructs), 3D provided a substantial improvement in read speed and accuracy compared to 2D. More specifically, participants were able to read over 20% more of the 3D diagram with over twice the accuracy compared to 2D in the same amount of time. These results were very encouraging and inspired further exploration of this new method of visualisation.

The key difference in our approach compared to current 2D extensions is the separation of domains. BPMN can remain relatively unaltered, being represented without change across two axes as seen in the left of Fig. 12.

Cyber security requirements can then be represented across the x, y and z axes, as seen in the right of Fig. 12. This way, the security requirements are a completely separate entity to the BPMN diagram but are still represented at a similar abstraction level with meaningful relationships to their respective BPMN elements. This effectively splits complexity management into two manageable components rather than entangled clutter as with current approaches.

(In order to represent BPMN and security requirements in 3D, it is necessary to remap BPMN to the x and z axes. Where x and y are commonly used for 2D visualisation, the third dimension (z) is used to add depth. Therefore to make the diagram more readable and maintain manageable rotational information, the coordinates must be remapped. See mapping of BPMN diagram on x and z plane in Fig. 12.)

For our solution, we build on from the 3D examples in our experiment [22]. That being, each BPMN element will have its own unique holder capable of specifying any and all security requirements. Representing 79 concepts at once on a single BPMN element, however, will almost always cause cognitive overload and incur several complexity issues on its own. Therefore, the incorporation of modularisation and hierarchy structuring, alongside 3D will allow for a more manageable and therefore comprehensible diagram.

In our solution, we display six concepts at the highest level on each BPMN element (Fig. 13a), respective to the six key concepts in the ontology [11]. These symbols then act as individual buttons to modularise their subconcepts. Once a symbol is selected, the remaining five will collapse and the next level of concepts will display (Fig. 13b). This functionality will then continue for the lower levels (Fig. 13c–d). However, instead of collapsing the other symbols at lower levels, they will be hidden. This is to ensure complexity is still managed. Once collapsed, the symbols become unidentifiable anyway, to hide them after the top level will ensure cognitive overload does not ensue.

To further iterate the concept hierarchy on top of *brightness, shape* and *size*, we include another visual variable: *vertical position*. Once a symbol is selected, the subconcepts display at a decreased size respectively to the lowest level (Fig. 13d). They also appear below the parent symbol giving the impression of a tree structure and that a lower vertical position indicates a lower concept level. However, when no symbol is selected, the six key concepts are displayed vertically as well. To ensure the user does not infer a similar hierarchy, new links (lines) are used to connect parent and child concepts (Fig. 13). Along with the fact the core six concepts also have different colours and are the same size (not reduced sizes like their children), we are confident this issue will not arise.

Along with *vertical position* we also use *horizontal position*. Unlike the majority of extensions (and modelling languages), our extension always places constructs in the exact same position relative to their associated BPMN element, explicitly. For example, if we were to number each of the red symbols in Fig. 13d, one to six respectively. Symbol six (bottom right) will always appear in the same position irrelevant of whether or not symbols four and five are specified. This effectively means that if every symbol looked exactly the same, as they all have a unique position, a user could still infer the construct from this alone.

Of the eight visual variables our extension utilises seven of them, dismissing only *texture*. Thereby making our solution one of the first to explore and utilise the full toolset at a modelling languages disposal. Our method of visualisation also ensures the satisfaction of the **structure** requirement. With little explanation necessary, obser-

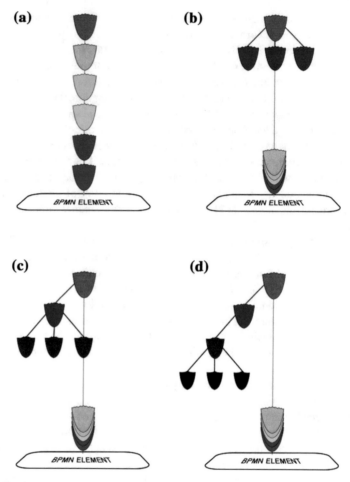

Fig. 13 Notation - visual grammar

vation of Fig. 13 demonstrates how both a novice and expert can utilise the extension. Dropping to lower level concepts to specify more detail as expertise increases. The visual grammar of our solution also ensures **complexity management** as discussed earlier. By separating the domains and utilising principles such as modularisation and hierarchy, we are able to represent just under 80 security concepts in our extension without incurring complexity issues. Comparing to existing extensions, it increased the number of security concepts drastically but with better management.

4.1.5 Policy Language Framework

The policy language framework isn't as visual as the core and extension frameworks. Nevertheless, it still requires due attention. For this section, the language developer must decide on what validation to include within the policies as well as the method of verification. By validation we mean, as an example, if a user specifies *user consent* is required only *once*. They are no longer able to specify it as being required *every time*. This will ensure no poorly or vulnerable implemented functionality when the system is developed.

As for the verification rules, these define how the policy is used to evaluate the diagram security. This component alone represents a very large and important section of cyber security. As such, it is not something we will over discuss within this chapter. For our solution, we used the policy verification as a non-visual security extension. Security experts who dislike modelling or simply prefer a classic form input for specifying requirements can do so within our policy creation. This can then be used by the modeller to specify security requirements within the diagram. The policy acting as a form of validation to ensure all requirements are included.

4.2 Application Developer—Technology Framework

Although the language developer is undoubtedly the most important role in our framework, the application developer brings their work into fruition. While the previous section was based around the visual and conceptual construction of the languages, this portion of our framework focuses on the technical requirements for creating the application. This portion of our framework focuses on the technical requirements for creating the application. As previously mentioned, current approaches to security extensions have all opted to extend existing tools with their new domain. However, our experimentation found this method is a poor approach to the area and can quickly lead to high levels of graphic complexity. Therefore, the only way to successfully extend an existing language with security requirements is to create a new visualisation and thereby application.

When it comes to interactive digitally generated real-time 3D scenes projected onto 2D display, game technology provides a range of technologies that support and simplify the development of interactive visualisation. Technical advancements in game technology include rendering, realistic physics, lighting, audio, graphical user interfaces (GUI), head-up displays (HUD), inputs and scripting [23]. Therefore, for our solution, we opted to build our application using the Unity game engine.

4.2.1 File Serialisation

One of the key technologies required for the development of a security extension (or software in general) is some form of middleware serialiser. Unfortunately, as we are adding a new domain (security) to an existing language, the middleware used for existing core languages will not be designed to save this new information. Therefore, we must create new schemas for both the security extension file and the policy file. These schemas will of course be based around our ontology. Given that the concepts are already structured in a hierarchy, this is more a process of remapping the ontology to the applicable middleware and specifying any necessary positional data for drawing each construct.

For our solution, as most game engines already contain multiple middleware serialisers, the only component we have to deal with is the schema creation.

4.2.2 Rendering

Another technology required is a renderer. The middleware files contain all the necessary data to redraw their respective diagrams but without some form of symbol generator and rendering tool, this data is useless. Therefore, the application developer must create or utilise the necessary technologies for translating this raw data into their respective diagrammatic counterparts.

4.2.3 Tools

The tools system of the technology framework is of vital importance, as these represent the interactions an end-user can perform with the application. This section is divided into three concepts based on end-user requirements. These being: the ability to specify security requirements, create a security policy and some form of viewport navigation.

Within our application, security constructs are specified by highlighting a BPMN element and giving it a *holder*. Once an element has a *holder*, the application will give the user access to the six key concepts. (Until a *holder* is added, this functionality is disabled.) The user then simply needs to add their choice of construct by pressing the respective button in the *build* toolbar.

However, this only works for the key six concepts. If the user wishes to add a concept of a lower level, they must first select the parent construct by pressing it with the left mouse button. This will then change the set of constructs in the *build* toolbar to the children of the highlighted construct. Taking *access control* as an example parent. If we highlight this construct, the security requirements in the *build* toolbar will change from the core six to *authentication, identification* and *authorisation*. This is another way of managing the complexity of the application along with the usability and speed at which a modeller can specify their requirements. When familiar with the notation hierarchy, a modeller will be able to quickly add their requirements by selecting parent and child constructs. Compared with traditional methods of long scrollable lists of constructs, our approach is much more manageable.

Given that our proposed solution will include 3D visualisation, navigation of the scene (3D space) is a potentially problematic area [24]. Nevertheless, we propose using a similar method as that used in most 3D games and game engines. Wherein, the user can "fly" a camera around the scene using WSAD keys and mouse input configuration [25]. However, this may not be to all users' preferences and some users will inevitably struggle to use this setup. Therefore, we will also include functionality to allow the user to focus and align the camera to specific BPMN and security elements with the push of a button.

4.2.4 Functionality

This component of the framework refers more to system functionality opposed to manual user functionality, although the two are very closely related. As discussed in the previous section, modularising the concepts to assist with complexity management is controlled by the application itself. Not only within the visualisation but in how the user adds new concepts to the diagram. This requirement and thereby functionality should be solved by the developer at implementation. A complexity managed extension is one that requires the least input from the end-user. At no point should the user have to worry about arranging elements on the diagram. Their only concern should be what security to include; the extension (application) should deal with the positioning and structuring of the elements.

The same can be said for how the application notifies the user of missing security when verifying a diagram against a policy. The specification of security and creation of a policy are individual requirements on their own. The verification of the policy against the diagram and the feedback of this verification is another functionality in itself. Although a typical programming error log may suffice, given that modelling languages are a visual medium and aim to avoid text as much as possible. The inclusion of some form of visual feedback as well will provide the most robust solution.

The modularisation of the constructs in our extension was accomplished by assigning each construct its own family tree as mentioned earlier. In this example (Fig. 14), the highlighted concept is *authentication*, located inside Fig. 14a's red box.

As the parent must also be highlighted (*access control*) the remaining concepts in the key six will collapse (Fig. 14b). (Refer to the element in the right side of the figure for an example of the key six expanded.) You will also be able to see by viewing Fig. 14a, how level two and lower concepts in the hierarchy hide their siblings when highlighted opposed to collapsing them. *Authentication* is sibling to *identification* and *authorisation*. However, as *authentication* has been highlighted in this instance, *identification* and *authorisation* are hidden from view. This is done as a way of managing the complexity of a diagram and reducing the visual clutter when trying to view a specific concept and its children.

For most constructs, specifying a link to a single BPMN element is sufficient. However, there are some security concepts (*separation of duty* and *binding of duty*) which require linking to multiple BPMN elements. Given that each construct can already link to one element through the holder, the missing functionality is the ability to specify a second or third element.

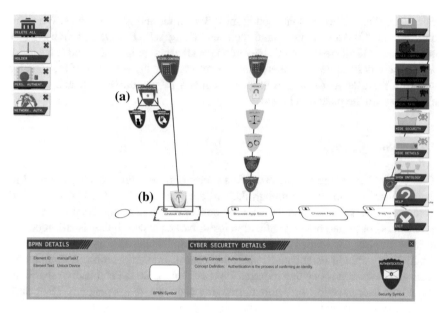

Fig. 14 Symbol hiding and collapsing

To overcome this issue, we added new functionality for each respective construct (*separation of duty* and *binding of duty*). Once a user links another BPMN element, the link is visually represented by a line across the diagram. The only way a user can access this functionality, however, is if the constructs themselves are visible on screen. When the hierarchy is collapsed and *binding of duty* is hidden, the links are no longer visible. An example of how this looks within the application be seen in Fig. 15).

As for the verification feedback, our application notifies the user in two ways, both textual and visual. The text-based feedback is similar to a programming error log. The system will list discrepancies between the diagram and policy, detailing how the user can fix each issue. The visual feedback uses a warning icon to highlight the BPMN (or security) element the current error is associated with. Although this is not robust enough on its own to inform the user of what the error is. Alongside the text description, it speeds up the time required to identify which element needs addressing.

4.2.5 Front End

Finally, the last component of the technology framework is the front end of the application. Otherwise referred to as the graphical user interface. Although menus could be categorised under GUI, given the importance of the GUI within the diagram creation portion of the application, we deemed it necessary to make a clear distinction

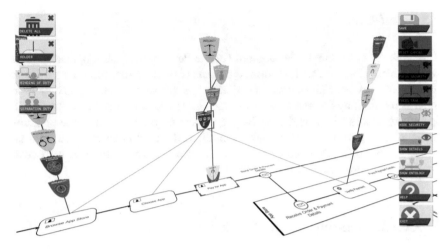

Fig. 15 *Binding of duty* diagram element linking

between the two. In previous sections, we've already discussed some of our GUI, in how we add security requirements to our diagram and the verification feedback. Along with these, there is another requirement discussed in Section III that can be addressed; coherence. As discussed, current extensions at times have a difference of opinion on what a concept is and thereby how it should be used. To overcome this issue, extensions would benefit from explicitly specifying concept meanings and consequently their use. This can be implemented into an extension through a details toolbar (GUI). Allowing the user access to various information about symbols which would otherwise be difficult to represent through a notation; such as the definition of a concept.

In our extension, we also included another level of detail in this toolbar. Although our ontology [11] might be comprehensive to what a security notation should graphically represent, there is still room for more detail to be specified. For example, representing the security requirement for *virtual private network* in some cases may be adequate. However, there is more detail that could be specified such as *L2TP* or *IKE* [18]. Providing the functionality to specify such detail gives the modeller even more freedom to explicitly define their requirements. We represent such detail as text in a toolbar opposed to a graphical symbol to ensure graphic economy is maintained. An example of the toolbar within our application can be seen in Figs. 14 and 15, with Fig. 15 showing how the user specifies other BPMN elements that requiring linking to the respective security construct.

4.3   End-User

The end-user is the final role required for the development and application of a security extension. You will see from the framework the components are far fewer than for other roles. This is done intentionally, as this section represents how little input is required by the end-user. All of the issues and challenges associated with specifying security in a modelling language have been addressed in the previous sections. This portion of the framework outlines the only input required from an end-user. That being the specification of their chosen elements for each respective domain (core language, security and policy).

5   Conclusions and Future Works

Current research surrounding the visualisation of cyber security requirements has so far been very limited in terms of design rationale. Authors have typically focused heavily on their choice of semantics and put very little thought into the notation design, totally disregarding the complexity issues associated with adding a new extension into existing modelling languages.

Throughout this chapter, we identified both the positive and negative aspects of existing extensions in BPMN, highlighting the key requirements an extension needs to meet to be considered both comprehensive to the domain and usable as a modelling language. From these requirements, we were able to create a framework not only for BPMN, but for any other modelling languages requiring an extension for visualising security requirements. Using BPMN as a case study, we created our own application based on this framework, acting not only as the first comprehensive security extension to BPMN but also as a way of validating our framework. Utilising the third dimension we were able to include 79 security requirements within BPMN, at a similar abstraction level, whilst still maintaining complexity management. It overcomes the issues experienced by current extensions and proves our framework as a usable means of extending a language with security requirements visualisation.

For our future work, we plan to test our solution with end-users to further clarify its ability in meeting the aforementioned requirements. Following this, our work has various directions it can take. We eventually envisage the creation of a single application which allows the modelling of both BPMN and security requirements, opposed to using two separate applications for each domain, as in this instance. We also plan to explore the application of artificial intelligent technologies to achieve automatic and intelligent security reasoning based on past knowledge and experience. In this way, security requirements can be added to the scenario automatically without human intervene.

6 Questions

1. What are security requirements and why they are fundamental in designing and defending IT system against cyber attacks?
2. Why graphical frameworks are important in cyber security?
3. What is BPMN, and how it can be utilised in cyber security application?
4. What are the security extension of BPMN? Explain at least three.
5. Explain five components of security notation extension.
6. Explain the essential properties of security requirements.
7. What modelling languages are available for cyber security requirements?
8. Why the comprehensive ability is the fundamental property in any modelling language?
9. Why icon design for symbols increases usability, recognition and familiarity?
10. What is the relation between application and language developer in the proposed framework?

References

1. Chinosi M, Trombetta A (2012) Bpmn: an introduction to the standard. Comput Stand Interfaces 34(1):124–134
2. Bocciarelli P, Dambrogio A (2011) A bpmn extension for modeling non functional properties of business processes. In: 2011 symposium on theory of modeling & simulation: DEVS integrative M&S symposium, pp 160–168
3. omg: business process model and notation (BPMN), Version 2.0 (2015). Object management group. http://www.bpmn.org/
4. Salnitri M, Dalpiaz F, Giorgini P (2014) Modeling and verifying security policies in business processes. Enterprise, business-process and information and information systems modeling, vol 17. Springer LCBIP, Berlin, pp 200–214
5. Rodriguez A, Fernandez-Medina E, Piattini M (2007) A bpmn extension for the modeling of security requirements in business processess. IEICE Trans Inf Syst 90(4):745–752
6. Saleem MQ, Jaafar JB, Hassan MF (2012) A domain-specific language for modelling security objectives in a business process models of soa applications. Int J Adv Inf Sci Serv Sci 4(1):353–362
7. Leitner M, Miller M, Rinderle-Ma S (2013) An analysis and evaluation of security aspects in the business process model and notation. In: 2013 international conference on availability, reliability and security, pp 262–267
8. Moody D (2009) The "physics" of notations: toward a scientific basis for constructing visual notations in software engineering. IEEE Trans Softw Eng 35(6):756–779
9. Genon N, Heymans P, Amyot D (2010) Analysing the cognitive effectiveness of the bpmn 2.0 visual notation. Software language engineering. Springer LNCS, Berlin, pp 377–396
10. Popescu G, Wegmann A (2014) Using the physics of notations theory to evaluate the visual notation of the systemic enterprise architecture methodology. In: 16th IEEE conference on business informatics, pp 166–173
11. Maines C, Llewellyn-Jones D, Tang S, Zhou B (2015) A cyber security ontology for bpmn-security extensions. In: 13th IEEE international conference on dependable, autonomic and secure computing, pp 1756–1763
12. Pfleeger CP, Pfleeger SL (2006) Security in computing, 4th edn. Prentive Hall PTR

13. Colblindor: tritanopia - blue-yellow color blindness (2014). http://www.colorblindness.com/tritanopia-blue-yellow-color-blindness/
14. Labda W, Sampaio P (2014) Modeling of privacy-aware business processes in bpmn to protect personal data. In: 29th ACM symposium on applied computing, pp 1399–1405
15. Koh SS, Zhou B (2015) Bpmn security extensions for healthcare process. In: 13th IEEE international conference on dependable, autonomic and secure computing, pp 2340–2345
16. zur Muehlen M, Recker J (2013) We still don't know how much bpmn is enough, but we are getting closer. Seminal contributions to information systems engineering, pp 445–451
17. Microsoft: visio home (2016). https://products.office.com/en-gb/visio/flowchart-software
18. Sharma T, Yadav R (2015) Security in virtual private network. Int J Innov Adv Comput Sci (IJIACS) 4:669–675
19. Kascak L, Ave N, Rebola CB, Sanford JA (2013) Icon design for user interface of remote patient. In: 31st ACM international conference on design of communication, pp 77–83
20. Amini F, Rufiange S, Hossain Z, Ventura Q, Irani P, McGuffin MJ (2015) The impact of interactivity on comprehending 2d and 3d visualizations of movement data. IEEE Trans Vis Comput Graphics 21(1):122–135
21. Brown R (2011) Using virtual worlds for collaborative business process modeling. Bus Process Manag 17(3):546–564
22. Maines C, Zhou B, Tang S, Shi Q (2016) Adding a third dimension to bpmn as a means of representing cyber security requirements. In: 2016 international conference on developments of E-systems engineering (DeSE), pp 105–110
23. Maines C, Tang S (2015) An application of game technology to virtual university campus tour and interior navigation. In: 2015 international conference on developments of E-systems engineering (DeSE), pp 341–346
24. Hinckley K, Tullio J, Pausch R, Proffitt D, Kassell N (1997) Usability analysis of 3d rotation techniques. In: 10th annual ACM symposium on user interface software and technology - UIST, pp 1–10
25. Technologies U.: Scene view navigation: unity manual (2016). https://docs.unity3d.com/Manual/SceneViewNavigation.html

Big Data and Cyber Security: A Visual Analytics Perspective

Suvodeep Mazumdar and Jing Wang

Abstract With organisations and governments significantly investing in cyber defenses, there is an urgent need to develop tools and technologies to help security professionals understand cyber security within their application domains. A critical aspect of this is to develop and maintain situation awareness of security aspects within cyber infrastructures. Visual analytics provide support to security professionals to help understand evolving situations and the overall status of systems, particularly when dealing with large volumes of data. This chapter explores situation awareness in cyber security in more detail, aligning design recommendations for visual analytics to assist security professionals with progressive levels of situation awareness.

1 Introduction

As organisations move toward the digitisation of legacy systems and data processes, an increased use of online Web-enabled and mobile-based services, always available data and resources, large volumes of network data are constantly generated. An increasingly important aspect of an organisation is the security of their systems. In addition, many countries have already invested significant amounts in cyber security infrastructures.[1] The International Data Corporation estimates that by the year 2020, worldwide spending on security hardware, software and services will grow to over

---

[1]The US Department of State Security budget for FY2016 was almost $480 million (https://www.dhs.gov/sites/default/files/publications/FY_2016_DHS_Budget_in_Brief.pdf) The UK has committed to spend over 1.9 billion over five years till 2021 to transform UK cyber security infrastructure.

S. Mazumdar (✉) · J. Wang
Department of Computing, Sheffield Hallam University, Sheffield, UK
e-mail: s.mazumdar@shu.ac.uk

J. Wang
e-mail: j.wang@shu.ac.uk

© Springer International Publishing AG, part of Springer Nature 2018
S. Parkinson et al. (eds.), *Guide to Vulnerability Analysis for Computer Networks and Systems*, Computer Communications and Networks,
https://doi.org/10.1007/978-3-319-92624-7_16

367

$100bn annually.[2] In an ever-challenging world, and with a significantly increasing online presence of individuals and organisations, the risk to online privacy, security and personal information is becoming a key concern. The desire for organisations to process personal data for provisioning personalised services further increases security and privacy risks. In addition, personal crowdsourced data is at the very core of business models for many organisations in the service industry. For example, Uber, Deliveroo, TripAdvisor etc. In recent times, attacks on such organisations have seen major data breaches, personal information leaked[3] resulting in an increased level of risk to millions of users worldwide.[4] At the same time, as a part of transformation strategies to harness digital technologies, tools and capabilities, to transform governance and facilitate democratisation of policy-making,[5] governments and local authorities are moving to an increase online presence and services. This has also significantly increased the need for more robust cyber security and threat assessment processes. In addition, this risks a large change in political landscapes as countries and governments may often be vulnerable to cyber attacks and malicious agents. The recent events surrounding the US elections highlight the risks of external organisations interfering in democratic processes within countries [1], eventually escalating tensions [2]. The risks of cyber attacks to organisations and Governments are increasing and there is a developing urgency in mitigating, which is emphasised considering the extent of significant economic, political and long-term impacts.

The security of an organisation relies on the monitoring capabilities and threat assessments of the security professions to maintain network and systems security and integrity, particularly the ability to detect and respond to cyber attacks. Organisations are often the target of a wide range of attacks, varying from ransomware and Denial of Service to exfiltration of sensitive data by insiders. With varying types of attacks and ever-evolving threats, it is critical that security experts have access to effective monitoring tools to automatically as well as semi-automatically detect attacks [3]. The significant investments by organisations and governments are also due to the very nature of the evolving landscape of cyber attacks as cyber crimes are becoming more sophisticated, intelligent, complex and destructive [4]. With the access to large volumes of data constantly generated and being available to security experts, there is a need for tools and systems that can help analysts and decision makers take critical decisions effectively and efficiently. The growing volume of data often challenges traditional analytical process and there is a need for scalable solutions that can deal with large heterogeneous datasets—a 'big data' challenge.

Big data is characterised as large collections of diverse datasets which are often large scale, complex, multidimensional and multivariate [4, 5]. Typically, big data

---

[2]https://www.idc.com/getdoc.jsp?containerId=prUS41851116.

[3]www.theverge.com/2017/11/21/16687796/uber%2Dcyberattack%2Ddata%2Dbreach%2Dexposed%2Dusers%2D57%2Dmillion.

[4]http://fortune.com/2016/05/18/linkedin%2Ddata%2Dbreach%2Demail%2Dpassword/.

[5]www.gov.uk/government/news/the%2Dfuture%2Dof%2Dpublic%2Dservice%2Dgovernment%2Dtransformation%2Dstrategy%2Dlaunched.

characteristics are defined by the 6Vs—velocity, volume, variety, veracity, vocabulary and value [6, 7]. Velocity refers to the high speed of generation and processing of the data, while volume indicates the vast amounts of data being generated and required to be consumed. Variety indicates the large number of types of data. Veracity indicates how trustworthy is the data being consumed—often, big data is characterised by data that have a combination of different trustworthiness of data. Vocabulary indicates that the data often conforms to different schema, models and ontologies, while value refers to the cost of acquiring the data and the value (importance) and insight that can be potentially gained from the data. Big data analytics is a set of well-established tools and techniques that can leverage the useful (and often, hidden) information inside the raw data [4, 8]. The advent of big data analytics has been significant and there has been enormous impacts on several domains. Big data analytics has significant potential in changing the landscape of security technologies and forensics and has attracted the interests of the security community [9]. One of the critical issues in big data analytics is the well-known phenomenon of information overload, where analysts are provided with too much information to be processed.

Visual analytics aims to bridge this gap by using intelligent means in the analysis process, essentially turning information overload into an opportunity [10]. While analytical processes aim to extract critical information and insight from the data, visualisations help analysts understand large volumes of data by presenting more data in a single view while maintaining understandability. Visual analytics is the science of analytical reasoning facilitated by interactive visual interfaces [11]. Reference [10] defines visual analytics as *"combines automated analysis techniques with interactive visualisations for effective understanding, reasoning and decision-making on the basis of very large and complex data set"*.

In the next section, we explore the wider field of cyber security and discuss the variety of big data sources that analysts can use to help understand their cyber infrastructure security risks and vulnerabilities. We then discuss Endsley's theoretical model of situation awareness, aligned to the cyber security domain. Finally, based on the literature and our experience in other domains, we provide a set of design guidelines, interaction and visualisation techniques that can potentially help solution developers design tools to help support cyber security analysts achieve situation awareness.

2 The Cyber Security Domain

This section provides a high-level overview of the cyber security domain, highlighting the various aspects of security that needs to be understood as well as the different types of cyber attacks and risks encountered by security experts. During the last decades, the cyber threats landscape has been massively extended from desktop computers to portable platforms and cloud services. Information security has become a major concern for businesses and consumers. A variety of technologies have been adopted and adapted to tackle challenging cyber threats. As a result, a key activity for cyber analysts and security experts in such efforts is establishing situation awareness [12]— knowing the kinds of threats is an important indicator to improving security solutions, while knowing the threat vectors targeting different domains help analysts develop better defensive solutions [13]. For example:

Intrusion Detection Systems (IDS) [14] are based on the hypothesis that cyber-threats can be detected through monitoring the network activities to distinguish abnormal patterns. Any such patterns, as malicious activities, are reported and collected by event management systems. Using frequent analyses, IDS watches the attacks from outside and inside cyber systems. However, IDS could create a significant high false alarm rate due to data noise such as broken packages and software bugs.

Wireless Sensor Network for Vulnerabilities: Wireless connectivity, such as mobile networks, has grown significantly during this decade, which requires critical security monitoring in the hostile cyber environments. Using sensor nodes (event capturing) and base stations (event analysis and processing) in large networks enables a flexible solution for different application objectives. The aim of using sensor network is to provide a low cost, self-indication and diagnosis network environment. However, it also limits the wireless speed performance in many applications [15].

Cloud Security: With organisations and businesses moving to Cloud-based solutions, significant new challenges have emerged over the past decade. The cloud integrates a wide range of services across user devices, network, servers, applications/services and storage [16]. As more mission-critical operations are moved to the cloud and more early movers take advantage of cloud computing, cloud service providers need to have right protocols and security defences to handle customer data security and privacy.

Cyber criminals are continually exploring new ways to bypass security solutions to access computer systems and networks. Hence, it is important to understand the various types of cyber attacks. Some of the common cyber attacks are [17]: Spamming involves sending unsolicited bulk messages to multiple recipients [18]; Search Poisoning [19] involves dishonest use of search engine optimisation techniques to falsely improve ranking and thereby direct traffic to typically short-lived Web pages; Botnets [20] are networks of malware-infected compromised computers; Denial-of-Service (DoS) attacks renders a system or network resource inaccessible to its users [21]; Phishing fraudulently acquires confidential user data by mimicking communication [22] such as email and Web spoofing [23]; Malware is a software that perform and propagate malicious activities such as viruses, worms and trojans [24]; Website threats refer to attackers exploiting vulnerabilities in legitimate Websites, infecting them and indirectly attacking visitors via SQL injections, ads, search result redirections.

3 Big Data Sources

The cyber security domain needs to analyse massive volumes of data to assess threats and take preventive measures. For example, analysts collect large volumes of data on the systems and networks they monitor, including large-scale measurements to identify securities, e.g. IPv4 address space [25]. Organisations such as Computer Emergency Response Teams (CERTs) and security companies monitoring cyber infrastructures also publicly share information. Finally, cyber security experts also have access to large volumes of publicly available and shared data for further analyses. While the availability and the potential of combining such large volumes of data is promising, there is a need for appropriate analytic tools and capabilities within security organisations to extract actionable intelligence and insights [26]. With the large volumes of data being available, conventional cyber security systems often struggle to perform operations as well as analysis of security data simultaneously. As a result, Big data analytics applied to the cyber security domain is an area of growing interest. We discuss a few potential data sources within the cyber infrastructure that security experts need to consider:

Computer-based: It includes passive data generated by computer hardware and software such as IP Address, E-health certificates, keyboard typing and clickstream. There are also some attacks targets on acoustic emanations produced by electronic devices, which are a known source of concern and present a threat to user privacy [27].

Mobile-based Data and Travel Data: Mobile information, such as GPS location, has become a vulnerable target for cyber attacks. Current approaches, such as user active authorisation, provide a possible solution. However, it raises new concerns on verifying personal identities and distinguishing behaviours.

Physical Data of Users: This includes time and location of physical access records of network, such as SIEM data, which can be utilised to control the access to the network through monitoring the access record. On the other hand, protecting such data means keeping associated evidences in secured storage to be later used as raw information for security defence.

Human Resource Data: Given the highly sensitive nature of human resource (HR) data, especially the value of some private information, HR data is one of the primary targets of cybercrime. Also, users of the data, such as HR teams, usually do not control network activities—hence, much effort needs to be focused on internal threats and network attacks.

Credentials: It includes data such as usernames and password, which highlights the crackability, correlation and security of these information. The safety of the data does not only imply the problem of creating a "strong" password but also analysis about users' perceptions of password security [28].

One-Time Passwords: Using one-time passwords can prevent recurrent attacks. However, as with credential data, one-time passwords are vulnerable to social engineering attacks such as fishing.

Digital Certificates are electronic keys that allow different parties to transfer information securely over the Internet and has been recognised as a critical aspect of cyber security.

Biometrics: Using biometric data, such as fingerprint, facial features, voice and handwriting, can locate a specific person and their private information and hence has severe implications on personal security.

Social Media: User activities on social media can be used/abused to analyse their social and professional networks and infer personal information. Integrated with many other big data resources mentioned above such as locations, passwords and biometric data, such datasets can potentially provide identifiable information about individuals, thereby having enormous implications to security.

4 Situation Awareness in Cyber Security

Endsley [12] proposed a theoretical model of situation awareness (SA) in decision-making, based on analysing operational practices across various domains, such as operational civil, commercial and military aircraft, air traffic control, large systems operations, tactical and strategic systems. A key success factor in such domains is to achieve and maintain situation awareness, i.e. "accurate, complete and real-time information about an incident" [29], to understand "the current local and global situation and how this may evolve over time" [12, 30]. The goal of situation awareness is to rapidly answer [31]:

- What is happening?
- Why is it happening?
- What will happen next?
- What can I do about it?

As seen in the Fig. 1, Endsley separates the decision-making process and performance from situation awareness.

Understanding the state of a system or environment is an iterative process, which is in turn informed by situation awareness, decisions and performance. While achieving situation awareness is critical to good decision-making, various factors (e.g. training on proper procedures, tactics, established protocols etc.) are also involved in taking the right decisions. At the same time, human factors (e.g. attention, working memory, confidence level), task and system factors (e.g. system design, interface design, stress, workload, complexity) can also influence an individual's ability to achieve situation awareness. It is, therefore, important to be aware of the significance of these technical and cognitive factors when taking critical decisions based on situation awareness.

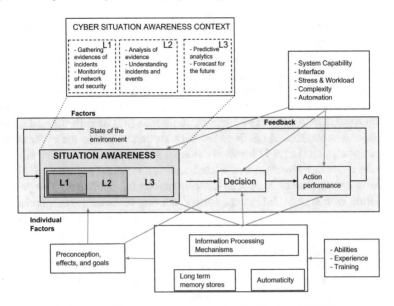

Fig. 1 Theoretical model of situation awareness based on Endsley's model [12]

Studies have also shown that developing and maintaining a high level of situation awareness can vary significantly between people and tasks [32].

Endsley's situation awareness model consists of three levels , in the order of progressively increasing awareness—"perception", "comprehension" and "projection". Level 1 involves perceiving the critical factors in the environment that are important to the decision maker. Level 2 involves comprehending what the Level 1 factors mean and requires the integration and correlation of disjointed elements that are required to be understood by the decision maker to make an informed decision. Level 3 involves predicting the impact of the various elements in the future. This is typically done by managing the knowledge of the status and dynamics of various factors and comprehending the situation (Level 1 and 2) to predict the state of the environment in the future. In dynamic environments, decision-making is based upon timely, sensible and accurate situation awareness.

Within the context of cyber security, understanding how to attain situational awareness has been a well recognised area of research [33]. Much of the early work in this field originates from the late 90s [34, 35]. This paper [36] highlights seven aspects of situation awareness for cyber defense: awareness of the current situation; impact assessment; evolution of situations; awareness of the actors behaviour; awareness of why and how the situation is caused (causality); awareness of the quality and veracity of the information contributing toward the existing situation awareness; and assess plausible future situations. Cyber situation awareness can be reached by using IT sensors (such as intrusion detection systems, network sniffing, Web crawlers) or more traditional sensors such as human informants indicating an imminent attack, either using computational techniques such as data fusion or even manual interpretation by decision makers [37].

Endsley's model is critical to understand how cyber security experts and analysts can make critical decisions based on threats and various network parameters being monitored. Reference [38] views cyber situation awareness as a three-phase process: situation recognition; situation comprehension; situation projection, aligning with Endsleys situation awareness model. Reference [33] describes Endsleys situation awareness model and the three levels of awareness within the cyber security domain: Perception (Level 1) involves evidence gathering of the various situations within the cyber infrastructure, understanding timed incidents reported by intrusion detection systems, firewall logs, scan reports and security monitoring. This produces information with meaningful representations offering the bases for comprehension. Comprehension (Level 2) involves the analysis of the evidences to understand threat levels, attack types and associated risks. This requires various techniques and procedures to analyse, synthesise, correlate and aggregate evidences and perceived threats. Finally, project (Level 3) involves predictive analyses and forecast to address future incidents and mitigation of potential risks, based on the knowledge extracted from the dynamics of the network (Level 1) and comprehension (Level 2). Extending Endsleys model applied in cyber security, [39] proposed a fourth level, resolution, which involves the countermeasures taken to mitigate and resolve security threats. Cyber situation awareness requires a holistic approach to synthesize perception, understanding and projection, while at the same time needs to manage uncertainty [36].

5   Visual Analytics and the Cyber Security Domain

While situation awareness contributes towards critical decision-making, the decision-making process itself requires humans in the loop—hence, much of the research highlights the essential role of humans and human factors in cyber situation awareness [33, 36, 37, 40]. With the need to understand human factors, it is important to consider the cognitive processes involved in the different levels: Level 1 (perception) involves the analyst acquiring the data about the environment/system, inspecting data to detect activities of interest; Level 2 involves analysts moving from a perception of threats/events of interest to comprehension, where the analyst integrates new information with their knowledge and experience, examining further sources of information and additional data to determine actual incidents or threat levels; Level 3 involves the analyst performing correlations, threat analysis reviews, adding data from intelligence sources to project future threats to take mitigation steps, which are fed back to the start of the analysis as new cues for detection. Visual analytics within the cyber security domain aims to enhance situation awareness to support informed decision-making [41, 42] and has been employed in various application areas, with industrial control systems using much of the matured solutions [37, 43].

The visual analytics community aims to create tools and techniques that help users derive information and gain insight from complex and large heterogeneous, multi-dimensional, spatiotemporal data to detect the expected and unexpected incidents and events [44]. Several researchers have conducted thorough reviews of the various ways visualisations and visual analytics have been used in the cyber security domain for various uses such as network security, malware analysis, log visualisation [44–47]. These studies highlight several excellent examples how visualisations can be used to support decision-making. While much research exists on how visualisations are currently being used in the cyber security domain, we believe there is a need for a systematic approach toward designing visualisations and visual analytic solutions for the domain. Based on prior research, we analyse this in two dimensions: generic visualisation principles for support situation awareness and domain-specific situation awareness.

Over the past many decades, the information visualisation, human–computer interaction, psychology and design communities have produced excellent examples of visualisations and design principles that can be employed while designing systems for various domains, including cyber security situation awareness [48]: A key factor in designing visualisations is the visual representations—representations translate data items into visual objects, encoded by visual properties such as color, shape, size, intensity, texture, motion. Reference [49] can be captured by our preattentive processes. It is important to design visual representations and encodings in a meaningful way to help users gain insight without requiring much learning and interpretation. Considering visualisation and interpretation, two phases of our cognitive systems come into play—preattentive phase (low-level process prior to processing sensory information) and interpretive phase (representations that are learned). The preattentive phase occurs at Norman's visceral level [50, 51] and is responsible for rapid understanding and hence employing certain visual principles can help quickly spot anomalies, outliers (or, in our context, threats or incidents). Much of these principles can be drawn from Healey's experiments [52–54]—for example, hue and form (shape) can be used as a mechanism to rapidly and accurately determine targets. However, varying hue can affect the ability to determine form-defined targets, while the converse is not necessarily true. Several other cognitive aspects also impact on our understanding of visualisations such as minimalistic approach [55], symmetrical layouts, golden ratio [56, 57]. Reference [55] also identified key guidelines for attractive displays such as properly chosen format and design, using combinations of words, numbers and drawing, balance and proportionality in design, content-free decoration. Gestalt laws of organisation which describe how humans perceive visual components as organised patterns or wholes as opposed to different parts should also be respected when designing solutions [58, 59].

While much of the principles discussed so far explore individual visualisations and interfaces as a whole, it is important to note that Visual Analytic systems are not merely visualisations but tools that facilitate analytical process and reasoning. The well-established information seeking mantra of *"overview first, zoom/filter, details on demand"* [60] finds much resonance within several visual analytic systems. In fact, with large volumes of data and visual analytic needs, the information-seeking

SA Level	Description	Cyber Security Context	Cognitive task	Design Recommendations
1	Perception of the elements in the environment User has to clearly perceive the status of the most relevant elements in the context Strongly influenced by the user's memory	Evidence gathering of incidents Monitoring of network and security	Acquire data about the environment /system Inspecting monitoring data to determine activities of interest	1.1 Simple separate displays to focus on one element 1.2 Filtering mechanisms for focussing on an element of interest 1.3 Highlight trends and spikes in the data 1.4 Provide real-time alerts 1.5 Use familiar visual metaphors and representations
2	Comprehension of the current situation Recognised elements are perceived in the context of the user's goals	Analysis of evidence collected Understanding incidents and events	Integration of information from multiple sources Aligning new information with prior experience	2.1. Represent information in the right context (temporal, spatial) to support viewing information based on different perspectives 2.2. Provide interconnecting displays to analyse information 2.3. Provide up-to-date information with provenance information
3	Projection of future status Anticipate the consequences that elements can have on the context	Predictive analysis and forecast for the future	Perform correlations, threat analysis reviews, project future threats based on experience and past data	3.1. Provide possibilities to highlight and follow-up correlations between different elements 3.2. Cluster elements to highlight implicit relations 3.3. Integrate multiple features in a single display 3.4. Provide multiple points of access, exploration, retrievable at later stages 3.5. Provide flexible pathways for exploring related information

Fig. 2 Design recommendations for Endsley's levels of situation awareness for cyber security

paradigm was adapted with a visual analytic focus to *"analyse first - show the important - zoom/filter - details on demand"* [10]. Reference [61] further proposed 12 interactions, organised in three categories (Data & view specification, View Manipulation and Process & Provenance), which provide an excellent guidance to help visual analytic solution developers design cyber security solutions.

Within the domain of cyber security situation awareness, while much research has been done in categorising and organising visual analytic systems, there has been limited work on linking design recommendations with Endsleys situation awareness model. Taking inspiration from a previous work [62] by one of the authors of this chapter for the emergency response domain, and our review of the literature, we propose the following design recommendations to serve as a starting direction for addressing this gap (Fig. 2).

As can be seen from Fig. 2, much of the design recommendations can be aligned with visualisations, interface design or even features within visual analytic solutions.

Level 1 aims to inform the analyst's perception of the environment and high-level overviews are essential for providing a summary of various system states. Typically, this can be visualised as category views such as pie charts or bar charts [63]. Treemaps and matrix views are also useful in summarising large volumes of data [64, 65]. Geographical visualisations on maps or 3D spaces are also common in the domain, to highlight areas of attack or potential threats [66]. At this level, it is also important to provide means for analysts to inform of issues or developing situations—visual [67] or even sonic alerts [3] are often useful in highlighting this information. Level 2 aims to support comprehension by providing means for analysis and understanding. Typically, various interaction mechanisms and a visual design can help support analysis in level. Providing means to quickly filter the underlying data to visualise only particular categories or specific sections of data would also be helpful for analysts [63]. The use of multiple coordinated visualisations [68] can also help analysts understand the wider context of the underlying data as well as how the various facets of the data are related [69]. Level 3 aims to provide means for visualising projected views of simulations, future status and expected threats. The Level 3, owing to the direct links between visualisations and data analysis and prediction, requires considerable focus on visualisation of uncertainty [70, 71]. This level also involves visualisation of correlations between unrelated data—often, the use of multiple visualisations and composite visualisations [72, 73] can provide much support for visualising potential links between facets in the data.

While design and visualisation recommendations have been derived from literature and previous work in the Emergency Response domain, it is important to note that attaining situation awareness process is a continuous process, and hence, systems need to be flexible and support seamless navigation between Endsley's levels and situation awareness state. It is also important to note that visual analytic systems should consider the generic principles and recommendations discussed earlier. We believe that although these recommendations are not comprehensive, aligning visual design guidelines with theoretical models can help develop visualisation models that could be generic and applied in a variety of domains.

6 Summary and Conclusions

With growing interest, and much effort being put on developing and advancing the field of cyber security analytics, the scope for visual analytics research in the cyber security domain is enormous. While there has been some research into studying how visual analytics has been employed within the domain at large, there is a need for a consolidated understanding on how the research fits in with theoretical models of situation awareness. This chapter is a first step toward that direction. Several visualisations have been employed in the field for very specific purposes. However, it is also critical to understand the challenges of cyber security visualisation and develop approaches to address them. To this end, the paper by [74] highlights seven challenges within the field, noting the challenges characterised by big data, particularly volume, variety and quality (veracity). Furthermore, the authors note the challenges in understanding the cadence of the network and the progression of threat escalation. The final challenge noted by the authors highlight the need for analysts to understand how to balance the costs for acquiring further evidence and information with the confidence of the threat.

At the same time, cyber security experts may often have a preference for command line analysis rather than visualisations [75]. As a result, personal preferences may also affect the adoption of visual analytics solutions, which needs to be considered with care while designing solutions. While this chapter attempts to align design and visualisation recommendations with Endley's situation awareness model, understanding how visualisations and visual analytics has been used is out of scope. The wider challenges in the domain, while briefly mentioned, also require a much more critical and in-depth understanding, beyond the scope of the chapter. As a part of future work, we aim to extend our visual design recommendations into a much more formalised representation.

7 Questions

1. What is the purpose of Visual Analytics within the cyber security domain?
2. Describe the vulnerabilities that can occur in Wireless Sensor Network.
3. What is Intrusion Detection System?
4. Define Search Poisoning, its impact and how to prevent it?
5. Discuss two methods of Big Data Analytics.
6. What are the five potential big data sources? Elaborate two of them.
7. What are the factors involved in understanding the security of a system or environment?
8. What are the seven aspects of Situation Awareness for cyber defense?
9. Describe Endsley's Situation Awareness model.
10. What the available tools and methods to aid cyber security visualisation?

References

1. Jasper S, (2017) Russia sanctions are insufficient: use active cyber defense
2. Kreps S, Das D (2017) Warring from the virtual to the real: assessing the publics threshold for war over cyber security. Res Politics 4(2). https://doi.org/10.1177/2053168017715930
3. Axon L, Nurse JR, Goldsmith M, Creese S (2017) A formalised approach to designing sonification systems for network-security monitoring
4. Terzi DS, Terzi R, Sagiroglu S (2017) Big data analytics for network anomaly detection from netflow data. In: 2017 International conference on computer science and engineering (UBMK), IEEE, USA, pp 592–597
5. Chen VY, Razip AM, Ko S, Qian CZ, Ebert DS (2015) Multi-aspect visual analytics on large-scale high-dimensional cyber security data. Inf Vis 14(1):62–75

6. Lakshen GA, Vraneš S, Janev V (2016) Big data and quality: A literature review. In: 2016 24th Telecommunications forum (TELFOR), IEEE, USA, pp 1–4
7. Tsai C-W, Lai C-F, Chao H-C, Vasilakos AV (2015) Big data analytics: a survey. J Big Data 2(1):21
8. Sanjay M, Alamma B (2016) An insight into big data analyticsmethods and application. In: International conference on inventive computation technologies (ICICT), vol 1. IEEE, USA, pp 1–5
9. Cardenas AA, Manadhata PK, Rajan SP (2013) Big data analytics for security. IEEE Secur Priv 11(6):74–76
10. Keim DA, Mansmann F, Schneidewind J, Thomas J, Ziegler H (2008) Visual analytics: scope and challenges. Visual data mining, Springer, Berlin, pp 76–90
11. Cook KA, Thomas JJ (2005) Illuminating the path: the research and development agenda for visual analytics
12. Endsley MR (1995) Toward a theory of situation awareness in dynamic systems. Hum Factors 37(1):32–64
13. Garae J, Ko RK (2017) Visualization and data provenance trends in decision support for cyber-security. Data analytics and decision support for cybersecurity, Springer, Berlin, pp 243–270
14. Hamed T, Ernst JB, Kremer SC (2018) A survey and taxonomy on data and pre-processing techniques of intrusion detection systems. Computer and network security essentials, Springer, Berlin, pp 113–134
15. Butun I, Morgera SD, Sankar R (2014) A survey of intrusion detection systems in wireless sensor networks. IEEE Commun Surv Tutor 16(1):266–282
16. Mell P, Grance T, et al. (2011) The nist definition of cloud computing
17. Mahmood T, Afzal U (2013) Security analytics: big data analytics for cybersecurity: a review of trends, techniques and tools. In: 2013 2nd National conference on information assurance (ncia), IEEE, USA, pp 129–134
18. Banday MT, Qadri JA (2011) Spam–technological and legal aspects. arXiv preprint arXiv:1112.5621
19. Lu L, Perdisci R, Lee W (2011) Surf: detecting and measuring search poisoning. In: Proceedings of the 18th ACM conference on computer and communications security, ACM, USA, pp 467–476
20. Stone-Gross B, Cova M, Cavallaro L, Gilbert B, Szydlowski M, Kemmerer R, Kruegel C, Vigna G (2009) Your botnet is my botnet: analysis of a botnet takeover. In: Proceedings of the 16th ACM conference on computer and communications security, ACM, USA, pp 635–647
21. Gu Q, Liu P (2007) Denial of service attacks. Handbook of computer networks: distributed networks, network planning, control, management, and new trends and applications, vol 3. Wiley, USA, pp 454–468
22. Jakobsson M, Myers S (2006) Phishing and countermeasures: understanding the increasing problem of electronic identity theft. Wiley, USA
23. Shi J, Saleem S (2012) Computer security research reports: phishing. University of Arizona, USA
24. Carter III RB, Lall PK, Oitment G, Maha D, Hasan J (2016) Method and system for protecting against unknown malicious activities by determining a reputation of a link. Google Patents, US Patent 9,317,680
25. Durumeric Z, Adrian D, Mirian A, Bailey M, Halderman JA (2015) A search engine backed by internet-wide scanning. In: Proceedings of the 22nd ACM SIGSAC conference on computer and communications security, ACM, USA, pp 542–553
26. Le Pochat V, Van Goethem T, Joosen W (2018) Towards visual analytics for web security data
27. Halevi T, Saxena N (2015) Keyboard acoustic side channel attacks: exploring realistic and security-sensitive scenarios. Int J Inf Secur 14(5):443–456
28. Ur B, Bees J, Segreti SM, Bauer L, Christin N, Cranor LF (2016) Do users' perceptions of password security match reality? In: Proceedings of the 2016 CHI conference on human factors in computing systems, ACM, USA, pp 3748–3760
29. Winerman L (2009) Social networking: crisis communication. Nat News 457(7228):376–378

30. Endsley MR (1988) Design and evaluation for situation awareness enhancement. In: Proceedings of the human factors society annual meeting, vol 32. SAGE Publications Sage: Los Angeles, CA, pp. 97–101
31. Erbacher RF (2012) Visualization design for immediate high-level situational assessment. In: Proceedings of the ninth international symposium on visualization for cyber security, ACM, USA, pp 17–24
32. Endsley MR, Garland D (2000) Theoretical underpinnings of situation awareness: a critical review. Situat Aware Anal Meas 1:24
33. Tianfield H (2016) Cyber security situational awareness. In: 2016 IEEE International conference on internet of things (iThings) and IEEE green computing and communications (Green-Com) and IEEE cyber, physical and social computing (CPSCom) and IEEE smart data (Smart-Data), IEEE, USA, pp 782–787
34. Bass T (1999) Multisensor data fusion for next generation distributed intrusion detection systems
35. Bass T (2000) Intrusion detection systems and multisensor data fusion. Commun ACM 43(4):99–105
36. Barford P, Dacier M, Dietterich TG, Fredrikson M, Giffin J, Jajodia S, Jha S, Li J, Liu P, Ning P (2010) Cyber sa: situational awareness for cyber defense. Cyber situational awareness, Springer, Berlin, pp 3–13
37. Franke U, Brynielsson J (2014) Cyber situational awareness-a systematic review of the literature. Comput Secur 46:18–31
38. Tadda G, Salerno JJ, Boulware D, Hinman M, Gorton S (2006) Realizing situation awareness within a cyber environment. Multisensor, multisource information fusion: architectures, algorithms, and applications 2006, vol 6242. International society for optics and photonics, p 624204
39. McGuinness B, Foy L (2000) A subjective measure of sa: the crew awareness rating scale (cars). In: Proceedings of the first human performance, situation awareness, and automation conference, Savannah, Georgia, vol 16
40. McNeese M, Cooke NJ, DAmico A, Endsley MR, Gonzalez C, Roth E, Salas E (2012) Perspectives on the role of cognition in cyber security. In: Proceedings of the human factors and ergonomics society annual meeting, vol 56. SAGE Publications Sage CA: Los Angeles, CA, pp 268–271
41. Paxson V (1999) Bro: a system for detecting network intruders in real-time. Comput Netw 31(23–24):2435–2463
42. Bou-Harb E, Debbabi M, Assi C (2014) Cyber scanning: a comprehensive survey. IEEE Commun Surv Tutor 16(3):1496–1519
43. Goodall JR (2009) Visualization is better! a comparative evaluation. In: 2009 6th International workshop on visualization for cyber security, VizSec, IEEE, USA, pp 57–68
44. Varga M, Winkelholz C, Träber-Burdin S The application of visual analytics to cyber security
45. Shiravi H, Shiravi A, Ghorbani AA (2012) A survey of visualization systems for network security. IEEE Trans Vis Comput Graph 18(8):1313–1329
46. Wagner M, Fischer F, Luh R, Haberson A, Rind A, Keim DA, Aigner W, Borgo R, Ganovelli F, Viola I (2015) A survey of visualization systems for malware analysis. In: EG conference on visualization (EuroVis)-STARs, pp 105–125
47. Vaarandi R, Niziński P (2013) Comparative analysis of open-source log management solutions for security monitoring and network forensics. In: Proceedings of the 2013 European conference on information warfare and security, pp 278–287
48. Lavigne V, Gouin D (2014) Visual analytics for cyber security and intelligence. J Def Model Simul 11(2):175–199
49. Ware C (2012) Information visualization: perception for design, Elsevier, USA
50. Norman DA (2004) Emotion design: why we love (or hate) everyday things. Basic books
51. Marriott K, Purchase H, Wybrow M, Goncu C (2012) Memorability of visual features in network diagrams. IEEE Trans Vis Comput Graph 18(12):2477–2485

52. Healey CG, Booth KS, Enns JT (1993) Harnessing preattentive processes for multivariate data visualization. Graphics interface, Citeseer, pp 107–107
53. Healey CG, Booth KS, Enns JT (1995) Visualizing real-time multivariate data using preattentive processing. ACM Trans Model Comput Simul (TOMACS) 5(3):190–221
54. Healey CG, Booth KS, Enns JT (1996) High-speed visual estimation using preattentive processing. ACM Trans Comput-Hum Interact (TOCHI) 3(2):107–135
55. Tufte ER (1985) The visual display of quantitative information. J Healthc Qual 7(3):15
56. Fishwick P, Diehl S, Prophet J, Löwgren J (2005) Perspectives on aesthetic computing. Leonardo 38(2):133–141
57. Eichelberger H (2003) Nice class diagrams admit good design? In: Proceedings of the 2003 ACM symposium on software visualization, ACM, USA, p 159
58. Tufte ER (1990) Envisioning information. Graphics Press, USA
59. Koffka K (2013) Principles of gestalt psychology, vol 44. Routledge, Abingdon
60. Shneiderman B (2003) The eyes have it: a task by data type taxonomy for information visualizations. The craft of information visualization, Elsevier, USA, pp 364–371
61. Heer J, Shneiderman B (2012) Interactive dynamics for visual analysis. Queue 10(2):30
62. Lanfranchi V, Mazumdar S, Ciravegna F (2014) Visual design recommendations for situation awareness in social media
63. Hao L, Healey CG, Hutchinson SE (2013) Flexible web visualization for alert-based network security analytics. In: Proceedings of the tenth workshop on visualization for cyber security, ACM, USA, pp 33–40
64. Fischer F, Fuchs J, Mansmann F, Keim DA (2015) Banksafe: visual analytics for big data in large-scale computer networks. Inf Vis 14(1):51–61
65. Koike H, Ohno K, Koizumi K (2005) Visualizing cyber attacks using IP matrix. In: IEEE workshop on visualization for computer security (VizSEC 05), IEEE, USA, pp 91–98
66. Hideshima Y, Koike H (2006) Starmine: a visualization system for cyber attacks. In: Proceedings of the 2006 Asia-Pacific symposium on information visualisation, vol 60. Australian computer society, Inc. pp 131–138
67. Livnat Y, Agutter J, Moon S, Erbacher RF, Foresti S (2005) A visualization paradigm for network intrusion detection. In: Proceedings from the sixth annual IEEE SMC information assurance workshop (IAW'05), IEEE, USA, pp 92–99
68. Roberts JC (2007) State of the art: coordinated and multiple views in exploratory visualization. In: Fifth international conference on coordinated and multiple views in exploratory visualization (CMV'07), IEEE, USA, pp 61–71
69. Noel S, Jacobs M, Kalapa P, Jajodia S (2005) Multiple coordinated views for network attack graphs. In: IEEE workshop on visualization for computer security (VizSEC 05), IEEE, USA, pp 99–106
70. Brodlie K, Osorio RA, Lopes A (2012) A review of uncertainty in data visualization. Expanding the frontiers of visual analytics and visualization, Springer, Berlin, pp 81–109
71. Spiegelhalter D, Pearson M, Short I (2011) Visualizing uncertainty about the future. Science 333(6048):1393–1400
72. Javed W, Elmqvist N (2012) Exploring the design space of composite visualization. In: 2012 IEEE pacific visualization symposium (PacificVis), IEEE, USA, pp 1–8
73. Mazumdar S, Ciravegna F, Gentile AL, Lanfranchi V (2012) Visualising context and hierarchy in social media. In: International workshop on intelligent exploration of semantic data (IESD2012) at EKAW, vol 2012
74. Best DM, Endert A, Kidwell D (2014) 7 key challenges for visualization in cyber network defense. In: Proceedings of the eleventh workshop on visualization for cyber security, ACM, USA, pp 33–40
75. Fink GA, North CL, Endert A, Rose S (2009) Visualizing cyber security: usable workspaces. In: 6th international workshop on visualization for cyber security (VizSec 2009), IEEE, USA, pp 45–56

Index

A
Access control, 159
Action model, 165
Active probing, 63
Algorithms
    A*, 195
    decision tree, 307
    extreme gradient boosting, 308
    K-Nearest Neighbour, 306
    logistic regression, 307
    random forest, 308
    support vector machines, 304
Analytical attack modelling, 109
Attack graphs, 112
Attacks
    advanced persistent threats, 67
    DDoS, 67
    DoS, 67
    malicious software, 67
    man-in-the-middle , 67
    password pilfering, 67
    ransomware, 317
    replay attack, 67
Automated planning, 19, 169

B
Behaviour-based detection, 324
Big data sources for cyber security, 371
BPMN security extensions, 340
Business Process Model and Notation
    (BPMN), 339

D
Deep neural network, 213

E
Endsley's situation awareness model, 373
Evasion attack, 223

F
Firewall, 66
Function call graph, 261

H
Hidden Markov models, 34

I
Incident management, 70
Industrial Control System (ICS), 61
Intrusion detection systems, 70, 93
Iterative cardinal reduction, 146

L
Linear discriminant analysis, 43

M
Machine learning, 17
Malware detection, 322
Masquerade attack, 301
Modelling
    file system access controls, 163
    malware, 184

P
Passive scanning, 62

© Springer International Publishing AG, part of Springer Nature 2018
S. Parkinson et al. (eds.), *Guide to Vulnerability Analysis for Computer Networks and Systems*, Computer Communications and Networks,
https://doi.org/10.1007/978-3-319-92624-7

PDDL, 170
Penetration testing, 69
Perceptual discriminability, 341
Principal Component Analysis (PCA), 38
Profile Hidden Markov models, 36
Pruning vulnerabilities, 193

R
Reciprocity measure, 248

S
SCADA, 61
    countermeasures, 69
    privacy, 74
Signature-based detection, 322
SQL injection, 8

T
Tools
    aircrack, 12
    burp suite, 13
    metasploit, 12
    Nessus, 64

Nmap, 13, 63
Passive Vulnerability Scanner (PVS), 64
Shodan, 64
SQLMap, 13
wireshark, 13
Zmap, 64
Trust assessment frameworks, 90
Trustless security system, 143

V
Vector quantization, 42
Vishing, 241
Visual analytics and the cyber security domain, 374
Vulnerabilities assessment
    cloud computing, 84
Vulnerability assessment
    assistive, 12
    automated, 16
    manual, 6

Z
Zero trust, 131

Printed in the United States
By Bookmasters